peaceful uses of atomic energy are also treated prominently.

In addition the reader will find ample documentation of the changing status of Germany, the crisis in the Formosa Straits, bilateral negotiations with Red China, developments in the Near and Middle East as well as the texts of the Austrian State Treaty, international economic agreements and the communiqué of the Bandung Conference of Asian-African countries.

With DOCUMENTS ON AMERICAN FOREIGN RELATIONS at hand each year, any interested reader can keep abreast of the ever-changing, always-fascinating picture of America in her relationships with the world.

SOME PUBLICATIONS OF THE

COUNCIL ON FOREIGN RELATIONS

FOREIGN AFFAIRS (quarterly), edited by Hamilton Fish Armstrong.

THE UNITED STATES IN WORLD AFFAIRS (annual). Volumes for 1931, 1932, and 1933, by Walter Lippmann and William O. Scroggs; for 1934-1935, 1936, 1937, 1938, 1939 and 1940, by Whitney H. Shepardson and William O. Scroggs; for 1945-1947, 1947-1948 and 1948-1949, by John C. Campbell; for 1949, 1950, 1951, 1952, 1953, and 1954, by Richard P. Stebbins.

DOCUMENTS ON AMERICAN FOREIGN RELATIONS (annual). Volume for 1952 edited by Clarence W. Baier and Richard P. Stebbins; for 1953, and 1954, edited by Peter V. Curl.

POLITICAL HANDBOOK OF THE WORLD (annual), edited by Walter H. Mallory.

RUSSIA AND AMERICA: Dangers and Prospects, by Henry L. Roberts.

STERLING: Its Meaning in World Finance, by Judd Polk.

KOREA: A Study of U. S. Policy in the United Nations, by Leland M. Goodrich.

FOREIGN AFFAIRS BIBLIOGRAPHY, 1942-1952, by Henry L. Roberts.

AMERICAN AGENCIES INTERESTED IN INTERNATIONAL AFFAIRS, compiled by Ruth Savord and Donald Wasson.

JAPANESE AND AMERICANS: A Century of Cultural Relations, by Robert S. Schwantes.

THE FUTURE OF UNDERDEVELOPED COUNTRIES: Political Implications of Economic Development, by Eugene Staley.

THE UNDECLARED WAR, 1940-1941, by William L. Langer and S. Everett Gleason.

THE CHALLENGE TO ISOLATION, 1937-1940, by William L. Langer and S. Everett Gleason.

MIDDLE EAST DILEMMAS: The Background of United States Policy, by J. C. Hurewitz.

BRITAIN AND THE UNITED STATES: Problems in Cooperation, a joint report prepared by Henry L. Roberts and Paul A. Wilson.

TRADE AND PAYMENTS IN WESTERN EUROPE: A Study in Economic Cooperation, 1947-1951, by William Diebold, Jr.

THE ECONOMICS OF FREEDOM: The Progress and Future of Aid to Europe, by Howard S. Ellis.

WAR AND THE MINDS OF MEN, by Frederick S. Dunn.

PUBLIC OPINION AND FOREIGN POLICY, by Lester Markel and Others.

THE PRICE OF POWER, by Hanson W. Baldwin.

OUR FARM PROGRAM AND FOREIGN TRADE, by C. Addison Hickman.

THE FOREIGN AFFAIRS READER, edited by Hamilton Fish Armstrong.

THE STUDY OF INTERNATIONAL RELATIONS IN AMERICAN COLLEGES AND UNIVERSITIES, by Grayson Kirk.

THE PROBLEM OF GERMANY, by Hoyt Price and Carl E. Schorske.

FOREIGN AFFAIRS BIBLIOGRAPHY, 1932-1942, by Robert Gale Woolbert.

THE UNITED STATES IN A MULTI-NATIONAL ECONOMY, by Jacob Viner and Others.

THE FAR EASTERN CRISIS, by Henry L. Stimson.

THE STRUGGLE FOR AIRWAYS IN LATIN AMERICA, by William A. M. Burden.

LIMITS OF LAND SETTLEMENT, prepared under the direction of Isaiah Bowman.

SURVEY OF AMERICAN FOREIGN RELATIONS (in four volumes, 1928-1931), prepared under the direction of Charles P. Howland.

DOLLARS IN LATIN AMERICA, by Willy Feuerlein and Elizabeth Hannan.

NEW DIRECTIONS IN OUR TRADE POLICY, by William Diebold, Jr.

INTERNATIONAL AIR TRANSPORT AND NATIONAL POLICY, by Oliver J. Lissitzyn.

DOCUMENTS ON AMERICAN FOREIGN RELATIONS

1955

EDITED BY

PAUL E. ZINNER

Published for the

COUNCIL ON FOREIGN RELATIONS

by

HARPER & BROTHERS

NEW YORK

1956

The Council on Foreign Relations is a non-profit institution devoted to study of the international aspects of American political, economic and strategic problems. It takes no stand, expressed or implied, on American policy.

The authors of books published under the auspices of the Council are responsible for their statements of fact and expressions of opinion. The Council is responsible only for determining that they should be presented to the public.

DOCUMENTS ON AMERICAN FOREIGN RELATIONS, 1955

For information address Council on Foreign Relations,
58 East 68th Street, New York 21

The Colonial Press Inc., Clinton, Mass.

Library of Congress catalog card number: LC 39-28987

PREFACE

THIS volume of the annual *Documents on American Foreign Relations* is the seventeenth in a series initiated by the World Peace Foundation in 1939 and published under the auspices of the Council on Foreign Relations since 1952. The purpose of each volume has been to provide concise yet comprehensive documentation of the foreign relations of the United States in a given calendar year.

The task of selection within reasonable limits of space—a consideration which for better or for worse cannot be lightly overlooked—has grown steadily more difficult. American responsibilities throughout the world continue to expand. International relations in general grow more complex each year. Finally, increasing use of public diplomacy—news conference statements, public addresses, conferences largely taken up by lengthy speeches intended for public consumption—tends to swell the total volume of wordage to be considered without producing a commensurate yield of hard and fast documents, i.e. treaties, agreements, notes.

Consider, for example, the Geneva Meeting of Heads of Government in July 1955. It was far and away the most important diplomatic event of the year. It marked a turning point in the "cold war." It must of necessity occupy a central place in this volume. Yet it yielded a minimum of documents in the usual sense of the word. Its most notable contribution was a change in the "climate" of international relations, in the "spirit" in which the free countries and the Soviet bloc faced each other across the conference table. Much the same can be said of the Geneva Conference of Foreign Ministers, a natural aftermath of the "Meeting at the Summit."

The composition of this volume, then, reflects the diversity and complexity of the problems with which the United States had to cope in 1955 and the character of present-day diplomacy. In addition to the two Geneva conferences, the disarmament talks (carried on for the most part under the aegis of the United Nations) and deliberations concerning the peaceful uses of atomic energy are treated prominently. But issues and events such as the Formosa crisis, bilateral negotiations with Communist China, the changing status of Germany, the conclusion of an Austrian State Treaty and many others are also accorded due attention.

In preparing the volume for publication, the editor frequently had occasion to call on the assistance of more seasoned members of the Council staff. Such assistance as was asked for was in all cases readily forthcoming and proved of inestimable value. The library staff under the able guidance of Ruth Savord invariably came up with any needed document. The business office was more than accommodating in arranging the schedule for publication. Elaine P. Adam helped in a variety of useful ways. Special thanks are due to Richard P. Stebbins, editor of the Council's annual analytical treatise on the *United States in World Affairs,* a friend of long standing whose discerning eye and infallibly good judgment helped to smooth over many a rough spot.

The responsibility for selecting the documents, however, rested with the editor alone and no one sought to exercise undue influence in this respect. Consequently the blame for any shortcoming from which this volume may suffer should be directed at me alone.

The discerning reader may detect throughout the text a variety of minor stylistic and orthographic discrepancies. While some of these undoubtedly result from human error in reading the proofs, the vast majority of them reflect a deliberate decision on the part of the editor to preserve the text of the document in its original form.

May 1956 PAUL E. ZINNER

CONTENTS

CHAPTER ONE

THE UNITED STATES: PRINCIPLES AND POLICIES

A. Annual Review.

Message of the President on the State of the Union, January 6, 1955.[1]

(Excerpts)

In the past year, there has been progress justifying hope for the ultimate rule of freedom and justice in the world. Free nations are collectively stronger than at any time in recent years.

Just as nations of this hemisphere, in the historic Caracas[2] and Rio Conferences,[3] have closed ranks against imperialistic communism and strengthened their economic ties, so free nations elsewhere have forged new bonds of unity.

Recent agreements between Turkey and Pakistan have laid a foundation for increased strength in the Middle East.[4] With our understanding support, Egypt and Britain, Yugoslavia and Italy, Britain and Iran have resolved dangerous differences. The security of the Mediterranean has been enhanced by an alliance among Greece, Turkey, and Yugoslavia.[5] Agreements in Western Europe have paved the way for unity to replace past divisions which have undermined Europe's economic and military vitality. The defense of the West appears likely at last to include a free, democratic Germany, participating as an equal in the councils of NATO.[6]

In Asia and the Pacific, the pending Manila Pact[7] supplements our treaties with Australia, New Zealand, the Philippines, Korea and Japan and our prospective treaty with the Republic of China.[8] These pacts stand as solemn warning

[1] House Document 1, 84th Cong., 1st Sess.
[2] *Documents on American Foreign Relations, 1954,* pp. 407-411.
[3] *Ibid.,* pp. 419-420.
[4] *Ibid.,* pp. 376-378.
[5] *Ibid.,* pp. 186-190.
[6] See below, p. 93.
[7] *Documents on American Foreign Relations, 1954,* pp. 319-323.
[8] See below, pp. 299-305.

that future military aggression and subversion against the free nations of Asia will meet united response. The Pacific Charter, also adopted at Manila, is a milestone in the development of human freedom and self-government in the Pacific area.[9]

Under the auspices of the United Nations, there is promise of progress in our country's plan for the peaceful use of atomic energy.[10]

Finally, today the world is at peace. It is, to be sure, an insecure peace. Yet all humanity finds hope in the simple fact that for an appreciable time there has been no active battlefield on earth. This same fact inspires us to work all the more effectively with other nations for the well-being, the freedom, the dignity, of every human on earth. In the ultimate achievement of this great purpose lies the only sure promise of security and permanent peace for any nation, including our own.

These developments are heartening. But sobering problems remain.

The massive military machines and ambitions of the Soviet-Communist bloc still create uneasiness in the world. All of us are aware of the continuing reliance of the Soviet Communists on military force, of the power of their weapons, of their present resistance to realistic armament limitation, and of their continuing effort to dominate or intimidate free nations on their periphery. Their steadily growing power includes an increasing strength in nuclear weapons. This power, combined with the proclaimed intentions of the Communist leaders to communize the world, is the threat confronting us today.

To protect our nations and our peoples from the catastrophe of a nuclear holocaust, free nations must maintain countervailing military power to persuade the Communists of the futility of seeking to advance their ends through aggression. If Communist rulers understand that America's response to aggression will be swift and decisive—that never shall we buy peace at the expense of honor or faith—they will be powerfully deterred from launching a military venture engulfing their own peoples and many others in disaster. Now this, of course, is a form of world stalemate. But in this stalemate each of us—every American—may and must exer-

[9] *Documents on American Foreign Relations, 1954,* pp. 318-319.
[10] See below, p. 461 ff.

cise his high duty to strive in every honorable way for enduring peace.

The military threat is but one menace to our freedom and security. We must not only deter aggression; we must also frustrate the effort of Communists to gain their goals by subversion. To this end, free nations must maintain and reinforce their cohesion, their internal security, their political and economic vitality, and their faith in freedom.

In such a world, America's course is clear:

We must strengthen the collective defense under the United Nations Charter and gird ourselves with sufficient military strength and productive capacity to discourage resort to war and protect our Nation's vital interests.

We must continue to support and strengthen the United Nations. At this moment, by vote of the United Nations General Assembly, its Secretary General is in Communist China on a mission of deepest concern to all Americans: seeking the release of our never-to-be-forgotten American aviators and all other United Nations prisoners wrongfully detained by the Communist regime.[11]

We must also encourage the efforts being made in the United Nations to limit armaments and to harness the atom to peaceful use.

We must expand international trade and investment and assist friendly nations whose own best efforts are still insufficient to provide the strength essential to the security of the free world.

We must be willing to use the processes of negotiation whenever they will advance the cause of just and secure peace.

In respect to all these matters, we must, through a vigorous information program, keep the peoples of the world truthfully advised of our actions and purposes. This problem has been attacked with new vigor during the past months. I urge that the Congress give its earnest attention to the great advantages that can accrue to our country through the successful and expanded operations of this information program.

We must carry forward our educational exchange program.

Now, to advance these many efforts, the Congress must act in this session on appropriations, legislation, and treaties. Today I shall mention especially our foreign economic and military programs.

The recent economic progress in many free nations has

[11] See below, pp. 305-307.

been heartening. The productivity of labor and the production of goods and services are increasing in ever-widening areas. There is a growing will to improve the living standards of all men. This progress is important to all our people. It promises us allies who are strong and self-reliant; it promises a growing world market for the products of our mines, our factories, our farms.

But only through steady effort can we continue this progress. Barriers still impede trade and the flow of capital needed to develop each nation's human and material resources. Wise reduction of these barriers is a long-term objective of our foreign economic policy—a policy of an evolutionary and selective nature, assuring broad benefits to our own and to other peoples.

We must gradually reduce certain tariff obstacles to trade. These actions should, of course, be accompanied by a similar lowering of trade barriers by other nations, so that we may move steadily together toward economic advantage for all. We must further simplify our customs procedures. We must facilitate the flow of capital and continue technical assistance, both directly and through the United Nations. This must go to less developed countries to strengthen their independence and raise their living standards. Many another step must be taken in the free world to release forces of private initiative.

On January 10, by special message, I shall submit specific recommendations for carrying forward the legislative phases of our foreign economic policy.[12]

Our many efforts to build a better world include the maintenance of our military strength. This is a vast undertaking. Over 4 million Americans—servicemen and civilians—are on the rolls of the Defense Establishment. During the past 2 years, by attacking duplication and overstaffing, by improved procurement and inventory controls, by concentrating on the essentials, many billions of dollars have been saved on these defense activities. I should like to mention certain fundamentals underlying this vast program.

First, I repeat that a realistic limitation of armaments and an enduring, just peace remain our national goals; we maintain powerful military forces because there is no present alternative—they are forces designed for deterrent and defensive purposes, able instantly to strike back with destructive power in response to any attack.

Second, we must stay alert to the fact that undue reliance

[12] See below, pp. 24-31.

on one weapon or preparation for only one kind of warfare simply invites an enemy to resort to another. We must, therefore, keep in our Armed Forces balance and flexibility adequate to our needs.

Third, to keep our Armed Forces abreast of the advances of science, our military planning must be flexible enough to utilize the new weapons and techniques which flow ever more speedily from our research and development programs. The forthcoming military budget therefore emphasizes modern airpower in the Air Force, Navy, and Marine Corps and increases the emphasis on new weapons, especially those of rapid and destructive striking power.

It seeks continuous modernization of our Army. It accelerates the continental defense program and the buildup of military reserve forces. It continues a vigorous program of stockpiling strategic materials and strengthening our mobilization base. It provides for reduction of forces in certain categories and their expansion in others, to fit them to the military realities of our time. These emphases in our defense planning have been made at my personal direction after long and thoughtful—even prayerful—study. In my judgment, they will give our Nation a defense accurately adjusted to the national need.

Fourth, pending a world agreement on armament limitation, we must continue to expand our supplies of nuclear weapons for our land, naval, and air forces. We shall continue our encouraging progress, at the same time, in the peaceful use of atomic power.

Fifth, in the administration of these costly programs, we demand the utmost efficiency. We must assure our people not only of adequate protection but also of a defense that can and will be resolutely carried forward from year to year until the threat of aggression has disappeared.

To help maintain this kind of armed strength and to improve its efficiency, I urge the enactment of several important measures.

The first concerns the Selective Service Act which expires next June 30. For the foreseeable future, our standing forces must remain much larger than voluntary methods can sustain. We must, therefore, extend the statutory authority to induct men for 2 years of military service.

The second kind of measure concerns the rapid turnover of our most experienced servicemen. This process seriously weakens the combat readiness of our Armed Forces and is unnecessary and extravagantly expensive. To encourage more trained servicemen to remain in uniform, I shall, on the 13th of this month, propose a number of measures to increase the attractions of a military career. These measures will include more adequate medical care for dependents, survivors' benefits, more and better housing, and selective adjustments in military pay and allowances.

And, third, I shall present a program to rebuild and strengthen the civilian components of our Armed Forces. Because it will go far in assuring fair and equitable participation in military service, it is of particular importance to our combat veterans. In keeping with our historic military policy, the program is designed to build civilian reserves capable of effective military service in an emergency in lieu of maintaining active forces in excess of the Nation's immediate need.

Through this program the individual will be able to discharge one of his obligations to the Nation; equally, the Nation will be able to discharge one of its obligations to a potential future serviceman; namely, to give him the greatest possible chance of survival in time of war.

An effective defense requires continuance of our aggressive attack on subversion at home. In this effort we have, in the past 2 years, made real progress. FBI investigations have been reinforced by a new Internal Security Division in the Department of Justice; the security activities of the Immigration and Naturalization Service have been revitalized; an improved security system is in effect throughout the Government; the Department of Justice and the FBI have been armed with new legal weapons forged by the 83d Congress.

We shall continue to ferret out and to destroy Communist subversion.

We shall, in the process, carefully preserve our traditions and the basic rights of every American citizen.

Our civil defense program is also a key element in the protection of our country. We are developing cooperative methods with State governors, mayors, and voluntary citizen groups, in building the civil defense. The significance of this organization in time of war is obvious; its swift assistance in disaster areas last year proved its importance in time of peace.

An industry capable of rapid expansion and essential materials and facilities available in time of emergency are indispensable. I urge, therefore, a 2-year extension of the Defense Production Act and title II of the First War Powers Act of

1941. These are cornerstones of our program for the development of an adequate mobilization base.

At this point, I should like to make this additional observation.

Our quest for peace and freedom necessarily presumes that we who hold positions of public trust, must rise above self and section—that we must subordinate to the general good our partisan and our personal pride and prejudice. Tirelessly, with united purpose, we must fortify the material and spiritual foundations of this land of freedom. As never before, there is need for unhesitating cooperation among the branches of our Government.

At this time the executive and legislative branches are under the management of different political parties. This fact places both parties on trial before the American people.

In less perilous days of the past, division of governmental responsibility among our great parties has at times produced indecision approaching futility. We must not let this happen in our time. We must avoid a paralysis of the will for peace and international security.

Now in the traditionally bipartisan areas—military security and foreign relations—I can report to you that I have already, with the present leaders of this Congress, exchanged assurances of unreserved cooperation. Yet, the security of our country requires more than maintenance of military strength and success in foreign affairs; these vital matters are in turn dependent upon concerted and vigorous action in a number of supporting programs.

I say, therefore, to the 84th Congress:

In all areas basic to the strength of America, there will be —to the extent I can insure them—cooperative, constructive relations between the executive and legislative branches of this Government. Let the general good be our yardstick on every great issue of our time. In that pledge I should include, also, the similar pledge of every head of department or independent agency in this Government.

* * *

B. Basic Foreign Policy Strategy.

1. *The Peace We Want: Address by the President before the American Bar Association, Philadelphia, August 24, 1955.*[1]

(Excerpts)

[The address was made in connection with a series of meetings celebrating the John Marshall Bicentennial. The omitted portion of the President's speech consists of a tribute to John Marshall.]

* * *

The central fact of today's life is the existence in the world of two great philosophies of man and of government. They are in contest for the friendship, loyalty, and support of the world's peoples.

On the one side, our Nation is ranged with those who seek attainment of human goals through a government of laws administered by men. Those laws are rooted in moral law reflecting a religious faith that man is created in the image of God and that the energy of the free individual is the most dynamic force in human affairs.

On the other side are those who believe—and many of them with evident sincerity—that human goals can be most surely reached by a government of men who rule by decree. Their decrees are rooted in an ideology which ignores the faith that man is a spiritual being, which establishes the all-powerful state as the principal source of advancement and progress.

The case of the several leading nations on both sides is on trial before the bar of world opinion. Each of them claims that it seeks, above all else, an enduring peace in the world. In that claim, all identify themselves with a deep-seated hunger of mankind. But the final judgment on them—and it may be many years in coming—will depend as much on the march of human progress within their own borders, and on their proved capacity to help others advance, as on the tranquillity of their relations with foreign countries.

Mankind wants peace because the fruits of peace are manifold and rich, particularly in this atomic age; because war

[1] *Department of State Bulletin,* v. 33 (September 5, 1955), pp. 375-378.

could be the extinction of man's deepest hopes; because atomic war could be race suicide.

The world is astir today with newly awakened peoples. By the hundreds of millions, they march toward opportunity to work and grow and prosper, to demonstrate their self-reliance, to satisfy their aspirations of mind and spirit. Their advance must not and cannot be stopped.

These hundreds of millions help make up the jury which must decide the case between the competing powers of the world.

The system, or group of systems, which most effectively musters its strength in support of peace and demonstrates its ability to advance the well-being, the happiness of the individual, will win their verdict and their loyal friendship.

You of the American Bar Association will play a critical part in the presentation of freedom's case.

The many thousands of men and women you represent are, by their professional careers, committed to the search for truth, that justice may prevail and human rights may be secured. Thereby, they promote the free world's cause before the bar of world opinion. But let us be clear that, in the global scene, our responsibility as Americans is to present our case as tellingly to the world as John Marshall presented the case for the Constitution to the American public more than a hundred years ago. In this, your aptitude as lawyers has special application.

In his written works and innumerable decisions, John Marshall proved the adequacy and adaptability of the Constitution to the Nation's needs. He was patient, tireless, understanding, logical, persistent. He was—no matter how trite the expression—a crusader; his cause, the interpretation of the Constitution to achieve ordered liberty and justice under law.

Now America needs to exercise, in the crusade for peace, the qualities of John Marshall. Peace and security for all can be established—for the fearful, for the oppressed, for the weak, for the strong. But this can be done only if we stand uncompromisingly for principle, for great issues, with the fervor of Marshall—with the zeal of the crusader.

We must not think of peace as a static condition in world affairs. That is not true peace, nor in fact can any kind of a peace be preserved that way. Change is the law of life, and unless there is peaceful change, there is bound to be violent change.

Our Nation has had domestic tranquility largely through

its capacity to change peacefully. The lone exception was when change, to meet new human concepts, was unduly resisted.

Our founders would scarcely recognize the Nation of today as that which they designed; it has been so greatly changed. But the change has been peaceful and selective, and always conforming to the principles of our founding documents. That has made it possible to conserve the good inherited from the past while adjusting to meet constantly rising goals. In that way we have kept in the front ranks of those who respect human dignity, who produce increasingly, and who share fairly the fruits of their labors.

This is the kind of peace that we seek. Our program must be as dynamic, as forward looking, as applicable to the international problems of our times as the Constitution, under John Marshall's interpretations, was made flexible and effective in the promotion of freedom, justice, and national strength in America.

That is the spirit in which the American delegation went to Geneva.[2] We asserted then—and we shall always hold—that there can be no true peace which involves acceptance of a status quo in which we find injustice to many nations, repressions of human beings on a gigantic scale, and with constructive effort paralyzed in many areas by fear.

The spirit of Geneva, if it is to provide a healthy atmosphere for the pursuit of peace, if it is to be genuine and not spurious, must inspire all to a correction of injustices, an observance of human rights, and an end to subversion organized on a worldwide scale. Whether or not such a spirit as this will thrive through the combined intelligence and understanding of men, or will shrivel in the greed and ruthlessness of some, is for the future to tell. But one thing is certain. This spirit and the goals we seek could never have been achieved by violence or when men and nations confronted each other with hearts filled with fear and hatred.

At Geneva we strove to help establish this spirit.

Geneva spells for America, not stagnation, then, but opportunity—opportunity for our own people and for people everywhere to realize their just aspirations.

Eagerness to avoid war—if we think no deeper than this single desire—can produce outright or implicit agreement that injustices and wrongs of the present shall be perpetuated in the future. We must not participate in any such false agree-

[2] See below, p. 171 ff.

ment. Thereby, we would outrage our own conscience. In the eyes of those who suffer injustice, we would become partners with their oppressors. In the judgment of history, we would have sold out the freedom of men for the pottage of a false peace. Moreover, we would assure future conflict!

The division of Germany cannot be supported by any argument based on boundaries or language or racial origin.

The domination of captive countries cannot longer be justified by any claim that this is needed for purposes of security.

An international political machine, operating within the borders of sovereign nations for their political and ideological subversion, cannot be explained away as a cultural movement.

Very probably the reason for these and other violations of the rights of men and of nations is a compound of suspicions and fear. That explains; it cannot excuse. In justice to others and to ourselves, we can never accept those wrongs as a part of the peace that we desire and seek.

We must be firm but friendly. We must be tolerant but not complacent. We must be quick to understand another's viewpoint, honestly assumed. But we must never agree to injustice for the weak, for the unfortunate, for the underprivileged, well knowing that if we accept destruction of the principle of justice for all, we cannot longer claim justice for ourselves as a matter of right.

The peace we want—the product of understanding and agreement and law among nations—is an enduring international environment based on justice and security. It will reflect enlightened self-interest. It will foster the concentration of human energy—individual and organized—for the advancement of human standards in all the areas of mankind's material, intellectual, and spiritual life.

Can we achieve that sort of peace? I think we can. At times it may seem hopeless, far beyond human capacity to reach. But has any great accomplishment in history begun with assurance of its success? Our own Republic is a case in point. Through a long generation there was almost a unanimous world conviction that the United States of America was an artificial contrivance that could not long endure.

And the Republic survived its most perilous years—the experimental years—because of dedicated efforts by individuals, not because it had a built-in guaranty of success or a path free from obstacles.

Our case for peace, based on justice, is as sound as was John Marshall's for the Constitution and the Union. And it will be as successful—if we present it before the bar of world opinion with the same courage and dedicated conviction that he brought to his mission.

In our communities we can, each according to his capacity, promote comprehension of what this Republic must be—in strength, in understanding, in dedication to principle—if it is to fulfill its role of leadership for peace.

In the search for justice, we can make our system an ever more glorious example of an orderly government devoted to the preservation of human freedom and man's individual opportunities and responsibilities.

No matter how vigorously we propose and uphold our individual views in domestic problems, we can present abroad a united front in all that concerns the freedom and security of the Republic, its dedication to a just and prosperous peace.

Above all, conscious of the towering achievements manifest in the Republic's history under the Constitution, assured that no human problem is beyond solution—given the will, the perseverance, and the strength—each of us can help arouse in America a renewed and flaming dedication to justice and liberty, prosperity and peace among men.

So acting, we shall prove ourselves—lawyers and laymen alike—worthy heirs to the example and spirit of John Marshall. Like him in his great mission, we shall succeed.

2. *The New Phase of Struggle with International Communism: Address by the Secretary of State (Dulles) before the Illinois Manufacturers' Association, Chicago, December 8, 1955.*[3]

We are, it seems, in a new phase of the struggle between international communism and freedom.

The first postwar decade was a phase of violence and threat of violence. There was the continued Soviet military occupation of northern Iran, the Communist guerrilla war in Greece, the Soviet blockade of Berlin, the Communist takeover in Czechoslovakia under the menace of armed invasion, the war against Korea, the war against Indochina, the warfare in the Formosa Straits, and the hostile threats against West-

[3] Department of State Press Release 683, dated December 8, 1955.

ern Europe when the German Federal Republic acted to join the West.

Since last spring, this phase of violence seems to have undergone an eclipse. But we should remember that one of the doctrines taught by Lenin and constantly emphasized by Stalin was the need for "zigzag." Repeatedly Stalin drove home the idea that it is as important to know when to retreat as when to attack, and that when blocked in one course it is necessary to find another.

Stalin is dead. But for 30 years his writings have been the Communist creed, and Stalinism in fact, though not in name, is still a potent influence in Russia. In prudence, therefore, we must act on the assumption that the present Soviet policies do not mark a change of purpose but a change of tactics.

We do not, however, want policies of violence to reappear. Therefore, it is useful to have clearly in mind what are the free-world policies which have caused the Soviet Union to shift from tactics of violence and intimidation as being unproductive.

The free nations have adopted and implemented two interrelated policies for collective security. The first policy is to give clear warning that armed aggression will be met by collective action. The second policy is to be prepared to implement this political warning with deterrent power.

The Political Warning System

The first major political warning to the Soviet Union was expressed in the North Atlantic Treaty, a product of the Democrat-Republican cooperation of 1948 and 1949. By the North Atlantic Treaty, the parties told the Soviet rulers that, if they attacked any one, they would have to fight them all. If the Kaiser and Hitler had known in advance that their aggressions would surely bring against them the full power of the United States, they might never have begun their armed aggression. As it was, they did what despots readily do—they miscalculated. The North Atlantic Treaty left no room for such miscalculation. That, said Senator Vandenberg, was "the most practical deterrent to war which the wit of man has yet devised."

But the North Atlantic Treaty was not enough. With that alone, it might be inferred that we were relatively indifferent to what occurred elsewhere, notably in Asia. And, indeed, less than a year after the North Atlantic Treaty came into force, the Communists attacked the Republic of Korea.

But now, except for countries of South Asia which choose "neutralism," the gaps in the political warning system have been closed. The United States with bipartisan cooperation has made mutual security treaties with the Philippines, Japan, the Republic of Korea, and with the Republic of China on Taiwan. We have entered into the ANZUS [Australia-New Zealand-U.S.] Pact. We have joined with seven other nations to make the Southeast Asia Collective Defense Treaty. There is the Balkan alliance of Yugoslavia, Greece, and Turkey and the Baghdad Pact, which includes the "northern tier" of Turkey, Iraq, Iran, and Pakistan.[4]

All of these treaties are made pursuant to what the United Nations Charter calls the "inherent right of collective self-defense." Together they constitute a worldwide political warning system. They prevent the despots from miscalculating that they can use Red armies to conquer weaker nations, one by one.

The Deterrent of Retaliatory Power

It is, however, not enough to have a political warning system. It must have backing if it is effectively to deter. That poses a difficult problem.

"With more than 20 nations strung along the 20,000 miles of iron curtain, it is not possible to build up static defensive forces which could make each nation impregnable to such a major and unpredictable assault as Russia could launch. To attempt this would be to have strength nowhere and bankruptcy everywhere. That, however, does not mean that we should abandon the whole idea of collective security and merely build our own defense area. . . . Fortunately, we do not have to choose between two disastrous alternatives. It is not necessary either to spread our strength all around the world in futile attempts to create everywhere a static defense, nor need we crawl back into our own hole in the vain hope of defending ourselves against all of the rest of the world. . . . As against the possibility of full-scale attack by the Soviet Union itself, there is only one effective defense, for us and for others. That is the capacity to counterattack. That is the ultimate deterrent. . . . The arsenal of retaliation should include all forms of counterattack with a maximum flexibility. . . . In such ways, the idea of collective security can be given sensible and effective content."

[4] See below, pp. 342-344.

What I have just been saying is what I said 5 years ago.[5]

That program has now become a reality. We have developed, with our allies, a collective system of great power which can be flexibly used on whatever scale may be requisite to make aggression costly. Our *capacity* to retaliate must be, and is, massive in order to deter all forms of aggression. But if we have to *use* that capacity, such use would be selective and adapted to the occasion.

"To deter aggression, it is important to have the flexibility and the facilities which make various responses available. In many cases, any open assault by Communist forces could only result in starting a general war. But the free world must have the means for responding effectively on a selective basis when it chooses. It must not put itself in the position where the only response open to it is general war. The essential thing is that a potential aggressor should know in advance that he can and will be made to suffer for his aggression more than he can possibly gain by it. This calls for a system in which local defensive strength is reinforced by more mobile deterrent power. The method of doing so will vary according to the character of the various areas."

What I have been saying is from an article I wrote about 2 years ago.[6]

Our mutual security arrangements help provide the local defensive strength needed to preserve internal order against subversive tactics and to offer a resistance to aggression which would give counterattacking, highly mobile forces time to arrive.

Thus we have collective defense policies which, on the one hand, are calculated to deter armed aggression and which, on the other hand, we can, if need be, live with indefinitely.

The two elements I have described—on the one hand, a political warning system and, on the other hand, selective retaliatory power—constitute in combination a firm foundation for peace. If we want peace to continue, we must preserve that foundation intact.

We earnestly strive for some dependable system of limitation of armament. Until we succeed in such efforts, however, we and our allies must constantly maintain forces, weapons, and facilities necessary to deter armed aggression, large or small. That is an indispensable price of peace.

[5] *Department of State Bulletin,* v. 25 (January 15, 1951), pp. 85-89.
[6] *Documents on American Foreign Relations, 1954,* pp. 7-15.

The Struggle for Justice

But we dare not assume that the only danger is that of armed aggression and that, if armed aggression can be deterred, we can otherwise relax. There still exist grave injustices to be cured and grave dangers to be averted.

President Eisenhower, speaking last August,[7] pointed out that—

"Eagerness to avoid war—if we think no deeper than this single desire—can produce outright or implicit agreement that injustices and wrongs of the present shall be perpetuated in the future. We must not participate in any such false agreement. Thereby, we would outrage our own conscience. In the eyes of those who suffer injustice, we would become partners with their oppressors. In the judgment of history we would have sold out the freedom of men for the pottage of a false peace. Moreover, we would assure future conflict!"

And the President went on to point to the division of Germany and the domination of captive countries as an illustration of the injustices of which he spoke.

We shall not seek to cure these injustices by ourselves invoking force. But we can and will constantly keep these injustices at the forefront of human consciousness and thus bring into play the force of world opinion which, working steadily, will have its way. For no nation, however powerful, wishes to incur, on a steadily mounting basis, the moral condemnation of the world.

This force was a potent factor in bringing Austria its freedom. Last May, after 7 years of delay, the Soviet Union signed the Austrian Treaty, the Red forces were withdrawn, and Austria was liberated.[8]

We face a similar problem with respect to the reunification of Germany. The July meeting of the Heads of Government at Geneva had brought this problem to the forefront.[9] There the four Heads of Government had explicitly agreed that "the reunification of Germany by means of free elections shall be carried out." However, at the second Geneva conference last month, the Soviet Union repudiated that agreement, despite Western offers which gave maximum assurances that a reunified Germany would not create insecurity for the Soviet Union and any of Germany's neighbors.[10] Apparently the

[7] See above, pp. 8-12.
[8] See below, pp. 127-156.
[9] See below, pp. 182-213.
[10] See below, pp. 256-266.

Soviets realized that all-German elections would surely remove from power the puppet regime which it has installed in East Germany. This, in turn, would have repercussions throughout the Soviet satellite world.

Therefore, the Soviet Union took the rigid position that it could accept no proposals for Germany, however reasonable, if they might enable the German people to get rid of those whom the Soviet has picked to rule in the Eastern Soviet Zone of Germany.

The result is that the West must continue to maintain the pressure of world opinion for the undoing of the present injustice which separates 17 million Germans from the great body of their fellows.

Western Unity

The Western European nations need also to continue to develop their own unity, not merely for defense, but also for well-being. It is the past divisions of Western Europe, and the rivalries of these nations, which has been the greatest cause of war and economic weakness.

The North Atlantic Treaty Organization serves greatly, not only to protect Europe but to provide a sense of unity and fellowship. I shall be sharing in that next week when Secretary Humphrey, Secretary Wilson, and I go to Paris for the December NATO Ministerial Council meeting. These meetings enable the Ministers of Foreign Affairs, of Finance, and of Defense to consult together and tighten the bonds which join the 15 NATO partners. These bonds are strong and tested. NATO is more than a mere military defense. Its members are constantly seeking and finding useful ways, other than military, to give expression to the closeness and warmth of their relationship.

But there is also need for unity on a more intimate basis among the continental European nations themselves. The six nations of France, Germany, Italy, Belgium, the Netherlands, and Luxembourg already have begun to create common institutions, notably the Coal and Steel Community. I was glad to find on my last visit to Europe that the movement to develop along these lines is taking on new vitality. That movement must obtain its strength primarily from the peoples concerned. It is, however, a development in which the United States has a deep interest and which it is prepared to support if opportunity offers.

As this movement develops, it is bound to exert a powerful influence on the Eastern European countries. If the Western European countries find, in unity, increased prosperity, there will be increasing pressure in the satellite countries for independent governments responsive to the needs and aspirations of the people.

This may speed the day when the Soviet rulers will come to realize that to hold these Eastern European nations in subjugation involves an obsolete reactionary practice, entailing costs, moral and material, far outweighing the seeming advantages.

The Less Developed Countries

New tasks also confront us in the less developed areas of the world. There, hundreds of millions of people lack what could and should be theirs.

These areas have always been a target of Soviet communism.

Today, as the Soviet rulers are balked in their effort to extend their influence by force, they have picked these areas as targets of their guile. The Soviet peoples seriously lack many of the commodities of everyday living. The satellite peoples are particularly exploited, and their standards of living have been seriously reduced. But the Soviet rulers find it easy to neglect these needs while professing concern for the welfare of those whom they call "colonial and dependent peoples" whose "amalgamation" into the Soviet Communist orbit has always been an open goal of Soviet policy.

The Soviet rulers, themselves exponents of a materialistic philosophy, have concentrated their educational efforts on training scientists. By now, the Soviet output of trained technical personnel is large. Also these technicians are always at the command of their government, to do whatever their government wants. They are thus available to go into the other areas, as a symbol of promises which are alluring.

We need not become panicky because Soviet communism now disports itself in this new garb. We need not assume, as some seem to assume, that the leaders in the Asian countries are unaware of danger and easily duped by false promises. These leaders have, indeed, had much political experience and have helped to win great political successes for their countries.

But the peoples of free countries which are not adequately developed do need the kind of help which matured industrial economies have historically provided for less developed economies. The flow of private capital partly meets that need. But government also has an important role to play.

We have indeed for several years had a governmental program for economic and technical assistance, much of which is directed to the less developed areas. That program is manned by a splendid corps of dedicated men and women. Congress has appropriated substantial funds to finance this program and to provide economic aid, much of which goes to the less developed areas. We expect to ask the Congress this coming year for as much money for this purpose as we think can usefully be spent, and we expect that the Congress will, as in the past, patriotically respond. Also we shall seek somewhat more flexibility than heretofore.

We are helping in other ways too. For example, our scientists, with the help of those from other free countries, had the imagination to see the immense possibilities in fissionable material. We were the first to crack the atom and to find the way to harness its vast power. We are in the lead in developing President Eisenhower's program of atoms for peace.

However, the coming years pose a challenge to our Nation and its people. A grudging response will not be enough. Nor will public money alone provide the answer. An effective response will call for a revival of the crusading spirit of our past.

We need to recapture the spirit which animated our missionaries, our doctors, our educators, and our merchants who, during the last century, went throughout the world carrying the benefits of a new way of life. For the most part these persons were not seeking to make money for themselves, although the profit motive was an honorable incentive. What they sought, and what they gained, was the unique joy that comes from creating and from sharing.

It would indeed be tragic if our people, and particularly our youth, now became so attracted by mercenary considerations, by the lure of the market place, that they lost the missionary spirit, the sense of destiny, which has been characteristic of our Nation since its beginning and which has made it great.

I frequently think of the scriptural promise that material things will be added unto those who seek first the Kingdom of God and His righteousness. This Nation has from its earliest days been influenced by religious ideals. Our forebears believed in a Divine Creator who had endowed all men with certain inalienable rights. They believed in a moral law and in its concepts of justice, love, and righteousness. They had a sense of mission in the world, believing it their duty to help men everywhere to be and to do what God designed. They saw a great prospect and were filled with a great purpose.

Under the impulsion of that faith, there developed here an area of spiritual, intellectual, and economic vigor the like of which the world had never seen. It was no exclusive preserve. Indeed, sharing was a central theme. Millions were welcomed from other lands to share equally the opportunities of the founders and their heirs. Through missionary activities and the establishment of schools and churches American ideals were carried throughout the world. Our Government gave aid and comfort to those elsewhere who sought to increase human freedom.

Meanwhile, material things were added to us. Now we must take care lest those byproducts of great endeavor seem so good that they become promoted to be the all-sufficient end.

That is the danger against which we must always be on guard. That is particularly the case today, when a huge materialistic state like the Soviet Union, thwarted in its efforts to aggrandize itself by force, coldly and cruelly calculates on how to exploit, for its selfish ends, the aspirations of the peoples of less developed lands.

What the world needs to know at this juncture is that our Nation remains steadfast to its historic ideals and follows its traditional course of sharing the spiritual, intellectual, and material fruits of our free society, in helping the captives to become free and helping the free to remain free, not merely in a technical sense but free in the sense of genuine opportunity to pursue happiness, in the spirit of our Declaration of Independence.

And may we never forget that, as Lincoln said, that declaration was not something exclusive to us, but there was "something in that declaration giving liberty, not alone to the people of this country, but hope for the world for all future time. It was that which gave promise that in due time the weights should be lifted from the shoulders of all men, and that all should have an equal chance."

That was the spirit in which our Nation was conceived. May it also be the spirit in which we live.

C. Military Requirements in a Changing World.

1. *Letter from the Secretary of Defense (Wilson) to the President, January 3, 1955.*[1]

Dear Mr. President:

For nearly two years we have discussed the various problems relating to the armed services and in particular the need for the conservation and proper utilization of our manpower, both military and civilian. Just before Christmas you again discussed the question of personnel strengths with me and the Joint Chiefs of Staff.

I have found so much value in the views underlying your decisions as to the personnel strengths of the armed services that I wonder if you would give me the gist of them in written form. I should like very much to have them available during the next year to guide me in my consideration of those matters and to be able to make them available to all of the interested people who are considering this problem.

With great respect, I am

Faithfully Yours,
CHARLES E. WILSON.

2. *Letter from the President to the Secretary of Defense (Wilson), January 5, 1955.*[2]

Dear Mr. Secretary:

Responding to your request I shall, in this note, briefly summarize the views on our general needs in military strength, including personnel, that I expressed verbally to you and the Joint Chiefs of Staff in December. Needless to say, these convictions on how best to preserve the peace were formed after earnest consideration of the oral and written views of our military advisers.

In approaching this problem, we should keep ever before us the realization that the security of the United States is inextricably bound up with the security of the free world. For this reason, one of our tasks is to do everything possible to promote unity of understanding and action among the free nations so that each may take its full and proper part in the cooperative process of establishing a lasting and effective security.

[1] *Department of State Bulletin,* v. 32 (January 17, 1955), p. 87.
[2] *Ibid.,* pp. 87-88.

Certain considerations, applying more specifically to our own country's military preparations, are these:

First, the threat to our security is a continuing and many-sided one—there is, so far as we can determine, no single critical "danger date" and no single form of enemy action to which we could soundly gear all our defense preparations. We will never commit aggression, but we must always be ready to defeat it.

Second, true security for our country must be founded on a strong and expanding economy, readily convertible to the tasks of war.

Third, because scientific progress exerts a constantly increasing influence upon the character and conduct of war, and because America's most precious possession is the lives of her citizens, we should base our security upon military formations which make maximum use of science and technology in order to minimize numbers in men.

Fourth, due to the destructiveness of modern weapons and the increasing efficiency of long-range bombing aircraft, the United States has reason, for the first time in its history to be deeply concerned over the serious effects which a sudden attack could conceivably inflict upon our country.

Our first objective must therefore be to maintain the capability to deter an enemy from attack and to blunt that attack, if it comes—by a combination of effective retaliatory power and a continental defense system of steadily increasing effectiveness. These two tasks logically demand priority in all planning. Thus we will assure that our industrial capacity can continue throughout a war to produce the gigantic amounts of equipment and supplies required.

We can never be defeated so long as our relative superiority in productive capacity is sustained.

Other essential tasks during the initial period following a possible future attack would require the Navy to clear the ocean lanes and the Army to do its part in meeting critical land situations. Our forces in NATO and elsewhere could be swiftly engaged. To maintain order and organization under the conditions that would prevail in attacked areas of our country would of itself constitute a major challenge. Improved Reserve programs would help greatly—in fact might prove the decisive margin—in these as in other major tasks.

To provide for meeting lesser hostile action—such as local aggression not broadened by the intervention of a major aggressor's forces—growing reliance can be placed upon the forces now being built and strengthened in many areas of the free world. But because this reliance cannot be complete, and because our own vital interests, collective security and pledged faith might well be involved, there remain certain contingencies for which the United States should be ready with mobile forces to help indigenous troops deter local aggression, direct or indirect.

In view of the practical considerations limiting the rapid deployment of large military forces from the continental United States immediately on outbreak of war, the numbers of active troops maintained for this purpose can be correspondingly tailored. For the remainder we may look primarily to our Reserves and our mobilization base, including our stockpile of critical materials.

All these capabilities have a double value—they serve our aim in peacetime of preventing war through their deterrent effect; they form the foundation of effective defense if aggressors should strike.

Both in composition and in strength our security arrangements must have long-term applicability. Lack of reasonable stability is the most wasteful and expensive practice in military activity. We cannot afford intermittent acceleration of preparation and expenditure in response to emotional tension, inevitably followed by cutbacks inspired by wishful thinking. Development of sound, long-term security requires that we design our forces so as to assure a steadily increasing efficiency, in step with scientific advances, but characterized by a stability that is not materially disturbed by every propaganda effort of unfriendly nations.

It is, of course, obvious that defensive forces in America are maintained to defend a way of life. They must be adequate for this purpose but must not become such an intolerable burden as to occasion loss of civilian morale or the individual initiative on which, in a free country, depends the dynamic industrial effort which is the continuing foundation of our nation's security.

It is at this point that professional military competence and political statesmanship must join to form judgments as to the minimum defensive structure that should be supported by the nation. To do less than the minimum would expose the nation to the predatory purposes of potential enemies. On the other hand, to build excessively under the impulse of fear could, in the long run, defeat our purposes by damaging the growth of our economy and eventually forcing it into regimented controls.

It is for the reasons so briefly touched upon above that I have decided to present to the Congress, on behalf of the Administration, a program which has been under development during the past two years. That program contemplates an active personnel strength of the armed forces at June 30, 1955, of approximately 3,000,000, within which the Air Force will be increased to about 975,000.

Experience will determine to what extent the personnel strengths set for June 1955 can be further reduced. It would not be wise at this time to fix rigid targets for 1956. As a goal, I suggest a strength of the order of 2,850,000—with any further material reductions dependent upon an improved world situation. To reach such figures without injuring our combat strength will require continuing close scrutiny of all defense elements, with particular emphasis on administrative overhead.

Essential to this entire program is economy in operation. If we are to support active and effective forces of the order indicated over a period which may last for decades, we must practice a strict austerity in day-to-day operations. This is an insistent and constant mission of every responsible official, military and civilian, in the Defense Department.

In this time of rapidly developing technology and frequent changes in the world situation, we should in our efforts for peace and security continuously re-shape our programs to changing conditions and avoid fixed or frozen ideas. The threat of modern war calls for constant modernization.

Since your request to me and this reply both deal with matters on which our citizenry ought to be as fully informed as considerations of security permit, I am directing the public release of the two documents.

Sincerely,
DWIGHT D. EISENHOWER.

D. Foreign Economic Policy and Mutual Security.

1. *Message of the President on Foreign Economic Policy, January 10, 1955.*[1]

The Nation's enlightened self-interest and sense of responsibility as a leader among the free nations require a foreign

[1] House Document 63, 84th Cong., 1st Sess.

economic program that will stimulate economic growth in the free world through enlarging opportunities for the fuller operation of the forces of free enterprise and competitive markets. Our own self-interest requires such a program because (1) economic strength among our allies is essential to our security; (2) economic growth in underdeveloped areas is necessary to lessen international instability growing out of the vulnerability of such areas to Communist penetration and subversion; and (3) an increasing volume of world production and trade will help assure our own economic growth and a rising standard of living among our own people.

In the world wide struggle between the forces of freedom and those of communism, we have wisely recognized that the security of each nation in the free world is dependent upon the security of all other nations in the free world. The measure of that security in turn is dependent upon the economic strength of all free nations, for without economic strength they cannot support the military establishments that are necessary to deter Communist armed aggression. Economic strength is indispensable, as well, in securing themselves against internal Communist subversion.

For every country in the free world, economic strength is dependent upon high levels of economic activity internally and high levels of international trade. No nation can be economically self-sufficient. Nations must buy from other nations, and in order to pay for what they buy they must sell. It is essential for the security of the United States and the rest of the free world that the United States take the leadership in promoting the achievement of those high levels of trade that will bring to all the economic strength upon which the freedom and security of all depends. Those high levels of trade can be promoted by the specific measures with respect to trade barriers recommended in this message, by the greater flow of capital among nations of the free world, by convertibility of currencies, by an expanded interchange of technical counsel, and by an increase in international travel.

From the military standpoint, our national strength has been augmented by the overall military alliance of the nations constituting the free world. This free-world alliance will be most firmly cemented when its association is based on flourishing mutual trade as well as common ideals, interests, and aspirations. Mutually advantageous trade relationships are not only profitable, but they are also more binding and more enduring than costly grants and other forms of aid.

Today numerous uneconomic, man-made barriers to mutually advantageous trade and the flow of investment are preventing the nations of the free world from achieving their full economic potential. International trade and investment are not making their full contribution to production, employment, and income. Over a large area of the world currencies are not yet convertible.

We and our friends abroad must together undertake the lowering of the unjustifiable barriers to trade and investment, and we must do it on a mutual basis so that the benefits may be shared by all.

Such action will add strength to our own domestic economy and help assure a rising standard of living among our people by opening new markets for our farms and factories and mines.

The program that I am here recommending is moderate, gradual, and reciprocal. Radical or sudden tariff reductions would not be to the interest of the United States and would not accomplish the goal we seek. A moderate program, however, can add immeasurably to the security and well-being of the United States and the rest of the free world.

Trade Agreement Authority

I request a 3-year extension of Presidential authority to negotiate tariff reductions with other nations on a gradual, selective, and reciprocal basis. This authority would permit negotiations for reductions in those barriers that now limit the markets for our goods throughout the world. I shall ask all nations with whom we trade to take similar steps in their relations with each other.

The 3-year extension of the Trade Agreements Act should authorize, subject to the present peril and escape clause provisions:[2]

1. Reduction, through multilateral and reciprocal negotiations, of tariff rates on selected commodities by not more than 5 percent per year for 3 years;

2. Reduction, through multilateral and reciprocal negotiations, of any tariff rates in excess of 50 percent to that level over a 3-year period; and

[2] *Public Law* no. 86, 84th Cong., 1st Sess. (June 21, 1955). "Trade Agreements Extension Act of 1955."

3. Reduction, by not more than one-half over a 3-year period, of tariff rates in effect on January 1, 1945, on articles which are not now being imported or which are being imported only in negligible quantities.

The General Agreement on Tariffs and Trade

For approximately 7 years the United States has cooperated with all the major trading nations of the free world in an effort to reduce trade barriers. The instrument of cooperation is the General Agreement on Tariffs and Trade. Through this agreement the United States has sought to carry out the provisions and purpose of the Trade Agreements Act.

The United States and 33 other trading countries are now reviewing the provisions of the agreement for the purpose of making it a simpler and more effective instrument for the development of a sound system of world trade. When the current negotiations on the revision of the organizational provisions of the General Agreement are satisfactorily completed, the results will be submitted to the Congress for its approval.

Customs Administration and Procedure

Considerable progress has been made in freeing imports from unnecessary customs administrative burdens. Still more, however, needs to be done in the three areas I mentioned in my message last year: (1) the simplification of commodity definitions, classification, and rate structures; (2) improvement in standards for the valuation of imports; and (3) further improvement of procedures for customs administration.

An important step toward simplification of the tariff structure was taken by the Congress last year with the passage of the Customs Simplification Act, which directs the Tariff Commission to study the difficulties of commodity classification of imports.[3] The interim report of the Tariff Commission to be made by next March 15 should help enable the Congress to determine whether further legislative steps should then be taken or should await submission of the final report.

The uncertainties and confusion arising from the complex system of valuation on imported articles cause unwarranted delays in the determination of customs duties. I urge the

[3] *Public Law* no. 768, 83rd Cong., 2nd Sess. (Sept. 1, 1954). "Customs Simplification Act of 1954."

Congress to give favorable consideration to legislation for remedying this situation.

The improvement of customs administration requires continuous effort, as the Congress recognized by enacting the Customs Simplification Acts of 1953 and 1954. The Treasury Department in its annual report to the Congress will review the remaining reasons for delay or difficulty in processing imported articles through customs and will propose still further technical amendments to simplify customs procedures.

United States Investment Abroad

The whole free world needs capital; America is its largest source. In that light, the flow of capital abroad from our country must be stimulated and in such an manner that it results in investment largely by individuals or private enterprises rather than by government.

An increased flow of United States private investment funds abroad, especially to the underdeveloped areas, could contribute much to the expansion of two-way international trade. The underdeveloped countries would thus be enabled more easily to acquire the capital equipment so badly needed by them to achieve sound economic growth and higher living standards. This would do much to offset the false but alluring promises of the Communists.

To facilitate the investment of capital abroad, I recommend enactment of legislation providing for taxation of business income from foreign subsidiaries or branches at a rate 14 percentage points lower than the corporate rate on domestic income, and a deferral of tax on income of foreign branches until it is removed from the country where it is earned.

I propose also to explore the further use of tax treaties with the possible recognition of tax concessions made to foreign capital by other countries. Under proper safeguards, credit could be given for foreign income taxes which are waived for an initial limited period, as we now grant credit for taxes which are imposed. This would give maximum effectiveness to foreign tax laws designed to encourage new enterprises.

As a further step to stimulate investment abroad, I recommend approval by the Congress at the appropriate time of membership in the proposed International Finance Corporation, which will be affiliated with the International Bank for

Reconstruction and Development.[4] This corporation will be designed to increase private investment in less developed countries by making loans without Government guaranties. Although the corporation will not purchase stock, it will provide venture capital through investing in debentures and similar obligations. Its operation will cover a field not dealt with by an existing institution.

The executive branch will continue through our diplomatic representatives abroad to encourage a climate favorable to the private enterprise concept in investment.

We shall continue to seek other new ways to enlarge the outward flow of capital.

It must be recognized, however, that when American private capital moves abroad, it properly expects to bring home its fair reward. This can only be accomplished in the last analysis by our willingness to purchase more goods and services from abroad in order to provide the dollars for these growing remittances. This fact is a further compelling reason for a fair and forward-looking trade policy on our part.

Technical Cooperation

The United States has a vast store of practical and scientific know-how that is needed in the underdeveloped areas of the world. The United States has a responsibility to make it available. Its flow for peaceful purposes must remain unfettered.

United States participation in technical cooperation programs should be carried forward. These programs should be concerned with know-how rather than large funds. In my budget message next week I shall recommend that the Congress make available the funds required to support the multilateral technical cooperation programs of the United Nations. The bilateral programs of the United States should be pressed vigorously.

International Travel

The United States remains committed to the objective of freedom of travel throughout the world. Encouragement given to travel abroad is extremely important, both for its cultural and social importance in the free world and for its economic benefits. Travel abroad by Americans provides an important source of dollars for many countries. The execu-

[4] See below, pp. 68-71

tive branch shall continue to look for ways of facilitating international travel and shall continue to cooperate with private travel agencies.

One legislative action that would be beneficial in this field is the increase of the present duty-free allowances for tourists from $500 to $1,000 exercisable every 6 months. I recommend the passage of such legislation.

Trade Fairs

International trade fairs have been of major importance to foreign countries for many years, and most of the trading nations have strengthened the promotional aspects of their industrial displays in many fairs with a central exhibit designed to emphasize the industrial progress and achievement of the nation.

Soviet and satellite exhibits, for example, have been costly, well planned, and housed in expensive structures designed to convey the impression that the U.S.S.R. is producing on a large scale for peace and is creating a paradise for workers.

The United States, which has a larger volume of international trade than any other nation, until recently has been conspicuous by its absence at these trade fairs. American visitors and participants have pointed out the failure of their Government to tell adequately the story of our free enterprise system and to provide effective international trade promotion cooperation.

As a result, I have undertaken an international trade fair program under the direction of the Department of Commerce. Since the inauguration of this program in August [1954], participation has been authorized in 11 fairs to be held before June 30 [1955]. Sixteen additional fairs are being considered for exhibition purposes in the latter part of the year. The first fair in which the United States presented a central exhibit is that at Bangkok, which opened December 7, 1954. At it our exhibit was awarded first prize. Over 100 American companies supplied items for inclusion in it.

I shall ask the Congress for funds to continue this program.

Convertibility

Convertibility of currencies is required for the development of a steadily rising volume of world trade and investment. The achievement of convertibility has not been possible in the post-war period due to dislocations caused by the war, inflation, and other domestic economic difficulties in many countries, which have contributed to an imbalance in international trade and payments. However, steady progress, particularly by Western European countries, is being made toward our mutual objective of restoring currency convertibility. The foreign economic program proposed here will make an important contribution to the achievement of convertibility.

Agriculture

No single group within America has a greater stake in a healthy and expanding foreign trade than the farmers. One-fourth to one-third of some major crops, such as wheat, cotton, and tobacco, must find markets abroad in order to maintain farm income at high levels.

If they are to be successful, programs designed to promote the prosperity of agriculture should be consistent with our foreign economic program. We must take due account of the effect of any agricultural program on our foreign economic relations to assure that it contributes to the development of healthy, expanding foreign markets over the years.

Conclusion

The series of recommendations I have just made are all components of an integrated program, pointing in a single direction. Each contributes to the whole. Each advances our national security by bringing added strength and self-sufficiency to our allies. Each contributes to our economic growth and a rising standard of living among our people.

2. *The Mutual Security Program.*

a. *Message of the President on the Mutual Security Program for 1956, April 20, 1955.*[5]

To the Congress of the United States:

I recommend that the Congress authorize, for the Fiscal Year ending June 30, 1956, the Program for Mutual Security outlined in this message. The program reflects the greatly improved conditions in Europe and provides for the critical needs of Asia. It encourages private overseas investment and private enterprise abroad, fosters an increase in cooperative effort, emphasizes loans rather than grants wherever possible. I consider the program an indispensable part of a realistic and enlightened national policy.

[5] House Document 144, 84th Cong., 1st Sess.

The fixed, unwavering objective of that policy is a just, prosperous, enduring peace. On this fundamental position, we base our broad approach toward our world trade, our military alliances, our exchange of information and of persons, our partnership with free nations through the Mutual Security Program. This partnership is rooted in the facts of economic and defense interdependence and also in the understanding and respect of each partner for the cultural and national aspirations of the other.

The recommendations in this message are an essential complement to the foreign economic program outlined in my message of January 10, 1955. That program is designed to develop the economic strength and the security of the free world through healthy trade expansion among the free nations and through an increased flow of investment capital particularly to underdeveloped areas. The lessening of barriers to trade in the free world is a vital component for the successful implementation of our national policy for security and peace.

We must recognize, however, that certain free world countries, because of the aftermath of war and its continuing threat or because of less developed economies, require assistance which will help them achieve stable national health and essential defensive strength. The Mutual Security Program is designed to deal with these specific problems in the national interest and in the cause of peace. The program stands on its demonstrated worth.

Its cumulative success is especially evident in Western Europe today. The free nations there have attained new levels of production, larger volumes of trade, expanded employment, and rising standards of living. They have established strong defense forces which, although deficient in some respects, now constitute a significant deterrent to aggression and add substantially to the free world's defensive power. Their own national efforts and their cooperation with each other are the prime reasons for their success. However, the United States Mutual Security Program and its predecessor, the European Recovery Program, deserve an important portion of the credit.

The program I now recommend to you for Fiscal Year 1956 proposes no economic aid for the original Marshall Plan countries in Western Europe. These nations are capable of meeting current defense goals without such support. Deliveries of arms from previous appropriations will continue under constant review to insure that the latest weapon developments and strategic thinking are taken into account. Our initial contribution toward the arming of German forces is already funded by previous Congressional action.

In Spain and Yugoslavia, which were not in the Marshall Plan, defense programs can be successful only with further strengthening of their economic base. New appropriations are needed to continue our cooperation with them. Likewise the special circumstances of the city of Berlin require continued support for that outpost of freedom.

But the immediate threats to world security and stability are now centered in Asia. The preponderance of funds requested of the Congress will be used to meet the threat there. Within the vast arc of free Asia, which extends from the Republic of Korea and Japan to the Middle East, 770 million people, one-third of the world's population, reside. Most of them are citizens of newly independent states. Some have been engaged in recent war against the Communists. All are threatened. Capital is very scarce. Technical and administrative skill is limited. Within the area, however, abundant resources and fertile lands are ready for development.

Now is the time for accelerated development of the nations along the arc. The major responsibility must necessarily lie with the countries themselves. At best, foreign capital as well as foreign aid can only launch or stimulate the process of creating dynamic economies. In this light, the United States has the capacity, the desire, the concern to take the lead in friendly help for free Asia.

For example, we can assist in providing and mobilizing capital for useful and constructive development. We can encourage our successful private industry to join with the people of free Asia in building their private industry and facilitate the way. We can consult and advise on the means by which a free nation builds upon the initiative of independent farmers to achieve a steady advance toward better standards of living, in contrast to the mounting failures of collectivist agriculture.

It is clear that most of the nations of free Asia prefer to quicken their cooperative march toward these objectives through the Colombo Plan Consultative Group which was established in 1950 to promote mutual economic development. We welcome this initiative. As a member of the Group, we shall continue to work in strengthening its cooperative efforts.

The varied nature of national situations requires that our cooperation be essentially bilateral. Some of the nations are members of the Manila Pact and their treaty obligations give rise to special economic problems. Most are members of the Colombo Plan. Most, except for Japan, have very little industrial capacity.

The requested authorization includes substantial funds to further our mutual objectives in this area. Of these funds I suggest that we can achieve the maximum return if $200 million is set aside for the establishment of a President's Fund for Asian Economic Development, with broad rules enacted by Congress for its use through loans and grants, and with adequate latitude to meet changing circumstances and to take advantage of constructive opportunities.

To help assure the most effective use of these funds, this appropriation should be available for use over a period of years. Wisdom and economy in their use cannot be achieved through speed. A small, firm, annual commitment out of this $200 million may prove in many instances to be the most fruitful method.

Because of the continuing threat of aggression and subversion in Asia, a large part of the amounts requested for military assistance and direct forces support is to build and maintain the defensive forces of our allies there. This includes the substantial costs of maintaining and improving the defenses of the Nationalist Government of China in Formosa and provides for military equipment and supplies for Korea.

The newly achieved stability in Iran has decreased the Communist threat and has opened the way to the use of oil resources. These eventually will bring revenues to the nation for the further development of the land and the opening of new opportunities for its people. Pending resumption of sufficient revenues from oil, however, limited defense and economic support must be provided.

In the Near East, our stalwart North Atlantic Treaty Organization allies, Greece and Turkey, are both making significant progress. But neither of them can alone support the substantial armed forces which they maintain for their own defense and for the NATO force goals in that area. Their initiative in promoting security arrangements in the Balkans, and Turkey's vigorous efforts for Middle East defense, reinforce the need for continued support of their efforts. Iraq's action in joining with Turkey in a defensive security arrangement is another favorable development.[6]

The continuing tension between the Arab States and Israel handicaps the peoples of all Near East nations.[7] We should continue to work with the governments and peoples on both sides to improve their economic status and accelerate their progress toward lasting peace between them. Our cooperation is beginning to bring results, particularly in the development of water resources. Such developments in the Palestine area can go far to remove present causes of tension.

In the vast continent of Africa the long-range effect of our cooperation is extremely significant. This continent and its resources, the progress of its people and their relationship to the free world are of growing importance. Requested appropriations for this area are needed in the effort to promote welfare and growth for the peoples of Africa.

In Latin America, I recommend intensification of our technical cooperation program. In this area more than a decade ago, technical cooperation was first undertaken in a systematic manner. The programs have proved their high value in many of our sister republics. No international programs have ever had such widespread welcome and support. Indispensable to the economic development of many free nations, they also reflect the deep humanitarian spirit of the American people.

Technical cooperation programs have contributed effectively to the efforts of the other American Republics to strengthen and expand their national economies. These efforts have likewise been aided by our very large inter-American trade, substantial private investment, more extensive lending by the Export-Import Bank, and credits by the International Bank for Reconstruction and Development. As a result, Latin America has achieved a remarkable rate of economic development. In addition to the technical cooperation programs for Latin America, I recommend a continuation of our modest contribution to the Organization of American States and further economic support to meet the critical situations in Guatemala and Bolivia.

Our programs of national action are not in any manner a substitute for United Nations action in similar fields. Every instance of effective measures taken through the United Nations on a human problem improves the ultimate prospect

[6] See below, pp. 342-344.
[7] See below, pp. 348-358.

of peace in the world. Therefore, I strongly recommend that the United Nations Technical Assistance Program, in which sixty governments participate and which is carried out by the United Nations and its specialized agencies be supported in a continuing and adequate manner. The United Nations Children's Fund has carried out an especially appealing and significant work. We have done our full share to make this work possible. We should continue to do so.

Persons who have escaped from totalitarian oppression, often at great peril, and refugees uprooted by war and disaster deserve further support in 1956 through programs administered by the United States, the United Nations, and the Intergovernmental Committee for European Migration.

One of the unique, least expensive, and most fruitful aspects of the Mutual Security Program is the participation, largely in humanitarian projects, of forty-seven voluntary organizations representing many millions of our citizens. These organizations do an exceptionally effective work in helping the escapees and refugees become self-supporting. They distribute large quantities of food on a people-to-people basis. But certain costs for transporting food, and for supplies beyond their own voluntary resources, are needed and should be provided.

In total, for Fiscal Year 1956, I recommend that the Congress approve funds totaling $3,530 million for the Mutual Security Program, as proposed in the Budget Message. Of this amount $712.5 million is for economic programs, including $172 million for a continuation of Technical Cooperation programs, $175.5 million for special programs, $165 million for development assistance, $200 million for the special President's Fund. $100 million is for a worldwide contingency fund. I request $1,000.3 million for Defense Support which serves both economic and defense purposes by supplementing the efforts of countries, particularly in Asia, carrying out defensive measures beyond their current financial capacity. $1,717.2 million is for military assistance and direct forces support. Included in this amount is $500 million to cover expected losses to present military assistance programs by operation of the Supplemental Appropriation Act, 1955.

The Foreign Operations Administration has proved to be an effective and efficient instrument for conducting the Mutual Security Program. An able and devoted group of men and women have successfully conducted the program under direct line authority from the President.

The Congress provided in the Mutual Security Act of 1954 for the termination of the Foreign Operations Administration by June 30 of this year.[8] As I indicated in my letter to the Secretary of State of April 15,[9] I shall issue an Executive Order effective June 30, 1955, transferring the affairs of the Foreign Operations Administration to the Department of State, except for certain military aspects which will be transferred to the Department of Defense.[10]

This transfer to permanent Departments of the Government will reflect the significance of this program as an integral part of our foreign policy. In the implementation of the program, the facilities of all agencies of the Executive Branch will be used where appropriate, and to the maximum possible extent on a contract basis. However, it is essential that responsibility for the non-military operations continue unified; to fragment this responsibility among several agencies would seriously detract from their effectiveness. The reorganization will continue the role of the Institute of Inter-American Affairs in carrying out cooperative programs for the advancement of the well-being of the peoples in the other American Republics.

The continuity of operations and the adjustments of internal relationships within the Department of State after June 30, 1955, will require a period of transition. I recommend that the Mutual Security Act of 1955 include broad authority to revise the organization during a period of six months following June 30, 1955.

The International Cooperation Administration will be a new semi-autonomous unit within the Department of State. Its Director will report directly to the Secretary of State and will, on the Secretary's behalf, give supervision and direction to the mutual security operations performed within the Department of State.

This responsibility will require that the International Cooperation Administration have the capacity to make and carry out operating decisions within broad policy guides established by the Secretary of State. It will likewise require that the Director of the International Cooperation Administration have his own complement of supporting staff and program personnel, both in Washington and in the field. It will be his responsibility to assure that appropriate policy

[8] *Documents on American Foreign Relations, 1954,* p. 53.
[9] *Department of State Bulletin,* v. 32 (May 2, 1955), pp. 715-716.
[10] Executive Order 10610, May 9, 1955, 20 Federal Register 3179; also Executive Order 10625, August 2, 1955, 20 Federal Register 5571.

guide lines are secured from the Secretary of State, and within those guide lines he will issue the necessary instructions to the field to carry out is policy.

Based on the experience of the past two years, three out of every four dollars appropriated for the entire Mutual Security Program will be immediately spent within the United States for commodities, services, machinery, and other items. Insofar as feasible and consistent with the effective meeting of our goals overseas, the commodities will include food, cotton, coal, and other goods for which our capacity or surplus supply most readily matches requirements. Approximately $350 million of agricultural products are expected to be used in the Fiscal Year 1955. This includes a significant export of major surplus crops. Shipments under the Mutual Security Program will be in addition to but coordinated with sales of surplus agricultural commodities for foreign currencies under the Agricultural Trade Development and Assistance Act.

The other twenty-five percent of the dollars will be spent overseas in a manner that will add directly to the accomplishments of the Mutual Security Program. For example, the offshore procurement contracts assist in establishing a defense production base in key points in the free world. In addition, these expenditures will indirectly add to the power of other nations subsequently to purchase with these dollars other needed goods from the United States.

I recommend continuance of the authority in the present Mutual Security Act to meet unexpected events by transfer of funds, appropriated for one geographic area or purpose, to another geographic area or purpose. Experience in recent years has demonstrated that flexible authority is highly desirable to move with dispatch to meet new circumstances, to overcome new dangers, or to capitalize upon favorable developments.

New procedures approved by the Congress last year now make possible maximum integration of domestic procurement of military equipment for our own and allied forces, increased flexibility in the flow of military equipment to our allies and greatly simplified procurement and accounting arrangements. Under the new procedures, the military departments procure most of the equipment for this program as a part of their regular procurement operations, with military assistance funds reserved to repay the Services at the time the equipment is delivered. Under present law, military assistance funds which are reserved remain available for obligation and expenditure until June 30, 1957. To further improve the present arrangements, I recommend that current and proposed military assistance funds be made available until expended, as is now provided in the case of most Department of Defense appropriations for procurement.

In conclusion, I wish again to emphasize the essential role of the Mutual Security Program. The program for the arc of free Asia has had a thorough review by all the Departments of the Government concerned, and it has been recommended to me by the Council on Foreign Economic Policy and the National Security Council after extensive study.

We are making renewed and intensified efforts to develop a successful basic policy on the question of disarmament and we will persist in this effort. But until success is assured beyond doubt, the best prospects of peace and the grim essentials of security together demand the continuance of both our national and mutual defense programs.

The other free nations need the United States, and we need them, if all are to be secure. Here is a clear case of interwoven self-interest. The necessary expenditures to equip and maintain United States armed forces of air and land and sea at strategic points beyond our borders are never called aid. The necessary expenditures to enable other free nations associated with us to equip and maintain vital armed forces at these same strategic points beyond our borders should not be considered as aid. These, in fact, are defense alliance expenditures clearly safeguarding in the most desirable manner, and at times in the only possible way, the security of the United States and of other free nations.

Our economy cannot be strong and continue to expand without the development of healthy economic conditions in other free nations, and without a continuous expansion of international trade. Neither can we be secure in our freedom unless, elsewhere in the world, we help to build the conditions under which freedom can flourish by destroying the conditions under which totalitarianism grows—poverty, illiteracy, hunger and disease. Nor can we hope for enduring peace until the spiritual aspirations of mankind for liberty and opportunity and growth are recognized as prior to and paramount to the material appetites which Communism exploits.

Apart from any obstacles created by the Communists, this is a long-term process. Patience, resourcefulness and dedication are required as well as the creative application of knowledge, skill and material resources to the solution of fundamental human problems, ancient in their origin. In that spirit, the Mutual Security Program is designed for the benefit of all free nations.

DWIGHT D. EISENHOWER

THE WHITE HOUSE,
April 20, 1955.

b. *Review of Achievements of the Foreign Operations Administration: Final Report to the President, June 30, 1955.*[11]

(Excerpts)

* * *

V. *The Major Results*

Today we are able to take stock of our partnership policies and programs to see the results which have been building up over a period of years. Toward many of these results the Mutual Security Program has made a significant and effective contribution.

In *strategic and military affairs,* the United States and its partners have been able to accomplish this: (a) the overwhelming balance of power—population, raw materials, and industrial resources, the bases of military strength—remains on this side of the Iron Curtain; (b) collective defense arrangements have joined together the United States and most of the free-world nations; (c) the almost universal weakness which prevailed in 1949 among the military forces of free nations is being transformed into positive strength. At the present time our allies are bringing into being more than 180 divisions, over 550 combat vessels, and about 250 air squadrons as well as related supporting units that we are helping to equip and support.

As a result of the large and rapid growth of free-world defense strength, the leaders of the Soviet bloc must take into consideration an ever-increasing element of risk in using force to achieve their desires for world domination.

In *economic affairs,* the composite picture of the free-world

[11] *Report to the President on the Foreign Operations Administration, January 1953 to June 1955,* submitted on June 30, 1955 by Harold E. Stassen, Director.

situation is brighter today than at any time in the twentieth century.

In Western Europe, most economic indicators—industrial and agricultural production, trade, exchange reserves—point to alltime highs. Europe's gross national product in 1954, in terms of constant prices, was almost 19 percent above prewar on a per capita basis, and nearly 30 percent above 1948, the start of the Marshall plan. Although Western Europe's external payments position with the dollar area is delicately balanced and still dependent upon extraordinary U.S. expenditures, the original Marshall plan countries of the area no longer require economic aid. The average European today enjoys a higher standard of living than ever before.

In the underdeveloped areas, notable gains in economic development have been scored, despite the fact that the rate of progress lags far behind population needs. Particularly good advances have been made in food production, and prospects are favorable for further forward movement in other vital sectors of the economy.

In the vast arc of countries stretching from South Asia through the Far East live some 770 million people, 45 percent of the entire free-world population. It is in this far-spread region that signs of forward movement are especially heartening. Agricultural production in the Asian arc is at record levels. Output of food grains in 1953-54 was 8 percent above the 1952-53 crop year, and 10 percent above prewar. Population, however, has increased to such an extent that the per capita share of all agricultural production is only 90 percent of prewar.

Most encouraging is the growing evidence that the countries in the underdeveloped areas are overcoming the obstacles which, for centuries past, have kept living standards at the lowest levels of human existence. Increased initiative and enterprise are being demonstrated by the people and the governments in these areas in pushing ahead with measures for economic development. It has been estimated that public expenditures for development in South and Southeast Asia, for example, are currently more than double what they were in 1951-52.

World attention has been focused on India, the largest free-world nation striving to better the lot of its people through representative government and democratic means. In the first 3 years of its current Five-Year Plan, per capita income has been raised by 8 percent.

The situation in India is in striking contrast to that in Red China where production gains are being made by subordinating the will of the individual to the will of the Communist State and by regimenting labor by force and fiat. Only by the most callous repression of consumer wants, and by a grossly disproportionate emphasis on heavy industry, has Red China been able to achieve a more rapid rate of industrialization than India. But even in industry, despite recent gains, Communist China fails to match India's per capita levels of output.

Noteworthy progress is also being made in other areas. In Latin America, despite the highest rate of population growth in the world and the continued difficult economic position of "one-crop" countries, living standards in general are moving constantly upward.

In *political affairs,* much progress has been made in clearing up many misunderstandings about the U.S. position which prevailed at the time of your inauguration. There is a growing recognition, I believe, throughout the entire world of the enduring reality of U.S. interests in world peace and world prosperity and in our willingness to take constructive action toward those goals in concert with other nations.

We have seen during the last 2½ years some evidences of progress toward the dream of Europe's greatest statesmen—European unity. NATO has moved forward. The Coal and Steel Community is an accomplished fact. Western Germany has regained its sovereignty and is fast becoming a full-fledged partner in military, economic, and political affairs in Europe.

In Asia, many new nations—formerly colonies—are achieving conditions of true independence and national sovereignty and are now not only enjoying the privileges of independence but are also taking on new responsibilities. The recent conferences in Bandung[12] (Indonesia) and in Simla (India) give constructive evidence of this. We have seen many recent evidences—few of them of overwhelming magnitude but all of them pointing in the right direction—of reduced Communist strength in the free world: shop steward elections in Northern Italy; elections in India in the State of Andhra; events in Guatemala, Iran, and France—all of these, and others, indicate progress away from the false answers of totalitarian propaganda.

In the United States, the full effects of economic gains abroad are likely to be felt only in the longer span of time.

[12] See below, pp. 332-341.

It is apparent, nevertheless, that the U.S. economy is already experiencing substantial economic benefits from results of the Mutual Security Program.

Foreign economic conditions played an important part in stemming our own business contraction in 1953-54. Analysis of the factors that brought about a reversal of the downward trend in our own economy, shows that the continuing recovery of Western Europe helped to augment our exports and to bolster the prices of internationally traded raw materials. This was in sharp contrast to the historical pattern of foreign economic developments whenever downswings occurred in the United States. Formerly, foreign economies were acutely affected by the downward spiral of demand in this country and were forced to contract their imports from us, thus adding to the severity of our own decline.

During the 2 years ended June 30, 1955, expenditures for goods under the Mutual Security Program were approximately $8.7 billion—$6.3 billion for military assistance and direct forces support and $2.4 billion for other mutual security programs. Of these amounts, more than three-quarters represented payments for goods or services procured in the United States. During fiscal years 1954 and 1955, FOA paid a total of approximately $90 million to U.S. flag vessels for the transportation of nonmilitary supplies.

In conducting the program of FOA, there have been occasions when special consideration has been given to the needs of distressed sectors of the American economy. For example, about a year ago, much of the U.S. railroad equipment industry was idle. At that time the Government of India requested that a substantial portion of its aid allotment be made available to purchase 100 locomotives. To help the ailing U.S. industry in these circumstances, FOA directed that 50 percent of a $38.5 million order be placed in this country.

To relieve unemployment in the coal-producing regions of the United States, a $20 million coal revolving fund was authorized last winter to finance coal shipments abroad. We estimate that over 4 million tons of American coal were authorized for purchase during the fiscal year under the revolving fund and the regular FOA Program.

In the past 2 years, U.S. agricultural surpluses have been put to constructive use on an increasing scale under the Mutual Security Program. Surplus farm products have been sold abroad to friendly countries who pay in their own currencies. In fiscal year 1954, some $245 million worth of surpluses were sold by FOA and the proceeds realized from such surplus sales are now being used for military assistance, defense support, development assistance, and other purposes which forward the objectives of the Mutual Security Program.

In fiscal year 1955, $380 million of surplus agricultural sales was authorized with the sales proceeds earmarked for Mutual Security Program purposes. These sales are in addition to the surplus commodity sales concluded under the Agricultural Trade Development and Assistance Act, administered by the Department of Agriculture.

With the conclusion of the Korean war, world supply of many items changed abruptly from shortage to overabundance. FOA then promptly shifted the focus of its agricultural development programs. The underdeveloped areas were encouraged to expand production of items for which there was a growing demand. Cocoa, coffee, fish, and forestry products, for example, were emphasized in program planning.

LOOKING AHEAD

The list of free-world accomplishments—to many of which our programs of mutual security have made a significant contribution—is long. It shows that we have left many milestones behind on the road to free-world security and prosperity. But you have wisely and repeatedly emphasized that these gains, real and gratifying though they are, should not be allowed to obscure the dimensions of the tasks that lie ahead.

The Mutual Security Program has a come a long way toward meeting its objectives but, as you stated in your recent message to the Congress,[13] our task is far from complete.

May I summarize this outlook in relation to the present status of the Mutual Security Program.

NATO is unquestionably an effective deterrent and retaliatory fighting force. So long as there is any threat of aggression, it must remain so. But this will call for continuing materiel and training aid by the United States to supplement the significant defense efforts of our European partners. Technology in the military sciences is dynamic and ever-changing. If NATO is not to lapse into obsolescence, it must be made continually stronger by the latest that modern industry can produce.

In the Near East, the Northern Tier (Turkey, Iran, Iraq, Pakistan), blocking Soviet access to this vital area and its

[13] See above, pp. 31-40.

people, is in the incipient stages of development as an alliance and as a military force. Here, too, the United States will have an opportunity of helping to build a strategic bulwark of free-world defense.

In Asia and the Pacific, nations are allied with us to defend their homelands, their institutions, and their peoples against the encroachments of Communist dictatorship. The Southeast Asia Collective Defense Treaty can lead to a powerful barrier to further aggression on the Asian periphery of the Communist bloc. We must continue to help the still-free peoples of Asia to keep that freedom.

But all of these nations have competing demands on their resources—demands for economic and social betterment which cannot go unheeded. The task of building peace must not be confined primarily to armaments and alliances. There will be little hope for enduring world tranquillity unless the vast segments of humanity in the underdeveloped areas succeed in lifting themselves onto a higher economic plane and develop political and social institutions responsive to their cultural and spiritual values.

The less developed nations are in the throes of a vast technological and social evolution. It is in our interest, as well as in theirs, to help them succeed.

U.S. Economic Interests

There is no doubt that the United States can, in the next 10 years, raise its national output from the current level of about $370 billion to more than $500 billion, in dollars of the same buying power. We have, unquestionably, the capacity and ingenuity to achieve this expansion, but our progress toward this goal and its actual attainment will present new and difficult problems affecting our relations with the rest of the world.

This projected one-third increase in national output over a 10-year period would mean a very substantial increase in our requirements for raw materials. To a large extent, these expanded needs can be met through greater production at home of minerals, fibers, and synthetic products. We cannot meet our full requirements, however, without a great increase in imports of foreign materials.

Concurrently with our own rising imports, there will be competing demands for the needed materials from other developed regions and from the producing areas themselves as they move to higher levels of production and consumption.

Most of the basic materials which we import originate in the underdeveloped areas of the world. Therefore, aside from numerous other compelling reasons, we have a vital interest in helping these areas to achieve a substantial increase in their capacity to produce.

Furthermore, as we increase our national output to one-third or more above present levels, we must find new markets for some products—particularly for certain agricultural items where domestic demand is relatively inelastic.

This brings us to the second major aspect of our future economic relations with the rest of the world—exports. The present need to increase our own imports in order that we may increase exports has been described often and effectively. There is, however, a problem of developing purchasing power abroad which can be capable of absorbing a portion of our increased output. If we assume no change in the present relationship between U.S. exports and national output 10 years from now, and if we assume further that we reach a $500-billion production level, we should then be seeking markets abroad capable of buying each year an additional $5 billion of U.S. merchandise over and above our present level of exports.

To market these goods successfully in a way that will bring reasonable returns to American producers, there must first be a sizable expansion abroad of commercial and personal buying power. But this expansion will be achieved only if foreign nations are helped to secure additional capital to accelerate their economic development and if the results of such development are widely shared.

Europe's Economic Future

As I have outlined above, Western Europe has made remarkable progress since the end of the war in rehabilitating its economy and in attaining new heights in production. Productivity and personal consumption have gained, but the rate of progress in these respects has lagged behind that in other developed areas. If Europe is to strengthen, or even maintain, its economic position, it must keep pace with technical progress elsewhere in the world. That applies not only to progress in industrial and agricultural methods, but to distribution and marketing as well.

Continued technical assistance from the United States in support of European efforts to lower costs of production and distribution, to improve management education, and to strengthen free trade unions will help not only to assure Western Europe's competitive position in world markets, but will also permit further increases in wages and living standards for workers in the area and greater imports of U.S. products.

Capital Needs Abroad

To a very large degree, foreign nations requiring development capital will be able to secure it from their own resources. There will be, however, a sizable capital deficiency unless external private capital, including United States capital, can be encouraged to move abroad on a substantially greater scale than at the present time. The problem is difficult but not insurmountable. In time, we may hope that a further relaxation of international tensions will overcome some of today's hesitancy of private capital. Currency and other restrictions have eased in recent years and there are encouraging prospects for further progress in this direction in the near future. One of the biggest problems appears to be that of creating a better understanding between foreign governments and external capital sources. Only through joint ventures of foreign and local capital and skills can the capital gap of the underdeveloped areas of the world be adequately bridged. Acceptance by foreign investors of a *minority* position is one of the best means of giving recognition to the ascending status of the now underdeveloped areas and to their position as active partners in the free world.

This and other forms of joint investment in which foreign capital can participate constructively without dominating, would go far to calm the fears of newly independent nations that private investment may be used as an entering wedge for a new colonialism.

Aid to Underdeveloped Areas

In the period ahead, certainly for several years, there is little possibility that the underdeveloped areas can meet unaided their minimum capital requirements for economic development. Many of these areas still lack the resources to finance the expansion necessary even to keep up with normal population increases. As a result, living standards may not only fail to move upward; they may decline.

To preclude these developments, which would have extremely adverse consequences on free-world security, our Government should continue to supplement technical assistance with capital funds for basic economic development and industrial expansion. Moreover, our technical assistance programs for the underdeveloped areas should emphasize increasingly the improvement of public services and public institutions. If the now free governments of the world are to remain free, they must demonstrate an ever-growing capacity to serve the needs of their people. The underdeveloped areas are on the threshold of epochal change and the will and initiative to accomplish this change are steadily gaining momentum.

The path before us is clear; the task of building an enduring peace must be based not only upon a lowering of tension and lessening of armament with safety, but also upon the creation of expanding economies throughout the world.

As men everywhere are able to create more of the material goods they need, as they are increasingly able to exchange the fruits of their labor and to share experiences and cultural values, we will come even closer to the goal you have so often and eloquently described—an atomic age of peace with freedom.

c. *Eighth Semiannual Report to Congress on the Mutual Security Program, August 25, 1955.*[14]

(Excerpts)

As the mutual security program moved into a new fiscal year of operation in mid-1955, there was increasing evidence of solid gains achieved through joint efforts with some 70 countries and territories throughout the free world. The contribution of a portion of our military, economic, and technical resources to buttress the undertakings of other free nations has made it possible for them to carry out specific measures for preparing stiffer defenses against aggression and for building stronger economies. Added together, these measures have brought the free world as a whole to a position of measurably greater security and have made the ground firmer for further forward movement.

Events of the past six months, particularly in Europe, but also in Asia and other parts of the free world, have given additional demonstration that the United States investment in cooperative programs abroad is paying worthwhile dividends in stronger and more self-reliant partner nations and

[14] House Document 266, 84th Cong., 1st Sess.

a lessening of international tensions. Today's greater opportunities for peaceful economic growth flow in great measure from our steadfast policy of a partnership approach in solving the difficult problems of our time.

Stronger Military Posture of the Free World

The bulk of mutual security funds has been used to help put the free world into a stronger position to discourage armed aggression as a means of gaining world power. Through June 30, 1955, the United States had shipped $11.4 billion worth of military equipment to bolster the defense efforts of more than 35 friendly countries. These shipments included 7,575 planes, 38,400 tanks and combat vehicles, and 1,079 Navy vessels; they also included artillery pieces, small arms, machine guns, electronic equipment, and other military supplies.

The United States has placed about $2.8 billion worth of contracts in friendly countries for procurement of certain types of military items to be used by recipient governments for mutual security purposes. Such contracts overseas have helped our allies to develop their own capabilities for military production, reduce their dependence on this country for replacements and spare parts, and provide a close-in supply line in case of war.

In Europe.—The most powerful concentration of free world strength outside of the United States has been established in Western Europe. The free nations of Europe, linked with the United States and Canada through the North Atlantic Treaty Organization, have continued to move ahead in creating a strong deterrent force and in building their military capabilities to the point where they will be able to meet successfully any attempt to seize their lands and resources by armed force. The addition in May of a sovereign Germany to the free world community and to NATO opened up new avenues to increased unity and strength on the European continent.[15]

European NATO nations (excluding Greece and Turkey) are spending about $12.3 billion a year on military production and maintenance of their armed forces. These outlays for defense, which are double what they were in 1950, are being made on an increasingly self-supporting basis. No new economic dollar aid to these European NATO countries is

[15] See below, p. 93.

planned after June 30, 1955. Economic aid expenditures from previous appropriations are also declining rapidly.

Europe's invigorated defense effort, reinforced by our assistance, has been reflected in the impressive increase in NATO capabilities. The armed forces committed to the defense of the North Atlantic Treaty area today number about 100 divisions, active and in mobilizable reserves, as compared to NATO's total manpower complement of 12 divisions in 1949. There are now more than 6,000 planes available for defense of the NATO area.

The quality of weapons for the NATO arsenal has steadily improved. The latest types of jet planes, guided missiles, and atomic artillery are available in increased quantity for NATO defense. The basis has been laid for consideration of atomic capabilities in NATO planning. Hundreds of joint training exercises have developed more effective fighting power and promoted smoother operational coordination among the land, air, and sea forces committed to NATO.

Mutual security funds have been used for the United States contribution to a military construction program financed jointly by all the NATO nations and designed to provide NATO with more effective logistic support. Through this program, NATO now has 142 airfields which could be used in an emergency. Communications and transportation networks have been modernized and extended, and construction on a 3,800-mile inland distribution pipeline for fuel is well advanced.

Elsewhere in the Free World.—Heartening progress toward a stronger defense posture also has been made in other areas of the free world. In underpinning defense efforts outside Europe, the mutual security program not only has helped build greater defense capabilities in individual countries; it also has been effective in developing an atmosphere for better cooperation in working toward regional defense arrangements.

New links have strengthened and lengthened our security chain in Asia and the Pacific. The latest link, the Southeast Asia Collective Defense Treaty, rounds out our mutual defense treaties with Korea, Japan, and the Republic of China on Formosa.

The Republic of Korea now has a strong force of 21 ground divisions on active duty. The free Chinese forces on Formosa are better trained and better equipped today, in great part because of United States military aid. Pakistan's defense establishment has received its first shipments of army equipment as a result of a military assistance agreement signed with this country in early 1954.[16] The Philippines and Thailand have also substantially raised their defense capabilities because of our mutual security programs. Cambodia concluded a military assistance agreement with the United States in May 1955.[17]

* * *

Use of Funds in Fiscal Year 1955

During fiscal year 1955, obligations and reservations under the military assistance program accounted for $3.3 billion of mutual security funds. In addition, $523 million was allotted for direct forces support in the form of soft goods consumed by the military, such as petroleum and cloth for uniforms. A total of $795 million was allotted for defense support to reinforce the economies of those nations joined with us in programs of military assistance so that they could sustain their military contributions to free world defense; $125 million was allotted for joint technical cooperation projects, and $256 million for development assistance. The remainder was used for activities such as the United States share of international programs of technical assistance and children's welfare, the escapee and refugee programs, and aid to West Berlin.

During the fiscal year, agreements were made with 11 countries which provided for $214.5 million of mutual security assistance to be furnished on a loan basis. Collections from all countries on previous loans made under mutual security programs amounted to about $150 million as of the end of June 1955. These were mainly interest payments, since under the terms of the original loans repayments of principal generally do not begin to fall due until 1956.

By far the largest portion of expenditures made under the mutual security program has been for goods and services procured in the United States. In fiscal year 1955, over 75 percent of all program expenditures were paid to American suppliers.

During the 1955 fiscal year also, over $467 million worth of United States surplus agricultural commodities were sold to friendly countries which have contracted to pay in their

[16] *Documents on American Foreign Relations, 1954,* pp. 379-383.
[17] *Department of State Bulletin,* v. 32 (May 30, 1955), p. 891.

own currencies. These surplus sales were concluded in accordance with the provisions of Section 402 of the Mutual Security Act of 1954,[18] and the sales proceeds have been earmarked for use in mutual security operations. Together with transactions made in the previous fiscal year under a similar provision, over $700 million of our agricultural surpluses have been sold to friendly countries in direct connection with mutual security activities. Such sales were in addition to the surplus commodity sales carried out under Title I of the Agricultural Trade Development and Assistance Act of 1954.[19]

The New International Cooperation Administration

In compliance with the Congressional provision that the Foreign Operations Administration be terminated as an independent agency by the end of June 1955, Executive Order 10610 was issued on May 9, 1955, which transferred FOA activities to the Department of State. Certain military aspects of the mutual security program were transferred for administration to the Department of Defense.

Under the Executive Order, which took effect at the close of June 30, the International Cooperation Administration was established as a semiautonomous organization in the State Department, and the President directed that the mutual security program be carried out by and under ICA. The Institute of Inter-American Affairs, the International Development Advisory Board, and the Office of Small Business, all of which formerly were under the Foreign Operations Administration, were attached to or made part of ICA.

The President selected John B. Hollister as the Director of the International Cooperation Administration. Mr. Hollister took office on July 1, and Harold E. Stassen, former Director of the Foreign Operations Administration, became Special Assistant to the President to help develop basic policy on disarmament. As Director of the new organization, Mr. Hollister will report directly to the Secretary of State and will supervise and direct the nonmilitary mutual security operations. He also has the responsibility for coordinating the entire program, although the Department of Defense will continue to administer United States assistance furnished directly to the armed forces of other nations. Such military

[18] *Public Law* no. 665, 83d Cong., 1st Sess. (August 16, 1954).
[19] *Public Law* no. 480, 83d Cong., 1st Sess. (July 10, 1954).

assistance now includes "direct forces support," previously administered by the Foreign Operations Administration.

The International Cooperation Administration was established within the State Department in conformance with the wide recognition that the development of military and economic strength through our mutual security program is an integral part of United States foreign policy. In working out arrangements for the new organization, however, care had to be taken to maintain the central planning and the coherent direction necessary to insure coordinated and effective program action. To effect this, the Executive Order specified that the International Cooperation Administration be made semiautonomous, with its own supporting staff and program personnel both in Washington and in the field. Within guide lines established by the Secretary of State, the Director of the ICA will perform the operations necessary to carry out our national policy objectives.

3. *United States Participation in the General Agreement on Tariffs and Trade.*

a. *Message of the President Recommending Participation in the Organization for Trade Cooperation, April 14, 1955.*[20]

THE WHITE HOUSE
April 14, 1955.

To the Congress of the United States:

The United States continuously seeks to strengthen the spiritual, political, military, and economic bonds of the free nations. By cementing these ties, we help preserve our way of life, improve the living standards of free peoples, and make possible the higher levels of production required for the security of the free world. With this objective in view, I recommended to the Congress in my message of January 10, 1955,[21] the enactment of legislation designed to promote a healthy trade expansion and an increased flow of private capital for economic development abroad.

Consistent with that broad purpose, the United States over the past seven years has participated in the multilateral trade agreement known as the General Agreement on Tariffs and

[20] House Document 140, 84th Cong., 1st Sess.
[21] See above, pp. 24-31.

Trade. This key element in the nation's foreign economic policy has been carried on under the authority vested in the President by the Congress in the trade agreements legislation. After several months of intensive review of the trade rules in the General Agreement, the United States and 33 other participating countries last month agreed upon certain revisions of those rules.[22] A new instrument was also drafted which would set up a simple international organization, to be known as the Organization for Trade Cooperation, whose purpose is the administration of the General Agreement.[23]

I should like to recall the circumstances that gave rise to the General Agreement and this country's participation in it. I should also like to stress some of its benefits to us which justify the continued existence of the General Agreement and United States membership in the Organization for Trade Cooperation.

The economic and political dislocations produced by World War II jeopardized, in the postwar years, the re-establishment of healthy, expanding international trade. Many countries had little to export and lacked the means to buy the products of other countries. Widespread resort to restrictions on imports and to discriminatory bilateral trade arrangements threatened a return to economic isolationism and narrow channels of government-directed trade. There was a great need for cooperative efforts to reduce unjustifiable trade restrictions and to establish a set of principles, mutually beneficial to the free nations of the world, for the reconstruction of world trade.

In this state of world affairs, the United States and a group of friendly nations negotiated a series of tariff agreements among themselves. They also negotiated a set of trade principles or rules to protect the tariff concessions. These tariff agreements and trade rules were incorporated in a multilateral trade agreement, the General Agreement on Tariffs and Trade.[24]

The trade rules consist basically of provisions which this nation, since 1934, has incorporated in bilateral trade agreements to protect our interest in the tariff concessions granted to us in such agreements. They provide, for example, that tariff concessions should not be nullified by the imposition

[22] *Department of State Bulletin*, v. 32 (March 21, 1955), p. 495; also *ibid.* (April 4, 1955), p. 577.
[23] See below, pp. 59-68.
[24] Concluded on October 30, 1947.

of other restrictions; that quantitative restrictions should not be imposed on imports; that trade restrictions, when used, should be nondiscriminatory as between countries; and that concessions granted to one country should be extended to like products of other countries in accordance with the unconditional most-favored-nation principle.

To provide the degree of flexibility required to meet the varying needs of participating countries, the General Agreement provides for specific exceptions to the basic rules. Under certain circumstances waivers may be granted to countries to depart from these basic rules. The United States has obtained such a waiver to restrict imports of agricultural products on which we have government programs.

The General Agreement through the trade rules and the tariff negotiations sponsored under it has served well the purpose for which it was designed: the orderly expansion of international trade. Thirty-four countries, whose trade accounts for nearly four-fifths of the world's total trade, are now participating in this cooperative effort. World trade has expanded at a rapid rate, and for many countries foreign trade now represents a higher ratio to total output of goods than in the prewar years.

An important benefit to this country results from participation in multilateral trade negotiations under the General Agreement. Doing so makes it possible for us to obtain more tariff concessions on our exports than would be forthcoming from bilateral negotiation. This country, as a party to the multilateral agreement, obtains benefits from concessions which other countries would be unwilling to negotiate except in a multilateral undertaking.

Some measure of the value of these multilateral trade agreement negotiations to the United States is indicated by the fact that we have been able to obtain concessions covering about 50 percent in value of our exports.

Another advantage to this country through our participation in the General Agreement has been manifest during the past two years. Restrictions on the part of other countries against dollar imports are permitted under the trade rules for genuine balance of payments reasons, and as the balance of payments position of other countries has improved, we have been able to persuade them to relax such restrictions. Between 1953 and the beginning of 1955 ten Western European countries had removed quantitative restrictions on dollar imports amounting to about 60 percent of such imports. Since the beginning of this year additional restrictions have been removed. In the absence of the General Agreement it would be more difficult to persuade these countries to relax such controls. We are thus moving toward full realization of the tariff concessions that have been granted our exports since 1948. It is the policy of this Government to utilize the consultative procedures of the General Agreement to press for the discharge of these commitments for the benefit of our foreign trade.

In addition to the general relaxation of restrictions on dollar imports that has been accomplished, we have been successful in persuading other countries to remove discriminatory restrictions against imports of particular dollar goods. This Government has protested the inconsistency between the discriminatory action in those cases and the principles of the General Agreement. Certain discriminatory restrictions have thus been removed on imports from this country of such items as coal, apples, cigarettes, lumber, potatoes, textiles, automobiles, tobacco, petroleum, wool, and motion pictures.

A further important contribution of the General Agreement to the extension of trade is the assurance against wholesale increases in tariff rates in export markets. Our exporters, therefore, can proceed with their plans for sales in markets abroad with a greater degree of certainty as to tariff rates. Participating countries may, of course, consistently with the trade rules, raise tariff rates in individual cases where serious injury to domestic industry is threatened.

The revised General Agreement has been thoroughly reviewed within the Executive Branch of the Government. I believe it has been improved and strengthened. It protects the legitimate interests of this country and provides a firm basis for orderly trade expansion among the free nations of the world. The necessity for the United States to restrict imports of agricultural products with regard to which we have government programs is fully recognized. The right of this country to protect the legitimate interests of its industries and labor is clearly provided for. The rules of trade regarding the imposition of discriminatory import controls have been tightened and should assist in the efforts to remove and to prevent discriminatory restrictions against United States exports. The spirit with which the participating countries cooperated in the task of review and revision of the General

Agreement was heartening and augurs well for its future vitality.

The United States and the other participating countries concluded on the basis of seven years' experience that the organizational provisions of the General Agreement should be changed to provide a continuous mechanism for the administration of the trade rules and the discussion of mutual trade problems. Under present arrangements these activities are confined largely to the annual sessions of the parties to the Agreement. The participating countries therefore have proposed to set up an Organization for Trade Cooperation for more effective administration of the trade rules and related activities.

The Organization for Trade Cooperation would be established by a separate agreement among the participating countries. In addition to administering the General Agreement, it would provide a mechanism through which arrangements for trade negotiations could be facilitated. It would also serve as a forum for the discussion of trade matters and for the amicable adjustment of problems involving the trade rules. The Organization would have no supra-national powers. It would conduct no trade negotiations; this would be done by the countries who chose to participate in the negotiations and to whatever extent they choose.

The United States delegation which took part in the revision of the General Agreement was specifically instructed to reject all efforts to expand the functions of the new organization into fields other than trade. One measure of the success of the negotiations from the standpoint of the United States is the fact that the proposed Organization for Trade Cooperation is thus limited in its functions. Its effectiveness, in my judgment, will be enhanced by the fact that it has such specific and limited responsibilities.

I believe the reasons for United States membership in the proposed Organization are overwhelming. We would thus demonstrate to the free world our active interest in the promotion of trade among the free nations. We would demonstrate our desire to deal with matters of trade in the same cooperative way we do with military matters in such regional pacts as the North Atlantic Treaty Organization, and with financial matters in the International Monetary Fund and in the International Bank for Reconstruction and Development. We would thus cooperate further with the free world, in the struggle against Communist domination, to the greater security and the greater prosperity of all.

Such action would serve the enlightened self-interest of the United States. As a member of this Organization we could work more effectively for the removal of discriminatory restrictions against our exports. We could help establish conditions favorable to convertibility of currencies. We could further the expansion of markets abroad for the products of our mines, our farms and our factories. We could assist in the development of conditions conducive to the international flow of investment capital so urgently needed to expand production throughout the free world, especially in its underdeveloped areas.

Failure to assume membership in the Organization for Trade Cooperation would be interpreted throughout the free world as a lack of genuine interest on the part of this country in the efforts to expand trade. It would constitute a serious setback to the momentum which has been generated toward that objective. It would strike a severe blow at the development of cooperative arrangements in defense of the free world. It could lead to the imposition of new trade restrictions on the part of other countries, which would result in a contraction of world trade and constitute a sharp setback to United States exports. It could result in regional re-alignments of nations. Such developments, needless to say, would play directly into the hands of the Communists.

I believe the national interest requires that we join with other countries of the free world in dealing with our trade problems on a cooperative basis.

I herewith transmit copies of the agreement providing for an Organization for Trade Cooperation, and I recommend that the Congress enact legislation authorizing United States membership in that organization.[25]

DWIGHT D. EISENHOWER

[25] On July 14, 1955 the Chairman of the [House] Committee on Ways and Means informed the President that hearings on H.R. 5550 authorizing U.S. membership in the Organization for Trade Cooperation would be postponed. The President acknowledged the reasons for the delay and urged that H.R. 5550 be "among the very first measures" to be considered by the Committee in 1956. See *Department of State Bulletin*, v. 33 (August 1, 1955), p. 188.

b. *Text of Agreement on Organization for Trade Cooperation, Geneva, March 10, 1955.*[26]

PART I—GENERAL

Article 1—Establishment

The Organization for Trade Cooperation (hereinafter referred to as "the Organization") is hereby established to further, as provided for in the General Agreement and herein, the achievement of the purposes and objectives set forth in the General Agreement on Tariffs and Trade (herein referred to as "the General Agreement").

Article 2—Membership

The Members of the Organization shall be the contracting parties to the General Agreement. Governments which become or cease to be contracting parties to the General Agreement shall become or cease to be Members of the Organization. The Organization may, by a two-thirds majority of the votes cast, invite governments which are not or which cease to be contracting parties to the General Agreement to participate in such activities of the Organization and on such terms as it shall decide; *Provided* that in no case shall such participation involve the right to vote or to be counted in determining the fulfilment of the relevant voting requirements when the Organization is exercising any function relating directly to the General Agreement.

Article 3—Functions

(a) The Organization shall administer the General Agreement and generally facilitate the operation of that Agreement.

(b) In addition, the Organization shall have the following functions:

(i) to facilitate intergovernmental consultations on questions relating to international trade;
(ii) to sponsor international trade negotiations;
(iii) to study questions of international trade and commercial policy and, where appropriate, make recommendations thereon;

[26] *Department of State Bulletin,* v. 32 (April 4, 1955), pp. 579-582.

(iv) to collect, analyse and publish information and statistical data relating to international trade and commercial policy, due regard being paid to the activities in this field of other international bodies.

(c) The Organization shall, in carrying out these functions, endeavour to give full effect to the provisions of Article 1 of this Agreement.

(d) The Organization shall have no authority to amend the provisions of the General Agreement; no decision or other action of the Assembly or any subsidiary body of the Organization shall have the effect of imposing on a Member any new obligation which the Member has not specifically agreed to undertake.

PART II—STRUCTURE AND ADMINISTRATION OF THE ORGANIZATION

Article 4—Structure in General

The Organization shall have an Assembly, an Executive Committee and a Secretariat.

Article 5—The Assembly

(a) The Assembly shall consist of all the Members of the Organization.

(b) It shall be the responsibility of the Assembly to carry out the functions of the Organization.

(c) The Assembly shall determine the seat of the Organization.

(d) The Assembly shall meet in regular annual session and in such special sessions as may be convened in accordance with the rules of procedure.

(e) The Assembly shall establish its own rules of procedure and shall approve the rules of procedure of the Executive Committee and of any other subsidiary body.

Article 6—The Executive Committee

(a) The Executive Committee shall consist of seventeen Members of the Organization elected periodically by the Assembly. Each election shall be for a single term and each Member shall be eligible for re-election. In such elections, the Assembly shall be guided by the following criteria:

(i) the Executive Committee shall include the five members of chief economic importance, in the determination of which particular regard shall be paid to their shares in international trade;

(ii) the Executive Committee shall be representative of the broad geographical areas to which the Members belong;

(iii) the Executive Committee shall be representative of different degrees of economic development, different types of economies and different economic interests.

(b) The Executive Committee shall exercise the powers and perform the duties assigned to it by the Assembly by a majority of two-thirds of the votes cast. Decisions or recommendations of the Executive Committee shall be subject to a right of appeal to the Assembly by any Member in accordance with rules to be prescribed by the Assembly.

(c) Any Member of the Organization which is not a member of the Executive Committee shall be entitled to participate, without the right to vote, in the discussion by the Executive Committee of any matter of concern to it.

Article 7—The Secretariat

(a) The Assembly shall appoint a Director-General as chief administrative officer of the Organization. The powers, duties, conditions of service and term of office of the Director-General shall conform to regulations approved by the Assembly.

(b) The Director-General or his representative shall be entitled to participate, without the right to vote, in all meetings of the Assembly and subsidiary bodies of the Organization.

(c) The Director-General shall appoint the members of the staff, and shall fix their duties and conditions of service in accordance with regulations approved by the Assembly.

(d) The selection of the members of the staff shall as far as possible be made on a wide geographical basis and with due regard to the various types of economy represented by Member countries. The paramount consideration in the selection of candidates and in determining the conditions of service of the staff shall be the necessity of securing the highest standards of efficiency, competence, impartiality and integrity.

(e) The responsibilities of the Director-General and of the members of the staff shall be exclusively international in character. In the discharge of their duties, they shall not seek or receive instructions from any government or from any other authority external to the Organization. They shall refrain from any action which might reflect on their positions as international officials. The Members shall respect the international character of the responsibilities of these persons and shall not seek to influence them in the discharge of their duties.

Article 8—Voting

(a) At meetings of the Assembly each Member of the Organization shall be entitled to have one vote and, except as otherwise provided for in the General Agreement or in this Agreement, decisions of the Assembly shall be taken by a majority of the votes cast.

(b) Each member of the Executive Committee and of other subsidiary bodies shall have one vote therein; *Provided* that the rules of procedure may require that parties to a dispute shall abstain from voting.

Article 9—Budget and Contributions

(a) The Director-General shall present to the Assembly, through the Executive Committee, the annual budget estimates and financial statement of the Organization. The Assembly shall approve the accounts and the budget.

(b) The Assembly shall apportion the expenditures of the Organization among the Members, in accordance with a scale of contributions to be fixed by the Assembly, and each Member shall contribute promptly to the Organization its share of these expenditures.

(c) If a Member is in arrears in the payment of its contributions by an amount which equals or exceeds the amount of contributions due from it in respect of the preceding two completed financial years, the Member shall have no vote, and shall not be counted in the determining of the fulfilment of the relevant voting requirements, in the organs of the Organization. If the Assembly is satisfied that the failure to pay is due to circumstances beyond the control of the Member, it may, nevertheless, permit such a Member to vote, and then such Member shall be counted accordingly.

Article 10—Status

(a) The Organization shall have legal personality.

(b) The Organization shall enjoy in the territory of each

of the Members such legal capacity, privileges and immunities as may be necessary for the exercise of its functions.

(c) The representatives of the Members, and the officials of the Organization shall similarly enjoy such privileges and immunities as may be necessary for the independent exercise of their functions in connexion with the Organization.

(d) The privileges and immunities to be accorded by a Member to the Organization, to its officials and to the representatives of its Members shall be similar to those accorded by that Member to specialized agencies of the United Nations, to their officials and to the representatives of their members, under the Convention on the Privileges and Immunities of the Specialized Agencies, or under similar arrangements.

Article 11—Relations with other Organizations

(a) The Organization shall make arrangements with intergovernmental bodies and agencies which have related responsibilities to provide for effective cooperation and the avoidance of unnecessary duplication of activities.

(b) In pursuance of the provisions of the preceding paragraph, the Organization may, by an agreement approved by the Assembly, be brought into relationship with the United Nations, as one of the specialized agencies referred to in Article 57 of the Charter of the United Nations.

(c) The Organization may make suitable arrangements for consultation and cooperation with non-governmental organizations concerned with matters within the scope of the Organization.

PART III—SPECIAL PROVISIONS RELATING TO THE ADMINISTRATION OF THE GENERAL AGREEMENT

Article 12—Administration in General

The Organization shall give effect to those provisions of the General Agreement which provide for action by the Organization, and shall carry out such other activities in relation to the General Agreement which involve joint action. This shall include the taking of decisions, the sponsorship of negotiations and consultations, the conduct of studies, the circulation of proposals and the receipt of reports, in any case in which such action is required or appropriate to carry out the purposes of the General Agreement.

Article 13—Waivers in Exceptional Circumstances

In exceptional circumstances, not elsewhere provided for in this Agreement, nor provided for in the General Agreement, the Assembly may waive an obligation imposed upon a contracting party by the General Agreement; *Provided* that any such decision shall be approved by a two-thirds majority of the votes cast and that such majority shall comprise more than half of the Members. The Assembly may also by such a vote (i) define certain categories of exceptional circumstances to which other voting requirements shall apply for the waiver of obligations imposed by the General Agreement upon a contracting party thereto, and (ii) prescribe such criteria as may be necessary for the application of this Article.

Article 14—Nullification and Impairment

(a) If a claim that a benefit accruing directly or indirectly under the General Agreement is being nullified or impaired, or that the attainment of any objective of that Agreement is being impeded, is referred to the Organization in accordance with the provisions of that Agreement, the Organization shall promptly investigate the matter and shall make appropriate recommendations to the contracting parties to the General Agreement which it considers to be concerned, or give a ruling on the matter, as appropriate. The Organization may consult with contracting parties, with the Economic and Social Council of the United Nations, and with any appropriate intergovernmental organization in cases where it considers such consultation necessary.

(b) If the Organization considers that the circumstances are serious enough to justify such action, it may authorize a contracting party or parties to suspend the application to any other contracting party or parties of such concessions or other obligations under the General Agreement as it determines to be appropriate in the circumstances. If the application to any contracting party of any concession or other obligation is in fact suspended, that contracting party shall then be free, not later than sixty days after such action is taken, to give written notice to the Director-General of the Organization of its intention to withdraw from the General Agreement and such withdrawal shall take effect on the sixtieth day following the day on which such notice is received by him.

Article 15—Continued Application of Provisions of this Part

The Members shall not, acting as contracting parties to the General Agreement, amend the General Agreement so as to provide therein for procedures, other than consultation, negotiation or recommendation, applicable to the general situations to which Articles 13 and 14 relate.

PART IV—OTHER PROVISIONS

Article 16—Amendments

Amendments to this Agreement shall become effective, in respect of those Members which accept them, upon acceptance by two-thirds of the Members of the Organization and thereafter in respect of each other Member upon acceptance by it.

Article 17—Entry into Force

(a) This Agreement shall be deposited, subject to the provisions of Article 21, with the Director-General of the Organization.

(b) This Agreement shall be opened at Geneva on 10 March 1955 for acceptance, by signature or otherwise, by contracting parties to the General Agreement and by any other government which has, in accordance with such rules of procedure as may be established by the Organization, notified the Director-General of its intention to accede.

(c) Without prejudice to the principle laid down in Article 2, this Agreement shall enter into force, as among those governments which are then contracting parties to the General Agreement and which have accepted this Agreement, on the thirtieth day following the day on which it has been accepted by governments named in the Annex to this Agreement the territories of which account for 85 per centum of the total external trade of the territories of such governments, computed in accordance with the appropriate column of percentage set forth therein. This Agreement shall enter into force for each other government which is a contracting party to the General Agreement on the thirtieth day following the day on which it has been accepted thereby. It shall enter into force for each other government which has accepted it when such government accedes to the General Agreement.

Article 18—Notification and Registration

(a) The Director-General of the Organization shall promptly furnish a certified copy of this Agreement and a notification of its entry into force, and of each acceptance thereof, to each contracting party to the General Agreement.

(b) This Agreement shall be registered in accordance with the provisions of Article 102 of the Charter of the United Nations.

PART V—TRANSITIONAL PROVISIONS

Article 19—Relation to Amendments to the General Agreement

If this Agreement enters into force before the entry into force of amendments to the General Agreement contained in the Protocol of Organizational Amendments to the General Agreement on Tariffs and Trade dated 10 March 1955, this Agreement shall, until the entry into force of such amendments, be applied as if all references in the General Agreement to "the CONTRACTING PARTIES" were references to the Organization.

Article 20—Provisional Application

Without prejudice to the principle laid down in Article 2, if by 15 November 1955 this Agreement shall not have entered into force pursuant to paragraph (c) of Article 17, those governments, being contracting parties to the General Agreement, which are prepared to do so may nevertheless decide to apply it; *Provided* that the territories of such governments account for the percentage of trade required for the entry into force of this Agreement under paragraph (c) of Article 17.

Article 21—Temporary Exercise of Depository Functions

Pending the entry into force of this Agreement, the title "Director-General of the Organization" in paragraph (b) of Article 14, paragraphs (a) and (b) of Article 17 and paragraph (a) of Article 18, shall read "Executive Secretary to the CONTRACTING PARTIES to the General Agreement."

IN WITNESS WHEREOF the respective representatives, duly authorized to that effect, have signed the present Agreement.

DONE at Geneva, in a single copy, in the English and

	Column I (Contracting parties on 1 March 1955)	*Column II* (Contracting parties on 1 March 1955 and Japan)
Australia	3.1	3.0
Austria	0.9	0.8
Belgium-Luxemburg	4.3	4.2
Brazil	2.5	2.4
Burma	0.3	0.3
Canada	6.7	6.5
Ceylon	0.5	0.5
Chile	0.6	0.6
Cuba	1.1	1.1
Czechoslovakia	1.4	1.4
Denmark	1.4	1.4
Dominican Republic	0.1	0.1
Finland	1.0	1.0
France	8.7	8.5
Germany, Federal Republic of	5.3	5.2
Greece	0.4	0.4
Haiti	0.1	0.1
India	2.4	2.4
Indonesia	1.3	1.3
Italy	2.9	2.8
Netherlands, Kingdom of the	4.7	4.6
New Zealand	1.0	1.0
Nicaragua	0.1	0.1
Norway	1.1	1.1
Pakistan	0.9	0.8
Peru	0.4	0.4
Rhodesia and Nyasaland	0.6	0.6
Sweden	2.5	2.4
Turkey	0.6	0.6
Union of South Africa	1.8	1.8
United Kingdom	20.3	19.8
United States of America	20.6	20.1
Uruguay	0.4	0.4
Japan	....	2.3
	100.0	100.0

NOTE: These percentages have been computed taking into account the trade of all territories in respect of which the General Agreement on Tariffs and Trade is applied.

French languages, both texts authentic, this tenth day of March, one thousand nine hundred and fifty-five.[27]

ANNEX—PERCENTAGE SHARES OF TOTAL EXTERNAL TRADE TO BE USED FOR THE PURPOSE OF MAKING THE DETERMINATION REFERRED TO IN ARTICLE 17

(based on the average of 1949-1953)

If, prior to the accession of the Government of Japan to the General Agreement, the present Agreement has been accepted by contracting parties the external trade of which under column I accounts for the percentage of such trade specified in paragraph (c) of Article 17, column I shall be applicable for the purposes of that paragraph. If the present Agreement has not been so accepted prior to the accession of the Government of Japan, column II shall be applicable for the purposes of that paragraph.[28]

4. *United States Participation in the Proposed International Finance Corporation.*

a. *Announcement of the International Bank for Reconstruction and Development Summarizing the Principal Features of the Proposed International Finance Corporation, April 15, 1955.*[29]

The International Bank for Reconstruction and Development (World Bank) announced on April 15 that the charter of the International Finance Corporation, proposed new affiliate of the Bank, is now ready for acceptance by prospective member governments.

By authorization of the Bank's Board of Executive Directors, the text of the charter, or Articles of Agreement, together with a memorandum explaining its main features, is being transmitted to the 56 governments which are members of the Bank. The next step will be for those governments desiring to join the new organization to take whatever legislative or other action may be required to accept membership and to subscribe their respective share of IFC's capital.

[27] The United States signed the Agreement *ad referendum* on March 21, 1955.
[28] Japan became a Contracting Party to the General Agreement on Tariffs and Trade on September 10, 1955. The tariff concessions negotiated between the United States and Japan became effective on the same date. See *Department of State Bulletin*, v. 32 (June 27, 1955), pp. 1051-1054; *ibid.*, v. 33 (August 8, 1955), pp. 226-230, and (September 5, 1955), p. 397.
[29] *Department of State Bulletin*, v. 32 (May 23, 1955), pp. 845-847.

In a letter transmitting the charter, Eugene R. Black, President of the World Bank, said:

"The Executive Directors have devoted several months to the formulation of the proposed Articles of Agreement and explanatory memorandum and have approved them for submission to Governments. Although the Executive Directors' action has not committed Governments to join the International Finance Corporation, the various views expressed by Governments have been carefully considered and fully discussed. It is my opinion that the proposed Articles of Agreement afford a most satisfactory framework for the establishment and functioning of the new institution. I therefore recommend the proposed Articles of Agreement for early and favorable consideration. . . ."

The main features of the proposed Corporation are as follows:

Purposes—The basic objective of IFC will be to encourage the growth of productive private enterprises in its member countries, particularly in the less developed areas of the world. The Corporation—

(a) will invest in productive undertakings, in association with private investors and without government guaranty, in cases where sufficient private capital is not available on reasonable terms;

(b) as suitable opportunities for productive investment come to its attention, will seek to recruit capital from private sources and, if necessary, to find experienced management; and

(c) in general, will seek to stimulate, and to help create conditions which will stimulate, the flow of both domestic and international private investment into productive enterprises in IFC's member countries.

Membership and Capital—Membership in the Corporation will be open to governments which are members of the World Bank. IFC will have an authorized capital of $100 million, available for subscription by members in amounts proportionate to their subscriptions to the capital of the Bank. Subscriptions will be paid in gold or United States dollars.

The United States would be the largest shareholder in the Corporation; its subscription would amount to $35,168,000. The United Kingdom would be the next largest shareholder, with a subscription of $14,400,000.

Establishment—The Corporation will come into being when at least 30 governments have subscribed at least $75 million to its capital.

Affiliation With the Bank—IFC will be affiliated with the Bank in the following ways:

(a) Membership in the Bank will be a prerequisite to membership in the Corporation.

(b) Each Governor of the Bank representing a government which joins the Corporation will become a member of the Board of Governors of the new institution.

(c) IFC's Board of Directors will be composed of those Executive Directors of the Bank who represent at least one government which joins the IFC.

(d) The President of the World Bank, who is Chairman of the Bank's Executive Directors, will also be Chairman of the Corporation's Board of Directors.

The Corporation will, however, be an entity separate and distinct from the Bank. The assets of the two institutions will be kept entirely separate, and the Corporation is prohibited from borrowing from the Bank.

Management—The new institution will have its own President. He will be appointed by its Board of Directors on the nomination of the Chairman. Subject to the policy direction of the Board and the Chairman, the President will be responsible for the conduct of the Corporation's business.

IFC's principal office will be in Washington, together with the headquarters of the Bank. It is expected, therefore, that IFC will be able to make extensive use of the experience and personnel of the Bank. IFC will pay for services rendered it by the Bank.

Methods of Operation—The Corporation will make its investments without governmental guaranty. It will be authorized to make both fixed-interest loans and investments of other kinds. It may, for instance, buy securities which would give the Corporation a right to participate in the profits of an enterprise and which, when sold by IFC, could be converted by the purchasers into capital stock. The Corporation itself, however, will not be authorized to invest in capital stock, nor will it assume responsibility for managing the enterprises in which it invests.

IFC's charter gives it more latitude in financing private enterprise than the World Bank has. The Bank may lend to private borrowers only with a governmental guarantee;

this has deterred both private entrepreneurs and governmental sponsors from seeking loans for private projects. Secondly, the Bank makes only fixed-interest loans, whereas the type of financing required for the establishment or expansion of a private enterprise is often venture capital as well as fixed obligations.

The Corporation will have authority to invest in any kind of productive private enterprise, including agricultural, financial, and commercial undertakings, but its main emphasis is likely to be on industry. In addition to its financing operations, IFC will serve as a clearinghouse to bring together investment opportunities, private capital, and experienced management.

In the case of an entrepreneur looking for capital and for technical skills from abroad, for instance, the Corporation would seek to interest investors outside the country who would be able to provide management experience as well as capital. Conversely, in the case of an entrepreneur interested in establishing or expanding an operation abroad, the Corporation would seek to recruit domestic capital and local partners in the country of investment.

In either case, the Corporation itself might invest in the enterprise. But it would do so only if it were satisfied that the private interests concerned were contributing a full share of the funds required and that the remaining requirements could not be met from other private sources on reasonable terms. The Corporation will supplement, and not substitute for, private investment; as far as financing is concerned, it will regard itself as the last resort.

Sales of Securities—The Corporation will seek to revolve its funds by selling its investments to private investors whenever it can appropriately do so on satisfactory terms. The Corporation will be authorized to raise additional funds by selling its own obligations in the market, but it is not likely to do so in the early years of its operations.

Status—Enterprises in which IFC invests will not, by reason of that investment, have any special status under domestic laws and regulations. Although the Corporation itself will have substantially the same privileges and immunities as the World Bank, its charter does not exempt it from applicable foreign exchange regulations on the transfer of earnings and of repayments of principal on its investments. In this respect, IFC will be in the same position as private investors generally.

b. *Message of the President Recommending United States Participation in the International Finance Corporation, May 2, 1955.*[30]

To the Congress of the United States:

The establishment of the International Finance Corporation and our participation in it will strengthen the partnership of the free nations. In my message to the Congress, January 10, 1955, on the foreign economic policy of the United States and in my annual Economic Report transmitted to you January 20, 1955, I stated that I would recommend at the appropriate time legislation to permit United States participation in the Corporation as part of our effort to increase the flow of United States private investment funds abroad.

I now forward to you the Articles of Agreement of the International Finance Corporation and an Explanatory Memorandum approved by the Executive Directors of the International Bank for Reconstruction and Development.[31] I recommend that the Congress enact legislation authorizing me to accept membership in the Corporation for the United States and providing for the payment of our subscription of $35,168,000 to the $100 million capital stock of the corporation as set forth in the Articles of Agreement. The subscription was included in the Budget.

The entire free world needs capital to provide a sound basis for economic growth which will support rising standards of living and will fortify free social and political institutions. Action to that end by cooperating nations is essential.

In its own enlightened self-interest, the United States is vitally concerned that capital should move into productive activities in free countries unable to finance development needs out of their own resources.

Government funds cannot, and should not, be regarded as the basic sources of capital for international investment. The best means is investment by private individuals and enterprises. The major purpose of the new institution, consequently, will be to help channel private capital and experienced and competent private management into productive investment opportunities that would not otherwise be developed. Through the Corporation, we can cooperate more effectively with other people for mutual prosperity and

[30] House Document 152, 84th Cong., 1st Sess.
[31] Not printed here. See House Document 152, 84th Cong., 1st Sess.

expanding international trade, thus contributing to the peace and the solidarity of the free world.

Economic recovery, notably in Western Europe, enables nations other than the United States to participate substantially in furnishing capital to the less developed areas. The International Finance Corporation is an undertaking in which all nations, as members of the International Bank for Reconstruction and Development, will be able to pool some of their resources to spur such investment. All subscriptions to the Corporation will be paid in gold or dollars.

The Corporation, as an affiliate of the International Bank, will serve as an international agency, which will provide, in association with local and foreign private investors, risk capital for financing the establishment, improvement, and expansion of productive private enterprises in member countries when other sources of funds are not available on reasonable terms. This type of risk or venture capital is most urgently needed.

By providing the margin of capital needed to attract other funds, the Corporation will help expand private investment abroad. It will make its investments without guarantee of repayment by the member governments concerned. Accordingly, it will complement the activities of existing international investment institutions.

The Corporation will not duplicate the operations of the International Bank for Reconstruction and Development, for the investments of the International Bank are guaranteed by its member governments and are of fixed-interest nature in projects not usually attractive to risk capital.

Since the Executive Directors of the International Bank would serve *ex-officio* as Directors of the Corporation, and the President of the Bank would serve as Chairman of the Corporation's Board, effective collaboration between the two agencies and operating economy is assured.

Nor will the Corporation's operations duplicate the work of the Export-Import Bank. That Bank, an agency of the United States Government, is an instrumentality of our foreign and trade policy. It is not designed to provide venture capital; its loans are at definite interest rates with fixed schedules of repayment.

The Corporation will not hold capital stock nor participate in operating control but will rely on private management. It will not be a holding company retaining its investments on a long-term basis, but will dispose of its holdings to private investors as opportunity offers so that it can reinvest its funds in new activities. Since its main mission is to supply risk capital where it is needed, its investments will be highly flexible.

In some cases the Corporation may take fixed interest obligations, in others it may receive obligations bearing a return related to the earnings of the enterprises, and in others its holdings may be obligations convertible into stock when sold by it to private investors. Thus, the Corporation will supplement private investment, and will operate only in association with private interests which are willing to carry a large share of the total investment in each enterprise. In no event will it supply capital for an enterprise which could reasonably be expected to obtain the funds from private sources.

United States participation in the International Finance Corporation will be a step forward in our foreign economic policy in cooperation with the other free nations. It is, however, only one step among several which we must take. In my message to the Congress on January 10, 1955, I outlined other important steps.

These actions—such as extension of the Trade Agreements Act, United States membership in the Organization for Trade Cooperation, simplification and improvement of customs valuation procedures, increased tourist allowances, changes in the law concerning the taxation of income from foreign sources and further developments in tax treaties designed to encourage private investment abroad, continued technical cooperation with other countries, and necessary programs of foreign assistance—are essential to a sound and foresighted foreign economic policy for the United States.

I urge the Congress to enact promptly the legislation permitting the United States to join with the other free nations in organizing the International Finance Corporation—an important part of our foreign economic program which will foster more rapid advance by free people everywhere as they strive to improve their material well-being.[32]

DWIGHT D. EISENHOWER

[32] Following Congressional approval (by the Senate on June 21, 1955 and the House on August 1, 1955) an Instrument of Acceptance signed by the President was deposited with the International Bank for Reconstruction and Development on December 5, 1955.

E. The Administration of Foreign Affairs: The Treaty-Making Power.

1. *Resolution on Amending the Treaty-Making Power Filed by the Senator from Ohio (Bricker), January 6, 1955.*[1]

S. J. Res. 1, 84th Congress, 1st Session

JOINT RESOLUTION

Proposing an amendment to the Constitution of the United States, relating to the legal effect of certain treaties and other international agreements.

Resolved by the Senate and House of Representatives of the United States of America in Congress assembled (two-thirds of each House concurring therein), That the following article is proposed as an amendment to the Constitution of the United States, which shall be valid to all intents and purposes as part of the Constitution when ratified by the legislatures of three-fourths of the several States:

"ARTICLE—

"SECTION 1. A provision of a treaty or other international agreement which conflicts with this Constitution, or which is not made in pursuance thereof, shall not be the supreme law of the land nor be of any force or effect.

"SEC. 2. A treaty or other international agreement shall become effective as internal law in the United States only through legislation valid in the absence of international agreement.

"SEC. 3. On the question of advising and consenting to the ratification of a treaty, the vote shall be determined by yeas and nays, and the names of the persons voting for and against shall be entered on the Journal of the Senate.

"SEC. 4. This article shall be inoperative unless it shall have been ratified as an amendment to the Constitution by the legislatures of three-fourths of the several States within seven years from the date of its submission."

[1] Congressional Record, 84th Cong., 1st Sess., v. 101, No. 2 (January 6, 1955), pp. 81-83.

2. *Statement by the Secretary of State (Dulles) on Amending the Treaty-Making Power, before the Subcommittee on Constitutional Amendments of the Senate Judiciary Committee, May 2, 1955.*[2]

S. J. Res. 1 of the 84th Congress would amend the United States Constitution in regard to the making of treaties and the conduct of foreign affairs generally.

The resolution has two substantive sections. Section 1 says (a) that "A provision of a treaty or other international agreement which conflicts with this Constitution . . . shall not be the supreme law of the land nor be of any force or effect"; and (b) that the same is true if the treaty or international agreement "is not made in pursuance" of the Constitution.

Section 2 would do away with the present provision that treaties are the "law of the land" and require (a) that treaties or other international agreements "shall become effective as internal law . . . only through legislation"; and (b) that the legislation must be legislation which would be "valid in the absence of international agreement."

Section 1

The portion of section 1 which deals with the supremacy of the Constitution is urged on the ground that the Constitution does not now indicate the relative supremacy of the Constitution itself and treaties made "under the authority of the United States." It is suggested that recent developments in the field of international relations and recent judicial opinions make it desirable that the Constitution itself make it clear that, if there is a conflict between a treaty or executive agreement and the Constitution, the Constitution will prevail.

Senator Bricker, in his able statement before this Committee on April 27, 1955, said that "the most important part of the amendment" is that which provides that "an executive agreement which conflicts with the Constitution shall not be of any force and effect." He went on to say, "The next most important objective is to prevent treaties from overriding the Constitution."

Thus, the most important and next most important objectives of the proponents of the Constitutional amendment would be accomplished by so much of section 1 as provides:

[2] Department of State Press Release 238, dated May 2, 1955.

"A provision of a treaty or other international agreement which conflicts with this Constitution . . . shall not be . . . of any force or effect."

Many feel that decisions of the United States Supreme Court now adequately and authoritatively establish a proper balance between treaties and the Constitution and make it clear that the Constitution cannot be violated by treaties or executive agreements. Nevertheless, as President Eisenhower has said, there does exist within the country a certain fear that treaties, or even executive agreements, might supersede the Constitution. Therefore, the President has said that he would find it acceptable to have a Constitutional amendment reaffirming that any provision of a treaty or international agreement which conflicts with the Constitution should not be of any force or effect. I fully concur in this position.

Section 1 of the proposed amendment goes, however, considerably beyond this. It says that treaties or international agreements are of no effect unless made "in pursuance" of the Constitution. This further condition was not embodied in S. J. Res. 1 (83d Cong.) as reported by this Committee.

The Constitution now distinguishes between Federal laws and national treaties. Federal laws must be made "in pursuance" of the Constitution. But treaties are only required to be made "under the authority of the United States." There are different theories to explain that difference.

One theory is that the present language was designed merely to preserve treaties which had been concluded prior to coming into force of the Constitution and which, therefore, could not have been made "pursuant to" it. One example is the Treaty of Peace of 1783 between the United States and Great Britain, which gave this Nation its independence.

Thus, it may be that the effect of this portion of the proposed Constitutional amendment is merely to invalidate treaties made before the adoption of the Constitution in 1788.

However, there is another theory, which is that suggested in the Migratory Bird Case of *Missouri* v. *Holland*. It was there indicated that the phrase "in pursuance" of the Constitution was used relative to statutory laws because the Federal branch of the Nation was limited to the exercise of expressly delegated powers; but that different language was used in relation to treaties because, in the field of foreign affairs, the President and the Senate were to act for the Nation as a whole.

If this interpretation is accepted, the result of applying the "pursuant to" clause to treaties might be to invalidate that large part of our existing treaty structure which is applicable to States and to create, for the future, the very situation of impotence which the Constitution was designed to end.

As President Eisenhower pointed out on April 27, 1955, "The Constitution had as one of its principal reasons for coming into being the conduct of the foreign affairs of the United States as a single unit, not as 48 States."

I shall discuss this point further in relation to section 2 of the proposed amendment, which raises the problem explicitly.

Section 2

Section 2 of the proposed joint resolution reads:

"A treaty or other international agreement shall become effective as internal law in the United States only through legislation valid in the absence of international agreement."

This is a revolutionary provision. Under our Federal system of government, certain legislative powers are vested in the Federal Government and other legislative powers are vested in the States. However, our Constitution does not project this division of power into our international relations. There the Nation is one. The States are forbidden to make treaties, and the President and the Senate, acting by a two-thirds vote, speak for the Nation as a whole.

In the Senate the States are represented on a basis of sovereign equality designed to enable them to preserve their residual sovereignty [Federalist No. 62]. Thus, 17 of the 48 States can prevent any treaty from exercising the powers reserved to the States.

The proposed amendment undoes that Constitutional concept of the Nation acting as a unit in relation to foreign affairs. It would make it impossible, in the absence of legislation by the Congress and by the 48 States, to conclude and make effective many traditional types of treaties. These would include the treaties of friendship, commerce and navigation, which secure numerous and substantial benefits for our citizens abroad in return for a promise of the same treatment for foreign nationals in this country. They would include treaties on extradition, narcotics control, the right to inherit property, and the right to collect debts.

A survey of all treaties entered into by the United States

since 1789 shows that approximately 30 percent of them could not have been concluded and effectuated under the Constitutional amendments now proposed in the absence of legislative action by all of the States, as well as by the Congress.

Section 2 would impair the historic prerogatives of the Senate by giving the House of Representatives a veto over many treaties. It may be recalled that the Constitutional Convention in 1787 rejected a proposal that "no treaty shall be binding on the United States which is not ratified by a law."

The present proposal goes far beyond that rejected by the Founding Fathers, for it would require State legislation as well as Federal legislation to make many types of treaties effective.

By applying not only to treaties but to other international agreements, section 2 would infringe the President's powers as Commander in Chief and in the conduct of our foreign relations. It speaks of agreements in terms of their being "effective as internal law." This phrase has no settled meaning. It might be construed to mean affecting the determination of issues in judicial or administrative proceedings.

In this sense most international agreements have some effect which our courts will recognize.

As Senators are well aware, the executive branch of the Government, in carrying on the Nation's business with foreign countries, negotiates and concludes numerous agreements and other arrangements that do not reach the dignity of treaties. Among these are military armistices and recognitions of foreign governments. All of these have legal effects which our courts recognize. If the proposed section 2 is to end that, then the President would be unable properly to conduct foreign relations. The President's powers in this respect would be shared by the Congress; it would become deeply involved in the impossible task of itself trying to manage the current conduct of foreign affairs, and the traditional balance of powers between the executive and legislative branches of government would be impaired.

It should also be observed that section 2 invites substituting executive agreements for treaties. An executive agreement implemented by an act of Congress under this amendment would have the same effect as a treaty which requires a two-thirds vote in the Senate. This would give the Executive the option to use treaties or executive agreements.

Section 3

Section 3 in S. J. Res. 1 provides for a roll-call vote in the Senate on treaties. This seems a clearly desirable procedure to be followed in matters of such importance. The result, of course, may be obtained without resorting to Constitutional amendment. A change in the Senate rules will suffice. I understand proposals to this effect have been introduced in the Senate.

United Nations and ILO Treaties

Some of the support for proposals to amend the Constitution in regard to treaties and the conduct of foreign relations comes from those who fear the activities of the United Nations, particularly in relation to certain cultural, economic, humanitarian, and social matters.

The administration has felt that a number of these activities were not fit subjects for the treaty-making power and has acted accordingly. We have made clear that the United States will not sign or become a party to the covenants on human rights, the convention on the political rights of women, and certain other proposed multilateral agreements.

Two years ago, I said to the Committee:[3]

"This administration is committed to the exercise of the treatymaking power only within traditional limits. By "traditional" I do not mean to imply that the boundary between domestic and international concerns is rigid and fixed for all time. I do mean that treaties are contracts with foreign governments designed to promote the interests of our Nation by securing action by others in a way deemed advantageous to us. I do not believe that treaties should, or lawfully can, be used as a device to circumvent the Constitutional procedures established in relation to what are essentially matters of domestic concern."

The policies expressed in that statement have been incorporated in a Department of State order known as Circular 25. I believe that it reflects a pattern which will be followed by the executive branch of government and enforced, if need be, by judicial determination that, under our system, "treaties" are contracts between nations in their corporate capacity and not means for writing domestic law.

In order that the problem may be seen in proper perspective, some statistics may be useful.

[3] *Department of State Bulletin,* v. 28 (April 20, 1953), pp. 592-595.

Since the establishment of the United Nations nearly 10 years ago, a total of 14 treaties have been formulated by United Nations organs and committees and opened for signature or acceptance. The United States has signed 6 and ratified 4 of these 14 treaties. One of the four relates to the control of drugs. The three remaining treaties are concerned only with the transfer to the United Nations of procedural functions under prior treaties on narcotic drugs, suppression of the white slave traffic, and suppression of the circulation of obscene publications.

Some fears have been expressed regarding conventions drafted by the International Labor Organization. It may be of interest to record that, in the 21 years while the United States has been a member of the International Labor Organization, this country has become a party to only five conventions that have been formulated by that Organization. Four of these five conventions relate to maritime subjects and are limited in their application to matters entirely within the authority of the Federal Government. The other convention relates to the discharge by the United Nations of secretarial functions entrusted by earlier conventions to the League of Nations.

Conclusion

Two years ago, in appearing before this Committee, I sought to analyze the significance of the treaty power and the President's traditional authority in the field of foreign affairs in relation to the world situation facing the United States. What I said then applies equally now. My statement was:

"Today about 50 free countries, representing approximately two-thirds of the peoples and natural resources of the world, face a grave threat. That threat comes from a single totalitarian dictatorship which rules one-third of the peoples and natural resources of the world. This single despotic power has enormous advantages, unless the free nations can work together. This cooperation of the free cannot be achieved by imposed unity. It must be achieved largely through treaties and executive agreements which will coordinate the military and economic strength of the free world and promote friendly cooperation and understanding. The ability of the United States to use treaties and agreements to effect this result can become a matter of national survival.

"We need national power to make treaties with our potential enemies in order to mitigate our dangers and to ease our burdens through measures which would effectively control armaments. Such treaties do not now seem likely, but their possibility should not be excluded.

"If we should be attacked and, unhappily, there should be war, the President as Commander in Chief would need the power through executive agreements to achieve unity of purpose and of action with our allies. And when victory was won, we would need national power to make treaties of peace which would heal the wounds of war."

Such considerations show the unwisdom of adopting Constitutional amendments which weaken the capacity of the United States to act with unity and certainty in its dealings with other nations. That capacity has been a strong bulwark in the past, and it is needed for the future.

I do not question the sincerity of those who fear that our Constitution might hereafter fail us. But I cannot believe that those fears have sufficient basis to justify those provisions of the proposed amendment which would mean reverting to a situation comparable to that which existed under the Articles of Confederation. That situation was found intolerable at that time when there were only 13 States and when we enjoyed what George Washington referred to as a "detached and distant situation." Today we are 48 States, and our Nation is no longer "detached" or "distant" from either the friendly or the hostile forces of the world. More than ever we need national power to deal quickly, authoritatively, and unitedly with these forces.

Our Constitution was designed "to form a more perfect Union." Let us not bring imperfection to that Union.

CHAPTER TWO

EUROPE

A. The Atlantic Community.

1. *United States Policy Toward the Western European Union: Message from the President to the Prime Ministers of the Seven Nations Signatory to the Protocols Establishing the Western European Union, March 10, 1955.*[1]

At the time when there was under consideration the Treaty to establish a European Defense Community, I made a public announcement of certain principles which would guide United States policies and actions with respect to Western Europe in the event that Treaty should be ratified.[2] Now, in substitution for that Community, a plan has been evolved for a Western European Union. Obviously that Union and related arrangements signed at Paris on October 23, 1954[3] when brought into force, will serve the vital interests not only of the members of the Union, but of the peoples of the free world, including the United States. The United States has twice been drawn into wars which originated in Europe and today it maintains forces there to help minimize the possibility of another war. It is in the interest of the United States to help reduce such dangers.

To this end the United States committed itself to the North Atlantic Treaty. This Treaty is in accordance with the basic security interests of the United States, and the obligations which the United States has assumed under the Treaty will be honored.

The member nations are seeking to make the Atlantic alliance an enduring association of free peoples within which all members can concert their efforts toward peace, prosperity and freedom. The success of that association will be determined in large measure by the degree of practical cooperation realized among the European nations themselves. The Western European Union and the related arrangements agreed

[1] *Department of State Bulletin,* v. 32 (March 21, 1955), pp. 464-465.
[2] *Documents on American Foreign Relations,* 1954, pp. 85-87.
[3] *Ibid.,* pp. 145-164.

upon in Paris are designed to ensure this cooperation and thereby to provide a durable basis for consolidating the Atlantic relationship as a whole.

It is my belief that the proposed arrangements when effective:

Will promote progress toward unity in Western Europe and draw together those whose past differences have led to recurrent war and gravely depleted Europe's human, material and moral strength;

Will restore sovereignty to the Federal Republic of Germany, a sovereignty which has now been withheld for ten years, during which time the Government and people of that Republic have demonstrated that they are capable of worthily discharging their responsibilities as a self-governing member of the free and peaceful world community;

Will, by controlling armament levels through an appropriate Agency of the Western European Union, assure against militarism;

Will provide a core of unity at the heart of the North Atlantic Treaty Organization, thus permitting adoption of practical defensive measures which offer good hope that any enemy attack could be stopped at the threshold;

Will enable the Federal Republic of Germany to make its appropriately measured contribution to international peace and security, in keeping with the spirit of the North Atlantic Treaty Organization;

Will, through action of the North Atlantic Treaty Council, assure a closer integration of the armed forces in Europe of the member countries, thereby giving assurance that these forces cannot be used for nationalistic aggression or otherwise than for the security purposes envisaged by the North Atlantic Treaty.

At London on September 29, 1954, the United States Secretary of State in order to facilitate efforts to produce an effective collective defense of Western Europe, indicated the conditions under which the United States might be prepared to make a policy declaration similar to that which was announced when the earlier European Defense Community plan was under consideration.[4] I am glad to affirm that when the Paris Agreements have been ratified and have come into force, it will be the policy of the United States:

(1) To continue active in the various organic arrangements established under the North Atlantic Treaty Organization

[4] *Documents on American Foreign Relations, 1954*, p. 122.

and to consult with other members of NATO on questions of mutual concern, including the level of forces from the respective NATO countries to be placed at the disposal of the Supreme Allied Commander Europe;

(2) To consult, if so desired, with the Agency for the Control of Armaments of the Western European Union with a view to assisting in the achievement of its objective of controlling armament and preventing unjustified military preparations within the members of the Union;

(3) To continue to maintain in Europe, including Germany, such units of its armed forces as may be necessary and appropriate to contribute its fair share of the forces needed for the joint defense of the North Atlantic area while a threat to that area exists, and will continue to deploy such forces in accordance with agreed North Atlantic strategy for the defense of this area;

(4) To cooperate in developing the closest possible integration among the forces assigned to NATO in Western Europe, including those contributed by the German Federal Republic, in accordance with approved plans developed by the military agencies and the Supreme Commanders of the North Atlantic Treaty Organization in accordance with the Resolution adopted by the North Atlantic Council on October 22, 1954;[5]

(5) To continue to cooperate toward Atlantic Security by sharing information authorized by Congress with respect to the military utilization of new weapons and techniques for the improvement of the collective defense;

(6) In consonance with its policy of encouraging maximum cooperation among the free nations of Europe and in recognition of the contribution which the Brussels Treaty, as amended, will make to peace and stability in Europe, to regard any action from whatever quarter which threatens the integrity or unity of the Western European Union as a threat to the security of the parties to the North Atlantic Treaty calling for consultation in accordance with Article IV of that Treaty.

In accordance with the basic interest of the United States in the North Atlantic Treaty, as expressed at the time of ratification, the Treaty was regarded as of indefinite duration rather than for any definite number of years. The United States calls attention to the fact that for it to cease to be a party to the North Atlantic Treaty would appear quite con-

[5] *Ibid.*, pp. 169-172.

trary to our security interests when there is established on the Continent of Europe the solid core of unity which the Paris Agreements will provide.

2. *The North Atlantic Treaty Organization.*

a. *Draft Agreement between the Parties to the North Atlantic Treaty for Cooperation Regarding Atomic Information, Approved by the North Atlantic Council, Paris, March 2, 1955.*[6]

PREAMBLE

The Parties to the North Atlantic Treaty, signed at Washington on 4th April, 1949,

Recognising that their mutual security and defence requires that they be prepared to meet the contingencies of atomic warfare, and

Recognising that their common interests will be advanced by making available to the North Atlantic Treaty Organization information pertinent thereto, and

Taking into consideration the United States Atomic Energy Act of 1954, which was prepared with these purposes in mind,

Acting on their own behalf and on behalf of the North Atlantic Treaty Organization,

Agree as follows:

ARTICLE I

1. While the North Atlantic Treaty Organization continues to make substantial and material contributions to the common defence efforts, the United States will from time to time make available to the North Atlantic Treaty Organization, including its civil and military agencies and commands, atomic information which the Government of the United States of America deems necessary to:

(a) the development of defence plans;
(b) the training of personnel in the employment of and defence against atomic weapons; and
(c) the evaluation of the capabilities of potential enemies in the employment of atomic weapons.

2. As used in this Agreement so far as concerns information provided by the United States, "atomic information"

[6] *Department of State Bulletin,* v. 32 (April 25, 1955), pp. 687-689.

means Restricted Data, as defined in Section 11 r of the United States Atomic Energy Act of 1954, which is permitted to be communicated pursuant to the provisions of Section 144 b of that Act, and information relating primarily to the military utilisation of atomic weapons which has been removed from the Restricted Data category in accordance with the provisions of Section 142 d of the United States Atomic Energy Act of 1954.

3. All transfers by the Government of the United States of America of atomic information will be made in compliance with the provisions of the United States Atomic Energy Act of 1954, and subsequent applicable United States legislation. Under this Agreement there will be no transfers of atomic weapons or special nuclear material, as these terms are defined in Section 11 d and Section 11 t of the United States Atomic Energy Act of 1954. (The sections of the United States Atomic Energy Act of 1954 referred to in paragraphs 2 and 3 of this Article are attached.)

ARTICLE II

1. Atomic information which is transferred to the North Atlantic Treaty Organization will be made available through the channels now existing for providing classified military information to the North Atlantic Treaty Organization.

2. Only those persons within the North Atlantic Treaty Organization whose duties require access to atomic information may be the original recipients of such information. Atomic information will be authorised for dissemination within the North Atlantic Treaty Organization only to persons whose North Atlantic Treaty Organization responsibilities require them to have access to such information. Information will not be transferred by the North Atlantic Treaty Organization to unauthorised persons or beyond the jurisdiction of that Organization. The Government of the United States of America may stipulate the degree to which any of the categories of information made available by it may be disseminated, may specify the categories of persons who may have access to such information, and may impose such other restrictions on the dissemination of information as it deems necessary.

ARTICLE III

1. Atomic information will be accorded full security protection under applicable North Atlantic Treaty Organization

regulations and procedures, and where applicable, national legislation and regulations. In no case will recipients maintain security standards for the safeguarding of atomic information lower than those set forth in the pertinent North Atlantic Treaty Organization security regulations in effect on the date this Agreement comes into force.

ARTICLE IV

1. Atomic information which is transferred by the Government of the United States of America pursuant to Article I of this Agreement shall be used exclusively for the preparation of and in implementation of North Atlantic Treaty Organization defence plans.

2. The North Atlantic Treaty Organization will from time to time render reports to the Government of the United States of America of the use which has been made of the information. These reports will contain pertinent information requested by the Government of the United States of America and will in particular contain a list of the persons possessing certain categories of information, in accordance with the provisions of paragraph 2 of Article II, and a list of the documents which have been transferred.

ARTICLE V

1. The Parties to the North Atlantic Treaty, other than the United States, will to the extent that they deem necessary, make available to the North Atlantic Treaty Organization information in the same categories as may be made available by the United States under Article I of this Agreement. Any such information will be supplied on the same or similar conditions as those which apply under this Agreement with respect to the United States.

ARTICLE VI

1. The Agreement shall enter into force upon notification to the United States by all Parties to the North Atlantic Treaty that they are bound by the terms of the Agreement.

2. If any other State becomes a Party to the North Atlantic Treaty no information made available to the North Atlantic Treaty Organization under this Agreement will be provided to any person who is a national of, or who is employed by, the new Party to the North Atlantic Treaty until the new Party has notified the Government of the United States of America that it is bound by the terms of this Agreement, and

upon such notification, this Agreement will enter into force for the new Party.

3. The Government of the United States of America will inform all Parties to the North Atlantic Treaty of the entry into force of this Agreement under paragraph 1 of this Article and of each notification received under paragraph 2 of this Article.

4. This Agreement shall be valid as long as the North Atlantic Treaty is in force.

In witness whereof the undersigned Representatives have signed the present Agreement on behalf of their respective States, members of the North Atlantic Treaty Organization, and on behalf of the North Atlantic Treaty Organization.

Done at Paris this day of 1955, in the English and French languages, both texts being equally authoritative, in a single original which shall be deposited in the archives of the Government of the United States of America.[7] The Government of the United States of America shall transmit certified copies thereof to all the signatory and acceding States.

For the Kingdom of Belgium:
For Canada:
For the Kingdom of Denmark:
For France:
For the Kingdom of Greece:
For Iceland:
For Italy:
For the Grand Duchy of Luxembourg:
For the Kingdom of the Netherlands:
For the Kingdom of Norway:
For Portugal:
For Turkey:
For the United Kingdom of Great Britain
and Northern Ireland:
For the United States of America:

[7] Signed on June 22, 1955. United States notification of being bound by the terms of the agreement transmitted on December 28, 1955.

Sections of the United States Atomic Energy Act of 1954 referred to in the Agreement for Co-Operation Regarding Atomic Information

SECTION 11. DEFINITIONS

Section 11 d:

"Atomic weapon"

"d. The term 'atomic weapon' means any device utilizing atomic energy exclusive of the means for transporting or propelling the device (where such means is a separable and divisible part of the device), the principal purpose of which is for use as or for development of, a weapon, a weapon prototype, or a weapon test device."

Section 11 r:

"Restricted Data"

"r. The term 'Restricted Data' means all data concerning: (1) design, manufacture, or utilisation of atomic weapons; (2) the production of special nuclear material; or (3) the use of special nuclear material in the production of energy, but shall not include data de-classified or removed from the Restricted Data category pursuant to Section 142."

Section 11 t:

"Special nuclear material"

"t. The term 'special nuclear material' means (1) plutonium, uranium enriched in the isotope 233 or in the isotope 235, and any other material which the Commission, pursuant to the provisions of section 51, determines to be special nuclear material, but does not include source material; or (2) any material artificially enriched by any of the foregoing, but does not include source material."

SECTION 142. CLASSIFICATION AND DECLASSIFICATION OF RESTRICTED DATA

Section 142 d:

"d. The Commission shall remove from the Restricted Data category such data as the Commission and the Department of Defense jointly determine relates primarily to the military utilisation of atomic weapons and which the Commission and Department of Defense jointly determine can be adequately safeguarded as defense information: provided, however, that no such data so removed from the Restricted Data category shall be transmitted or otherwise made available to any nation or regional defence organization, while such data remains defence information, except pursuant to an agreement for co-operation entered into in accordance with subsection 144 b."

SECTION 144. INTERNATIONAL CO-OPERATION

Section 144 b:

"b. The President [of the United States of America] may authorize the Department of Defense, with the assistance of the [Atomic Energy] Commission to co-operate with another nation or with a regional defence organization to which the United States is a party, and to communicate to that nation or organization such Restricted Data as is necessary to:

"(1) the development of defence plans;
"(2) the training of personnel in the employment of and defence against atomic weapons; and
"(3) the evaluation of the capabilities of potential enemies in the employment of atomic weapons,

while such other nation or organization is participating with the United States pursuant to an international arrangement by substantial and material contributions to the mutual defence and security:

"Provided, however, That no such co-operation shall involve communication of Restricted Data relating to the design or fabrication of atomic weapons except with regard to external characteristics, including size, weight, and shape, yields and effects, and systems employed in the delivery or use thereof but not including any data in these categories unless in the joint judgment of the [Atomic Energy] Commission and the Department of Defense such data will not reveal important information concerning the design or fabrication of the nuclear components of an atomic weapon: And provided further, That the co-operation is undertaken pursuant to an agreement entered into in accordance with section 123."

b. *Letter from the President to the Chairman of the Joint [Congressional] Committee on Atomic Energy (Anderson) Transmitting Draft Agreement for NATO Cooperation on Atomic Information, April 13, 1955.*[8]

DEAR SENATOR ANDERSON: Pursuant to Section 123 of the Atomic Energy Act of 1954,[9] I hereby submit to the Joint Committee on Atomic Energy a proposed agreement for cooperation regarding the communication of atomic information to the North Atlantic Treaty Organization.

Under the terms of the proposed agreement, the United States will communicate to the North Atlantic Treaty Organization, so long as that Organization continues to make substantial and material contributions to the mutual defense effort, atomic information which the United States considers as necessary to

(1) the development of defense plans;
(2) the training of personnel in the employment of and defense against atomic weapons; and
(3) the evaluation of the capabilities of potential enemies in employment of atomic weapons.

Other members of the North Atlantic Treaty Organization agree to make atomic information available to the Organization on a similar basis.

Atomic information made available pursuant to the proposed agreement will not be transferred to unauthorized persons or beyond the jurisdiction of the North Atlantic Treaty Organization, and will be safeguarded by the stringent security regulations in force within the North Atlantic Treaty Organization. Under the terms of the proposed agreement, which will remain in force for the duration of the North Atlantic Treaty, transfers of atomic information by the United States will only be made in accordance with the Atomic Energy Act of 1954.

The North Atlantic Council strongly endorsed the proposed agreement, and I consider it to be a great stride forward in the strengthening of our common defense. It is my firm conviction that the proposed agreement will enable the North Atlantic Treaty Organization, consistent with the security and defense of the United States, to evolve more

[8] *Department of State Bulletin,* v. 32 (April 25, 1955), p. 686.
[9] *Public Law* no. 703, 83d Congress.

effective defense plans concerning the use of atomic weapons than have heretofore been achieved. Accordingly, I hereby determine that its performance will promote and will not constitute an unreasonable risk to the common defense and security, and approve the proposed agreement for cooperation. In addition, I hereby authorize, subject to the provisions of the Atomic Energy Act of 1954, the Honorable George W. Perkins, United States Permanent Representative to the North Atlantic Council, to execute the proposed agreement and the Department of Defense, with the assistance of the Atomic Energy Commission, to cooperate with the North Atlantic Treaty Organization and to communicate Restricted Data to that Organization under the agreement.[10]

Sincerely,

DWIGHT D. EISENHOWER

c. *Communiqué on the Ministerial Session of the North Atlantic Council, Paris, May 11, 1955.*[11]

The North Atlantic Council, under the chairmanship of Mr. Stephanos Stephanopoulos, Foreign Minister of Greece, met in Ministerial Session in Paris on May 9th, 10th and 11th, 1955.

I

To welcome the accession of the Federal Republic of Germany to the North Atlantic Treaty, the Council held an opening public session. In speeches made on that occasion, the texts of which have already been made public, Ministers stressed the significance they attach to the entry of the Federal Republic as a democratic and sovereign state into the North Atlantic Community. The Federal Chancellor, replying to the welcome extended him by his colleagues, emphasised the full harmony existing between the objectives of the North Atlantic Treaty and the ardent desire for peace, security and freedom felt by the German people including the eighteen million in East Germany.

II

The Council reaffirmed the purely defensive character of the Atlantic Alliance. It recorded its deep satisfaction at the

[10] Atomic agreements for mutual defense patterned on the agreement signed with the North Atlantic Treaty Organization were concluded with Canada and the United Kingdom on June 15, 1955. See *Department of State Bulletin*, v. 33 (July 11, 1955), pp. 59-64.

[11] *Department of State Bulletin*, v. 32 (May 23, 1955), pp. 831-832.

entry into force of the agreements which establish Western European Union and which promote peace and provide specific safeguards, including the control of armaments. The Council also noted the valuable mutual support made possible by close collaboration between NATO and Western European Union in their respective fields of activity.

The Council welcomed the declarations made by the Ministers of member governments signatory to the Italian Peace Treaty recalling the active part taken by Italy in the progress of Atlantic and European cooperation, and reaffirming that various discriminatory aspects of that Treaty were considered to be inconsistent with the position of Italy as an ally.

III

The Ministers examined major aspects of the international situation within and beyond the NATO area.

They discussed a report on the current negotiations regarding the Austrian State Treaty, and welcomed the indications that the Soviet Union may now join in concluding such a Treaty long sought by the Western Powers.

They were resolved to continue the policies followed heretofore in building and maintaining the strength and unity of the West.

The Council welcomed the initiative of France, the United Kingdom and the United States in proposing to the Soviet Union negotiations to find means for resolving outstanding issues. The Council hoped that this initiative would lead progressively to agreements which would remove sources of conflict and contribute to the security and liberty of all peoples. In particular, the Council hoped that such negotiations might help to bring about the peaceful unification of Germany in freedom, and promote progress toward reduction, under effective safeguards, of armaments and armed forces. The Council emphasised that this process of negotiation required careful preparation, and must be pursued with patience and determination.

The Council also reviewed the situation in the Middle East and Far East.

The Council received reports on the conclusion of various security pacts in these areas, including the Manila Pact and the Turco-Iraqi Pact.[12] The Council welcomed measures taken to strengthen the defence of the Middle East and Far East areas.

[12] See below, pp. 342-34.

A report was made to the Council on the Bandung Conference. The Council expressed the hope that there would be a cessation of hostilities in the Far East and no further resort to force, since this would so clearly endanger the peace of the world.

IV

Ministers expressed their satisfaction that the procedures followed in the Council had enabled them to have frank and free discussions and a thorough exchange of views. These discussions constitute a most significant proof of the solidarity of the Alliance and show the great value of the Council as a forum for political consultation on matters of common concern. They are resolved to continue to follow these procedures, which enable the member governments to develop their policies on common principles.

d. *Communiqué on the Ministerial Session of the North Atlantic Council, Paris, December 16, 1955.*[13]

The North Atlantic Council held its regular December Ministerial Session in Paris on the 15th and 16th of December. Member governments were represented by Foreign, Defence and Finance Ministers. Dr. Kristinn Gudmundsson, Foreign Minister of Iceland, acted as chairman.

I. The Council examined and assessed the present international situation.

It unanimously welcomed the vigour with which the three Western Ministers had presented to the second Geneva Conference the proposals already outlined at previous meetings of the North Atlantic Council. These proposals aimed at the reunification of Germany through free elections; left the unified German Government free to choose its own foreign policy and offered a security pact to the Union of Soviet Socialist Republics.

The Council noted with regret:

1. that the U.S.S.R. had repudiated the proposal to negotiate on the reunification of Germany through free elections, in spite of the directive agreed at the first Geneva conference.

2. that the U.S.S.R. was opposed to any effective system for the control of armaments including the air inspection plan proposed by President Eisenhower.

3. that the U.S.S.R. had given proof of its fear and hostility

[13] *Department of State Bulletin,* v. 33 (December 26, 1955), pp. 1047-1048.

with regard to the free exchange of information between the people of the Soviet Union and the free world.

The Council declared that the negative outcome of the Geneva Conference had in no way halted the efforts of the North Atlantic powers to secure the reunification of Germany in freedom, such reunification continuing to be held by them as an essential condition for the establishment of a just and lasting peace.

The Council reaffirmed that they consider the Government of the Federal Republic as the only German Government freely and legitimately constituted and therefore entitled to speak for Germany as the representative of the German people in international affairs; it stressed once again that the security and welfare of Berlin should be considered as essential elements of the peace of the free world in the present international situation; it urged the importance of consulting further within NATO on the question of German reunification and on the situation in Berlin.

The Council also reviewed recent provocative moves and declarations by the Soviet Union regarding the Middle East and Asia. They recognised that these tactics, coupled with a continued increase in Soviet military capability, created new problems and a new challenge to the Free World.

II. Following a report by the Secretary General on the work and activities of the Organization in the last eight months, the Council discussed future defence planning of NATO. It considered the Annual Review Report for 1955 and approved force goals for 1956, 1957 and 1958. The Council welcomed the German Federal Republic's participation for the first time in the NATO Annual Review. The Council adopted procedures designed to give new impulse and direction to the future defence planning of the Alliance and to ensure even closer co-operation in this field. The Council expressed the firm determination of all member governments to see the Atlantic forces equipped with the most modern weapons. The Council noted with satisfaction that substantial progress could be achieved in this respect as a result of the valuable assistance of the United States, the United Kingdom and Canada.

The Council devoted major attention to improving the arrangements for air defence and warning in Europe. It accepted recommendations for the re-organization and closer co-ordination of the air defence in NATO European countries, so as to integrate further NATO activities in this vital field.

The Council also received a report on a new type of communications system for air defence and warning. The United States offered to finance a pilot project for this new system.

III. The Council recognised that recent developments in the international situation made it more necessary than ever to have closer co-operation between the members of the Alliance as envisaged in Article 2 of the Treaty. They decided to instruct the Permanent Council to examine and implement all measures conducive to this end.

IV. In concluding its work, the Council declared that the North Atlantic Treaty Organization remains the essential foundation of the security of the fifteen associated nations. Such associations are in direct contrast to the obsolete system under which isolated nations are in danger of being subjugated, one by one, by despotic groups such as the Communist bloc.

B. The Changing Status of Germany.

1. *The Federal Republic of Germany.*

a. *Proclamation of the Allied High Commission on the Termination of the Occupation Statute, Bonn, May 5, 1955.*[1]

WHEREAS a new relationship between the French Republic, the United States of America, and the United Kingdom of Great Britain and Northern Ireland, on the one hand, and the Federal Republic of Germany, on the other, has been established by the Convention on Relations between the Three Powers and the Federal Republic of Germany and the Related Conventions which were signed at Bonn on 26 May 1952,[2] were amended by the Protocol on the Termination of the Occupation Regime in the Federal Republic of Germany signed at Paris on 23 October 1954,[3] and enter into force today,

NOW THEREFORE, We,

André François-Poncet, French High Commissioner for Germany,

James B. Conant, United States High Commissioner for Germany,

[1] HICOG Press Release, dated May 5, 1955.
[2] *Documents on American Foreign Relations, 1952,* pp. 211-238.
[3] *Ibid., 1954,* pp. 134-142.

Frederick Robert Hoyer Millar, United Kingdom High Commissioner for Germany,

Acting on behalf of, and duly authorized by, our Governments,

DO HEREBY JOINTLY PROCLAIM:

THAT the Occupation Statute[4] is revoked; and

THAT the Allied High Commission and the Offices of the Land Commissioners in the Federal Republic are abolished.

This Proclamation shall take effect at noon on the fifth day of May 1955.

Done at BONN, Mehlem, this 5th day of May 1955

A. FRANÇOIS-PONCET
JAMES B. CONANT
F. R. HOYER MILLAR

b. *Executive Order 10608 Defining United States Authority and Functions in Germany, May 5, 1955.*[5]

By virtue of the authority vested in me by the Constitution and the statutes, including the Foreign Service Act of 1946 (60 Stat. 999), as amended, and as President of the United States and Commander in Chief of the armed forces of the United States, it is ordered as follows:

1. Executive Order No. 10062 of June 6, 1949, and Executive Order No. 10144 of July 21, 1950, amending that order, are hereby revoked, and the position of United States High Commissioner for Germany, established by that order, is hereby abolished.

2. The chief of the United States Diplomatic Mission to the Federal Republic of Germany, hereinafter referred to as the Chief of Mission, shall have supreme authority, except as otherwise provided herein, with respect to all responsibilities, duties, and governmental functions of the United States in all Germany. The Chief of Mission shall exercise his authority under the supervision of the Secretary of State and subject to ultimate direction by the President.

3. The United States Military Commander having area responsibility in Germany, hereinafter referred to as the Commander, shall have authority with respect to all military responsibilities, duties, and functions of the United States in all Germany, including the command, security, and stationing of United States forces in Germany, the assertion and exercise

[4] *Ibid., 1949,* p. 109.
[5] 20 Federal Register 3093.

of their rights and discharge of their obligations therein, and emergency measures which he may consider essential for their protection or the accomplishment of his mission. The Commander may delegate the authority conferred upon him. If action by the Commander or any representative of the Commander, pursuant to the authority herein conferred, affects the foreign policy of the United States or involves relations or negotiations with non-military German authorities, such action shall be taken only after consultation with and agreement by the Chief of Mission or pursuant to procedures previously agreed to between the Chief of Mission and the Commander or his representative. Either the Chief of Mission or the Commander may raise with the other any question which he believes requires such consultation. If agreement is not reached between them, any differences may be referred to the Department of State and the Department of Defense for resolution.

4. The Chief of Mission and the Commander or his designated representatives shall, to the fullest extent consistent with their respective missions, render assistance and support to each other in carrying out the agreements and policies of the United States.

5. With regard to the custody, care, and execution of sentences and disposition (including pardon, clemency, parole, or release) of war criminals confined or hereafter to be confined in Germany as a result of conviction by military tribunals (A) the Chief of Mission shall share the four-power responsibility in the case of persons convicted by the International Military Tribunal, (B) the Chief of Mission shall exercise responsibility in the case of persons convicted by military tribunals established by the United States Military Governor pursuant to Control Council Law No. 10, and (C) the Commander shall exercise responsibility in the case of persons convicted by other military tribunals established by United States Military Commanders in Germany and elsewhere. The Commander shall, on request of the Chief of Mission, take necessary measures for carrying into execution any sentences adjudged against such persons in category (B) as to whom the Chief of Mission has responsibility and control. Transfer of custody of persons in categories (B) and (C) to the Federal Republic of Germany as provided in the Convention on the Settlement of Matters Arising out of the War and Occupation shall terminate the responsibility of the Chief of Mission and the Commander with respect to such

persons to the extent that the responsibility of the United States for them is thereupon terminated pursuant to the provisions of the said Convention.

6. If major differences arise over matters affecting the United States Forces in Germany, such differences may be referred to the Department of State and the Department of Defense for resolution.

7. This order shall become effective on the date that the Convention on Relations between the Three Powers and the Federal Republic of Germany and related Conventions, as amended, come into force.

[DWIGHT D. EISENHOWER]

THE WHITE HOUSE,
May 5, 1955.

c. *Statement by the Secretary of State (Dulles) on German Neutrality, May 24, 1955.*[6]

It is the view of the United States that a policy of neutrality has no application to a country of the character of Germany. It is all well to talk about neutrality for a country such as Austria, a small country with 7,000,000 people. But I do not believe that anybody realistically believes that the German people, 70 odd million of them, are destined to play the role of a neutral country. Furthermore, as President Eisenhower has pointed out, the kind of neutrality which was discussed in terms of Austria is an armed neutrality, and there is no limit in the Austrian State Treaty upon the size of the Austrian Army.[7] I do not think that the German people or the Soviet people or the Western European people want to see applied to Germany the concept of it being an independent State with an unlimited army.

d. *Mutual Defense Assistance Agreement between the United States and the Federal Republic of Germany, Signed at Bonn, June 30, 1955.*[8]

The United States of America and the Federal Republic of Germany,

Being parties to the North Atlantic Treaty signed at Washington on April 4, 1949;

[6] Department of State Press Release 290, dated May 24, 1955.
[7] See below, pp. 132-13
[8] Department of State Press Release 408, dated June 30, 1955.

CONSIDERING their reciprocal pledges under Article 3 of the North Atlantic Treaty separately and jointly with the other parties, by means of continuous and effective self-help and mutual aid, to maintain and develop their individual and collective capacity to resist armed attack;

CONSCIOUS of the desire to foster international peace and security through measures which further the ability of nations dedicated to the purposes and principles of the Charter of the United Nations to participate effectively in arrangements for collective self-defense in support of those purposes and principles, and conscious of the determination to give their full cooperation to United Nations collective security arrangements and measures and efforts to obtain agreement on universal regulation and reduction of armaments under adequate guarantees against violation or evasion;

CONSIDERING the support which the Government of the United States of America has brought to these principles by enacting the Mutual Security Act of 1954, which authorizes the furnishing of military assistance to certain nations;

DESIRING to set forth the conditions which will govern the furnishing of such assistance;

HAVE AGREED AS FOLLOWS:

ARTICLE I

1. The Government of the United States of America will make available to the Government of the Federal Republic of Germany such equipment, materials, services, or other assistance as the Government of the United States of America may authorize and in accordance with such terms and conditions as may be agreed. Such assistance as may be made available by the Government of the United States of America under the agreement will be furnished under the authority and subject to all of the terms, conditions and termination provisions of the Mutual Security Act of 1954, acts amendatory and supplementary thereto and appropriation acts thereunder. The furnishing and use of any such assistance shall be consistent with the principles of the Charter of the United Nations and with the principles of Article 3 of the North Atlantic Treaty.

2. The Government of the Federal Republic of Germany will make effective use of assistance received under this agreement for the purpose of promoting an integrated defense of the North Atlantic area in accordance with defense plans formulated by the North Atlantic Treaty Organization, and

will not use such assistance for any act inconsistent with the strictly defensive character of the North Atlantic Treaty, or, without the prior consent of the Government of the United States of America, for any other purpose. The two Governments will establish arrangements in which both Governments will participate to ensure that equipment and materials received under this agreement, other than equipment or material sold under Section 106 of the Mutual Security Act of 1954, and no longer required or used exclusively for the purpose for which they were furnished or in accordance with the terms and conditions under which they were furnished will be offered for return to the Government of the United States of America for appropriate disposition.

3. In the common security interest of the parties, the Government of the Federal Republic of Germany will not transfer to any person not an officer or agent of that Government, or to any nation other than the United States of America, title to or possession of any equipment, materials, property, information, or services furnished pursuant to this Agreement without the prior consent of the Government of the United States of America.

4. The Government of the Federal Republic of Germany may use equipment, materials, or services acquired from the Government of the United States of America on a reimbursable basis under the agreement (exchange of notes) of November 23, 1953,[9] for the purpose for which it will use equipment, materials, or services acquired under this Agreement.

ARTICLE II

1. The Government of the Federal Republic of Germany will make available to the Government of the United States of America and to such other governments as the parties hereto may in each case agree upon, such equipment, materials, services, or other assistance as may be authorized, in accordance with such terms and conditions as may be agreed between the two Governments. The furnishing and use of such assistance shall be consistent with the principles of the Charter of the United Nations and with the obligations under Article 3 of the North Atlantic Treaty.

2. In conformity with the principle of mutual aid, the Government of the Federal Republic of Germany will facilitate the production and transfer to the Government of the United States of America for such period of time, in such

[9] Department of State, Treaties and Other International Acts Series 2911.

quantities and upon such terms and conditions as may be agreed, of raw and semi-processed materials required by the United States of America as a result of deficiencies or potential deficiencies in its own resources, and which may be available in the territory of the Federal Republic of Germany. Arrangements shall give due regard to the requirements of the Federal Republic of Germany for domestic use and commercial export of such materials.

ARTICLE III

The two Governments will, upon the request of either of them, negotiate appropriate arrangements relating to the exchange of patent rights and technical information for defense, in order to expedite such exchanges and at the same time protect private interests and maintain necessary security safeguards.

ARTICLE IV

1. The Government of the Federal Republic of Germany will take such security measures as may be agreed between the two Governments in order to prevent the disclosure or compromise of classified equipment, materials, services, or information furnished pursuant to this Agreement.

2. Each Government will, consistent with security requirements, take appropriate measures to keep the public informed of operations under this Agreement.

ARTICLE V

The two Governments will establish procedures whereby the Government of the Federal Republic of Germany will so deposit, segregate or assure title to all funds allocated to or derived from any program of assistance undertaken by the Government of the United States of America so that such funds shall not, unless otherwise agreed hereafter, be subject to garnishment, attachment, seizure or other legal process by any person, firm, agency, corporation, organization or government.

ARTICLE VI

The Government of the Federal Republic of Germany will grant tax relief to activities of the Government of the United States of America under this Agreement, or any similar agreement between the Government of the United States of America and the government of any other country receiving military assistance, in accordance with the Agreement between the United States of America and the Federal Republic of Germany Concerning Tax Relief to be Accorded by the Federal Republic to United States Expenditures in the Interest of the Common Defense, signed at Bonn, October 15, 1954.[10]

ARTICLE VII

The Government of the Federal Republic of Germany will make available to the Government of the United States of America German currency for the use of the Government of the United States of America in adequate amounts for its administrative and operating expenditures in connection with this agreement. Discussions will be initiated forthwith with a view to determining the nature of the expenditures and the amount of such currency.

ARTICLE VIII

The Government of the Federal Republic of Germany will receive in its territory personnel of the Government of the United States of America, including personnel temporarily assigned, who will discharge the responsibilities of the Government of the United States of America with respect to the equipment, materials, and services furnished by the latter Government. Such personnel will operate as part of the Embassy of the United States of America under the direction and control of the Chief of the Diplomatic Mission of the United States of America. These personnel will be accorded authority and facilities to carry out continuous observation and review of operations under the program of assistance provided under this agreement, including the utilization of military assistance furnished by the Government of the United States of America, and the Government of the Federal Republic of Germany will provide any information as to these matters which may be requested by the Government of the United States of America. The personnel, including dependents, will be divided into two categories:

a) Upon appropriate notification by the Chief of the Diplomatic Mission of the United States of America, full diplomatic status will be granted to the senior military member and the senior Army, Navy and Air Force officer assigned thereto, and to their respective immediate deputies.

[10] Not printed.

b) The second category of personnel will enjoy privileges and immunities conferred by international custom, as recognized by each Government, to certain categories of personnel of the Embassy of the United States of America, such as the immunity from civil and criminal jurisdiction of the host country, immunity of official papers from search and seizure, right of free egress, exemption from custom duties or similar taxes or restrictions in respect of personally owned property imported into the host country by such personnel for their personal use and consumption, without prejudice to the existing regulations on foreign exchange, exemption from internal taxation by the host country upon salaries of such personnel. Privileges and courtesies incident to diplomatic status, such as diplomatic automobile license plates, inclusion on the "diplomatic list," and social courtesies may be waived by the Government of the United States of America for this category of personnel.

It is understood between the two Governments that the number of personnel in the two categories above will be kept as low as possible. In the event that the status, privileges and immunities of such personnel in any other North Atlantic Treaty country are modified pursuant to agreement with such other country, the Government of the United States of America will interpose no objection to amending this agreement in order that the status, privileges and immunities provided shall conform to those in such other North Atlantic Treaty country.

ARTICLE IX

The Government of the Federal Republic of Germany will consistent with its rights and obligations as a member of the North Atlantic Treaty Organization and under The Convention on Relations Between the Three Powers and the Federal Republic of Germany and its Related Conventions as amended by the Protocol on the Termination of the Occupation Regime in the Federal Republic of Germany:

a) join in promoting international understanding and good will and maintaining world peace; take such action as may be mutually agreed upon to eliminate causes of international tension; and fulfill the military obligations which it has assumed under multilateral or bilateral agreements, treaties or other instruments to which the United States of

America is a party or in which the United States of America has an interest;

b) make, consistent with its political and economic stability and international obligations the full contribution permitted by its manpower, resources, facilities, and general economic condition to the development and maintenance of its own defensive strength and the defensive strength of the free world and take all reasonable measures which may be needed to develop its defense capacities.

ARTICLE X

In order to safeguard the common interests and the resources of the two Governments, the Government of the Federal Republic of Germany will cooperate with the Government of the United States of America in the implementation of security controls agreed or to be agreed over the export of strategic goods.

ARTICLE XI

1. This Agreement shall enter into force upon the deposit of an instrument of ratification by the Federal Republic of Germany with the Government of the United States of America[11] and shall continue in force until one year after the receipt by either party of written notice of the intention of the other party to terminate it, except that the provisions of Article I, paragraphs 2 and 3, and arrangements entered into under Article I, paragraph 2, Article III, Article IV, paragraph 1, and Article V, shall remain in force unless otherwise agreed by the two Governments.

2. The two Governments shall, upon the request of either of them, consult regarding any matter relating to the application or amendment of this Agreement. Such consultation shall take into account, where appropriate, agreements concluded by either Government in connection with the carrying out of Article 9 of the North Atlantic Treaty.

3. The two Governments will, from time to time, negotiate detailed arrangements necessary to carry out the provisions of this Agreement.

4. This Agreement shall be registered with the Secretariat of the United Nations.

DONE at Bonn, in duplicate in the English and German

[11] The instrument of ratification was deposited on December 27, 1955. See Department of State Press Release 711, dated December 27, 1955.

languages, both texts authentic, this thirtieth day of June 1955.

For the United States of America
JAMES BRYANT CONANT
For the Federal Republic of Germany
V. BRENTANO

e. *"Normalization" of Relations between the Federal Republic of Germany and the Soviet Union: Communiqué on Talks between Government Delegations of the Soviet Union and the Federal Republic of Germany, Moscow, September 13, 1955.*[12]

From September 9 to 13 negotiations were held in Moscow between the Government delegation of the Soviet Union and the Government delegation of the German Federal Republic.

On the Soviet side there took part the Chairman of the Council of Ministers of the Soviet Union, Marshal [Nikolai A.] Bulganin, head of the delegation; [Nikita S.] Khrushchev, member of the Presidium of the Supreme Soviet of the Soviet Union; [Vyacheslav M.] Molotov, First Deputy Chairman of the Council of Ministers of the Soviet Union and Foreign Minister of the Soviet Union; [Michael G.] Pervukhin, First Deputy Chairman of the Council of Ministers of the Soviet Union; [Ivan G.] Kabanov, Minister of Foreign Trade; [Vladimir S.] Semyonov, Deputy Foreign Minister of the Soviet Union.

On the Federal German Republic side the following took part in the talks: Federal Chancellor Dr. [Konrad] Adenauer, head of the delegation; Minister of Foreign Affairs of the Federal German Republic Dr. [Heinrich] von Brentano; State Secretary of Foreign Affairs, [Professor Walter] Hallstein; State Secretary of the Office of the Federal Chancellor Dr. [Hans] Globke; chairman of the Lower House Foreign Affairs Committee and Minister-President of North Rhine-Westphalia, [Karl] Arnold; chairman of the Foreign Affairs Committee of the Bundestag, [Georg] Klesinger; deputy chairman of the Foreign Affairs Committee of the Bundestag, [Dr. Carlo] Schmid; envoy [Dr. Herbert] Blankenhorn; envoy [Felix] von Eckardt; Ministerial Director Dr. Greve.

During the talks, which took place in an atmosphere of mutual understanding, there took place a broad and frank

[12] *New York Times,* September 14, 1955.

exchange of views on the question of the mutual relations between the Soviet Union and the Federal German Republic. During the talks the question of the establishment of diplomatic relations between the Soviet Union and the Federal German Republic was discussed.

An agreement was reached and expressed in letters exchanged by the parties, with a view to obtaining the approval of the Federal Government and of the Bundestag, as well as of the Presidium of the Supreme Soviet, for the establishment of diplomatic relations between the two countries, and the setting up, to this end, of embassies respectively in Bonn and in Moscow, and to the exchange of diplomatic representatives of the rank of extraordinary and plenipotentiary ambassadors.

Both delegations agreed that the establishment of diplomatic relations would contribute to the development of mutual understanding and cooperation between the Soviet Union and the German Federal Republic in the interests of peace and security in Europe.

The parties are starting from the assumption that the establishment and development of normal relations between the Soviet Union and the Federal German Republic will further the settlement of pending problems affecting the whole of Germany, and must thus help the solution of the principal national problem of the German people—the re-establishment of the unity of the German democratic state.

In confirmation of the agreement reached, the Chairman of the Council of Ministers of the Soviet Union and Federal Chancellor of the German Federal Republic exchanged letters, the text of which is annexed.[13] The parties also agreed that negotiations should shortly be negotiated between the German Federal Republic and the Soviet Union on the problems of the development of trade.

2. *The Soviet Zone of Germany.*

a. *Treaty on Relations between the Union of Soviet Socialist Republics and the "German Democratic Republic," Moscow, September 20, 1955.*[14]

The Presidium of the Supreme Soviet of the Union of Soviet Socialist Republics and the President of the German Democratic Republic,

[13] Not printed here. See *Ibid.*

[14] *New Times* No. 39, September 22, 1955, Special Supplement.

Animated by a desire to promote close cooperation and further strengthen the friendly relations between the Union of Soviet Socialist Republics and the German Democratic Republic on a basis of equality, mutual respect for each other's sovereignty and non-interference in each other's internal affairs,

Mindful of the new situation brought about by the entry into force of the Paris agreements of 1954,

Convinced that concerting the efforts of the Soviet Union and the German Democratic Republic for the maintenance and strengthening of international peace and European security, and also for the reunification of Germany as a peaceful and democratic state and for a peace-treaty settlement with Germany, accords with the interests both of the Soviet and German peoples and of the other European peoples,

Cognizant of the obligations of the Soviet Union and the German Democratic Republic under existing international agreements relating to Germany as a whole,

Have decided to conclude the present Treaty and have appointed as their Plenipotentiaries:

The Presidium of the Supreme Soviet of the Union of Soviet Socialist Republics, N. A. Bulganin, Chairman of the Council of Ministers of the U.S.S.R.,

The President of the German Democratic Republic, Otto Grotewohl, Prime Minister of the German Democratic Republic,

Who, after presentation of their full powers, found in good and due form, have agreed as follows:

ARTICLE 1

The Contracting Parties solemnly reaffirm that the relations between them are based on full equality, mutual respect for each other's sovereignty and non-interference in each other's internal affairs.

The German Democratic Republic is accordingly free to decide questions of home and foreign policy, including its relations with the German Federal Republic and the development of relations with other states.

ARTICLE 2

The Contracting Parties declare their readiness to participate in a spirit of sincere cooperation in all international actions designed to ensure peace and security in Europe and the whole world and conforming with the principles of the United Nations Charter.

To this end they will consult with each other on all major international questions affecting the interests of the two countries and adopt all available measures to prevent violation of the peace.

ARTICLE 3

In accordance with the interests of the two countries and in pursuit of the principles of friendship, the Contracting Parties have agreed to develop and strengthen the existing economic, scientific-technical and cultural relations between the Union of Soviet Socialist Republics and the German Democratic Republic, to render each other all possible economic assistance, and to cooperate as shall be necessary in the economic, scientific and technical fields.

ARTICLE 4

The Soviet forces now stationed on the territory of the German Democratic Republic in accordance with existing international agreements shall temporarily remain in the German Democratic Republic with the consent of its Government and on conditions to be defined by supplementary agreement between the Government of the Soviet Union and the Government of the German Democratic Republic.

The Soviet forces temporarily stationed on the territory of the German Democratic Republic shall not interfere in the internal affairs or the social and political life of the German Democratic Republic.

ARTICLE 5

The Contracting Parties agree that their fundamental aim is to achieve through appropriate negotiation a peace settlement for all Germany. They will accordingly make the necessary effort for a peace settlement by treaty and for the reunification of Germany on a peaceful and democratic basis.

ARTICLE 6

The present Treaty shall remain in force until Germany is reunited as a peaceful and democratic state, or until the Contracting Parties agree to amend it or terminate its operation.

ARTICLE 7

The present Treaty is subject to ratification and shall enter into force on the day the instruments of ratification are exchanged, which shall be effected in Berlin at the earliest date.

Done in the city of Moscow on September 20, 1955, in two copies, each in the Russian and German languages, both texts being equally authentic.

For the Presidium of the Supreme Soviet of the U.S.S.R.
N. BULGANIN

For the President of the German Democratic Republic
OTTO GROTEWOHL

b. *Exchange of Letters between Soviet Deputy Foreign Minister (Zorin) and the Minister of Foreign Affairs of the "German Democratic Republic" (Bolz) on the Transfer of Certain Control Functions to the "German Democratic Republic," Moscow, September 20, 1955.*[15]

Dear Comrade Minister,[16]

The Government of the Soviet Union has instructed me to confirm that, as a result of the negotiations between the Government of the Soviet Union and the Government of the German Democratic Republic in Moscow, September 17 to 20, 1955, agreement has been reached on the following:

1. The German Democratic Republic shall exercise guard and control functions on the borders of the German Democratic Republic, on the demarcation line between the German Democratic Republic and the German Federal Republic, on the outer circuit of Greater Berlin, in Berlin, and also on the lines of communication between the German Federal Republic and West Berlin passing through the territory of the German Democratic Republic.

In connection with the exercises of guard and control functions on the lines of communication between the German Federal Republic and West Berlin passing through the territory of the German Democratic Republic, the German Democratic Republic shall provide for the settlement with the pertinent authorities of the German Federal Republic

[15] *New Times* No. 39, September 22, 1955, Special Supplement.
[16] A letter of identical text was addressed to V. Zorin (as Deputy Minister) by L. Bolz on behalf of the German Democratic Republic.

of all questions relating to the transit of rail, road and water traffic of the German Federal Republic or West Berlin, and their citizens or inhabitants, as well as of foreign states and their citizens, with the exception of personnel and freight of the armed forces of the U.S.A., Great Britain and France in West Berlin, to which reference is made below in clause 2 of this letter.

Accordingly, the function of issuing and formalizing shipping documents for traffic on the internal waterways of the German Democratic Republic, etc., shall be exercised fully by agencies of the German Democratic Republic.

2. Control of the movement between the German Federal Republic and West Berlin of military personnel and freight of the French, British and U.S. garrisons in West Berlin shall temporarily, pending the achievement of appropriate agreement, be exercised by the Command of the Soviet Army Group in Germany.

Furthermore, movement of military personnel and freight of the garrisons of the three Western Powers in West Berlin shall be permitted, in accordance with existing quadripartite decisions:

a) via the Berlin-Marienborn motor road;

b) via the Berlin-Helmstedt railway, with routing of empties via the Berlin-Oebisfelde line;

c) via the air corridors Berlin-Hamburg, Berlin-Bückeburg, and Berlin-Frankfort on Main.

V. ZORIN

c. *Joint Statement by the Foreign Ministers of the U.S., U.K. and France on Agreements Concluded between the Soviet Union and the "German Democratic Republic," New York, September 28, 1955.*[17]

The Foreign Ministers of the United States, the United Kingdom, and France wish to make known their view on certain points in connection with the agreements of September 20, 1955, as reported in the press, between the Soviet Union and the regime in the Soviet zone of Germany.

They wish in the first place to emphasize that these agreements cannot affect the obligations or responsibilities of the Soviet Union under agreements and arrangements between the Three Powers and the Soviet Union on the subject of

[17] *Department of State Bulletin,* v. 33 (October 10, 1955), pp. 559-560.

Germany and Berlin. The Soviet Union remains responsible for the carrying out of these obligations.

Secondly, the three Foreign Ministers reaffirm that the Federal Republic of Germany is the only German Government freely and legitimately constituted and therefore entitled to speak for Germany as the representative of the German people in international affairs. These three governments do not recognize the East German regime nor the existence of a state in the Soviet zone.

Finally, as regards a statement which has recently appeared in the Soviet press on the frontiers of Germany, the three Foreign Ministers reaffirm the repeatedly expressed position of their Governments that the final determination of the frontiers of Germany must await a peace settlement for the whole of Germany.

d. *United States Position on Soviet-East German Agreements: Exchange of Notes with the Soviet Union.*

(1) *Note Delivered by the American Embassy at Moscow to the Soviet Foreign Ministry, October 3, 1955.*[18]

The Government of the United States of America, in agreement with the Governments of the United Kingdom and France, wishes to make known its position with regard to the agreements concluded at Moscow on the 20th of September 1955 between Marshal Bulganin and Mr. Grotewohl, as published in the press.

The three Governments declare that these agreements cannot affect in any respect or in any way the obligations or responsibilities of the U.S.S.R. under agreements and arrangements on the subject of Germany, including Berlin, previously concluded between France, the United States, the United Kingdom and the U.S.S.R.

The three Governments consider that the U.S.S.R. remains bound by the engagements which it has assumed vis-a-vis the Three Powers concerning Germany, and that, in particular, the letters exchanged between Mr. Zorin and Mr. Bolz on the 20th of September 1955 cannot have the effect of discharging the U.S.S.R. from the responsibilities which it has assumed in matters concerning transportation and communications between the different parts of Germany, including Berlin.

[18] Department of State Press Release 584, dated October 4, 1955.

(2) *Soviet Note, October 18, 1955.*[19]

The Ministry of Foreign Affairs of the Union of Soviet Socialist Republics presents its compliments to the Embassy of the United States of America and in connection with the latter's note of October 3 has the honor to state the following:

On September 20 of this year the Government of the Soviet Union and the Government of the German Democratic Republic concluded "A Treaty on Relations Between the Union of Soviet Socialist Republics and the German Democratic Republic," which after ratification by the Parliaments of both countries has come into force. According to the treaty, relations between the Soviet Union and the German Democratic Republic are settled on a basis of full equality, mutual respect of sovereignty, and noninterference in internal affairs. The treaty provides for the cooperation of the Soviet Union and the German Democratic Republic in the interests of guaranteeing peace and security in Europe, and the reestablishment of the unity of Germany on a peace-loving and democratic basis.

In concluding the treaty with the German Democratic Republic, the Soviet Government at the same time made the decision on the abolition of the function of the High Commissioner of the U.S.S.R. in Germany, and also on the termination of the validity on territory of the German Democratic Republic of laws, directives, and decrees of the former Control Council in Germany issued by the occupying powers in the course of exercising rights of occupation of Germany.

At the same time, considering the actual situation which has come about at the present time, when on the territory of Germany there exist two independent sovereign states, the Soviet Union established diplomatic relations with the German Federal Republic. Thus, the Soviet Union has at the present time diplomatic relations with both states existing on the territory of Germany.

The Government of the United States of America has diplomatic relations with one German state—the German Federal Republic—with which it has concluded well-known treaties in violation of the obligations which it assumed under the four-power decisions in relation to Germany. Absence of normal relations of the United States of America

[19] *Department of State Bulletin,* v. 33 (November 7, 1955), pp. 734-735.

with the other part of Germany—with the German Democratic Republic—cannot, naturally, serve as an obstacle to the proper regulation of relations between the Soviet Union and the German Democratic Republic.

In signing the treaty on the relations between the U.S.S.R. and the German Democratic Republic, the parties proceeded from the premise that the German Democratic Republic exercises its jurisdiction on territory under its sovereignty, which, of course, also applies to communications on that territory.

As for control over the movement between the German Federal Republic and West Berlin of military personnel and freight of garrisons of the U.S.A., Great Britain, and France, quartered in West Berlin, in negotiations between the Governments of the U.S.S.R. and the German Democratic Republic, it was stipulated that this control would henceforth be carried out by the command of the Soviet military forces in Germany temporarily until the achievement of a suitable agreement.

It is self-understood that, in concluding the above-mentioned treaty, the Governments of the Soviet Union and the German Democratic Republic took into consideration the obligations which both have under existing international agreements relating to Germany as a whole.

In connection with the foregoing, the Ministry of Foreign Affairs of the U.S.S.R. has the honor to send the Embassy for its information texts of the "Treaty on Relations Between the Union of Soviet Socialist Republics and the German Democratic Republic" and documents connected therewith.[20]

(3) *United States Note, Delivered by the American Embassy at Moscow to the Soviet Foreign Ministry, October 27, 1955.*[21]

The Embassy of the United States of America presents its compliments to the Ministry of Foreign Affairs, and, with reference to the Ministry's note of October 18, 1955, concerning the agreements concluded on September 20, 1955, between Marshal Bulganin and Mr. Grotewohl, has the honor to state the following views of the Government of the United States.

As the Government of the United States has already made clear in its note of October 3, 1955, these agreements can in

[20] See above, pp. 108-112.
[21] *Department of State Bulletin,* v. 33 (November 7, 1955), p. 734.

no way be regarded as releasing the Soviet Government from its obligations under existing Four-Power Agreements, and in particular its responsibility for ensuring the normal functioning of communications between the different parts of Germany, including Berlin.

For its part, the United States Government cannot accept the allegation contained in the Ministry's note that, in treaties it has concluded with the Federal Government of Germany, it has violated the obligations it had assumed under quadripartite agreements.

(4) *Note from the United States Ambassador (Conant) to the Senior Soviet Diplomatic Representative in the Soviet Zone of Germany, [Ambassador] (Pushkin), Berlin, December 1, 1955.*[22]

On November 29, General Dasher, the United States Commandant in Berlin, called on General Dibrova, the Soviet Commandant, to protest against an incident which occurred on November 27.[23] This incident involved the unwarranted detention in the Soviet sector of Berlin of an American military vehicle of the Berlin command, and its occupants, including two members of the Congress of the United States of America.

I am informed that General Dibrova refused to accept General Dasher's protest and that in justification he made certain assertions concerning the applicability to this case of the laws of the "German Democratic Republic" and the relationship between the Soviet sector of Berlin and the "German Democratic Republic."

I must renew the protest made by General Dasher against interference with the freedom of Allied circulation in Berlin and against the grossly discourteous and threatening conduct displayed toward United States citizens by persons acting under Soviet authority and control. I do not consider the attempted justification of this incident to be acceptable.

As for General Dibrova's assertions, they are wholly inconsistent with the quadripartite status of Berlin. The position of my government as regards the status of Berlin, and its attitude to the so-called German Democratic Republic, are well known to you as a result of numerous

[22] Department of State Press Release 675, dated December 1, 1955.
[23] *Department of State Bulletin,* v. 33 (December 19, 1955), pp. 1012-1013.

communications on these subjects from my government to your government over a considerable period of time.

You will thus appreciate that the United States Government must continue to hold the Soviet authorities responsible for the welfare and proper treatment of all United States citizens during their presence in those areas, including the Soviet sector of Berlin, which are subject to Soviet authority and control.

(5) *Letter from the Soviet Ambassador (Pushkin) to the United States Ambassador (Conant), Berlin, December 14, 1955.*[24]

[Unofficial translation]

DEAR MR. AMBASSADOR: I acknowledge the receipt of your letter of December 1 of this year. This letter defends the action of a group of American citizens who used an automobile equipped with an unregistered radio transmitter on the territory of East Berlin under violation of the laws which are valid in the German Democratic Republic.

I know that the commandant of the American garrison of West Berlin, Major General Dasher, has been given an appropriate explanation, in which it was stated that the matter falls fully and completely under the competence of the presidium of the People's Police of East Berlin.

Concerning the other questions mentioned in your letter, I deem it necessary to tell you that under the treaty concluded September 20 between the German Democratic Republic and the Soviet Union, the German Democratic Republic exercises full and complete jurisdiction on its whole territory and regulates all questions arising from its relations with the German Federal Republic as well as with other states.

From the above-mentioned treaty and the documents relating to it—whose texts have been brought to the attention of the Governments of the United States, Britain and France—it can be seen that the German Democratic Republic exercises the guarding and control on the borders of the German Democratic Republic, the line of demarcation between the German Democratic Republic and the German Federal Republic, on the outer ring of Greater Berlin, in Berlin, as well as on the lines of communication between the German Federal Republic and West Berlin.

[24] *Department of State Bulletin,* v. 34 (January 9, 1956), p. 49.

In this connection it is well known that agreements exist between the Governments of the Soviet Union and the German Democratic Republic that the control of traffic of armed forces personnel and freight of the garrisons of the United States, Britain and France stationed in West Berlin between the German Federal Republic and West Berlin will be exercised temporarily until conclusion of an appropriate agreement by the command of the group of Soviet forces in Germany.

Sincerely yours,
G. PUSHKIN

(6) *Letter from the United States Ambassador (Conant) to the Soviet Ambassador (Pushkin), Berlin, December 16, 1955.*[25]

DEAR MR. PUSHKIN: I acknowledge receipt of your letter of December 14. The position of my Government has already been made clear in its note to the Soviet Government of October 3, 1955, namely that it continues to hold the Soviet Government responsible for the obligations assumed by it under quadripartite agreements on the subject of Germany, including Berlin.

The attitude of my Government remains unchanged.

Sincerely yours,
JAMES B. CONANT

C. Austria.

1. *Tripartite Declaration on the Possibilities of Concluding an Austrian State Treaty, New York, April 5, 1955.*[1]

For many years the Governments of the United Kingdom, the United States and France have sought to conclude an Austrian state treaty. They have made ceaseless efforts thus to bring about the restoration of Austrian freedom and independence at the earliest possible moment.

At the Berlin conference in 1954 the three governments expressed their readiness to sign the draft state treaty with the Soviet texts of the previously unagreed articles.[2] This would have resulted in the termination of the occupation and the withdrawal of all foreign troops within three months of

[25] *Ibid.*, p. 48.
[1] Department of State Press Release 187, dated April 5, 1955.
[2] *Documents on American Foreign Relations, 1954*, pp. 210-218.

the entry into force of the treaty. But the Soviet Government declined and insisted on putting forward new and unacceptable conditions which would have infringed Austrian sovereignty.

The three governments have followed closely the recent exchanges between the Austrian Government and the Soviet Government on matters relating to the state treaty. From these exchanges it appears that the Soviet Government may now have certain clarifications to offer regarding their policy toward Austria, in particular on the question of the independence and sovereignty of that country already provided for in the first five articles of the draft treaty. The three governments trust that the decision of the Austrian Government to accept the Soviet invitation to Moscow will result in useful clarifications.

Questions relating to the conclusion of the state treaty are of concern to the governments of all four responsible powers, as well as to the Austrian Government. The Governments of the United Kingdom, United States and France accordingly consider that if the Soviet Government should offer proposals which hold clear promise of the restoration of freedom and independence to Austria, these could appropriately be discussed by the four Ambassadors in Vienna with the participation of the Austrian Government.

It remains the earnest desire of the Governments of the United States, United Kingdom and France to conclude the state treaty as soon as possible in conformity with principles which would insure Austria's full freedom and independence.

2. *Communiqué on the Talks between Government Delegations of Austria and the Soviet Union, Moscow, April 15, 1955.*[3]

Negotiations were held in Moscow from April 12 to 15, 1955, between an Austrian Government Delegation, headed by Federal Chancellor Julius Raab and Vice-Chancellor Dr. Adolf Schärf, and a Soviet Government Delegation, headed by V. M. Molotov, Vice-Chairman of the Council of Ministers and Foreign Minister of the U.S.S.R., and A. I. Mikoyan, Vice-Chairman of the Council of Ministers of the U.S.S.R. The negotiations were conducted in a spirit of friendship.

As a result of the negotiations, the parties placed on record that both the government of the Soviet Union and the gov-

[3] *New Times* No. 17, April 23, 1955, Special Supplement.

ernment of the Republic of Austria favour the earliest possible conclusion of a State Treaty re-establishing an independent and democratic Austria, which would serve the national interests of the Austrian people and the promotion of peace in Europe.

The Austrian Delegation gave the assurance that the Republic of Austria, in keeping with the spirit of its statement at the Berlin Conference in 1954, does not intend to adhere to any military alliances or to allow the establishment of military bases on its territory. Austria will pursue in relation to all states an independent policy that will ensure the observance of this Declaration.

The Soviet government signified its consent to the withdrawal from Austria of the occupation forces of the Four Powers after the entry into force of the Austrian State Treaty, and not later than December 31, 1955.

In view of the statement published on April 5 of this year by the governments of the United States, France and Great Britain, intimating their desire for the speediest conclusion of the Austrian State Treaty, the Soviet and Austrian Delegations express the hope that conditions are now favourable for the settlement of the Austrian question by agreement between the Four Powers and Austria.

The Soviet government further agreed, in the spirit of the statement it made at the Berlin Conference in 1954, to accept the equivalent of the 150,000,000 dollars provided in Art. 35 of the State Treaty entirely in the form of Austrian goods.

In addition to the transfer of the German property in the Soviet zone of occupation in Austria, as provided for earlier, the Soviet government announced its readiness, immediately upon the coming into force of the State Treaty, to transfer to Austria, for suitable compensation, the property of the Danube Shipping Company (DDSG), including the Korneuburg shipyards and all vessels and port installations. It also consented to cede to Austria its rights, held under Art. 35[4] of the State Treaty, to the oil fields and refineries, including the Oil Products Trading Company (OROP), in exchange for deliveries of crude oil in quantities to be agreed upon between the parties.

Furthermore, it was agreed that negotiations would begin in the nearest future for the normalization of trade relations between Austria and the Soviet Union.

The Soviet Delegation informed the Austrian Delegation

[4] Article 22 in the final text of the State Treaty.

that the Presidium of the Supreme Soviet of the U.S.S.R. had agreed to give favourable consideration to the request made by the Austrian Federal President, Dr. Körner, for the repatriation of Austrians serving sentences passed by Soviet judicial bodies. After the withdrawal of the Soviet occupation forces from Austria, not a single prisoner of war or detained civilian of Austrian citizenship will remain on Soviet territory.

3. *Memorandum on the Results of Negotiations between Government Delegations of Austria and the Soviet Union, Moscow, April 15, 1955.*[5]

I

In the course of the discussions in Moscow, April 12-15, 1955, on the question of achieving early conclusion of the Austrian State Treaty, the Soviet and Austrian delegations agreed that, in consideration of the statements made by members of the Soviet Government V. M. Molotov, Vice-Chairman of the Council of Ministers and Minister of Foreign Affairs of the U.S.S.R., and A. I. Mikoyan, Vice-Chairman of the Council of Ministers of the U.S.S.R., Austrian Federal Chancellor Engineer Julius Raab, Vice-Chancellor Dr. Adolf Schärf, Minister of Foreign Affairs Dr. Leopold Figl, and State Secretary Dr. Bruno Kreisky will, in connection with the conclusion of the Austrian State Treaty, make it their concern to secure the adoption by the Austrian Federal Government of the following decisions and measures.

1. In the spirit of the statement made by Austria at the Berlin Conference in 1954 that she will not join any military alliances or permit any military bases on her territory, the Austrian Federal Government will make a Declaration, in a form imposing upon Austria an international obligation, that Austria will maintain permanent neutrality of the same type as that maintained by Switzerland.

2. The Austrian Federal Government will, in accordance with the provisions of the Federal Constitution, submit this Austrian Declaration for endorsement by the Austrian Parliament immediately upon the ratification of the Austrian State Treaty.

3. The Federal Government will take all appropriate steps to secure international recognition of the Declaration after its endorsement by the Austrian Parliament.

[5] *New Times* No. 22, May 28, 1955, Special Supplement.

4. The Austrian Federal Government will welcome a guarantee by the Four Great Powers of the integrity and inviolability of the territory of the Austrian State.

5. The Austrian Federal Government will make representations to the Governments of France, Great Britain and the United States of America, requesting such a statement of guarantee by the Four Great Powers.

6. After the transfer to Austria of the German assets in the Soviet zone of occupation, the Federal Government will take measures to preclude the transfer of these assets to foreign citizens, including private or public juridical persons. It will further make it its concern that no discriminatory measures are applied against persons employed in former USIA enterprises, or in the enterprises of the former Soviet oil company, OROP, or in the DDSG.

II

In consideration of the statements of the Austrian Government Delegation, Vice-Chairmen of the Council of Ministers of the U.S.S.R. V. M. Molotov and A. I. Mikoyan made the following statements on behalf of the Soviet Government:

1. The Soviet Government is prepared to sign the Austrian State Treaty without delay.

2. The Soviet Government agrees that, after the State Treaty enters into force, all the occupation forces of the Four Powers shall be withdrawn from Austria not later than December 31, 1955.

3. The Soviet Government considers Articles 6, 11, 15, 16b and 36 out of date or superfluous and is prepared to delete them. It is likewise prepared to delete Article 48b, provided Austria simultaneously renounces claims on the Soviet Union in connection with what is known as "civilian occupation expenses." In addition, it will support the efforts of the Austrian Government to secure further possible amendments of the draft State Treaty, and will agree to such amendments. However, it is understood that proposed amendments to the Treaty shall not unnecessarily prolong the negotiations of the Four Powers and Austria for the conclusion of the Austrian State Treaty.

4. The Soviet Government is prepared to recognize the Declaration of Austrian Neutrality.

5. The Soviet Government is prepared to participate in a guarantee by the Four Great Powers of the integrity and in-

violability of the territory of the Austrian State on the Swiss pattern.

III

After an exchange of opinions, the Delegations agreed as follows:

DELIVERY OF GOODS TO THE U.S.S.R. IN PAYMENT OF THE VALUE OF THE SOVIET ENTERPRISES IN AUSTRIA TRANSFERRED IN ACCORDANCE WITH THE AUSTRIAN STATE TREATY [ARTICLE 35[6]]

1. In conformity with the agreement it expressed at the Berlin Conference in 1954, the Soviet Government is prepared to accept entirely in the form of Austrian goods the equivalent of the total sum of 150,000,000 United States dollars mentioned in Article 35[6] of the State Treaty.

2. The Soviet Delegation takes note of the statement of the Austrian Delegation that it accepts the list of goods it received from the Soviet Delegation as a basis, and in this connection representatives of the Austrian Government will arrive in Moscow not later than the end of May of this year.

3. The Soviet Delegation likewise takes note of the statement of the Austrian Delegation that the Austrian Government will set up a special commission which will supervise the delivery of the goods to the Soviet Union at the proper times and of proper quality, and in the agreed quantities, to the total sum of 150,000,000 United States dollars, at the rate of 25,000,000 United States dollars annually.

4. The Austrian Delegation expressed its readiness to ensure that the representatives of the Soviet buyer have the opportunity to inspect and take delivery of the goods designated for consignment to the Soviet Union in payment of the afore-mentioned sum. It is understood that the goods will be delivered at world prices f.o.b. the Austrian border. The prices and quantities of goods will be determined by the Parties annually, three months before the beginning of the following year. The Austrian National Bank will issue promissory notes as security for the delivery of the goods to the sum of 150,000,000 United States dollars established in the Austrian State Treaty. The promissory notes of the Austrian National Bank will be returned as the sums mentioned in them are repaid in the form of goods.

[6] Article 22 in the final text of the State Treaty.

TRANSFER TO AUSTRIA OF OIL PROPERTIES BELONGING TO THE U.S.S.R. IN AUSTRIA

1. The Soviet Delegation accepts the proposal of the Austrian Delegation that the Austrian Government shall pay for the Soviet-owned oil fields and oil refineries transferred to Austria in the form of deliveries to the Soviet Union of crude oil to the extent of one million tons annually over a period of ten years, that is, ten million tons in all.

The Soviet Delegation takes note of the statement of the Austrian Delegation that the Austrian Government shall have the right to deliver to the Soviet Union the afore-mentioned quantity of oil in a shorter period. The oil will be delivered f.o.b. the Austrian border, free of tolls or duties.

2. The Austrian Delegation takes note of the statement of the Soviet Delegation that the oil enterprises and oil fields to be transferred by the Soviet Union to Austria will include the refineries and the Oil Products Trading Company (OROP).

TRANSFER TO AUSTRIA OF THE ASSETS OF THE DANUBE SHIPPING COMPANY LOCATED IN EASTERN AUSTRIA

The Soviet side will transfer to Austria all the assets of the Danube Shipping Company located in Eastern Austria, including the Korneuburg shipyards, ships and port installations, in return for which the Austrian Government will pay the Soviet Union a lump sum of 2,000,000 United States dollars simultaneously with the transfer of the assets to Austria.

TRADE BETWEEN THE SOVIET UNION AND AUSTRIA

1. It was agreed that the Soviet Union and Austria shall conclude a trade agreement for a period of five years, to be automatically prolonged if a statement abrogating the treaty is not made by either of the Parties.

2. It was agreed that the Soviet Union and Austria shall conclude a barter and payments agreement for a period of five years, and that the quantity of goods shall be defined by agreement annually.

Done in two copies, each in the Russian and German languages, both texts being equally authentic.

In witness whereof the present Memorandum is initialed:

For the Government Delegation
of the Soviet Union
V. MOLOTOV
A. MIKOYAN
For the Austrian Government Delegation
J. RAAB
A. SCHÄRF
L. FIGL
B. KREISKY

Moscow, April 15, 1955.

4. *Soviet Note on a Four-Power Conference with the Participation of Austria, Moscow, April 19, 1955.*[7]

The Soviet government considers it necessary to draw the attention of the government of the U.S.A. to the following.

Negotiations were held in Moscow on April 12-15 between the Soviet government and a Government Delegation of the Republic of Austria, headed by Federal Chancellor Julius Raab. An exchange of opinions revealed that the possibility now exists of completing the settlement of the Austrian question and concluding the State Treaty with Austria. This would permit the full restoration of the independence of a democratic Austrian state, which would be a substantial contribution to the strengthening of peace in Europe.

The Soviet government expresses the hope that the government of the U.S.A. will, on its part, assist the achievement of the necessary agreement between the governments of the Four Powers and the Austrian government on the conclusion of the State Treaty with Austria.

The Soviet government considers it advisable that a Conference of Foreign Ministers of the United States, France, Great Britain and the Soviet Union, with the participation of Austrian representatives, be arranged in the earliest future to examine the question of concluding the State Treaty reestablishing an independent and democratic Austria, and to sign the Treaty.

It is suggested that the Conference be held in Vienna.

The Soviet government would be grateful to the government of the U.S.A. for an early reply to this proposal.

Moscow, April 19, 1955.

[7] *New Times* No. 17, April 23, 1955, Special Supplement.

5. *United States Note to the Soviet Union on Concluding an Austrian State Treaty, delivered by the United States Embassy at Moscow to the Soviet Foreign Ministry, April 22, 1955.*[8]

The Government of the United States, in consultation with the British and French Governments, has considered the Soviet Government's note of April 19 proposing a conference of the Ministers of Foreign Affairs of the U.K., the Soviet Union, the U.S. and France, with Austrian representatives participating, in order to discuss the question of concluding a State Treaty for the reestablishment of an independent democratic Austria and in order to sign that Treaty.

The Government of the United States welcomes the Soviet Government's view that the possibility now exists of concluding the Austrian State Treaty. It would be pleased to participate at the earliest possible moment in a meeting of the Foreign Ministers of the four powers together with the representatives of Austria in order to sign the Treaty.

From the information it has received regarding the exchanges between the Austrian and Soviet Ministers in Moscow it is clear that some preparatory work still remains to be done. Recalling the tripartite declaration of April 5, it suggests that the Ambassadors of the four powers in Vienna should meet at a very early date, with the participation of Austrian representatives, in order to examine the results of the exchanges in Moscow and to reach the necessary agreements for the early signature of the State Treaty by the Foreign Ministers. It would therefore propose that the Ambassadors together with Austrian representatives should meet in Vienna on May 2.[9]

As soon as the necessary preparations have been completed, the earliest practicable date should then be set for the Foreign Ministers to meet and sign the treaty.

[8] Department of State Press Release 224, dated April 22, 1955.

[9] The Soviet Union on April 26 sent notes to the United States, France and the United Kingdom agreeing to an ambassadors' meeting in Vienna on May 2. The ambassadors completed their work on May 12.

6. *The Austrian State Treaty, Signed at Vienna, May 15, 1955.*[10]

STATE TREATY FOR THE RE-ESTABLISHMENT OF AN INDEPENDENT AND DEMOCRATIC AUSTRIA

PREAMBLE

The Union of Soviet Socialist Republics, the United Kingdom of Great Britain and Northern Ireland, the United States of America, and France, hereinafter referred to as "the Allied and Associated Powers," of the one part and Austria, of the other part;

Whereas on 13th March, 1938, Hitlerite Germany annexed Austria by force and incorporated its territory in the German Reich;

Whereas in the Moscow Declaration published on 1st November, 1943,[11] the Governments of the Union of Soviet Socialist Republics, the United Kingdom and the United States of America declared that they regarded the annexation of Austria by Germany on 13th March, 1938, as null and void and affirmed their wish to see Austria re-established as a free and independent State, and the French Committee of National Liberation made a similar declaration on 16th November, 1943;

Whereas as a result of the Allied victory Austria was liberated from the domination of Hitlerite Germany;

Whereas the Allied and Associated Powers, and Austria, taking into account the importance of the efforts which the Austrian people themselves have made and will have to continue to make for the restoration and democratic reconstruction of their country, desire to conclude a treaty re-establishing Austria as a free, independent and democratic State, thus contributing to the restoration of peace in Europe;

Whereas the Allied and Associated Powers desire by means of the present Treaty to settle in accordance with the principles of justice all questions which are still outstanding in connection with the events referred to above, including the annexation of Austria by Hitlerite Germany and participation of Austria in the war as an integral part of Germany; and

[10] *Department of State Bulletin,* v. 32 (June 6, 1955), pp. 916-932.
[11] *Documents on American Foreign Relations, 1943-1944,* p. 231.

Whereas the Allied and Associated Powers and Austria are desirous for these purposes of concluding the present Treaty to serve as the basis of friendly relations between them, thereby enabling the Allied and Associated Powers to support Austria's application for admission to the United Nations Organization;

Have therefore appointed the undersigned Plenipotentiaries who, after presentation of their full powers, found in good and due form, have agreed on the following provisions:

PART I

POLITICAL AND TERRITORIAL CLAUSES

ARTICLE 1

RE-ESTABLISHMENT OF AUSTRIA AS A FREE AND INDEPENDENT STATE

The Allied and Associated Powers recognize that Austria is re-established as a sovereign, independent and democratic State.

ARTICLE 2

MAINTENANCE OF AUSTRIA'S INDEPENDENCE

The Allied and Associated Powers declare that they will respect the independence and territorial integrity of Austria as established under the present Treaty.

ARTICLE 3

RECOGNITION BY GERMANY OF AUSTRIAN INDEPENDENCE

The Allied and Associated Powers will incorporate in the German Peace Treaty provisions for securing from Germany the recognition of Austria's sovereignty and independence and the renunciation by Germany of all territorial and political claims in respect of Austria and Austrian territory.

ARTICLE 4

PROHIBITION OF ANSCHLUSS

1. The Allied and Associated Powers declare that political or economic union between Austria and Germany is prohibited. Austria fully recognizes its responsibilities in this

matter and shall not enter into political or economic union with Germany in any form whatsoever.

2. In order to prevent such union Austria shall not conclude any agreement with Germany, nor do any act, nor take any measures likely, directly or indirectly, to promote political or economic union with Germany, or to impair its territorial integrity or political or economic independence. Austria further undertakes to prevent within its territory any act likely, directly or indirectly, to promote such union and shall prevent the existence, resurgence and activities of any organizations having as their aim political or economic union with Germany, and pan-German propaganda in favor of union with Germany.

ARTICLE 5

FRONTIERS OF AUSTRIA

The frontiers of Austria shall be those existing on 1st January, 1938.

ARTICLE 6

HUMAN RIGHTS

1. Austria shall take all measures necessary to secure to all persons under Austrian jurisdiction, without distinction as to race, sex, language or religion, the enjoyment of human rights and of the fundamental freedoms, including freedom of expression, of press and publication, of religious worship, of political opinion and of public meeting.

2. Austria further undertakes that the laws in force in Austria shall not, either in their content or in their application, discriminate or entail any discrimination between persons of Austrian nationality on the ground of their race, sex, language or religion, whether in reference to their persons, property, business, professional or financial interests, status, political or civil rights or any other matter.

ARTICLE 7

RIGHTS OF THE SLOVENE AND CROAT MINORITIES

1. Austrian nationals of the Slovene and Croat minorities in Carinthia, Burgenland and Styria shall enjoy the same rights on equal terms as all other Austrian nationals, includ-

ing the right to their own organizations, meetings and press in their own language.

2. They are entitled to elementary instruction in the Slovene or Croat language and to a proportional number of their own secondary schools; in this connection school curricula shall be reviewed and a section of the Inspectorate of Education shall be established for Slovene and Croat schools.

3. In the administrative and judicial districts of Carinthia, Burgenland and Styria, where there are Slovene, Croat or mixed populations, the Slovene or Croat language shall be accepted as an official language in addition to German. In such districts topographical terminology and inscriptions shall be in the Slovene or Croat language as well as in German.

4. Austrian nationals of the Slovene and Croat minorities in Carinthia, Burgenland and Styria shall participate in the cultural, administrative and judicial systems in these territories on equal terms with other Austrian nationals.

5. The activity of organizations whose aim is to deprive the Croat or Slovene population of their minority character or rights shall be prohibited.

ARTICLE 8

DEMOCRATIC INSTITUTIONS

Austria shall have a democratic government based on elections by secret ballot and shall guarantee to all citizens free, equal and universal suffrage as well as the right to be elected to public office without discrimination as to race, sex, language, religion or political opinion.

ARTICLE 9

DISSOLUTION OF NAZI ORGANIZATIONS

1. Austria shall complete the measures, already begun by the enactment of appropriate legislation approved by the Allied Commission for Austria, to destroy the National Socialist Party and its affiliated and supervised organizations, including political, military and para-military organizations, on Austrian territory. Austria shall also continue the efforts to eliminate from Austrian political, economic and cultural life all traces of Nazism, to ensure that the above-mentioned organizations are not revived in any form, and to prevent all Nazi and militarist activity and propaganda in Austria.

2. Austria undertakes to dissolve all Fascist-type organizations existing on its territory, political, military and para-military, and likewise any other organizations carrying on activities hostile to any United Nation or which intend to deprive the people of their democratic rights.

3. Austria undertakes not to permit, under threat of penal punishment which shall be immediately determined in accordance with procedures established by Austrian Law, the existence and the activity on Austrian territory of the above-mentioned organizations.

ARTICLE 10

SPECIAL CLAUSES ON LEGISLATION

1. Austria undertakes to maintain and continue to implement the principles contained in the laws and legal measures adopted by the Austrian Government and parliament since 1st May, 1945, and approved by the Allied Commission for Austria, aimed at liquidation of the remnants of the Nazi regime and at the re-establishment of the democratic system, and to complete the legislative and administrative measures already taken or begun since 1st May, 1945, to codify and give effect to the principles set out in Articles 6, 8 and 9 of the present Treaty, and insofar as she has not yet done so to repeal or amend all legislative and administrative measures adopted between 5th March, 1933, and 30th April, 1945, which conflict with the principles set forth in Articles 6, 8 and 9.

2. Austria further undertakes to maintain the law of 3rd April, 1919, concerning the House of Hapsburg-Lorraine.

ARTICLE 11

RECOGNITION OF PEACE TREATIES

Austria undertakes to recognize the full force of the Treaties of Peace with Italy, Roumania, Bulgaria, Hungary and Finland and other agreements or arrangements which have been or will be reached by the Allied and Associated Powers in respect of Germany and Japan for the restoration of peace.

PART II

MILITARY AND AIR CLAUSES

ARTICLE 12

PROHIBITION OF SERVICE IN THE AUSTRIAN ARMED FORCES OF FORMER MEMBERS OF NAZI ORGANIZATIONS, AND CERTAIN OTHER CATEGORIES OF PERSONS

The following shall in no case be permitted to serve in the Austrian Armed Forces:

1. Persons not of Austrian nationality;
2. Austrian nationals who had been German nationals at any time before 13th March, 1938;
3. Austrian nationals who served in the rank of Colonel or in any higher rank in the German Armed Forces during the period from 13th March, 1938, to 8th May, 1945;
4. With the exception of any persons who shall have been exonerated by the appropriate body in accordance with Austrian law, Austrian nationals falling within any of the following categories:

(a) Persons who at any time belonged to the National Socialist Party ("N.S.D.A.P.") or the "S.S.," "S.A.," or "S.D." organizations; the Secret State Police ("Gestapo") ; or the National Socialist Soldiers' Association ("N.S. Soldatenring"); or the National Socialist Officers' Association ("N.S. Offiziersvereinigung") .

(b) Officers in the National Socialist Fliers' Corps ("N.S.-F.K.") or the National Socialist Motor Corps ("N.S.-K.K.") of rank not lower than "Untersturmfuehrer" or its equivalent;

(c) Functionaries in any supervised or affiliated organizations of the N.S.D.A.P. of rank not lower than that equivalent to "Ortsgruppenleiter";

(d) Authors of printed works or scenarios placed by the competent commissions set up by the Government of Austria in the category of prohibited works because of their Nazi character;

(e) Leaders of industrial, commercial and financial undertakings who according to the official and authenticated reports of existing industrial, commercial and financial associations, trade unions and party organizations are found by the competent commission to have co-operated actively in the achievement of the aims of the N.S.D.A.P. or of any of its affiliated organizations, supported the principles of National Socialism or financed or spread propaganda for National Socialist organizations or their activities, and by any of the foregoing to have damaged the interests of an independent and democratic Austria.

ARTICLE 13

PROHIBITION OF SPECIAL WEAPONS

1. Austria shall not possess, construct or experiment with—(a) Any atomic weapon, (b) any other major weapon adaptable now or in the future to mass destruction and defined as such by the appropriate organ of the United Nations, (c) any self-propelled or guided missile or torpedoes, or apparatus connected with their discharge or control, (d) sea mines, (e) torpedoes capable of being manned, (f) submarines or other submersible craft, (g) motor torpedo boats, (h) specialized types of assault craft, (i) guns with a range of more than 30 kilometers, (j) asphyxiating, vesicant or poisonous materials or biological substances in quantities greater than, or of types other than, are required for legitimate civil purposes, or any apparatus designed to produce, project or spread such materials or substances for war purposes.

2. The Allied and Associated Powers reserve the right to add to this Article prohibitions of any weapons which may be evolved as a result of scientific development.

ARTICLE 14

DISPOSAL OF WAR MATERIEL OF ALLIED AND GERMAN ORIGIN

1. All war materiel of Allied origin in Austria shall be placed at the disposal of the Allied or Associated Power concerned according to the instructions given by that Power.

Austria shall renounce all rights to the above-mentioned war materiel.

2. Within one year from the coming into force of the present Treaty Austria shall render unusable for any military purpose or destroy:

all excess war materiel of German or other non-Allied origin;

in so far as they relate to modern war materiel, all German and Japanese drawings, including existing blueprints, prototypes, experimental models and plans;

all war materiel prohibited by Article 13 of the present Treaty; all specialized installations, including research and production equipment, prohibited by Article 13 which are not convertible for authorized research, development or construction.

3. Within six months from the coming into force of the present Treaty Austria shall provide the Governments of the Soviet Union, of the United Kingdom, of the United States of America, and of France with a list of the war materiel and installations enumerated in paragraph 2.

4. Austria shall not manufacture any war materiel of German design.

Austria shall not acquire or possess, either publicly or privately, or by any other means, any war materiel of German manufacture, origin or design except that the Austrian Government may utilize, for the creation of the Austrian armed forces, restricted quantities of war materiel of German manufacture, origin or design remaining in Austria after the Second World War.

5. A definition and list of war materiel for the purposes of the present Treaty are contained in Annex I.

ARTICLE 15

PREVENTION OF GERMAN REARMAMENT

1. Austria shall co-operate fully with the Allied and Associated Powers in order to ensure that Germany is unable to take steps outside German territory towards rearmament.

2. Austria shall not employ or train in military or civil aviation or in the experimentation, design, production or maintenance of war materiel:

persons who are, or were at any time previous to 13th March, 1938, nationals of Germany;

or Austrian nationals precluded from serving in the Armed Forces under Article 12;

Or persons who are not Austrian nationals.

ARTICLE 16

PROHIBITION RELATING TO CIVIL AIRCRAFT OF GERMAN AND JAPANESE DESIGN

Austria shall not acquire or manufacture civil aircraft which are of German or Japanese design or which embody major assemblies of German or Japanese manufacture or design.

ARTICLE 17

DURATION OF LIMITATIONS

Each of the military and air clauses of the present Treaty shall remain in force until modified in whole or in part by agreement between the Allied and Associated Powers and Austria or, after Austria becomes a member of the United Nations, by agreement between the Security Council and Austria.

ARTICLE 18

PRISONERS OF WAR

1. Austrians who are now prisoners of war shall be repatriated as soon as possible, in accordance with arrangements to be agreed upon by the individual Powers detaining them and Austria.
2. All costs, including maintenance costs, incurred in moving Austrians who are now prisoners of war from their respective assembly points, as chosen by the Government of the Allied or Associated Power concerned, to the point of their entry into Austrian territory, shall be borne by the Government of Austria.

ARTICLE 19

WAR GRAVES AND MEMORIALS

1. Austria undertakes to respect, preserve and maintain the graves on Austrian territory of the soldiers, prisoners of war and nationals forcibly brought to Austria of the Allied Powers as well as of the other United Nations which were at war with Germany, the memorials and emblems on these graves, and the memorials to the military glory of the armies

which fought on Austrian territory against Hitlerite Germany.

2. The Government of Austria shall recognize any commission, delegation or other organization authorized by the State concerned to identify, list, maintain or regulate the graves and edifices referred to in paragraph 1; shall facilitate the work of such organizations; and shall conclude in respect of the above-mentioned graves and edifices such agreements as may prove necessary with the State concerned or with any commission or delegation or other organization authorized by it. It likewise agrees to render, in conformity with reasonable sanitary requirements, every facility for the disinterment and despatch to their own country of the remains buried in the said graves, whether at the request of the official organizations of the State concerned or at the request of the relatives of the persons interred.

PART III

ARTICLE 20

WITHDRAWAL OF ALLIED FORCES

1. The Agreement on the Machinery of Control in Austria of 28th June, 1946[12] shall terminate on the coming into force of the present Treaty.

2. On the coming into force of the present Treaty, the Inter-Allied Command established under paragraph 4 of the Agreement on Zones of Occupation in Austria and the Administration of the City of Vienna of 9th July, 1945,[13] shall cease to exercise any functions with respect to the administration of the City of Vienna. The Agreement on Zones of Occupation of Austria shall terminate upon completion of the withdrawal from Austria of the forces of the Allied and Associated Powers in accordance with paragraph 3 of the present Article.

3. The forces of the Allied and Associated Powers and members of the Allied Commission for Austria shall be withdrawn from Austria within ninety days from the coming into force of the present Treaty, and in so far as possible not later than 31st December, 1955.

4. The Government of Austria shall accord to the forces of

[12] *Documents on American Foreign Relations, 1945-1946,* pp. 311-317.
[13] *Department of State Bulletin,* v. 13 (August 12, 1945), p. 221.

the Allied and Associated Powers and the members of the Allied Commission for Austria pending their withdrawal from Austria the same rights, immunities and facilities as they enjoyed immediately before the coming into force of the present Treaty.

5. The Allied and Associated Powers undertake to return to the Government of Austria after the coming into force of the present Treaty and within the period specified in paragraph 3 of this Article:

(a) All currency which was made available free of cost to the Allied and Associated Powers for the purpose of the occupation and which remains unexpended at the time of completion of withdrawal of the Allied forces;
(b) All Austrian property requisitioned by Allied forces or the Allied Commission and which is still in their possession. The obligations under this sub-paragraph shall be applied without prejudice to the provisions of Article 22 of the present Treaty.

PART IV

CLAIMS ARISING OUT OF THE WAR

ARTICLE 21

REPARATION

No reparation shall be exacted from Austria arising out of the existence of a state of war in Europe after 1st September, 1939.

ARTICLE 22

GERMAN ASSETS IN AUSTRIA

The Soviet Union, the United Kingdom, the United States of America and France have the right to dispose of all German assets in Austria in accordance with the Protocol of the Berlin Conference of 2nd August, 1945.[14]

1. The Soviet Union shall receive for a period of validity of thirty years concessions to oil fields equivalent to 60% of the extraction of oil in Austria for 1947, as well as property rights to all buildings, constructions, equipment, and other

[14] *Documents on American Foreign Relations, 1945-1946,* pp. 925-938.

property belonging to these oil fields, in accordance with list No. 1 and map No. 1 annexed to the Treaty.[15]

2. The Soviet Union shall receive concessions to 60% of all exploration areas located in Eastern Austria that are German assets to which the Soviet Union is entitled in conformity with the Potsdam Agreement and which are in its possession at the present time, in accordance with list No. 2 and map No. 2 annexed to the Treaty.[15]

The Soviet Union shall have the right to carry out explorations on the exploration areas mentioned in the present paragraph for 8 years and to subsequent extraction of oil for a period of 25 years beginning from the moment of the discovery of oil.

3. The Soviet Union shall receive oil refineries having a total annual production capacity of 420,000 tons of crude oil, in accordance with list No. 3.[15]

4. The Soviet Union shall receive those undertakings concerned in the distribution of oil products which are at its disposal, in accordance with list No. 4.[15]

5. The Soviet Union shall receive the assets of the Danube Shipping Company (D.D.S.G.), located in Hungary, Roumania and Bulgaria; and, likewise, in accordance with list No. 5, 100% of the assets of the Danube Shipping Company located in Eastern Austria.[15]

6. The Soviet Union shall transfer to Austria property, rights and interests held or claimed as German assets, together with existing equipment, and shall also transfer war industrial enterprises, together with existing equipment, houses and similar immovable property, including plots of land, located in Austria and held or claimed as war booty with the exception of the assets mentioned in paragraphs 1, 2, 3, 4 and 5 of the present Article. Austria for its part undertakes to pay the Soviet Union 150,000,000 United States dollars in freely convertible currency within a period of 6 years.

The said sum will be paid by Austria to the Soviet Union in equal three-monthly installments of 6,250,000 United States dollars in freely convertible currency. The first payment will be made on the first day of the second month following the month of the entry into force of the present Treaty. Subsequent three-monthly payments will be made on the first day of the appropriate month. The last three-monthly payment

[15] Not printed.

will be made on the last day of the six-year period after the entry into force of this Treaty.

The basis for payments provided for in this Article will be the United States dollar at its gold parity on 1st September, 1949, that is, 35 dollars for 1 ounce of gold.

As security for the punctual payment of the above-mentioned sums due to the Soviet Union the Austrian National Bank shall issue to the State Bank of the U.S.S.R. within two weeks of the coming into force of the present Treaty promissory notes to the total sum of 150,000,000 United States dollars to become payable on the dates provided for in the present Article.

The promissory notes to be issued by Austria will be non-interest-bearing. The State Bank of the U.S.S.R. does not intend to discount these notes provided that the Austrian Government and the Austrian National Bank carry out their obligations punctually and exactly.

7. Legal Position of Assets:[16]

(a) All former German assets which have become the property of the Soviet Union in accordance with paragraphs 1, 2, 3, 4 and 5 of the present Article shall, as the general rule, remain under Austrian jurisdiction and, in conformity with this, Austrian legislation shall apply to them.

(b) Where duties and charges, commercial and industrial rights and the levying of taxation are concerned, these assets shall be subject to conditions not less favorable than those which apply or will apply to undertakings belonging to Austria and its nationals and also to other states and persons who are accorded most-favored-nation treatment.

(c) All former German assets which have become the property of the Soviet Union shall not be subject to expropriation without the consent of the Soviet Union.

(d) Austria will not raise any difficulties in regard to the export of profits or other income (i. e. rents) in the form of output or of any freely convertible currency received.

(e) The rights, properties and interests transferred to the Soviet Union as well as the rights, properties and

[16] The provisions of this Article shall be subject to the terms of Annex II of this Treaty.

interests which the Soviet Union relinquishes to Austria shall be transferred without any charges or claims on the part of the Soviet Union or on the part of Austria. Under the words "charges and claims" is understood not only creditor claims arising out of the exercise of Allied control of these properties, rights and interests after 8th May, 1945, but also all other claims including claims in respect of taxes. The reciprocal waiver by the Soviet Union and Austria of charges and claims applies to all such charges and claims as exist on the date when Austria formalizes the rights of the Soviet Union to the former German assets transferred to it and on the date of the actual transfer to Austria of the assets relinquished by the Soviet Union.

8. The transfer to Austria of all properties, rights and interests provided for in paragraph 6 of the present Article, and also the formalizing by Austria of the rights of the Soviet Union to the former German assets to be transferred shall be effected within two months from the date of the entry into force of the present Treaty.

9. The Soviet Union shall likewise own the rights, property and interests in respect of all assets, wherever they may be situated in Eastern Austria, created by Soviet organizations or acquired by them by purchase after 8th May, 1945 for the operation of the properties enumerated in Lists 1, 2, 3, 4 and 5 below. [Not printed.]

The provisions as set forth in sub-paragraphs a, b, c, and d of paragraph 7 of the present Article shall correspondingly apply to these assets.

10. Disputes which may arise in connection with the application of the provisions of the present Article shall be settled by means of bilateral negotiations between the interested parties.

In the event of failure to reach agreement by bilateral negotiations between the Governments of the Soviet Union and of Austria within three months, disputes shall be referred for settlement to an Arbitration Commission consisting of one representative of the Soviet Union and one representative of Austria with the addition of a third member, a national of a third country, selected by mutual agreement between the two Governments.

11. The United Kingdom, the United States of America and France hereby transfer to Austria all property, rights and interests held or claimed by or on behalf of any of them in Austria as former German assets or war booty.

Property, rights and interests transferred to Austria under this paragraph shall pass free from any charges or claims on the part of the United Kingdom, the United States of America or France arising out of the exercise of their control of these properties, rights or interests after 8th May, 1945.

12. After fulfillment by Austria of all obligations stipulated in the provisions of the present Article or derived from such provisions, the claims of the Allied and Associated Powers with respect to former German assets in Austria, based on the Decision of the Berlin Conference of 2nd August, 1945, shall be considered as fully satisfied.

13. Austria undertakes that, except in the case of educational, cultural, charitable and religious property none of the properties, rights and interests transferred to it as former German assets shall be returned to ownership of German juridical persons or where the value of the property, rights and interests exceeds 260,000 schillings, to the ownership of German natural persons. Austria further undertakes not to pass to foreign ownership those rights and properties indicated in Lists 1 and 2 of this Article which will be transferred to Austria by the Soviet Union in accordance with the Austro-Soviet Memorandum of April 15, 1955.

ARTICLE 23

AUSTRIAN PROPERTY IN GERMANY AND RENUNCIATION OF CLAIMS BY AUSTRIA ON GERMANY

1. From the date of the coming into force of the present Treaty the property in Germany of the Austrian Government or of Austrian nationals, including property forcibly removed from Austrian territory to Germany after 12th March, 1938 shall be returned to its owners. This provision shall not apply to the property of war criminals or persons who have been subjected to the penalties of denazification measures; such property shall be placed at the disposal of the Austrian Government if it has not been subjected to blocking or confiscation in accordance with the laws or ordinances in force in Germany after 8th May, 1945.

2. The restoration of Austrian property rights in Germany

shall be effected in accordance with measures which will be determined by the Powers in occupation of Germany in their zones of occupation.

3. Without prejudice to these and to any other disposition in favor of Austria and Austrian nationals by the Powers occupying Germany, and without prejudice to the validity of settlements already reached, Austria waives on its own behalf and on behalf of Austrian nationals all claims against Germany and German nationals outstanding on 8th May, 1945 except those arising out of contracts and other obligations entered into, and rights acquired, before 13th March, 1938. This waiver shall be deemed to include all claims in respect of transactions effected by Germany during the period of the annexation of Austria and all claims in respect of loss or damage suffered during the said period, particularly in respect of the German public debt held by the Austrian Government or its nationals and of currency withdrawn at the time of the monetary conversion. Such currency shall be destroyed upon the coming into force of the present Treaty.

Article 24

Renunciation by Austria of Claims Against the Allies

1. Austria waives all claims of any description against the Allied and Associated Powers on behalf of the Austrian Government or Austrian nationals arising directly out of the war in Europe after 1st September, 1939, or out of actions taken because of the existence of a state of war in Europe after that date whether or not such Allied or Associated Power was at war with Germany at the time. This renunciation of claims includes the following:

(a) Claims for losses or damages sustained as a consequence of acts of armed forces or authorities of Allied or Associated Powers;

(b) Claims arising from the presence, operations or actions of armed forces or authorities of Allied or Associated Powers in Austrian territory;

(c) Claims with respect to the decrees or orders of Prize Courts of Allied or Associated Powers, Austria agreeing to accept as valid and binding all decrees and orders of such Prize Courts on or after 1st September, 1939 concerning ships or goods belonging to Austrian nationals or concerning the payment of costs;

(d) Claims arising out of the exercise or purported exercise of belligerent rights.

2. The provisions of this Article shall bar, completely and finally, all claims of the nature referred to herein, which shall henceforward be extinguished, whoever may be the parties in interest. The Austrian Government agrees to make equitable compensation in schillings to persons who furnished supplies or services on requisition to the forces of Allied or Associated Powers in Austrian territory and in satisfaction of noncombat damage claims against the forces of the Allied or Associated Powers arising in Austrian territory.

3. Austria likewise waives all claims of the nature covered by paragraph 1 of this Article on behalf of the Austrian Government or Austrian nationals against any of the United Nations whose diplomatic relations with Germany were broken off between 1st September, 1939 and 1st January, 1945, and which took action in co-operation with the Allied and Associated Powers.

4. The Government of Austria shall assume full responsibility for Allied military currency of denominations of five schillings and under issued in Austria by the Allied Military Authorities, including all such currency in circulation at the coming into force of the present Treaty. Notes issued by the Allied Military Authorities of denominations higher than five schillings shall be destroyed and no claims may be made in this connection against any of the Allied or Associated Powers.

5. The waiver of claims by Austria under paragraph 1 of this Article includes any claims arising out of actions taken by any of the Allied or Associated Powers with respect to ships belonging to Austrian nationals between 1st September, 1939 and the coming into force of the present Treaty as well as any claims and debts arising out of the Conventions on prisoners of war now in force.

PART V

PROPERTY, RIGHTS AND INTERESTS

ARTICLE 25

UNITED NATIONS PROPERTY IN AUSTRIA

1. In so far as Austria has not already done so, Austria shall restore all legal rights and interests in Austria of the

United Nations and their nationals as they existed on the day hostilities commenced between Germany and the United Nation concerned, and shall return all property in Austria of the United Nations and their nationals as it now exists.

2. The Austrian Government undertakes that all property, rights and interests falling under this Article shall be restored free of all encumbrances and charges of any kind to which they may have become subject as a result of the war with Germany and without the imposition of any charges by the Austrian Government in connection with their return. The Austrian Government shall nullify all measures of seizure, sequestration or control taken against United Nations property in Austria between the day of commencement of hostilities between Germany and the United Nation concerned and the coming into force of the present Treaty. In cases where the property has not been returned within six months from the coming into force of the present Treaty, applications for the return of property shall be made to the Austrian authorities not later than twelve months from the coming into force of the Treaty, except in cases in which the claimant is able to show that he could not file his application within this period.

3. The Austrian Government shall invalidate transfers involving property, rights and interests of any description belonging to United Nations nationals, where such transfers resulted from force exerted by Axis Governments or their agencies between the beginning of hostilities between Germany and the United Nation concerned and 8th May, 1945.

4. (a) In cases in which the Austrian Government provides compensation for losses suffered by reason of injury or damage to property in Austria which occurred during the German occupation of Austria or during the war, United Nations nationals shall not receive less favorable treatment than that accorded to Austrian nationals; and in such cases United Nations nationals who hold, directly or indirectly, ownership interests in corporations or associations which are not United Nations nationals within the meaning of paragraph 8 (a) of this Article shall receive compensation based on the total loss or damage suffered by the corporations or associations and bearing the same proportion to such loss or damage as the beneficial interest of such nationals bears to the capital of the corporation or association.

(b) The Austrian Government shall accord to United Nations and their nationals the same treatment in the allocation of materials for the repair or rehabilitation of their property in Austria and in the allocation of foreign exchange for the importation of such materials as applies to Austrian nationals.

5. All reasonable expenses incurred in Austria in establishing claims, including the assessment of loss or damage, shall be borne by the Austrian Government.

6. United Nations nationals and their property shall be exempted from any exceptional taxes, levies, or imposts imposed on their capital assets in Austria by the Austrian Government or by any Austrian authority between the date of the surrender of the German armed forces and the coming into force of the present Treaty for the specific purpose of meeting charges arising out of the war or of meeting the costs of occupying forces. Any sums which have been so paid shall be refunded.

7. The owner of the property concerned and the Austrian Government may agree upon arrangements in lieu of the provisions of this Article.

8. As used in this Article:

(a) "United Nations nationals" means individuals who are nationals of any of the United Nations, or corporations or associations organized under the laws of any of the United Nations, at the coming into force of the present Treaty, provided that the said individuals, corporations or associations also had this status on 8th May, 1945.

The term "United Nations nationals" also includes all individuals, corporations or associations which, under the laws in force in Austria during the war, were treated as enemy.

(b) "Owner" means one of the United Nations, or a national of one of the United Nations, as defined in sub-paragraph (a) above, who is entitled to the property in question, and includes a successor of the owner, provided that the successor is also a United Nation or a United Nations national as defined in sub-paragraph (a). If the successor has purchased the property in its damaged state, the transferor shall retain his rights to compensation under this Article, without prejudice to obligations between the transferor and the purchaser under domestic law.

(c) "Property" means all movable or immovable property, whether tangible or intangible, including industrial, literary and artistic property, as well as all rights or interests of any kind in property.

9. The provisions of this Article do not apply to transfers of property, rights or interests of United Nations or United Nations nationals in Austria made in accordance with laws and enactments which were in force as Austrian Law on 28th June, 1946.

10. The Austrian Government recognizes that the Brioni Agreement of 10th August, 1942 is null and void. It undertakes to participate with the other signatories of the Rome Agreement of 21st March, 1923, in any negotiations having the purpose of introducing into its provisions the modifications necessary to ensure the equitable settlement of the annuities which it provides.

ARTICLE 26

PROPERTY, RIGHTS AND INTERESTS OF MINORITY GROUPS IN AUSTRIA

1. In so far as such action has not already been taken, Austria undertakes that, in all cases where property, legal rights or interests in Austria have since 13th March, 1938, been subject of forced transfer or measures of sequestration, confiscation or control on account of the racial origin or religion of the owner, the said property shall be returned and the said legal rights and interests shall be restored together with their accessories. Where return or restoration is impossible, compensation shall be granted for losses incurred by reason of such measures to the same extent as is, or may be, given to Austrian nationals generally in respect of war damage.

2. Austria agrees to take under its control all property, legal rights and interests in Austria of persons, organizations or communities which, individually or as members of groups, were the object of racial, religious or other Nazi measures of persecution where, in the case of persons, such property, rights and interests remain heirless or unclaimed for six months after the coming into force of the present Treaty, or where in the case of organizations and communities such organizations or communities have ceased to exist. Austria shall transfer such property, rights and interests to appropri-

ate agencies or organizations to be designated by the Four Heads of Mission in Vienna by agreement with the Austrian Government to be used for the relief and rehabilitation of victims of persecution by the Axis Powers, it being understood that these provisions do not require Austria to make payments in foreign exchange or other transfers to foreign countries which would constitute a burden on the Austrian economy. Such transfer shall be effected within eighteen months from the coming into force of the present Treaty and shall include property, rights and interests required to be restored under paragraph 1 of this Article.

ARTICLE 27

AUSTRIAN PROPERTY IN THE TERRITORY OF THE ALLIED AND ASSOCIATED POWERS

1. The Allied and Associated Powers declare their intention to return Austrian property, rights and interests as they now exist in their territories or the proceeds arising out of the liquidation, disposal or realization of such property, rights or interests, subject to accrued taxes, expenses of administration, creditor claims and other like charges, where such property, rights or interests have been liquidated, disposed of or otherwise realized. The Allied and Associated Powers will be prepared to conclude agreements with the Austrian Government for this purpose.

2. Notwithstanding the foregoing provisions, the Federal Peoples' Republic of Yugoslavia shall have the right to seize, retain or liquidate Austrian property, rights and interests within Yugoslav territory on the coming into force of the present Treaty. The Government of Austria undertakes to compensate Austrian nationals whose property is taken under this paragraph.

ARTICLE 28

DEBTS

1. The Allied and Associated Powers recognize that interest payments and similar charges on Austrian Government securities falling due after 12th March, 1938, and before 8th May, 1945, constitute a claim on Germany and not on Austria.

2. The Allied and Associated Powers declare their intention not to avail themselves of the provisions of loan agreements made by the Government of Austria before 13th

March, 1938, in so far as those provisions granted to the creditors a right of control over the government finances of Austria.

3. The existence of the state of war between the Allied and Associated Powers and Germany shall not, in itself, be regarded as affecting the obligation to pay pecuniary debts arising out of obligations and contracts that existed, and rights that were acquired before the existence of the state of war, which became payable prior to the coming into force of the present Treaty, and which are due by the Government or nationals of Austria to the Government or nationals of one of the Allied and Associated Powers or are due by the Government or nationals of one of the Allied and Associated Powers to the Government or nationals of Austria.

4. Except as otherwise expressly provided in the present Treaty, nothing therein shall be construed as impairing debtor-creditor relationships arising out of contracts concluded at any time prior to 1st September, 1939, by either the Government of Austria or persons who were nationals of Austria on 12th March, 1938.

PART VI

GENERAL ECONOMIC RELATIONS

ARTICLE 29

1. Pending the conclusion of commercial treaties or agreements between individual United Nations and Austria, the Government of Austria shall, during a period of eighteen months from the coming into force of the present Treaty, grant the following treatment to each of the United Nations which, in fact, reciprocally grants similar treatment in like matters to Austria:

(a) In all that concerns duties and charges on importation or exportation, the internal taxation of imported goods and all regulations pertaining thereto, the United Nations shall be granted unconditional most-favored-nation treatment;

(b) In all other respects, Austria shall make no arbitrary discrimination against goods originating in or destined for any territory of any of the United Nations as compared with like goods originating in or destined for territory of any other of the United Nations or of any other foreign country;

(c) United Nations nationals, including juridical persons, shall be granted national and most-favored-nation treatment in all matters pertaining to commerce, industry, shipping and other forms of business activity within Austria. These provisions shall not apply to commercial aviation;

(d) Austria shall grant no exclusive or preferential rights to any country with regard to the operation of commercial aircraft in international traffic, shall afford all the United Nations equality of opportunity in obtaining international commercial aviation rights in Austrian territory, including the right to land for refuelling and repair, and, with regard to the operation of commercial aircraft in international traffic, shall grant on a reciprocal and non-discriminatory basis to all United Nations the right to fly over Austrian territory without landing. These provisions shall not affect the interests of the national defense of Austria.

2. The foregoing undertaking by Austria shall be understood to be subject to the exceptions customarily included in commercial treaties concluded by Austria prior to 13th March, 1938; and the provisions with respect to reciprocity granted by each of the United Nations shall be understood to be subject to the exceptions customarily included in the commercial treaties concluded by that State.

PART VII

SETTLEMENT OF DISPUTES

ARTICLE 30

1. Any disputes which may arise in giving effect to the Article entitled "United Nations Property in Austria" of the present Treaty shall be referred to a Conciliation Commission established on a parity basis consisting of one representative of the Government of the United Nation concerned and one representative of the Government of Austria. If within three months after the dispute has been referred to the Conciliation Commission no agreement has been reached, either Government may ask for the addition to the Commission of a third member selected by mutual agreement of the two Governments from nationals of a third country.

Should the two Governments fail to agree within two months on the selection of a third member of the Commission, either Government may request the Heads of the Diplomatic Missions in Vienna of the Soviet Union, of the United Kingdom, of the United States of America, and of France to make the appointment. If the Heads of Mission are unable to agree within a period of one month upon the appointment of a third member, the Secretary-General of the United Nations may be requested by either party to make the appointment.

2. When any Conciliation Commission is established under paragraph 1 of this Article, it shall have jurisdiction over all disputes which may thereafter arise between the United Nation concerned and Austria in the application or interpretation of the Article referred to in paragraph 1 of this Article and shall perform the functions attributed to it by these provisions.

3. Each Conciliation Commission shall determine its own procedure, adopting rules conforming to justice and equity.

4. Each Government shall pay the salary of the member of the Conciliation Commission whom it appoints and of any agent whom it may designate to represent it before the Commission. The salary of the third member shall be fixed by special agreement between the Governments concerned and this salary, together with the common expenses of each Commission, shall be paid in equal shares by the two Governments.

5. The parties undertake that their authorities shall furnish directly to the Conciliation Commission all assistance which may be within their power.

6. The decision of the majority of the members of the Commission shall be the decision of the Commission, and shall be accepted by the parties as definitive and binding.

PART VIII

MISCELLANEOUS ECONOMIC PROVISIONS

ARTICLE 31

PROVISIONS RELATING TO THE DANUBE

Navigation on the Danube shall be free and open for the nationals, vessels of commerce, and goods of all States, on a footing of equality in regard to port and navigation charges and conditions for merchant shipping. The foregoing shall not apply to traffic between ports of the same State.

ARTICLE 32

TRANSIT FACILITIES

1. Austria shall facilitate as far as possible railway traffic in transit through its territory at reasonable rates and shall be prepared to conclude with neighboring States reciprocal agreements for this purpose.

2. The Allied and Associated Powers undertake to support inclusion in the settlement in relation to Germany of provisions to facilitate transit and communication without customs duties or charges between Salzburg and Lofer (Salzburg) across the Reichenhall-Steinpass and between Scharnitz (Tyrol) and Ehrwald (Tyrol) via Garmish-Partenkirchen.

ARTICLE 33

SCOPE OF APPLICATION

The Articles entitled "United Nations Property in Austria" and "General Economic Relations" of the present Treaty shall apply to the Allied and Associated Powers and to those of the United Nations which had that status on 8th May, 1945, and whose diplomatic relations with Germany were broken off during the period between 1st September, 1939 and 1st January, 1945.

PART IX

FINAL CLAUSES

ARTICLE 34

HEADS OF MISSION

1. For a period not to exceed eighteen months from the coming into force of the present Treaty, the Heads of the Diplomatic Missions in Vienna of the Soviet Union, the United Kingdom, The United States of America and France, acting in concert, will represent the Allied and Associated Powers in dealing with the Government of Austria in all matters concerning the execution and interpretation of the present Treaty.

2. The Four Heads of Mission will give the Government of Austria such guidance, technical advice and clarification as may be necessary to ensure the rapid and efficient execution of the present Treaty both in letter and in spirit.

3. The Government of Austria shall afford to the said Four Heads of Mission all necessary information and any assistance which they may require in the fulfillment of the tasks devolving on them under the present Treaty.

ARTICLE 35

INTERPRETATION OF THE TREATY

1. Except where another procedure is specifically provided under any Article of the present Treaty, any dispute concerning the interpretation or execution of the Treaty which is not settled by direct diplomatic negotiations shall be referred to the Four Heads of Mission acting under Article 34, except that in this case the Heads of Mission will not be restricted by the time limit provided in that Article. Any such dispute not resolved by them within a period of two months shall, unless the parties to the dispute mutually agree upon another means of settlement, be referred at the request of either party to the dispute to a Commission composed of one representative of each party and a third member selected by mutual agreement of the two parties from nationals of a third country. Should the two parties fail to agree within a period of one month upon the appointment of the third member, the Secretary-General of the United Nations may be requested by either party to make the appointment.

2. The decision of the majority of the members of the Commission shall be the decision of the Commission, and shall be accepted by the parties as definitive and binding.

ARTICLE 36

FORCES OF ANNEXES

The provisions of the Annexes shall have force and effect as integral parts of the present Treaty.

ARTICLE 37

ACCESSION TO THE TREATY

1. Any member of the United Nations which on 8th May, 1945 was at war with Germany and which then had the status of a United Nation and is not a signatory to the present Treaty, may accede to the Treaty and upon accession shall be deemed to be an Associated Power for the purposes of the Treaty.

2. Instruments of accession shall be deposited with the Government of the Union of Soviet Socialist Republics and shall take effect upon deposit.

ARTICLE 38

RATIFICATION OF THE TREATY

1. The present Treaty, of which the Russian, English, French and German texts are authentic, shall be ratified. It shall come into force immediately upon deposit of instruments of ratification by the Union of Soviet Socialist Republics, by the United Kingdom of Great Britain and Northern Ireland, by the United States of America, and by France of the one part and by Austria of the other part. The instruments of ratification shall, in the shortest time possible, be deposited with the Government of the Union of Soviet Socialist Republics.

2. With respect to each Allied and Associated Power whose instrument of ratification is thereafter deposited, the Treaty shall come into force upon the date of deposit. The present Treaty shall be deposited in the archives of the Government of the Union of Soviet Socialist Republics, which shall furnish certified copies to each of the signatory and acceding States.

ANNEX I

DEFINITION AND LIST OF WAR MATERIEL

The term "war materiel" as used in the present Treaty shall include all arms, ammunition and implements specially designed or adapted for use in war as listed below.

The Allied and Associated Powers reserve the right to amend the list periodically by modification or addition in the light of subsequent scientific development.

Category I

1. Military rifles, carbines, revolvers and pistols; barrels for these weapons and other spare parts not readily adaptable for civilian use.

2. Machine guns, military automatic or auto-loading rifles, and machine-pistols; barrels for these weapons and other spare parts not readily adaptable for civilian use; machine gun mounts.

3. Guns, howitzers, mortars (Minenwerfer), cannon special

to aircraft, breechless or recoilless guns and flamethrowers; barrels and other spare parts not readily adaptable for civilian use; carriages and mountings for the foregoing.

4. Rocket projectors; launching and control mechanisms for self-propelling and guided missiles and projectiles; mountings for same.

5. Self-propelling and guided missiles, projectiles, rockets, fixed ammunition and cartridges, filled or unfilled, for the arms listed in sub-paragraphs 1-4 above, and fuses, tubes or contrivances to explode or operate them. Fuses required for civilian use are not included.

6. Grenades, bombs, torpedoes, mines, depth charges and incendiary materials or charges, filled or unfilled; all means for exploding or operating them. Fuses required for civilian use are not included.

7. Bayonets.

Category II

1. Armoured fighting vehicles; armoured trains, not technically convertible to civilian use.

2. Mechanical and self-propelled carriages for any of the weapons listed in Category I; special type military chassis or bodies other than those enumerated in sub-paragraph 1 above.

3. Armour plate, greater than three inches in thickness, used for protective purposes in warfare.

Category III

1. Aiming and computing devices for the preparation and control of fire, including predictors and plotting apparatus, for fire control; direction of fire instruments; gun sights; bomb sights; fuse setters; equipment for the calibration of guns and fire control instruments.

2. Assault bridging, assault boats and storm boats.

3. Deceptive warfare, dazzle and decoy devices.

4. Personal war equipment of a specialized nature not readily adaptable to civilian use.

Category IV

1. Warships of all kinds, including converted vessels and craft designed or intended for their attendance or support, which cannot be technically reconverted to civilian use, as well as weapons, armour, ammunition, aircraft and all other

equipment, material, machines and installations not used in peace time on ships other than warships.

2. Landing craft and amphibious vehicles or equipment of any kind; assault boats or devices of any type as well as catapults or other apparatus for launching or throwing aircraft, rockets, propelled weapons or any other missile, instruments or devices whether manned or unmanned, guided or uncontrolled.

3. Submersible or semi-submersible ships, craft, weapons, devices, or apparatus of any kind, including specially designed harbor defense booms, except as required by salvage, rescue or other civilian uses, as well as all equipments, accessories, spare parts, experimental or training aids, instruments or installations as may be specially designed for the construction, testing, maintenance or housing of the same.

Category V

1. Aircraft assembled or unassembled, both heavier and lighter than air, which are designed or adapted for aerial combat by the use of machine guns, rocket projectors or artillery, or for the carrying and dropping of bombs, or which are equipped with, or which by reason of their design or construction are prepared for, any of the appliances referred to in sub-paragraph 2 below. [Not printed.]

2. Aerial gun mounts and frames, bomb racks, torpedo carriers and bomb release or torpedo release mechanisms; gun turrets and blisters.

3. Equipment specially designed for and used solely by airborne troops.

4. Catapults or launching apparatus for shipborne, land-or-sea-based aircraft; apparatus for launching aircraft weapons.

5. Barrage balloons.

Category VI

Asphyxiating, vesicant, lethal, toxic or incapacitating substances intended for war purposes, or manufactured in excess of civilian requirements.

Category VII

Propellants, explosives, pyrotechnics or liquified gases destined for propulsion, explosion, charging, or filling of, or for use in connection with, the war materiel in the present categories, not capable of civilian use or manufactured in excess of civilian requirements.

Category VIII

Factory and tool equipment specially designed for the production and maintenance of the materiel enumerated above and not technically convertible to civilian use.

ANNEX II

Having regard to the arrangements made between the Soviet Union and Austria, and recorded in the Memorandum signed at Moscow on April 15, 1955, Article 22 of the present Treaty shall have effect subject to the following provisions:

1. On the basis of the pertinent economic provisions of the April 15, 1955 arrangements between the Soviet Union and Austria, the Soviet Union will transfer to Austria within two months from the date of entry into force of the present Treaty, all property, rights and interests to be retained or received by it in accordance with Article 22, except the Danube Shipping Company (D.D.S.G.) assets in Hungary, Roumania and Bulgaria.
2. It is agreed that in respect of any property, right or interest transferred to Austria in accordance with this Annex, Austria's rights shall be limited only in the manner set out in paragraph 13 of Article 22.

In faith whereof the undersigned Plenipotentiaries have signed the present Treaty and have affixed thereto their seals.

Done in the City of Vienna in the Russian, English, French and German languages this day of May 15, 1955.

VYACHESLAV MIKHAILOVICH MOLOTOV
IVAN I. ILYICHEV
HAROLD MACMILLAN
GEOFFREY WALLINGER
JOHN FOSTER DULLES
LLEWELLYN E. THOMPSON
A. PINAY
R. LALOUETTE
LEOPOLD FIGL

7. *Statement by the Secretary of State (Dulles) on the Austrian State Treaty, Made before the Senate Foreign Relations Committee, June 10, 1955.*[17]

It is with gratification that I appear before this Committee in support of the President's request that the Senate advise

[17] *Department of State Bulletin,* v. 32 (June 20, 1955), pp. 1013-1015.

and consent to the ratification of the Austrian State Treaty.[18] This treaty, signed on May 15, 1955, marks the ending of a long, hard trail. Austria's independence was lost in 1938, 17 years ago. The restoration of that independence was one of the objectives for which United States forces fought in the Second World War. In 1943, 11 years ago, the Soviet Union pledged itself, with the United Kingdom and the United States, to make Austria free and independent. France joined in that pledge. Since 1947, 8 years ago, negotiations for an independence treaty have been carried on.

The freedom of Austria has had to be won twice over—first on the battlefield and then through long years of diplomatic struggle in the "cold war."

In the 10 years that have elapsed since the conclusion of World War II, the Austrian Government and people have fully demonstrated their ability to practice democracy as we know it. They have rejected the manifold lures of communism. They have displayed remarkable patience and steadfastness under a lengthy and onerous military occupation. The courage and determination of the Austrian people have been the indispensable basic circumstance which finally enabled the United Kingdom, France, and the United States to bring about this treaty.

My report of May 27 to the President, which he in turn has transmitted to the Senate, gives in some detail an analysis of the treaty. Therefore, I shall today touch only briefly on the high points I believe to be of significance to your deliberations.

It may be well first to recall the tortuous history of the treaty. The four occupying powers noted in 1943 that Austria was the first victim of Hitler's imperialism and agreed that she should be reestablished as a free and independent nation. There was no reason why that intention should not have been carried out promptly, and indeed by the time of the 1947 Moscow meeting of the Council of Foreign Ministers it appeared that early agreement on a liberating treaty was possible. As in so many other fields, however, it soon became apparent that the Soviet Union had other intentions. The hopes of the Austrians and the three Western Powers were raised and dashed in 1947 and again in 1949. Throughout 8

[18] The Senate gave its advice and consent to ratification on June 17, 1955 by a vote of 63 to 3. The President ratified the treaty on June 24, 1955. Ratification was deposited on July 9, 1955 and the treaty entered into force on July 27, 1955.

years, approximately 400 four-power meetings were held at various levels. The Western Powers made every effort to conclude the treaty, but the Soviets, time after time, found new and irrelevant excuses for refusing agreement.

In the meantime the Soviet armed forces remained in strength in Eastern Austria, and there was intensive Soviet exploitation of the East Austrian economy. All of this was a severe burden for the Austrian people throughout the period to which I refer. Removals of capital equipment were particularly heavy in the early years, and the Austrians were denied the benefits of their oil and Danube shipping properties as well as some 300 business and industrial enterprises.

In 1952 the United Nations took cognizance of the situation and adopted a resolution calling upon the four powers to terminate the occupation and restore Austria's independence as the four powers had agreed to do in the Moscow Declaration of 1943. But the Soviet Union ignored that resolution.

Berlin Conference

At the Berlin Conference in February 1954 the Austrian Government and the three Western Powers dramatized Soviet perversity when they went to the length of offering to accept the Soviet versions of the only five articles that then remained unagreed in the draft treaty. The Soviet Foreign Minister, however, insisted upon his new demand that Soviet military occupation should continue indefinitely. That would have made a mockery of the treaty. These new Soviet conditions were refused by Austria.

In April of this year the Soviet Government suddenly altered its policy toward an Austrian treaty. That reversal coincided with the Western European parliamentary actions which assured the coming into force of the Paris Accords for restoring sovereignty to the Federal Republic of Germany, creating Western European Union, and bringing the Federal Republic into NATO. At that juncture the Soviet Government invited the Austrian Government to send representatives to Moscow. After exchanges of views with the three Western Powers the invitation was accepted.

It led to an understanding embodied in a memorandum of agreement dated April 15, 1955, which you have before you as an attachment to the President's message to the Senate, dated June 1, 1955. The Moscow agreement was the first positive indication that the Soviet attitude toward the treaty had changed and that it would be possible to realize a treaty which would bring about the withdrawal of Soviet armed forces to the East, their first retreat in Europe since 1945.

Final negotiations held at Vienna during the first half of May made it possible to obtain a treaty which, in major respects, is a more just and satisfactory document than the draft treaty as it stood from 1949 until the recent negotiations in Vienna. These Vienna negotiations were a model of Western unity in action, and the results are notable. Special recognition is due to Ambassador Llewellyn Thompson and his associates who comprised the United States delegation at Vienna during the concluding negotiations.

The Western Powers and the Austrian Government negotiated with the Soviet representatives on the basis of the principle that provisions that were either obsolete or that might in any serious way qualify Austria's sovereignty should be removed from the treaty. Also, account was taken of the Austrian Government's announced intention of assuming voluntarily a neutral status after her sovereignty was restored. It was thus important that the treaty should neither provide special opportunities for other nations to interfere in Austrian affairs nor render Austria incapable of defending and maintaining its independence and neutrality.

Briefly, here are some of the important ways in which the treaty was changed during 2 weeks of intensive negotiation:

The so-called "war guilt" clause in the preamble was removed.

The draft article concerning displaced persons and refugees formerly known as article 16 was deleted. Much concern had been voiced about it here and abroad, and it contained provision for Soviet activities inconsistent with Austria's status of independence.

The Austrian intention to adopt a neutral status also made inappropriate several of the military clauses as they had stood in prior years. Those clauses would have limited Austrian military forces so as to have made difficult an effective defense of a neutral Austria.

The terms of the draft treaty provided in former article 35, now 22, that the Soviet Government would retain for up to 30 years most of the valuable Austrian oil properties and would own in perpetuity Austrian Danube shipping with its docks. At Moscow in April the Soviets offered to restore these properties to Austria for payments of 10 million tons of oil over a period of 10 years and $2 million, respectively. However, the Soviet representative at the Vienna negotiations refused to modify article 35 correspondingly. Thus, so far as the treaty was concerned, the Soviet Government would have been free to assert a legal right to undertake an economic reoccupation of Austria on the basis of the treaty provisions after the treaty had entered into force. That danger seemed to me so great that, on May 10, 1955, I informed Ambassador Thompson that I would not come to Vienna to sign the treaty unless some way could be found to eliminate the risk. At the last the Soviet Government agreed to incorporate by reference in the treaty (article 22) the Moscow economic accord. This reference also covers the Moscow provision that Austria's payment to the Soviet Union of $150 million over 6 years for German assets other than the oil and shipping properties may be discharged in terms of Austrian goods.

With these and other changes, it is possible for me to say with complete assurance that the treaty that the President has submitted will, when ratified, make good its title, which reads "The State Treaty for the Reestablishment of an Independent and Democratic Austria." The treaty provides for the ending of the occupation within 90 days after the treaty comes into force and the reestablishment of Austria within its borders as they existed on January 1, 1938. The signatories declare their intention to respect Austria's independence and territorial integrity, and *Anschluss* with Germany is prohibited. The treaty also contains provision for the restoration of legal rights and interests in Austria of the United Nations and their nationals and for return of the property as it now exists. National treatment is provided for in case of war damage. Another article provides that Austria will make restoration or provide compensation to victims of nazism, who were largely those of Jewish faith.

Neutrality

As I reported to the President, the Austrian Government has indicated its intention to declare its perpetual neutrality and not to join any military alliances or permit any foreign military bases on its territory. The Austrian Parliament has by unanimous vote passed a resolution to that effect, calling upon the Government to submit a constitutional law, which I am informed will be acted on by the Parliament after the treaty has entered into force and the occupation troops have been withdrawn, so that the act will be that of a fully sovereign nation.

At that time the Austrian Government will call upon the governments with which it has diplomatic relations to signify that they will respect that neutrality. The Soviet Government has suggested that the four former occupying powers make a joint declaration that they will respect and observe the neutrality which Austria will have chosen for herself. The executive branch sees no objection in principle, as such action would in essence be merely a concrete application of the general undertakings which the United States has already given by the United Nations Charter to respect the principle of equal rights and self-determination of other peoples (article 1 (2)) and to refrain from the threat or use of force against the political independence of any state (article 2 (4)). It would also be consistent with the traditional attitude of the United States toward other neutral nations. The exact form in which the United States would make its intention known is, I believe, best left to a later date, that is, until after the Austrian request has actually been made.

It is important, I believe, to note that the Austrian Government has indicated its intention to raise a substantial armed force and its resolve to defend its independence and neutrality with all the resources at its command. The steadfast and courageous behavior of the Austrian people during the years of occupation gives every reason for confidence that the Austrian people and Government will hold to that intention.

The Soviet-Austrian memorandum of understanding agreed at Moscow on April 15 includes a statement that for its part Austria will request a guaranty by the United States, United Kingdom, France, and the Soviet Union of the inviolability and integrity of Austria's territory, and the Soviet Union has in the same memorandum expressed its willingness to grant such a guaranty. No proposal of this nature has been put forward as yet. When and if it is, the administration, aware of our constitutional provisions, would of course consult the Senate on any action that would seem appropriate for the United States to take. I should add that none of the parties to the treaty has made the ratification or implementation of the treaty dependent on a guaranty of Austria's territorial integrity.

Both houses of the Austrian Parliament have this week voted unanimously to ratify the State Treaty, and it has been signed by the President of the Austrian Republic.

I wish to associate myself with the President in urging that the Senate take early and favorable action with respect to the Austrian State Treaty, which, when it comes into force, will fulfill at last the Moscow Declaration of 1943. This result has been one for which the United States Government has long labored and toward which my predecessors in office, Secretaries Marshall and Acheson, made contributions which deserve to be recognized. President Eisenhower stated in his speech of April 16, 1953, and the United States Government has repeated on numerous occasions since, that Soviet agreement to the Austrian treaty, fulfilling the Moscow Declaration of 1943, would be considered a significant deed, as distinct from words. It may open the way to further cooperation to fulfill other wartime pledges. It is the hope of the President and myself that the United States will complete its ratification processes promptly and prior to the forthcoming meeting of the Heads of Government of the "Big Four." We hope that this will be done by a Senate vote which will evidence anew our own Nation's dedication to the lofty goals which were proclaimed during World War II and our determination to do all that peacefully lies within our power to achieve those goals.

8. *United States Recognition of Austrian Neutrality.*

a. *Austrian Note, Delivered by the Ambassador of Austria (Gruber) to the Acting Secretary of State (Hoover), Washington, November 14, 1955.*[19]

The Ambassador of Austria presents his compliments to the Honorable the Acting Secretary of State and upon instructions of the Austrian Federal Government has the honor to convey the following:

On October 26th 1955 the Austrian Parliament has passed the constitutional law concerning the neutrality of Austria. This law has entered into force on November 5, 1955 and has the following wording:

"ARTICLE I

(1) For the purpose of the lasting maintenance of her independence externally, and for the purpose of the inviola-

[19] Department of State Press Release 680, dated December 6, 1955.

bility of her territory, Austria declares of her own free will her perpetual neutrality. Austria will maintain and defend this with all means at her disposal.

(2) For the securing of this purpose in all future times Austria will not join any military alliances and will not permit the establishment of any foreign military bases on her territory.

ARTICLE II

The Federal Government is charged with the execution of this Federal Constitutional Law."

A copy of the authentic text in the German language is enclosed.

In bringing this constitutional law to the knowledge of the Government of the United States of America, the Austrian Federal Government has the honor to request that the Government of the United States of America recognize the perpetual neutrality of Austria as defined in the aforementioned law.

b. *United States Note, Handed by the Secretary of State (Dulles) to the Ambassador of Austria (Gruber), Washington, December 6, 1955.*[20]

The Secretary of State presents his complements to His Excellency the Ambassador of Austria and has the honor to acknowledge receipt of the note of the Embassy of Austria dated November 14, 1955, informing him that the Austrian Parliament approved on October 26, 1955, the federal constitutional law relative to the neutrality of Austria, which entered into force November 5, 1955.

The Secretary of State has the honor to inform the Austrian Ambassador, in compliance with the request expressed in the note under acknowledgement, that the Government of the United States has taken cognizance of this constitutional law and recognizes the perpetual neutrality of Austria as defined therein.

[20] *Ibid.*

D. Yugoslavia.

1. *Announcement of Yugoslav-Western Conferences, Belgrade, June 27, 1955.*[1]

Talks were held in Belgrade from June 24 to 27 between the Yugoslav Under Secretary of State for Foreign Affairs, M. Prica, the Ambassadors of the United States, the United Kingdom and France on the general international situation and questions of direct mutual concern.

These talks were a further step in a series of consultations, individual, or collective, between representatives of the three Western Governments and the Yugoslav Government.

This exchange of views, which took place in an atmosphere of cordiality and mutual confidence, confirmed the wide measure of agreement among the four Governments in their approach to the various international questions under review.

This meeting had special significance in view of the recent more favorable developments in the international situation.[2] The four Governments were agreed that solutions to outstanding problems should be sought by peaceful means and by negotiations based upon full respect for and recognition of the right of all nations to independence, equality, self-defense and collective security in conformity with the Charter of the United Nations. They will continue to promote such solutions.

The four Governments express their firm conviction that the existence of a strong and independent Yugoslavia and continued cooperation between them under conditions of full equality are a contribution to peace and stability. They consider that the fruitful cooperation being developed in all fields in the Balkan alliance is also an important contribution to peace and stability in this part of the world.

They believe that this method of exchange of views can

[1] *Department of State Bulletin,* v. 33 (July 11, 1955), pp. 49-50.

[2] One of the developments referred to was the easing of tensions between Yugoslavia and the Soviet Union. A Soviet delegation headed by the First Secretary of the Communist Party (Khrushchev) and including also the Chairman of the Council of Ministers (Bulganin) visited Marshal Tito from May 27, 1955 to June 2, 1955. The meetings between Soviet and Yugoslav leaders culminated a slow but gradual process of normalization of relations between their respective governments which began after the death of Joseph Stalin in March 1953. On the conclusion of the Soviet leaders' visit a joint declaration was issued which bespoke substantial agreement between the Soviet and Yugoslav governments on matters of foreign policy and outlined steps to be taken to achieve further improvement in the relations between the two states.

help to promote an even closer understanding between themselves and can also contribute to a further improvement in the general international situation and to world peace. They are confident that the good relations developed between them in recent years in so many fields will be maintained and further expanded.

2. *Visit of the Secretary of State (Dulles) with the President of the Federal People's Republic of Yugoslavia (Tito), Belgrade, November 6, 1955.*[3]

Announcement Concerning Visit

On November 6, 1955, the United States Secretary of State, John Foster Dulles, met with the President of the Federal People's Republic of Yugoslavia, Josip Broz-Tito, at Brioni. The President of the Republic entertained the Secretary of State and his party at luncheon.

Participating in the subsequent talks, held in the spirit of friendship and mutual understanding, were the Ambassador to Yugoslavia, James Riddleberger, and the Counselor of the State Department, Douglas MacArthur II, on the American side, and the Vice President of the Federal Executive Council, Edward Kardelj, the State Secretary for Foreign Affairs, Koca Popovic, and the Secretary General of the President of the Republic, Joza Vilfan, on the Yugoslav side.

Views were exchanged on the international situation and questions of mutual interest. The subjects that had been discussed were later outlined by the Secretary of State at his press conference.[4]

Agreement was noted on a series of issues, particularly as to the possibility and necessity of continued efforts to improve international relations and with regard to the further broadening of the friendly cooperation between the two countries.

The meeting proved once again the usefulness of such personal contacts for a better understanding of the mutual positions and for the promoting of the cause of peace and international cooperation under the charter of the United Nations.

[3] *Department of State Bulletin,* v. 33 (November 21, 1955), p. 833.

[4] The Secretary said in part: "The final subject of our talk was the problem of the States of Eastern Europe. We reached common accord on recognizing the importance of independence for these States, noninterference from the outside in their internal affairs, and their right to develop their own social and economic order in ways of their own choice."

Statement by the Secretary

I am happy to be in Yugoslavia, which I visit for the first time. I look forward with particular pleasure to meeting and talking with your President. His leadership has been conspicuous in that he has ardently sought to preserve the independence of his country, and in pursuit of that goal he has shown great courage and tenacity. These are qualities which command universal respect.

Oftentimes in the past and particularly during and since the first World War, our peoples have been associated when the independence of nations has been endangered by external threats. From that association has come mutual respect and regard, and I am glad to manifest that feeling on behalf of the United States by accepting the kind invitation to call upon President Tito.

E. Cyprus.

1. *State Department Announcement on Tension between the Governments of Greece and Turkey, September 18, 1955.*[1]

The U.S. Government regards as most regrettable recent evidences of tension between the Governments of Greece and Turkey. Present differences between these two countries resulted last week in widespread violence in the cities of Istanbul and Izmir. We have expressed to the Turkish Government our deep concern over these disorders, which have not only caused extensive physical damage but have also exerted an adverse influence on Turkish-Greek friendship at a time when these two allies are in great need of mutual understanding.

As an expression of the importance that the U.S. Government attaches to continued close cooperation between Greece and Turkey, Secretary Dulles has transmitted personal messages to Prime Minister Alexander Papagos of Greece and Prime Minister Adnan Menderes of Turkey.

[1] *Department of State Bulletin,* v. 33 (September 26, 1955), p. 496.

2. *Letter from the Secretary of State (Dulles) to the Prime Minister of Greece (Papagos), September 18, 1955.*[2]

I have followed with concern the dangerous deterioration of Greek-Turkish relations caused by the Cyprus question. Regardless of the causes of this disagreement, which are complex and numerous, I believe that the unity of the North Atlantic community, which is the basis of our common security, must be restored without delay.

Since the time, almost a decade ago, when Communist expansion first posed a serious threat to the free world, the close and friendly cooperation of Greece and Turkey has proved a powerful deterrent to Communist ambitions in the eastern Mediterranean. In Korea, Greek and Turkish troops fought valiantly, side by side, to repel the Communist aggressors.

I cannot believe that in the face of this record of common achievement, any problem will long disrupt the course of Greek-Turkish friendship. Nor can I believe that the unhappy events of the past two weeks will reverse policies of cooperation which were initiated twenty-five years ago under the far-sighted leadership of Eleftherios Venizelos and Kemal Ataturk.

Since 1947 the United States has made very considerable efforts to assist Greece and Turkey to maintain their freedom and to achieve greater social and economic progress. We have extended this assistance—and extend it now—because we believe that the partnership of Greece and Turkey constitutes a strong bulwark of the free world in a critical area.

If that bulwark should be materially weakened, the consequences could be grave indeed. I urge you therefore to make every effort to assure that the effectiveness of your partnership is not impaired by present disagreements.

I am confident that the spirit of close cooperation that Greece and Turkey have so often demonstrated in the past as fellow members of the United Nations, the North Atlantic Treaty Organization and the Balkan Alliance will enable you to transcend immediate differences in the interests of free world unity.

[2] *Ibid.* The text of the letter sent by the Secretary of State to the Prime Minister of Turkey (Menderes) is not reproduced. It is identical in language with the letter printed above except that the two countries are named in reverse order in each case.

3. *Letter from the President to the King of Greece (Paul), Delivered in Athens, September 29, 1955.*[3]

In the present difficult situation, I desire to assure Your Majesty that I remain deeply convinced of the paramount importance of the ties of strong friendship which unite Greece and the United States. Even if there are differences of opinion over how the Cyprus question should be handled, we shall not let this one issue trouble our deep friendship and sympathy for Greece.

With kindest personal assurances,

DWIGHT D. EISENHOWER

F. Portugal.

1. *News Conference Comments by the Secretary of State (Dulles) on Tension between India and Portugal over Goa, August 2, 1955.*[1]

The United States is concerned with tension in that area as it is with tension in any area. It has always been our policy to favor the settlement of disputes by peaceful means. That is, of course, a principle which is expressed in the Charter of the United Nations. That applies to Goa as well as to any other place in the world. We are pleased to note that, as I recall, Prime Minister Nehru affirmed that principle for his own Government, and I am confident that that is also the view that will be taken by the Government of Portugal.

2. *Communiqué on Talks between the Minister of Foreign Affairs of Portugal (Cunha) and the Secretary of State (Dulles), Washington, December 2, 1955.*[2]

In the course of the official visit of the Minister of Foreign Affairs of Portugal to Washington, conversations took place between Dr. Paulo Cunha and the Secretary of State, Mr. John Foster Dulles, and other officers of the United States Government on matters of mutual interest to both countries and also on other issues of general interest to their respective foreign policies.

The conversations were carried on in an atmosphere of

[3] *Department of State Bulletin,* v. 33 (October 10, 1955), p. 560.
[1] Department of State Press Release 471, dated August 2, 1955.
[2] Department of State Press Release 678, dated December 2, 1955.

excellent understanding, and they have therefore made a considerable contribution to the strengthening of Portuguese-American relations. Among other topics, problems of defense within the framework of NATO were discussed. The interdependence of Africa and the Western World was also emphasized.

Problems connected with the trade relations between the United States and Portugal, and certain points relating to the use of atomic energy for peaceful purposes were also considered.

Various statements attributed to Soviet rulers visiting in Asia, which included references to the policies of Western powers in the Far East and allegations concerning the Portuguese provinces in the Far East, were discussed by the two Foreign Ministers. They considered that such statements do not represent a contribution to the cause of peace. The two Ministers whose countries embrace many peoples of many races deplored all efforts to foment hatred between the East and West and to divide peoples who need to feel a sense of unity and fellowship for peace and mutual welfare.

3. *News Conference Comments by the Secretary of State (Dulles) on the Attitude of the United States toward Goa, December 6, 1955.*[3]

(Excerpts)

. . . You will recall that in an earlier statement, which I made I think the early part of August,[4] I indicated the interest of the United States in a peaceful solution of the problem. The statement which was issued here the other day[5] was primarily a statement directed against the introduction of hate and prejudice into a situation which needs to be dealt with in a spirit of calm. We did not take, or attempt to take any position on the merits of the matter. We did jointly express our concern at the atmosphere of hatred and prejudice which was sought to be created out of it.

* * *

I do not think that the Indian Government questions the status of these various portions of territory that are governed

[3] Department of State Press Release 681, dated December 6, 1955.
[4] See above, p. 168.
[5] See the preceding document.

by Portugal as being under Portuguese law "provinces." I believe that they are such under the Constitution of Portugal; and that the residents of these areas, which include not merely Goa but several others, such as Macao, have the full rights of the Portuguese citizens. They can be elected to office and serve in Portugal and also elsewhere. I do not think there is any particular controversy about the status of those areas under the Constitution of Portugal.

* * *

Well, we did give it very careful consideration.[6] The communiqué was not lightly issued. But we did feel that it was appropriate and right to indicate our attitude toward the emotionalism which was sought to be created by the Soviet rulers when they were in India. They were not in India at that time but had just left for Burma. But the creation and fomenting of that atmosphere of hatred was something we felt we should express ourselves against.

* * *

As you know, we have been strongly advocating the principles that these situations should not be settled by force. That general approach has, I think, been sympathetically shared by Prime Minister Nehru. We have taken that position in relation to all these situations where there are national claims that conflict. We did not think they should be settled by force. And we had the feeling that the statements which were made by the Russians in relation to this matter were designed to create an atmosphere which might generate efforts to invoke force. That was our objection.

* * *

[6] The answer is to a question which sought to ascertain whether the Secretary had anticipated the storm of protest which the Joint U.S.-Portuguese communiqué aroused in India.

CHAPTER THREE

EAST–WEST CONTACTS IN EUROPE

A. The Geneva Conference of Heads of Government (July 18-23, 1955).

1. *Preliminaries.*

a. *Tripartite Note to the Soviet Union Proposing a Heads of Government Conference, May 10, 1955.*[1]

The Governments of France, the United Kingdom and the United States believe that the time has now come for a new effort to resolve the great problems which confront us. We, therefore, invite the Soviet Government to join with us in an effort to remove sources of conflict between us.

We recognize that the solution of these problems will take time and patience. They will not be solved at a single meeting nor in a hasty manner. Indeed, any effort to do so could set back real progress toward their settlement. Accordingly, we think it would be helpful to try a new procedure for dealing with these problems.

In view of their complexity and importance, our suggestion is that these problems be approached in two stages. We think it would be fruitful to begin with a meeting of the Heads of Government, accompanied by their Foreign Ministers, for an exchange of views. In the limited time for which the Heads of Government could meet, they would not undertake to agree upon substantive answers to the major difficulties facing the world. Such a meeting could, however, provide a new impetus by establishing the basis for the detailed work which will be required.

For this purpose the Heads of Government could devote themselves to formulating the issues to be worked on and to agreeing on methods to be followed in exploring solutions. We further propose that the Foreign Ministers, to assist the Heads of Government in their task, should come together shortly in advance of the meeting of the Heads of Government and at the same place.

This first stage would lay the foundation for the second

[1] Department of State Press Release 257, dated May 10, 1955.

stage in which the problems would be examined in detail by such methods, organs, and participants as it appears will be most fruitful according to the nature of the issues. This work should be started as soon as practicable after the meeting of the Heads of Government.

This procedure would facilitate the essential preparation and orderly negotiation most likely to bring about agreements by progressive stages. The important thing is to begin the process promptly and to pursue it with patience and determination.

We hope that this proposal will commend itself to the Soviet Union as a useful basis for progress toward better relations between us. If the Soviet Union agrees that an early meeting of Heads of Government to explore such a program would be useful, we suggest that our Foreign Ministers settle through diplomatic channels or otherwise upon a time and place for such a meeting. The forthcoming meeting of the Foreign Ministers at Vienna for the signing of the Austrian State Treaty might provide an opportunity for preliminary discussion of this proposal.

b. *Soviet Note Accepting Invitation to the Conference, May 26, 1955.*[2]

The Ministry of Foreign Affairs of the U.S.S.R. presents its compliments to the Embassy of the U.S.A. and in connection with the Embassy's note of May 10 on the convening of a conference of the Heads of Government of the U.S.A., France, England and the Soviet Union has the honor to state the following:

The Soviet Government, as is known, regards positively the convening of a conference of the Heads of Government of the aforementioned powers, having in view that such a conference must facilitate the reduction of international tension and the strengthening of mutual confidence in relations between the states. The Soviet Government considers that a meeting of leading state figures can contribute to the establishment of conditions necessary for settling unresolved international problems, given a genuine desire for this of all the interested parties.

In this connection it is pertinent to recall that the display of readiness by interested states to contribute to the settlement of such problems permitted the bringing to an end of

[2] *The Geneva Conference of Heads of Government, July 18-23, 1955* (Department of State Publication 6044), pp. 7-9.

bloodshed in Korea and also to the stopping of military action in Indochina with the recognition of the lawful rights of the peoples of Indochina for independent development. By this, two dangerous hotbeds of war in the area of the Far East and Southeast Asia were successfully liquidated. Recently one of the most aggravated questions in Europe was also successfully resolved—the question of the Austrian State Treaty with recognition of the permanent neutrality of Austria, which was an important contribution to the cause of strengthening peace and lessening international tension.

Following its constant policy directed to securing peace, and striving for the strengthening of mutual confidence in relations between the states and the cessation of the "cold war," the Soviet Government on May 10 specifically set forth its position on the questions of disarmament, the banning of atomic weapons, and the elimination of the threat of a new war.[3] The achievement of an appropriate agreement on these questions first of all among the great powers would permit putting an end to the existing arms race, including the field of atomic and hydrogen weapons, freeing peoples from the ever growing burden of military expenditures and creating conditions for a peaceful and untroubled life for the people. In accordance with this, the Soviet Government expresses its agreement to the proposal of the Government of the U.S.A. and also to the Governments of France and Great Britain relative to carrying out in the very near future meetings of the Heads of Government of the Four Powers with the participation of the Ministers of Foreign Affairs. However, the Soviet Government in this connection cannot but draw attention to certain statements of leaders of the U.S.A. made after receipt by the Soviet Government of the aforementioned note of the Government of the U.S.A. In these statements it is pointed out that the Government of the U.S.A., while declaring for the convening of a conference of the Heads of Government of the Four Powers, approaches this conference "from a position of strength" which indicates a desire to exert inadmissible pressure on the conference. This is done in spite of the fact that the fruitlessness of similar attempts in negotiations with the Soviet Union has been repeatedly demonstrated.

The aforementioned leaders in the U.S. have even gone so far as to state the necessity of interference in the internal affairs of other states, making various thrusts and attacks in regard to the countries of the people's democracies, who are

[3] See below, pp. 417-430.

defending the freedom and independence of their peoples. At the same time it is completely evident that such attempts to interfere in the internal affairs of other states, which are incompatible with the principles of the U.N., must be rejected as expressions of the aggressive intentions of certain circles, which have as their aim further intensification of the arms race, prolongation of the "cold war" and still further exacerbation of international tension. Such statements cannot be evaluated as other than the tendency to discredit the very idea of convening a conference of the Four Powers.

In this manner, the U.S. Government on the one hand proposes to organize a meeting of the Heads of Government of the Four Powers for consideration of unresolved international problems and on the other hand is already proposing plans which deliberately doom the conference to failure. This can be explained only by the fact that the Government of the U.S.A., in spite of its statements, evidently does not in fact seek the settlement of aggravated international problems.

In such a situation a conference of the Four Powers not only cannot give positive results on which the peoples are naturally counting, but on the contrary, frustration of the conference, which is already being prepared, would lead to a further deepening of disagreements between the powers and a worsening of the international situation.

The Soviet Government, as it has stated repeatedly in the past, considers the task of a conference of the Heads of Government of the Four Powers to be the reduction of international tension and the strengthening of confidence between states. Such an aim can be attained only in the event all of the interested states strive for it. Only in this case can a conference of the Heads of Government give positive results. Regarding questions which should be the subject of consideration at the conference, taking the foregoing into consideration, the Heads of Government could themselves determine the range of questions and also determine ways of settling them and give appropriate instructions to the Ministers of Foreign Affairs.

The Soviet Government considers the most suitable place for the convening of a conference of the Heads of Government to be Vienna, which corresponds also to an invitation extended by the Federal Chancellor of Austria, J. Raab.

The Soviet Government assumes that the question of the time of convening a conference of the Heads of Government will be subject to further agreement.

Analogous notes of the Soviet Government are also being sent to the Governments of Great Britain and France.

c. *Tripartite Note to the Soviet Union Proposing Time and Place for the Conference, June 6, 1955.*[4]

The Governments of France, the United Kingdom, and the United States refer to their Notes of May 10, 1955, addressed to the Soviet Government proposing an early meeting of the four Heads of Government. They recall that during their informal conversations in Vienna on May 14 and 15, the four Foreign Ministers agreed upon the desirability of such a meeting, and the three Governments are pleased to find this view affirmed in the Note of May 26 from the Ministry of Foreign Affairs of the USSR.

With respect to the place for a meeting of the four Heads of Government, it will be recalled that at Vienna the Foreign Ministers of the three Governments suggested Lausanne, whereas the Soviet Foreign Minister suggested Vienna and the Soviet Government confirmed this suggestion in its Note of May 26. In light of the divergent views with respect to where the meeting might be held, the Governments of France, the United Kingdom, and the United States now propose that the four Heads of Government meet at Geneva, where there are excellent facilities for a meeting of this importance.

The three Governments accordingly propose that the four Heads of Government meet in Geneva from July 18 through July 21 inclusive.

An early reply would be very much appreciated in order to permit the necessary arrangements to be made with the Government of Switzerland, which has informed the three Governments that the holding of such a meeting in Geneva on the dates set forth above is agreeable.

d. *Soviet Note Agreeing on Time and Place for the Conference, June 13, 1955.*[5]

(Excerpt)

The Ministry of Foreign Affairs of the Union of Soviet Socialist Republics presents its compliments to the Embassy

[4] *The Geneva Conference*, etc., p. 9.
[5] *Ibid.*, p. 10.

of the United States of America and in connection with the Embassy's note of June 6 has the honor to state the following:

The Soviet Government, in its note of May 26 in reply to the note of the Government of the United States of America of May 10, has already stated its positive attitude to convene a conference of the Heads of Government of the United States of America, the Soviet Union, Great Britain, and France, having in mind that the objective of this conference is to lessen international tension and strengthen mutual trust in relations between states.

The Soviet Government agrees that the conference of the Heads of Government of the Four Powers should open July 18 in Geneva. At the same time, the Soviet Government cannot help but note that the note of the Government of the United States of America of June 6 displays concern that the conference should last for 3 to 4 days and also avoids the important question raised in the note of the Soviet Government of May 26 concerning the tasks of this conference. In the present situation, the efforts of the Governments of all Four Powers participating in the conference should be directed first of all to guaranteeing the fulfillment of the basic task of the conference—reducing tension in international relations.

* * *

e. *Radio-Television Address by the President before Leaving for the Conference, July 15, 1955.*[6]

Good evening, friends. Within a matter of minutes I shall leave the United States on a trip that in some respects is unprecedented for a President of the United States. Other Presidents have left the continental limits of our country for the purpose of discharging their duties as Commander-in-Chief in time of war or to participate in conferences at the end of the war, and to provide for the measures that would bring about a peace.

But now, for the first time, a President goes to engage in a conference with heads of other governments in order to prevent war; in order to see whether in this time of stress and strain, we cannot devise measures that will keep from us this terrible scourge that afflicts mankind.

Now, manifestly, there are many difficulties in the way of

[6] White House News Release, dated July 15, 1955.

a President going abroad for a period, particularly while Congress is in session. He has many constitutional duties. He must be here to perform them. I am able to go on this trip only because of the generous cooperation of the political leaders in Congress of both parties who have arranged their work so that my absence for a period will not interfere with the business of the Government.

On my part I have promised them that by a week from Sunday, on July twenty-fourth, I shall be back here ready to carry on my accustomed duties.

Now, it is manifest that in a period such as this, the time I am able to spend abroad, we cannot settle the details of the many problems that afflict the world. But, of course, I go for a very serious purpose. This purpose is to attempt, with my colleagues, to change the spirit that has characterized the intergovernmental relationships of the world during the past ten years.

Now, let us think for a moment about this purpose. Let us just enumerate a few of the problems that plague the world, the problem of armaments and the burdens that people are forced to carry because of the necessity for these armaments. The problem of the captive states, once proud people, that are not allowed their own form of government freely chosen by themselves and under individuals freely elected by themselves.

The problem of divided countries, people who are related to each other by blood kinship and divided by force of arms into two camps that are indeed expected to be hostile to each other. Then we have the problem of international interference in the internal affairs of free governments, bringing about a situation that leads to subversion, difficulties and recriminations within a country, sometimes even revolution.

These problems are made all the more serious by complications between governments. These problems of which I speak have often arisen as the aftermath of wars and conflicts. But governments are divided also by differing ambitions, by differing ideologies, but [*by*] mutual distrust and the alarms that these create, and because of the alarms, they build up armaments and place their trust for peace and protection in those armaments, and these armaments create greater alarm, and so we have a spiral of growing uneasiness, suspicion and distrust.

That is the kind of thing that the world faces today.

Now for these things there is no easy settlement. In the

brief time that this conference can exist, it is impossible to pursue all of the long and tedious negotiations that must take place before the details of these problems can be settled.

Our many post-war conferences have been characterized too much by attention to details; by an effort apparently to work on specific problems rather than to establish the spirit, and the attitude in which we shall approach them. Success, therefore, has been meager. Too often indeed these conferences have been mere opportunities for exploitation of nationalistic ambitions, or indeed only for sounding boards for the propaganda that the participants want to spread to the world.

If we look at this record we would say, "Why another conference? What hope is there for success?" Well now the first question I ask you "Do we want to do nothing? Do we want to sit and drift along to the inevitable end in such a contest of war or increased tensions?" We want peace. We cannot look at this whole situation without realizing first that pessimism never won any battle, whether it was in peace or it was in war.

Next we will understand that one ingredient has been missing from all these conferences. An honest intent to conciliate, to understand, to be tolerant, to try to see the other fellow's viewpoint as well as we see our own. I say to you if we can change the spirit in which these conferences are conducted we will have taken the greatest step toward peace, toward future prosperity and tranquillity that has ever been taken in all the history of mankind.

I want to give you a few reasons for hope in this project.

First, the people of all the world desire peace. This is peace for people everywhere. I distinguish between people and governments here for the moment when we know that the great hordes of men and women who make up the world do not want to go to the battlefield. They want to live in peace. Not a peace that is a mere stilling of the guns but a peace in which they can live happily, tranquilly, and in confidence that they can raise their children in a world of which they will be proud. That common desire for peace is something that is a terrific force in this world and to which I believe all political leaders in the world are beginning to respond. They must recognize it.

Another item; did you note this morning the speech made by Premier Bulganin in Moscow?[7] Every word he said was

[7] See below, pp. 180-182.

along the line that I am now speaking. He talked of conciliation and tolerance and understanding. I say to you—I say to all the world—if the words that he expressed are as truly reflective of the hearts and minds of the men in the Kremlin as we are sure they are reflective of the hearts and minds of all the people in Russia, as in the hearts and minds of all the people in the world everywhere, then there will be no trouble between the Russian delegation and our own at this coming conference.

Now I want to mention another item that is important in this problem. The free world is divided from the Communist world by an iron curtain. The free world has one great factor in common. We are not held together by force, but we are held together by this great factor, and it is this: The free world believes, under one religion or another, in a divine power. It believes in a Supreme Being. Now this, my friends, is a very great factor for conciliation and peace at this time because each of those religions, each one of them, has as one of its basic commandments the words, terminology that is similar to our Golden Rule. "Do unto others as you would have them do unto you." This means that the thinking of those people is based upon ideas of right and justice and mutual self-respect, consideration for the other man. And this means peace, because only in peace can such conceptions as these prevail.

This means that the free people of the world hate war, and they want peace and are fully dedicated to it. Now this country, as other free countries, maintains arms. We maintain formations of war and all the modern weapons. Why? Because we must. As long as this spirit that has prevailed up to now is going to prevail in the world, we cannot expose our rights, our privileges, our homes, our wives, our children, to the risk that would come to an unarmed country.

But we want to make it perfectly clear these armaments do not reflect the way we want to live; they merely reflect the way under present conditions we have to live.

Now it is natural for a people, steeped in a religious civilization, when they come to moments of great importance, maybe even crisis, such as now we face, to turn to the Divine Power that each has in his own heart, believes in his own heart, for guidance, for wisdom, for some help in doing the thing that is honorable and is right. I have no doubt that tonight, throughout this country, and indeed, throughout the free world, such prayers are ascending. This is a mighty force.

And this brings to me the thought that through prayer we could also achieve a very definite and practical result at this very moment. Suppose, on the next Sabbath Day observed by each of our religions, America, 165 million people of us, went to our accustomed places of worship and, crowding those places, asked for help, and by so doing demonstrated to all the world the sincerity and depth of our aspirations for peace.

This would be a mighty force.

None could then say that we preserve armaments because we want to—we preserve them because we must.

My friend, Secretary Dulles, and I go to this conference in the earnest hope that we may accurately represent your convictions, your beliefs, your aspirations. We shall be conciliatory because our country seeks no conquest, no property of others.

We shall be tolerant, because this nation does not seek to impose our way of life upon others. We shall be firm in the consciousness of your spiritual and material strength and your defense of the right.

But we shall extend the hand of friendship to all who will grasp it honestly and concede to us the same rights, the same understanding, the same freedom, that we accord to them.

We—the Secretary and I shall do our best with others there to start the world on the beginning of a new road, a road that may be long and difficult, but which, if faithfully followed, will lead us all into a better and fuller life.

Thank you. Good night.

f. *Statement by the Chairman of the Council of Ministers of the Soviet Union (Bulganin) before Leaving for the Conference, July 15, 1955.*[8]

The Soviet Government Delegation is going to Geneva in order frankly to discuss with the other Great Powers the cardinal questions of international affairs, find a common language and, through joint effort, ease international tension and strengthen confidence in relations between states.

The most ardent desire of all the peoples is for peace. And this is understandable. The first and second world wars imposed countless sacrifices on mankind. Today, the cold war policy, inflated military budgets and the arms drive are placing immense burdens on the masses and are breeding alarm and fear for the future. Men can breathe freely only

[8] *New Times,* No. 30, July 21, 1955, Special Supplement.

when they are sure of the morrow and firmly know that they and their children will not be menaced by the monstrous calamities of war, and that they will be able to live and work in tranquillity.

There is frequent talk in the West about a danger allegedly emanating from the Soviet Union. This has been made the pretext for building military blocs and for surrounding our country with military bases. It has never been our intention, nor is it our intention, to attack anyone—that runs counter to our principles, to our unswerving policy of peace. But, in view of the military preparations being made by other states, we, naturally, cannot but take measures to ensure the security of our country. We have an army, in our view a very good army, equipped with all the necessary technique.

However, now as always we do not want war, and we consider it our sacred duty to exert every effort in order that the present tension in international relations be succeeded by an atmosphere of confidence, mutual understanding and businesslike cooperation. This would enable the countries to convert the huge funds now spent on armaments to promoting the welfare of their peoples—to the building of homes, schools, factories, mills, power plants, to the development of science and culture.

The establishment in Europe of a system of collective security, in which other states, too, would participate, would represent a big victory for peace. We are deeply convinced that this is feasible: the peoples of Europe can live in peace and friendship, free of fear of each other.

It is sometimes said that peaceful settlement of controversial international questions is prevented by the existence of different social and governmental systems in the various countries. But the social and governmental system of any country is the domestic affair of its people. Some foreign leaders may not like much in our order of things, just as we may not like much in theirs. But why should the difference in social and governmental systems prevent the peoples from living in peace, from regarding each other with mutual respect, from promoting mutually advantageous trade and cultural intercourse?

Some believe that capitalism is better than socialism. We are convinced that the opposite is true. That controversy cannot be resolved by force, through war. Let each prove that he is right through peaceful economic competition.

There are many unsettled, controversial issues in the world.

They will exist in future too. Such is life. But we can and should discuss these issues with patience and loyalty at the conference table, and find peaceful solutions. It is said that even a bad peace is better than a good quarrel. But if we exert every effort and achieve not a bad, but a good, real peace, millions of peoples in all countries will heave a sigh of relief. They will be rid of the fear created by the danger of another war, they will be able to live and work in tranquillity and confidence, and this tranquillity and confidence will become the firm possession not only of our own generation, but of coming generations as well.

It is to achieve this that we are going to Geneva.

It would be naive to think that we can solve all the complex international problems at this Conference. But if all the conference participants display good will and sincerely work for agreement, there need be no doubt that we shall find a common language and chart realistic paths towards effective settlement of the cardinal issues upon which the peace and well-being of the peoples depend.

Undoubtedly, the attainment of the lofty aims of the conference will require much effort. The Soviet Delegation declares that, for its part, it will make this effort. We hope that the other conference participants will do likewise.

2. *Opening Statements at the Conference.*

a. *Statement by the President, July 18, 1955.*[9]

We meet here for a simple purpose. We have come to find a basis for accommodation which will make life safer and happier not only for the nations we represent but for people elsewhere.

We are here in response to a universal urge, recognized by Premier Bulganin in his speech of July 15, that the political leaders of our great countries find a path to peace. We cannot expect here, in the few hours of a few days, to solve all the problems of all the world that need to be solved. Indeed, the four of us meeting here have no authority from others that could justify us even in attempting that. The roots of many of these problems are buried deep in war, conflicts and history. They are made even more difficult by the differences in governmental ideologies and ambitions. Manifestly it is out of the question in the short time available to the Heads

[9] *The Geneva Conference, etc.*, pp. 18-22.

of Government meeting here to trace out the causes and origins of these problems and to devise agreements that could with complete fairness to all eliminate them.

Nevertheless, we can, perhaps, create a new spirit that will make possible future solutions of problems which are within our responsibilities. And, equally important, we can try to take here and now at Geneva the first steps on a new road to a just and durable peace.

The problems that concern us are not inherently insoluble. Of course, they are difficult; but their solution is not beyond the wisdom of man. They seem insoluble under conditions of fear, distrust, and even hostility, where every move is weighed in terms of whether it will help or weaken a potential enemy. If those conditions can be changed, then much can be done. Under such circumstances I am confident that at a later stage our Foreign Ministers will be able to carry on from where we leave off to find, either by themselves or with others, solutions to our problems.

No doubt there are among our nations philosophical convictions which are in many respects irreconcilable. Nothing that we can say or do here will change that fact. However, it is not always necessary that people should think alike and believe alike before they can work together. The essential thing is that none should attempt by force or trickery to make his beliefs prevail and thus to impose his system on the unwilling.

The new approach we of this conference should seek cannot be found merely by talking in terms of abstractions and generalities. It is necessary that we talk frankly about the concrete problems which create tension between us and about the way to begin in solving them.

As a preface, may I indicate some of the issues I think we should discuss.

First is the problem of unifying Germany and forming an all-German Government based on free elections. Ten years have passed since the German armistice and Germany is still divided. That division does a grievous wrong to a people which is entitled, like any other, to pursue together a common destiny. While that division continues, it creates a basic source of instability in Europe. Our talk of peace has little meaning if at the same time we perpetuate conditions endangering the peace. Towards Germany, the four of us bear special responsibilities. While any conclusions we reach would be invalid unless supported by majority opinion in

Germany this problem should be a topic for our meeting here. Must we not consider ways to solve it promptly and justly. [?]

In the interest of enduring peace, our solution should take account of the legitimate security interests of all concerned. That is why we insist a united Germany is entitled at its choice, to exercise its inherent right of collective self-defense. By the same token, we are ready to take account of legitimate security interests of the Soviet Union. The Paris agreements contain many provisions which serve this purpose. But we are quite ready to consider further reciprocal safeguards which are reasonable and practical and compatible with the security of all concerned.

On a broader plane, there is the problem of respecting the right of peoples to choose the form of government under which they will live; and of restoring sovereign rights and self-government to those who have been deprived of them. The American people feel strongly that certain peoples of Eastern Europe, many with a long and proud record of national existence, have not yet been given the benefit of this pledge of our United Nations wartime declaration, reinforced by other wartime agreements.

There is the problem of communication and human contacts as among our peoples. We frankly fear the consequences of a situation where whole peoples are isolated from the outside world. The American people want to be friends with the Soviet peoples. There are no natural differences between our peoples or our nations. There are no territorial conflicts or commercial rivalries. Historically, our two countries have always been at peace. But friendly understanding between peoples does not readily develop when there are artificial barriers such as now interfere with communication. It is time that all curtains whether of guns or laws or regulations should begin to come down. But this can only be done in an atmosphere of mutual respect and confidence.

There is the problem of international communism. For 38 years now, its activities have disturbed relations between other nations and the Soviet Union. Its activities are not confined to efforts to persuade. It seeks throughout the world to subvert lawful governments and to subject nations to an alien domination. We cannot ignore the distrust created by the support of such activities. In my nation and elsewhere it adds to distrust and therefore to international tension.

Finally, there is the overriding problem of armament. This

is at once a result and a cause of existing tension and distrust. Contrary to a basic purpose of the United Nations Charter, armaments now divert much of men's effort from creative to non-productive uses. We would all like to end that. But apparently none dares to do so because of fear of attack.

Surprise attack has a capacity for destruction far beyond anything which man has yet known. So each of us deems it vital that there should be means to deter such attack. Perhaps, therefore, we should consider whether the problem of limitation of armament may not best be approached by seeking —as a first step—dependable ways to supervise and inspect military establishments, so that there can be no frightful surprises, whether by sudden attack or by secret violation of agreed restrictions. In this field nothing is more important than that we explore together the challenging and central problem of effective mutual inspection. Such a system is the foundation for real disarmament.

As we think of this problem of armament, we need to remember that the present burden of costly armaments not only deprives our own people of higher living standards, but it also denies the peoples of underdeveloped areas of [*sic*] resources which would improve their lot. These areas contain much of the world's population and many nations now emerging for the first time into political independence. They are grappling with the urgent problem of economic growth. Normally they would receive assistance particularly for capital development from the more developed nations of the world. However, that normal process is gravely retarded by the fact that the more developed industrial countries are dedicating so much of their productive effort to armament. Armament reduction would and should insure that part of the savings would flow into the less developed areas of the world to assist their economic development.

In addition, we must press forward in developing the use of atomic energy for constructive purposes. We regret that the Soviet Union has never accepted our proposal of December 1953 that nations possessing stockpiles of fissionable material should join to contribute to a "world bank" so as, in steadily increasing measure, to substitute cooperation in human welfare for competition in means of human destruction.[10] We still believe that if the Soviet Union would according to its ability contribute to this great project, that act would improve the international climate.

[10] *Documents on American Foreign Relations, 1953,* pp. 45-52.

In this first statement of the Conference, I have indicated very briefly some of the problems that weigh upon my mind and upon the people of the United States and where solution is largely within the competence of the four of us. As our work here progresses I hope that all of us will have suggestions as to how we might promote the search for the solution of these problems.

Perhaps it would be well if each of us would in turn give a similar indication of his country's views. Then we can quickly see the scope of the matters which it might be useful to discuss here and arrange our time accordingly.

Let me repeat, I trust that we are not here merely to catalogue our differences. We are not here to repeat the same dreary exercises that have characterized most of our negotiations of the past ten years. We are here in response to the peaceful aspirations of mankind to start the kind of discussions which will inject a new spirit into our diplomacy; and to launch fresh negotiations under conditions of good augury.

In that way, and perhaps only in that way, can our meeting, necessarily brief, serve to generate and put in motion the new forces needed to set us truly on the path to peace. For this I am sure all humanity will devoutly pray.

b. *Statement by the President of the Council of Ministers of France (Faure), July 18, 1955.*[11]

(Excerpts)

Our meeting is of a highly exceptional nature. Until today none of us could say that he had met the other three, even individually. No such conference of Heads of Government has been held within the last ten years.

During this ten-year period a so-called "cold war" has developed. Our meeting may mark the end of this particular period of history. That is what the people hope. We must not disappoint them. Nevertheless, however important, vast, and difficult this task may seem to be, it is not the only one with which we are entrusted. Ten years ago the powers which we represent drew up a plan for organising peace and setting up among themselves a means of co-operating for the general welfare of the world.

The events that followed marked a long eclipse of this

[11] *The Geneva Conference, etc.*, pp. 22-31.

spirit, a suspension of these plans. In this statement I shall not, willingly, comment on these events, and shall say nothing that might impute responsibilities, for I believe that this questionable method would be detrimental to the effort which we are jointly undertaking. If we can now put an end to the period of tension and return to our point of departure, we shall once more find the general perspective which in 1945 we considered both essential and attainable.

—Put an end to the cold war.

—Organise peace and peaceful co-operation among the powers.

These are the two major aspects in which our problems and our duties present themselves today. These aspects are complementary and inseparable.

It would be a mistake to wish to take up, separately, the present causes of international tension or any one of them individually for new ones can always arise; moreover, every problem is easier to settle if we can arrive at a plan in which agreement is possible. If we, the four of us, can bring about a common desire for positive peaceful action with respect to one definite point, everything will be easier.

In the first part of this statement, I intend to deal with the problem of the cold war and the end of international tension; in the second part, with the more general problem of organising peace. These open vast fields. As a matter of fact, the first part, relating to the present tension, will be devoted primarily to the German problem.

The second part, relating to the organisation of peace, will be devoted to disarmament.

I realise that these two subjects will not be the only ones to be discussed. But if we progress towards their settlement we shall certainly have covered the most difficult part of a long road.

* * *

The present position of Germany is not the cause of the internation [*sic*] tension; it is, to a certain extent, the result of it. But it is a cause tending towards the perpetuation of this tension; it is an obstacle to the development of what might be called a "détente." I frankly believe that until the German problem is settled, even if there are some improvements elsewhere, there can be no real harmony in international relations.

First Question:

Should Germany be re-unified? Unquestionably, yes. There is no valid argument, whether political, economic or social, or of any kind at all, that could justify the permanent division of a nation into two sections and of a people into two fractions.

Moreover, I see that the other powers represented here have declared themselves in favour of the unification of Germany. They are not agreed as to the method for bringing about this unification, or on the consequences which could arise therefrom. But they do not disagree on the principle.

Second Question:

How can unification be achieved?

I believe that a decision as to procedure is really neither very serious nor very difficult. The Eden plan,[12] in its general outlines: elections, all German government, peace treaty, is incontestably logical, although it is not necessarily perfect in all its detail. I maintain it is only good sense that if we four want to re-unify Germany it is not questions of method that will prevent us from doing so. We must grasp the essentials, and this leads us to the third question.

Third Question:

Would the re-unification of Germany lead to a problem of security?

It is in this field that the real debate, the only real debate, arises. It is, as a matter of fact, in invoking security arguments that the Soviet Union rejected the stand taken by the three other powers, and it is also for security reasons that the United States, the United Kingdom and France have rejected the Soviet counter-proposal.

Nevertheless, no-one has ever claimed that the unification of Germany would create an entirely new security problem. This would imply that the present division of Germany is a sufficient guarantee for the security of all. The question which arises is to what extent and in which way the re-unification of Germany would change the basic facts of the problem of security as we see it to-day.

Since it is clear that re-unification will in any case involve the elimination of one cause of tension, even if it creates or

[12] *Documents on American Foreign Relations, 1954*, pp. 201-204.

aggravates certain risks, this point in its favour should not be forgotten.

Fourth Question:

In order to reply to this question, we must determine *what the status of a re-unified Germany will be from the military standpoint.*

Thus we come to our fourth question, which is sub-divided into two:

1) Can Germany be neutralised?
2) If not, what will its position be?

1) *Neutralisation of Germany*

This suggestion has been made. It simplifies the problem for certain people who consider that a neutralised Germany is a guarantee for peace. Others, on the contrary, consider that a neutralised Germany would constitute a power vacuum and would increase the risks of war.

However that may be, my belief is that Germany cannot and must not be neutralised for the following reasons.

a) In international law, it is impossible to inflict discriminatory and vexatious treatment on a country which has recovered its sovereignty and its rights with the signing of the peace treaty.
b) To designate neutralisation as the penalty of responsibility for the war would be to contradict the stand taken by the Allies in laying this responsibility upon the Nazi State and not upon the German people themselves. It would mean recognising to their detriment and in reverse the biological theory and the racial principle which we have renounced and fought.
c) Besides, no similar measure has been adopted with regard to other belligerents.
d) Apart from legal considerations, the facts are against neutralization [*sic*].
e) By making the German people an object of suspicion we would run the risk of creating a national complex of touchiness, resentment, and revenge.
f) The machinery of constraint and control which would be necessary for enforcing neutralisation would be materially and morally impossible to invent and apply.
g) It may be noted that up to now only small states have tried the experiment of neutrality, and that at their

own wish. It would be impossible for a nation like Germany, with extensive territory, a very special geographical position and a large population.

2) Having thus dismissed the neutralisation of Germany, what from the military standpoint will the administration of this country be once it is reunified?

For my part, I hold to the belief that a re-unified Germany would remain within Western European Union and NATO. This belief seems to me to be the most tenable for both legal and factual reasons. If this assumption is correct the question of security should be studied from the standpoint of the Soviet Union since the Western powers can obviously have no objection to it.

Fifth Question:

Does the re-unification of Germany entail risks to the security of the USSR? If so, can guarantees and satisfactory assurances be provided?

In my personal opinion the re-unification of a Germany which remained within the Western European Union and NATO would in no way involve insecurity nor aggravate risks.

These agreements are of a purely defensive nature. In addition they entail a limitation of, and publicity in regard to armaments which apply to Germany. In these conditions risks are not increased for anybody and one cause of tension is eliminated.

But I realise that at this meeting we should all try to study the problems not only from our own personal point of view but also from the other's point of view.

I also recognise the fact that the Soviet Union may have its own opinion about its own security, and that that opinion may be more exacting than the one I sincerely hold on this matter.

The answer to the question I have raised cannot, therefore, be an objective answer; it can only be a subjective answer, which must be sought by putting ourselves in the place of the state which is most concerned. Looked at from this angle, the re-unification of Germany would have the effect of increasing the general potential of a country which is a member of the Western system, and therefore of increasing the potential at the disposal of the Western system.

We must, therefore, find out whether the so-called risk which might result can be reduced or eliminated, and whether the apprehensions raised by this risk can be allayed.

At this stage I can only formulate a series of observations and suggestions on the matter.

1) In the first place, this increase in potential need not increase purely military potential. To ensure that, all that is needed is that we should agree to maintain the limitations laid down in Western European Union. In other words, the whole of Germany, after reunification, must not have forces greater than those held by the present two-thirds of Germany as a member of Western European Union.

2) In the second place, the Western powers must be ready to prove, by every means at their disposal, the purely defensive nature of the agreements.

In this spirit, I suggest that they should undertake to apply directly to the Soviet Union the undertakings provided for in the Paris Agreements, which deprive any aggressor government of the right to benefit from the guarantees and military aid envisaged in the North Atlantic Treaty.

In addition, the Paris Agreements took note of the declaration by the Government of the Federal Republic that it would not resort to force to achieve reunification or any change in the German frontiers.

The same undertakings should be given to the U.S.S.R.

3) Thirdly, I suggest we include Germany in a general security organisation. This organisation could be extended to include all the European states prepared to join. Thus it would superimpose new defense undertakings on those which already exist.

Such a solution would satisfy all the interested Powers. Germany would be submitted to a double limitation, but this limitation would be in no sense discriminatory. The Western Powers would keep the agreements they have signed and the organisations they have set up. The Soviet Union itself would benefit from a different type of guarantee than that deriving from a system—WEU—of which they may well be suspicious. Nothing would prevent us hoping that, in the future, these two security systems might be fused into one. The organisation set up in Eastern Europe should, therefore, be integrated into this system at the same time.

I must now add that a general European security organisation which included Germany would be particularly useful if my assumption is proved wrong and Germany does not remain within WEU. In that case, although unlikely, one of two situations might arise:

a) the entry of a unified Germany into the Eastern system;
b) the refusal by a unified Germany to join either system.

In the first case, the Western powers would find themselves in a position similar to that of the Soviet Union in the case we have just been discussing. There would therefore be an additional advantage for them in a new and common organisation. In the second case, neither the Western powers nor the Soviet Union would have any guarantee in regard to Germany. Only a European security organisation which includes Germany can fill such a void.

The observations I have just made are by way of an indication only. There may be other proposals. It seems to me essential that the importance of the three following principles be recognised:

(i) Germany must be reunified
(ii) Germany cannot be neutralised
(iii) The legitimate anxieties of each Power for its own security must receive the greatest possible consideration, and it must be accorded all the guarantees compatible with the first two requirements.

II. *The constructive organisation of peace: Disarmament.*

Disarmament is the core of any general organisation for peace. For a long time disarmament has been thought of as a Utopia. Today, the doubts of statesmen and the fears of the public faced with new forms of destruction are putting an end to scepticism.

The studies undertaken by the UNO sub-committee have made considerable progress, and it seems that agreement will soon be reached on the fixing of limited figures for manpower. But it is still not clear how the two main obstacles are to be surmounted, that is to say, control and sanctions.

How is control to be exercised by an external authority within any given country over armaments which may be camouflaged or dispersed over wide areas? How, in any case, are sanctions to be applied, even if such a control can be created, to any contraventions it may discover?

It is scarcely possible to imagine that such a procedure

could be effective within the framework of an agreement which had no other objective. Any effective limitation of armaments can be ensured only within an international organisation with a wider aim and adequate powers.

The answer may be a military organisation similar to WEU. Equally, it may be an economic organisation (for disarmament is by no means a matter of purely military concern) . It is along some such lines that we shall find a solution to difficulties which up to now have seemed insuperable.

It would not, at the present time, appear to be possible to unite the four powers we represent in one organisation endowed with common strategic machinery. But, on the other hand, I believe it would be possible to agree upon economic and social co-operation.

How could an economic organisation ensure military disarmament? To answer that question it is necessary only to give to the problem of disarmament its full significance—not to look merely at its traditional and negative aspect, but also at the positive aspect which is its essential complement.

The problem of disarmament must be linked with that of transferring the productive capacity which would then become available. A changeover from unproductive expenditure to productive expenditure is difficult within the framework of any one state, since security calculations do not depend upon that state alone. But it would become possible within a system of collective security, since that would cut down the cost of security.

Any reduction of arms potential makes certain budgetary credits and means of production available, which may, according to circumstances, take the form of working hours, power, or material assets.

Every State knows that if it reduces its expenditure on security it increases its means of production and its welfare. But no State dares take the risk, alone, of cutting down its expenditure on security. The problem of security is an international problem. Thus we must at the same time internationalise the reduction of expenditure on security and the disposal of the resources thus liberated, which would otherwise remain unused.

An international organisation would benefit from all the money and materials made available by an agreement to limit armaments for stock. These assets would be administered by a special, common organisation. My suggestion is that they be applied to the tasks of aiding and equipping underdeveloped territories and under-privileged people.

Such a system would solve the problem of control and sanctions. (The only problem which would not be changed by this solution would be that of fixing percentages but we have seen that this is the only one of the three which can be solved in present conditions.)

Control would become world control of a financial and budgetary nature. This is much easier than physical control, for the budget is a definite document. And, even if such control is not perfect, sanctions are automatically ensured and that is the essential point.

The common fund will consist of assets deriving from the application of the agreed percentage. If, therefore, one of the participants maintains his arms potential at a higher level, the concealment and the infringement of rules of which he is guilty will penalise to that exact extent. The sanction is certain. If at the beginning, it is not very considerable, the yearly increase, which is part and parcel of the system, will soon make it very formidable indeed.

This new machinery must not put a stop to the investigations which are now being made, particularly by UNO, into the technique of control. There is no need for this work to be interrupted, since it is quite compatible with the new formula we are proposing.

The machinery of international transfer also provides a guarantee against a fear of economic recession which often accompanies a policy of reducing armaments, since it is feared [*felt?*] that the contribution of each participant to the common fund could be furnished by its own national production.

In addition to its technical advantages, this system has a great moral advantage. It would stimulate the interest of world opinion in disarmament by appealing to sentiments other than those of fear and self-preservation, and by creating international rivalry in human generosity. I am not forgetting the objections that may be made. I do not want to go into details. The most important objection is in regard to the use of the resources available to the fund.

Some states will be disappointed that the charges levied upon them will be used for the benefit of peoples of other lands and of countries far away, instead of for their own national development or for the reduction of their taxes. There are two replies to that:

(i) There is nothing to prevent any State reducing its military expenditure as much as it likes and using this transfer of resources as it wishes. The only point with which we are concerned here is that of agreed and simultaneous reductions which would not have taken place otherwise—a special sort of saving. National production will continue as before, but part of it will be devoted to charitable aims instead of being put to unproductive use.

(ii) There is also nothing to prevent the fund being used to assist some of the participants, either because they themselves have charge of under-developed peoples, or for other reasons which may be laid down. These states, which will become applicants for aid after paying their dues, will therefore have to accept all the agreed controls both in regard to reducing armaments and in the use of the funds.

If these general ideas are commonly accepted, I suggest that our Conference should decide to adopt them and thus to promote a new doctrine with regard to disarmament. We could either, under our common UNO guarantee, put this forward to the Powers whose military potential may have to be reduced under agreement, or—and this seems to me preferable—we might ourselves decide in principle to set up a common organisation, with administrative organs.

It is said that our Conference is a first chance. It might be a first step.

In the course of our reflections on the question of disarmament, we cannot forget that it is almost exactly ten years to the day since the first atomic bomb was dropped. This terrible but brilliant invention may perhaps have hastened the end of the war, but it must on no account be allowed to threaten peace. France does not possess the atomic bomb, but my Government has decided to direct its nuclear researches towards the peaceful uses of atomic energy. We are in all the better position, therefore, for most solemnly demanding that we should seek together the means of controlling atomic armaments. In my view, we have no right to ignore the anxieties of a world whose fate has become one and indivisible.

The inventive genius which has conceived these incredible methods of destruction can also find the means of preventing their consequences and of using them for the common good.

The real enemy of man is not destruction, but distress. You and I can do a great deal today to achieve mankind's deliverance.

c. *Statement by the Prime Minister of the United Kingdom (Eden), July 18, 1955.*[13]

This Conference is unique in history because the conditions in which we meet are unmatched in human experience. We all know what unparalleled resources the scientific and technical discoveries of our age have placed within our reach. We have only to stretch out our hand and the human race can enter an age of prosperity such as has never been known. It is equally clear how utterly destructive must be the conditions of any conflict in which the Great Powers are engaged.

There was a time when the aggressor in war might hope to win an advantage and to realise political gain for his country by military action. The more overwhelming the military power the more tempting was the prize and the less might the aggressor expect to have to pay. We can each one of us think of examples of this in history. Nothing of the kind is possible now. No war can bring the victor spoils; it can only bring him and his victim utter annihilation. Neutrals would suffer equally with the combatants.

These are stern facts out of which we can perhaps win enduring peace at last. The deterrent against warlike action holds up a warning hand. But the deterrent cannot of itself solve international problems or remove the differences that exist between us. It is in an attempt to make progress with these problems and differences that we are met here today. And at this Conference we have to deal with them mainly in the context of Europe.

What is the chief among them? There can surely be no doubt of the answer. The unity of Germany. As long as Germany is divided, Europe will be divided. Until the unity of Germany is restored there can be neither confidence nor security in this continent. Within the limits of our Western Zone we have done all we can to unify Germany. We have broken down the barriers between our zones. We have treated the three Western areas as an economic unit and given them a federal Government. We have brought the occupation to an end.[14]

[13] *The Geneva Conference, etc.*, pp. 31-34.
[14] See above, pp. 97-98.

Quite apart from the larger issues of German reunification it would mark a real advance if, pending our negotiations for German unity, the Soviet Government felt able to relax the physical restrictions which now aggravate the division of Germany, and prevent contact between Germans in the East and West.

Now I must turn to the wider issues of German unification. What is the reason why the Berlin Conference failed a year ago? [15] We must examine this as dispassionately as we can in order to see what progress we can now make from the apparently fixed positions which the great Powers on both sides then felt obliged to take. At the Berlin Conference the West proposed the unification of Germany with free elections and the free right of Germany of [*to*] choose her own foreign policy. Under the so-called Eden Plan Germany could have chosen either association with the West or association with the East or neutrality. But the Soviet Government was unable to accept that plan. Yet we all know in our hearts that Germany must be united and that a great country cannot be permanently prevented from freely deciding its own foreign policy.

The reason why the Berlin Conference failed was because one of the Powers there believed that a united Germany, rearmed and exercising its choice to join the NATO alliance, would constitute an increased threat to its safety and security. I am not now going to argue whether those fears are justified. In these last ten years there have been plenty of occasions for suspicions and alarms. These have found expression in heavy armament programmes. To try to deal with these issues in their wider aspect we have all agreed to work through the Disarmament Commission of the United Nations. We welcome the substantial progress which has recently been made there and the important measure of common thinking which has now emerged between the various proposals of the Western Powers and those recently set before us by the Soviet Government. All these discussions will go on, but, as we know, the immediate need is to make a practical start.

The urgent problem is how to begin the process of reducing tensions and removing suspicion and fear. There is also the practical question of how we can devise and operate together an effective control of armaments and of armed forces.

To reunify Germany will not of itself increase or reduce any threat which may be thought to exist to European

[15] *Documents on American Foreign Relations, 1954,* pp. 200-229.

security. Everything will depend on the conditions under which reunification takes place. I wish therefore now to suggest that we should consider a number of inter-related proposals which are intended to do two things. First, they are calculated to meet the apprehension of increased danger which some at Berlin felt might follow the acceptance of our plan. Secondly, they are intended to make a practical experiment in the operative control of armaments. This, if locally successful in Europe, might, as it were, extend outwards from the centre to the periphery. If we can once establish a sense of security over the continent of Europe—if we can create an effective system to reduce tensions here—can we not hope that this first success will be the preliminary for wider and more far-reaching understanding? We have therefore had in mind certain ideas which we think could be helpful to this end.

As I have said, our purpose is to ensure that the unification of Germany and her freedom to associate with countries of her choice shall not involve any threat to anybody. There are no doubt many ways of doing this. To illustrate what I have in mind let me give some examples. These will consist partly of actions and partly of assurances. Let us take the latter first. We would be prepared to be parties to a security pact of which those round this [table] and a united Germany might be members. By its terms each country could declare itself ready to go to the assistance of the victim of aggression, whoever it might be. There are many forms which such a pact might take. We would be ready to examine them and to set out our views about them. We would propose to inscribe any such agreement under the authority of the United Nations. It would also be our intention that if any member country should break the peace that country would forfeit thereby any rights which it enjoys at present under existing agreements.

Secondly, we would be ready to discuss and try to reach agreement, as to the total of forces and armaments on each side in Germany and the countries neighbouring Germany. To do this it would be necessary to join in a system of reciprocal control to supervise the arrangement effectively. All those represented here would we hope be partners in this, together with a united Germany. It would be understood that any proposals in this field would not exclude or delay the work of the United Nations Disarmament Commission, to which we attach great importance.

Is there some further reassurance we can give each other? There is one which I certainly think should be considered. We should be ready to examine the possibility of a demilitarised area between East and West.

It is true that these ideas are limited in the first instance to the area of Europe, but I am sure that they could help us here in practice and perhaps as an example. I will sum them up. There is the suggestion of a mutual security pact. There is the prospect of an agreement about the total of forces and armaments of the two groups both in Germany and in the countries neighbouring Germany. This would be subject to reciprocal supervision. There is the concept of a demilitarised area.

If we could start work on these lines we should have a chance of providing a constructive and encouraging plan to ensure peace for Europe. These ideas would give real security: and it is for the lack of that security that Germany is kept divided today. I suggest that they should be further examined. I have given only the summary of them here.

There are other aspects of our work together which I could have mentioned. For instance we would warmly welcome any proposals which would result in a greater freedom of movement and exchange of contacts between our peoples.

But it seems to me that it will be by our success in achieving some practical results about the future of Germany and European security that this Conference will be judged. We want to agree on two things: the urgent need for the unification of Germany and the broad outline of the means by which it can be achieved. I do not pretend that our ideas are anything in the nature of a complete plan but they are the outline sketch which once agreed upon could surely be filled in. If we can draw up something like this before we leave Geneva at the end of this Conference, the peoples of the world will not be disappointed.

d. *Statement by the Chairman of the Council of Ministers of the Soviet Union (Bulganin), July 18, 1955.*[16]

(Excerpts)

* * *

The Conference of the Heads of the Governments of the Four Powers, convened in conformity with the desires of all

[16] *The Geneva Conference, etc.,* pp. 35-42.

the parties concerned, is taking place at a time when a certain relaxation of tension in international relations is in evidence and when more favourable conditions for the settlement of pending international issues have appeared.

What are the facts which have contributed to the relaxation of international tension?

The first thing to be mentioned is the termination of bloodshed in Korea and the cessation of hostilities in Indo-China[—]developments which undoubtedly represented considerable success for the forces of peace.

Furthermore, it is necessary to stress the significance of such events as: the conclusion of the State Treaty with Austria; the normalization of relations between the USSR and Yugoslavia, which has paved the way for the development of friendship and cooperation between the two countries; the success of the Conference of 29 Asian and African countries in Bandung;[17] the visit to the Soviet Union of Mr. Jawaharlal Nehru, the Prime Minister of India, as a result of which the friendly relations between the USSR and India have been strengthened still further; the proposal made by the Government of the Soviet Union to the Government of the German Federal Republic to establish diplomatic, commercial, and cultural relations between the USSR and the GFR.[18]

It is also necessary to stress particularly the importance of the proposal made by the Soviet Government on May 10th of this year on the reduction of armaments, the prohibition of atomic and hydrogen weapons, and the removal of the threat of a new war for the purpose of easing international tension. However, there are issues which divide us and which demand immediate settlement. It is because these issues have not been settled that, despite a certain improvement, the international situation as a whole is still tense and mutual trust, without which peoples cannot be sure of their future, has not yet been established.

It is a fact that the so-called "cold war" still continues, and it must be admitted that the use made in recent years of available opportunities to improve relations between our countries has been far from sufficient and that some of the steps taken by the Governments concerned, in the atmosphere of distrust and tension, led to a further deterioration of our relations.

All this makes it incumbent upon us, the statesmen of the

[17] See below, pp. 332-341.
[18] See above, pp. 107-108.

Four Powers assembled here, to consider the current situation in earnest and to do our best to facilitate the establishment of the confidence which is essential for relations between nations, both large and small.

* * *

The principal purpose of our Conference is to find ways to achieve the necessary understanding on the problems to be settled. The Delegation of the Soviet Union has come to this Conference with the desire to find through joint efforts by all the participants, solutions for the pending issues and, for its part, is prepared to give careful consideration to the proposals advanced by the other participants.

There can be no doubt that this is exactly what is expected of us by the people whose eyes are focussed on this Conference in Geneva. It is not fortuitous that many statesmen, recognizing the unbending will of the peoples toward peace, are coming out with ever growing determination in favour of having the unsolved problems settled on the basis of an adequate recognition of the legitimate rights of all the parties concerned.

* * *

The foreign policy of the Soviet Union is clear. We have always been in favour of peace among peoples and of peaceful co-existence between all nations, irrespective of their internal systems, regardless of whether the state concerned is a monarchy or a republic, whether it is capitalist or socialist, because the social and economic system existing in any country is the internal affair of its own people.

Recognition of this indisputable fact is of the greatest significance for the successful settlement of the unsolved international problems.

All those who are genuinely concerned about the present state of affairs, which is characterized by the armaments race, and the discovery of ever more dangerous and powerful weapons of mass destruction—a fact which increases the threat of a new war with its countless losses—are bound to uphold the demands to put an end to the arms race, to ban atomic weapons, and to limit atomic energy to peaceful uses for the benefit of mankind and civilization.

* * *

I would like to stress once again that the Soviet Government has accepted the proposal made by the three powers in regard to conventional armaments. Now we are entitled to expect that these powers would take a step which would ensure agreement on the prohibition of atomic weapons; that would put the whole problem of disarmament on firm ground.

In his statement M. Edgar Faure, Prime Minister of France, made a suggestion concerning the need to reduce military appropriations and set forth his reasons. We are of the opinion that these considerations are of interest and worthy of careful examination.

Furthermore, in the opinion of the Soviet Government the Four Powers would make a good beginning if they agreed even now to demobilize the military contingents which they are withdrawing from the territory of Austria as a result of the conclusion of the Austrian State Treaty, and correspondingly reduce the strength of their armed forces. The Soviet Government has decided to carry out such a measure and invite the Governments of the United States, France and Great Britain to follow suit.[19]

* * *

The Soviet Government is convinced that the best way to ensure peace and prevent new aggression in Europe is to establish a system of collective security with the participation of all European nations and the United States of America. The adoption of appropriate decisions to that end would invigorate the whole climate in Europe and would bring about normal living conditions for the peoples of that continent. Military groupings of some European nations directed against others should be replaced by a system of security based on the joint efforts of all the nations of Europe—a system the principles of which have been set forth in the well-known proposals of the Soviet Government.

The difficulties standing in the way of the establishment of such a system have to be reckoned with and, in particular, the fact that the powers engaged in the present talks are bound by military commitments in regard to other nations. The Soviet Government is, therefore, of the opinion that, in order to help reach agreement, the process of establishing a collective security system in Europe could be divided into two stages.

[19] On July 31, 1955 Marshal G. K. Zhukov, Minister of Defense of the Soviet Union, ordered the withdrawal of all Soviet troops from Austria by October 1, 1955. Simultaneously it was announced that the armed forces of the Soviet Union would be reduced by the number of troops withdrawn from Austria, i.e., by 44,000 men.

During the first stage the States-parties to the Treaty would not be relieved of the obligations assumed by them under existing treaties and agreements, but they would be bound to refrain from the use of armed force and to settle by peaceful means all the disputes that might arise between them.

It could be agreed that pending the conclusion of an agreement on the reduction of armaments and the prohibition of atomic weapons as well as the withdrawal of foreign troops from the territories of European countries, the States-parties to the Treaty undertake not to take any further steps to increase their armed forces stationed on the territories of other European States under treaties and agreements concluded by them previously.

During the second stage the States concerned would assume in full the treaty commitments related to the setting up of the collective security system in Europe, with the simultaneous complete termination of the North Atlantic Treaty, the Paris Agreements and the Warsaw Treaty,[20] and while the groupings of states created on the basis of these arrangements would be abolished and replaced by an all-European system of collective security.

* * *

The withdrawal of foreign troops from the territories of European states and the re-establishment in this respect of the situation which existed prior to the Second World War would in itself constitute a factor of great importance in consolidating peace, would radically improve the situation in Europe and would remove one of the principal, if not the primary, sources of the present distrust in international relations.

The significance of this step becomes even more evident if viewed in relation to the reduction of armaments and the prohibition of atomic weapons. The withdrawal of foreign troops from the countries of Europe would greatly facilitate agreement both on the reduction of conventional armaments of European, but not only European, nations and on the prohibition of the use of nuclear weapons.

* * *

[20] On May 14, 1955 the Soviet Union and seven of its European allies (Albania, Bulgaria, Czechoslovakia, East Germany, Hungary, Poland and Rumania) concluded a Mutual Defense Treaty at Warsaw. The treaty calls for the establishment of a joint military command under Soviet Marshal Ivan S. Konev and for the creation of a political consultative assembly. Ratifications were deposited on June 5, 1955 and the treaty entered into force on the same day.

In proposing the programme of disarmament and of establishing a system of European security the Soviet Government proceeds from the premise that the easing of tension in international relations and the creation of an effective system of security in Europe would largely facilitate the settlement of the German problem and would bring about the necessary prerequisites for the unification of Germany on peaceful and democratic principles.

The Soviet Government now, as in the past, favours the unification of Germany in conformity with the national interests of the German people and security in Europe. The unification of Germany as a peace-loving and democratic state would be of paramount importance both for the peace of Europe and for the German nation itself, a nation which has more than once suffered losses and devastation caused by war. It would offer the German people vast opportunities to develop their country's peace-time economy and culture and to improve the welfare of the population.

It must be admitted that the remilitarization of Western Germany and its integration into military groupings of the Western Powers now represent the main obstacles to its unification. It would be well to exchange views here, bearing in mind the need to seek a solution of the German problem even though under the present circumstances we may fail to reach immediate agreement on the reunification of Germany. In that case the problem should be solved step by step.

I believe it necessary to touch upon some other matters as well.

The Soviet Government is of the view that the States-parties to the North Atlantic Treaty and Paris agreements, on the one hand, and the States-parties to the Warsaw treaty, on the other, could assume mutual commitments not to use armed force against one another. It stands to reason that these commitments must not affect the inalienable right of states to individual and collective self-defence in case of armed attack as provided for by Article 51 of the UN Charter.

They could further assume an obligation to hold mutual consultations in case any differences or disputes arise among them which might constitute a threat to the maintenance of peace in Europe.

The Soviet government would like to call to the attention of the Governments of France, Great Britain, and the United States one important matter which is becoming ever more important.

It is a fact that for some time a movement in favour of a policy of neutrality, a policy of nonparticipation in military blocs and coalitions has been gaining ground in some countries. Experience shows that some states which pursued a neutral policy in time of war were able to ensure security for their peoples and play a positive role. This was confirmed, in particular, by the experience of the Second World War, although the neutrality of some countries was not beyond reproach.

The Soviet Government is also of the opinion that should any nation desiring to pursue a policy of neutrality and nonparticipation in military groupings, while these groupings exist, raise the question of having their security and territorial integrity guaranteed, the Great Powers should accede to these wishes. In any case, as far as the Soviet Union is concerned, it is prepared to take part in such guarantees as it has, for instance, declared in respect of Austria.

At this point mention was made of the countries of Eastern Europe—the people's democracies.[21] To raise this question at this Conference means interference in the internal affairs of these states.

It is common knowledge that the regime of people's democracies has been established in those countries by the people themselves of their own free will. Besides, nobody has authorized us to consider the state of affairs in those countries.

Thus, there are no grounds for discussing this question at our Conference.

The question of so-called "international Communism" has also been touched upon here. However, it is known that our Conference is convened to discuss problems of inter-State relations but not to discuss the activities of certain political parties in various countries or relations between those parties. Proceeding from this premise, we hold that raising this question at the Conference of the Heads of Government cannot be considered appropriate.

The Soviet Government has repeatedly stated its views on the need to settle the problems of Asia and the Far East. It has, in particular, drawn to the attention of the countries concerned the serious situation which has arisen in the region of Taiwan which has become a dangerous hotbed of complications in the Far East. The settlement of the situation in Asia and the Far East, including the Taiwan area, on the basis of the recognition of China's indisputable right to this island

[21] See above, p. 184.

would be of signal importance for the amelioration of the international situation as a whole.

In this connection I find it necessary to recall the well-known desire of the Government of the People's Republic of China to settle the Taiwan problem through direct negotiations between the United States and the People's Republic of China.

Note should also be taken of the important question of re-establishing the lawful rights of the People's Republic of China in the United Nations. The existing situation, under which Chiang Kai-shek's representative still acts in that Organisation while the great People's Republic of China is deprived of the possibility of occupying its seat[,] is not only abnormal but also inadmissible. This injustice should be rectified and the sooner that is done, the better.

The Soviet Government believes that in endeavouring to improve relations between countries the Four-Power Conference should pay due attention to the problem of strengthening economic ties between them and, in particular, to the development of trade. The present state of affairs when artificial restrictions of various kinds have been introduced in a number of countries with the result that economic and trade ties developed between many countries over many years have been broken, is one of the serious obstacles to the relaxation of international tensions. Such restrictions as are usually introduced when the economy of a state is subordinated to the interests of military preparations cannot be justified in any way if one is governed by a desire for the settlement of the unsolved international problems and for the termination of the "cold war." We point this out not because the Soviet Union's economy cannot do without the restoration of normal economic and trade relations with countries with which such relations were broken through no fault of ours. We mention this because in this field there are considerable possibilities for establishing normal and friendly international relations which may yield results favourable to the improvement of the welfare of peoples, the relaxation of international tension, and the strengthening of confidence among nations.

Accordingly, we have been and are still in favour of broad development of international contacts and cooperation in the field of culture and science and the removal of obstacles to intercourse among nations. We are convinced that broad development of international cultural, and scientific cooperation would answer the same purpose—the easing of tension in relations among states and the establishment of the necessary confidence among them.

These are the most important questions which, in the opinion of the Soviet Government, should be examined at our Conference and these are the considerations which it would like to put forward on these matters at the outset of our work.

We have listened here to the statements of the Heads of Government of the United States, France, and Great Britain. In those statements many important questions have been raised in respect of which we should have an exchange of views in order to find a basis for necessary agreement on them. Among these questions there are those that require further study. Besides there are questions on which we differ; this [*sic*] circumstances, however, should not, in our view, prevent our Conference from being successful.

The Soviet Government, for its part, will do all it can in order that the Conference may justify the people's craving for a peaceful and tranquil life.

3. *Germany and European Security.*

a. *Statement by the President, July 19, 1955.*[22]

Mr. President and members of the Conference, I have seen the record of the work of the Foreign Ministers at this morning's meeting and I, of course, concur in the decisions they tentatively reached and the subjects they have allotted for immediate and urgent study.

I note, of course, that my friend, Marshal Bulganin, takes certain exceptions and maintains that there are other questions that must be soon discussed. I would like to point out that I, too, raised certain questions which in his opening statement Mr. Bulganin said the Soviet Union would not consider appropriate here. But there is a very definite relationship between these two points. He mentions the "cold war" and its termination, neutrality, and the questions of the Far East. I brought up the questions of the situation of the satellites in Eastern Europe and of the activities of international communism in other places of the world.

Now, what I should like to call to the attention of all is that tensions are caused by different things in different countries. In my own country nothing causes greater tension than

[22] *The Geneva Conference, etc.*, pp. 45-47.

the two subjects that I brought up—than the satellites and international communism. This is so true that the Congress of the United States only within the past several days passed a resolution, I think by unanimous vote, deploring the situation of the satellite states and expressing the hope that they would have a free choice of their own form of government in the near future.[23] Nevertheless, Marshal Bulganin has consented to the temporary deferment of the three additional points he raises. I do the same. I will consent to the deferment. I will content myself, therefore, with merely the remark that I have read what the American Secretary of State had to say in the Foreign Ministers meeting this morning about these three points, which views I support.[24]

Now I would address myself, then, as others, to this German problem. I do not wish to go over the same ground that others have, but I would like to talk a little bit about NATO as it was conceived, as it has been organized, and as it has been administered, possibly a little bit from the political sense, but also from the military. I would particularly like my friend, Marshal Zhukov, to listen carefully to what I have now to say. I have known him for a long time and he knows that, speaking as soldier to soldier, I have never uttered a single word that I did not believe to be the truth.

In December of 1950, or January 1951, I returned to Europe as the head of SHAPE, the forces that the NATO countries had brought together into a single headquarters in Paris. I assure you that I accepted that job—because I had been retired—I accepted that job because I believed it to be a true agency for peace. Personally I have had enough of war and I would not have accepted that command had I conceived it to be an organization getting ready really to fight a war.

One of the great problems then facing the Western world was Germany. Germany, if allowed to become a military vacuum, if allowed to become again a fertile ground for the propagation of a Hitler, could be of the gravest danger. Now,

[23] Senate Resolution 127, 84th Cong., 1st Sess. (July 14, 1955). The resolution, adopted unanimously, declared it to be the sense of the Senate: "that the peoples who have been subjected to the captivity of alien despotisms shall again enjoy the right of self-determination within a framework which will sustain peace; that they shall again have the right to choose the form of government under which they will live, and that the sovereign rights of self-government shall be restored to them all in accordance with the pledge of the Atlantic Charter."

[24] The remarks of the Secretary of State (Dulles) are not printed. See *The Geneva Conference, etc.*, pp. 69-70.

admittedly, we were not at that moment thinking of danger to the Soviet Union: we were thinking of danger to Western Europe.

Let us not forget that our Allied friend within a matter of 85 years has three times been locked in mortal combat with Germany, and always as a result of German aggression.

Let us draw Germany into such a position that she would not be a prey to a Hitler, a dissatisfied, unhappy nation suffering from an inferiority complex, but one which could play a respectable part in its own defense, but which could not gain the power to attack.

Now, speaking politically for just a moment, all the world knows the main activities of every Western nation. There is free access to our great centers of activity by all the press of the world. There is news published about every main army camp, every great facility that we have, and this news goes all over the world. The scale of our military operations in our country is well known to everybody.

Now, within our country it is impossible for the Government, the Executive Government, to declare war. It can be done only by the Congress of the United States by free debate and vote. The only exception to this is when we ourselves are attacked with a full-scale military attack, as at Pearl Harbor, and then the reaction is merely that of self-defense.

Now, the treaties that bind the NATO nations together provide against aggression by any one of these nations, either among themselves or against anyone else. The treaty is purely defensive, and if any one of these nations attempts to act aggressively against any other, it is immediately moved against by all the remaining nations of NATO.

Militarily Germany, like all other nations in Western Europe, has certain limits set upon its forces, and, I must point out, these limits are maximum limits as well as minimum limits. In no case are any parts of the forces allowed to Germany complete or whole within themselves. They are all intertwined with the forces of the other Western nations, making it impossible for them to conduct any effective military operation of any kind by themselves.

My French colleagues can speak far better than can I about the preoccupations of the French Parliament concerning all of the measures and all of the agreements under the treaty that would prevent Germany from ever getting into a position where it would be strong enough again to attack France.

Now, besides all of these treaty provisions for making the

breaking of the peace by any nation impossible, I want to make one observation about the United States. The United States is a fairly important member of NATO, and I can assure you that under no circumstances is the United States ever going to be a party to aggressive war—against any nation. We believe in negotiation and friendly conference, and the only way that we will ever go to war is when we are attacked, as in our vital interests, in such a way that war would be the only alternative—and then it would have to be an alternative so desperate that only war could eventuate.

Perhaps I have talked overly long about my point, but my point is this. If there is any tendency to delay urgent consideration of the problem of German reunification because of the unhappiness or fear of the united Germany in NATO, then so far as it is possible for the United States to give the assurance of its pledged word, I say here and now: There is no need to fear that situation. . . .

b. *Soviet Proposal of a Collective Security Treaty in Europe, July 20, 1955.*[25]

I

[This portion of the Soviet draft proposal corresponds in substance to the Draft European Security Treaty submitted by the Soviet Union at the Berlin Conference in January and February, 1954,[26] except for the following changes:

After paragraph three of the Preamble add:

"Having in view that the establishment of a system of collective security in Europe would facilitate the earliest possible settlement of the German problem through the unification of Germany on a peaceful and democratic basis,".

Article 1: After "social systems" add "and the United States of America as well,".

Add new article 8: "The States-parties to the Treaty undertake to promote a broad economic and cultural cooperation among themselves as well as with other states through the development of trade and other economic relations and through the strengthening of cultural ties on a basis excluding any discrimination or restrictions which hamper such cooperation."

Article 9 (now 10): delete the reference to "the U.S.A.".]

[25] *Ibid.*, pp. 48-51.
[26] *Documents on American Foreign relations, 1954*, pp. 208-210.

II

12. The States-parties to the Treaty agree that during the first period (two or three years) of the implementation of measures for the establishment of the system of collective security in Europe under the present Treaty they shall not be relieved of the obligations assumed by them under existing treaties and agreements.

At the same time the States-parties to existing treaties and agreements which provide for military commitments shall refrain from the use of armed force and shall settle by peaceful means all the disputes that may arise between them. Consultations shall also take place between the parties to the corresponding treaties, and agreements in case any differences or disputes arise among them which might constitute a threat to the maintenance of peace in Europe.

13. Pending the conclusion of agreements on the reduction of armaments and the prohibition of atomic weapons and on the withdrawal of foreign troops from the territories of European countries, the States-parties to the Treaty undertake not to take any further steps to increase their armed forces on the territories of other European states under treaties and agreements concluded by them previously.

14. The States-parties to the Treaty agree that on the expiration of an agreed time-limit from the entry into force of the present Treaty, the Warsaw Treaty of May 14, 1955, the Paris Agreements of October 23, 1954, and the North Atlantic Treaty of April 4, 1949 shall become ineffective.

15. The duration of the Treaty shall be 50 years.

c. *Statement by the President, July 20, 1955.*[27]

Mr. Chairman and gentlemen of the Conference, as I listened to my colleague, Premier Bulganin,[28] it seemed to me that the principal point of difference between the thinking of the Soviet Delegation and the thinking of the United States Delegation is the urgency with which we view the need for a reunified Germany.

The Soviet Delegation seems to believe that the organization of some new and over-all pact, deferring for the moment any thought of reunifying Germany, would contribute to security. We believe that the division of Germany of itself

[27] *The Geneva Conference, etc.,* pp. 51-52.
[28] The speech referred to by the President is not printed.

contributes to the insecurity of Europe, and that seems to us to be the principal point of difference between what he has just said to the Conference and what we believe.

Now I certainly would be the last to minimize the importance of the over-all security of all Europe to the security of the world. Of course we agree to that, and I apologize for seeming to return to a question, the reunification of Germany, which we discussed at such length yesterday. But in our view these two matters are inseparable, and, therefore, I cannot help bringing them back. So I feel—this is my conviction—that to start this so-called security pact with this Conference, making no move toward starting the machinery or means for the reunifying of Germany, would appear to confirm instead of deploring that division, and, consequently, as we attack the broader question, which is of over-all security, it seems to me that we must, from our viewpoint, attack the problem of how do we get Germany back together.

Now, whether it will take one step or two steps or three steps, I admit my Soviet colleagues have studied it in greater detail than I, but I am sure that it would be a great mistake for us not to set up the machinery that proves once and for all that we confirm the necessity for so doing, and giving to some competent group or body the job of working out what needs to be done in order to bring this about. And I believe that until we do devise some such machinery we cannot by mere words, or saying we believe in the eventual reunification of Germany—I do not believe we can satisfy the situation that from our viewpoint confronts us, this Conference, and the world.

I think that is all I want to say at the moment because, I repeat, no one could applaud more than does the American Delegation the earnest protestations of the Soviet delegation that we seek peace through giving peace to all and not just to a part of this great world.

d. *Soviet Proposal of a Collective Security Treaty in Europe, July 21, 1955.*[29]

Guided by the desire to strengthen peace and recognizing the necessity to contribute in every possible way to reducing international tension and establishing confidence in relations between states,

The Governments of the Soviet Union, the United States

[29] *The Geneva Conference, etc.,* p. 54.

of America, France and the United Kingdom have agreed that the conclusion of a treaty between the member states of the North Atlantic Treaty Organization and the Western European Union on the one hand, and the parties to the Warsaw Treaty on the other, would be in the interest of the maintenance of peace in Europe. Such a treaty might be based on the following principles:

1. The member states of the North Atlantic Treaty Organization and of the Paris Agreements, on the one hand, and the parties to the Warsaw Treaty, on the other, undertake to refrain from the use of armed force against one another. This undertaking shall not infringe upon the right of states to individual or collective self-defense in the event of an armed attack, as provided in Article 51 of the Charter.

2. The parties to the Treaty undertake to consult one another in the event of differences and disputes which might constitute a threat to the maintenance of peace in Europe.

3. This Treaty is of a provisional nature and shall remain in effect until it is replaced by a treaty for the establishment of a system of collective security in Europe.

e. *Comments by the President on the Soviet Proposal of a Collective Security Treaty, July 21, 1955.*[30]

I personally believe, Mr. Chairman, that this matter [the Soviet proposal printed immediately above] must be studied by the Foreign Ministers before any action whatsoever can be taken by us, because it appears to me that there is here proposed the formulation of a treaty by four nations that affects some 25 or 30 nations. Now, this opens up to me an entirely new question, and certainly I am not prepared to talk about it intelligently today, much less take a decision upon it, and from my viewpoint it must be studied in more detail before I would want to say anything further about it.

4. *Disarmament.*

a. *Statement by the President Proposing Reciprocal Aerial Inspection, July 21, 1955.*[31]

Disarmament is one of the most important subjects on our agenda. It is also extremely difficult. In recent years the scien-

[30] *Ibid.*, pp. 54-55.
[31] *Ibid.*, pp. 56-59.

tists have discovered methods of making weapons many, many times more destructive of opposing armed forces—but also of homes, and industries and lives—than ever known or even imagined before. These same scientific discoveries have made much more complex the problems of limitation and control and reduction of armament.

After our victory as Allies in World War II, my country rapidly disarmed. Within a few years our armament was at a very low level. Then events occurred beyond our borders which caused us to realize that we had disarmed too much. For our own security and to safeguard peace we needed greater strength. Therefore we proceeded to rearm and to associate with others in a partnership for peace and for mutual security.

The American people are determined to maintain and if necessary increase this armed strength for as long a period as is necessary to safeguard peace and to maintain our security.

But we know that a mutually dependable system for less armament on the part of all nations would be a better way to safeguard peace and to maintain our security.

It would ease the fears of war in the anxious hearts of people everywhere. It would lighten the burdens upon the backs of the people. It would make it possible for every nation, great and small, developed and less developed, to advance the standards of living of its people, to attain better food, and clothing, and shelter, more of education and larger enjoyments of life.

Therefore the United States Government is prepared to enter into a sound and reliable agreement making possible the reduction of armament. I have directed that an intensive and thorough study of this subject be made within our own government. From these studies, which are continuing, a very important principle is emerging to which I referred in my opening statement on Monday.

No sound and reliable agreement can be made unless it is completely covered by an inspection and reporting system adequate to support every portion of the agreement.

The lessons of history teach us that disarmament agreements without adequate reciprocal inspection increase the dangers of war and do not brighten the prospects of peace.

Thus it is my view that the priority attention of our combined study of disarmament should be upon the subject of inspection and reporting.

Questions suggest themselves.

How effective an inspection system can be designed which would be mutually and reciprocally acceptable within our countries and the other nations of the world? How would such a system operate? What could it accomplish?

Is certainty against surprise aggression attainable by inspection? Could violations be discovered promptly and effectively counteracted?

We have not as yet been able to discover any scientific or other inspection method which would make certain of the elimination of nuclear weapons. So far as we are aware no other nation has made such a discovery. Our study of this problem is continuing. We have not as yet been able to discover any accounting or other inspection method of being certain of the true budgetary facts of total expenditures for armament. Our study of this problem is continuing. We by no means exclude the possibility of finding useful checks in these fields.

As you can see from these statements, it is our impression that many past proposals of disarmament are more sweeping than can be insured by effective inspection.

Gentlemen, since I have been working on this memorandum to present to this Conference, I have been searching my heart and mind for something that I could say here that could convince everyone of the great sincerity of the United States in approaching this problem of disarmament.

I should address myself for a moment principally to the Delegates from the Soviet Union, because our two great countries admittedly possess new and terrible weapons in quantities which do give rise in other parts of the world, or reciprocally, to the fears and dangers of surprise attack.

I propose, therefore, that we take a practical step, that we begin an arrangement, very quickly, as between ourselves—immediately. These steps would include:

To give to each other a complete blueprint of our military establishments, from beginning to end, from one end of our countries to the other; lay out the establishments and provide the blueprints to each other.

Next, to provide within our countries facilities for aerial photography to the other country—we to provide you the facilities within our country, ample facilities for aerial reconnaissance, where you can make all the pictures you choose and take them to your own country to study, you to provide exactly the same facilities for us and we to make these examinations, and by this step to convince the world that we are providing as between ourselves against the possibility of great surprise attack, thus lessening danger and relaxing tension. Likewise we will make more easily attainable a comprehensive and effective system of inspection and disarmament, because what I propose, I assure you, would be but a beginning.

Now from my statements I believe you will anticipate my suggestion. It is that we instruct our representatives in the Subcommittee on Disarmament in discharge of their mandate from the United Nations to give priority effort to the study of inspection and reporting. Such a study could well include a step by step testing of inspection and reporting methods.

The United States is ready to proceed in the study and testing of a reliable system of inspections and reporting, and when that system is proved, then to reduce armaments with all others to the extent that the system will provide assured results.

The successful working out of such a system would do much to develop the mutual confidence which will open wide the avenues of progress for all our peoples.

The quest for peace is the statesman's most exacting duty. Security of the nation entrusted to his care is his greatest responsibility. Practical progress to lasting peace is his fondest hope. Yet in pursuit of his hope he must not betray the trust placed in him as guardian of the people's security. A sound peace—with security, justice, well-being, and freedom for the people of the world—*can* be achieved, but only by patiently and thoughtfully following a hard and sure and tested road.

b. *Memorandum by the United Kingdom Delegation Proposing Joint Inspection of Forces in Specified Areas in Eastern and Western Europe, July 21, 1955.*[32]

The United Kingdom Delegation propose that, as a means of increasing mutual confidence in Europe, consideration should be given to the establishment of a system of joint inspection of the forces now confronting each other in Europe. In specified areas of agreed extent on either side of the line dividing Eastern and Western Europe joint inspecting teams would operate by mutual consent.

This project would provide opportunity for the practical test on a limited scale of international inspection of forces

[32] *Ibid.*, p. 59.

in being and would provide valuable experience and lessons for use over a wider field in the future.

The willingness of the Four Governments to accept such inspection would moreover demonstrate their determination to reduce international tension in Europe.

The system of inspection here proposed is without prejudice to the work of the United Nations Disarmament Sub-Committee. It is also distinct from the proposals put forward by the United Kingdom Delegation for the limitation, control and inspection of forces and armaments in connection with European security.

c. *Memorandum by the French Delegation Proposing Budgetary Control and Diversion of Funds toward International Economic Assistance, July 21, 1955.*[33]

At the opening session of the Geneva Conference, the French Prime Minister explained the reasons which lead him to believe that the first condition of a lasting peace is progress towards disarmament. Assistance to the peoples of the underdeveloped territories in improving their general living conditions constitutes a second reason.

The French Government believes that these two forms of activity should be carried out side by side, and that the possibility of establishing an organic link between them should be investigated. Such a link would make it possible, at least in part, to solve the problem of control and of sanctions in regard to disarmament.

The French Government proposes that a reduction in the amount of military expenditure borne by the states be agreed by them, and that the financial resources thus made available be, either in whole or in part, allocated to international expenditure on equipment and mutual aid.

The essentially financial aspect of these proposals must be stressed. It will allow an overall view to be taken of military problems at a high level, and will make possible the transfer of military expenditure to productive expenditure at international level, for which purpose the national framework has been shown to be too limited.

A variety of problems will be created by the application of these provisions—the collection and distribution of the financial resources, and the methods of administering them—

[33] *Ibid.*, pp. 60-62.

and this memorandum is designed to make certain proposals in that regard.

(1) In order to establish the basis of the contribution to be made, each of the governments concerned would declare annually the amount it intended to appropriate for military expenditure during a period of twelve months, in effect, the amount laid down in the budget.

The first statement would concern the twelve-monthly period covered by the budget for the current year.

The declarations made by the states would be sent to an International Secretariat, whose chief task would be to ensure that a common definition of military expenditure was interpreted in the same sense by all the states. In order to make this possible, the Secretariat would receive copies of the civil and military budgets presented by each government to the parliamentary organs which, according to the constitution of its own state, have to vote or approve the budget. The Secretariat would also lay down a common nomenclature for all states, and would draw up a list of the categories of military expenditure, subject to any agreements reached, and according to the programme for the progressive application and control of disarmament.

The percentage reduction of military expenditure in any annual budget in relation to a preceding budget could be laid down for future years by agreement between the governments concerned. This would make it possible to calculate the amounts to be allocated to the International Fund for Equipment and Mutual Aid.

The amounts to be levied during the years concerned should be progressive, in order to lay stress on the need for disarmament. These amounts could be related either to the figure of actual military expenditure, or, if the Powers fix a common "normal" level of military expenditure in relation either to their national expenditure or to some other criterion, they could apply to the excess of such expenditure over the normal figure thus defined. This second formula would have the advantage of linking the size of the allocation more closely to the unduly high level of military expenditure maintained by some states.

(2) The use of the resources of the I.F.E.M.A. would be supervised by the International Secretariat, whose task it would be to ensure their use according to four criteria:

(i) In order that the peoples of the states concerned may be associated with the results of disarmament, the amount of contribution due from each state should be reduced, on the basis of the formula laid down, by part of the reduction in expenditure effected in the military budget between one financial year and the next. Each country would thus be able to make internal transfers according to whatever method it liked.

(ii) Each state contributing to the fund should be in a position to use a portion of its contribution, to be defined, for the benefit of states or territories with which it is constitutionally linked. All that would be necessary would be to prove to the International Secretariat the need for such expenditure.

(iii) A part of the remainder of the available funds would have to be used to place orders of all kinds in the countries providing the funds. This provision would prevent the reduction of armament expenditure from reacting unfavourably on the level of economic activity of each country by guaranteeing the existence of a certain number of orders to take the place of orders for military supplies.

(iv) The balance would be used at international level, without any special restrictions, on equipment for under-developed territories. This allocation would be made in close cooperation with the international organisations within the framework of the United Nations, or even by those organisations themselves. It is, perhaps, worthwhile to stress the point that any states increasing their military expenditure would exclude themselves from the benefits to be obtained from the I.F.E.M.A.

(3) The United States, the U.S.S.R., the United Kingdom and France would, of course, be associated with the procedure to be laid down. As, however, these four nations are all represented on the Sub-Committee of the Disarmament Commission of the U.N. of which Canada is also a member, it might be best to entrust to that Sub-Committee the task of determining the methods of applying this plan for disarmament and transfer.

I should like to submit the following merely as suggestions:—

a) The administration of the fund could be carried out by a managerial organ associated with the International Secretariat. Both these bodies could come under a common political authority on which, for instance, the appropriate Ministers of the Four Powers might sit.

b) The use of the resources of the fund might be supervised by the managerial organ, which would not necessarily be composed only of representatives of the Four Powers and of the nations prepared to adhere to the principles set out in this memorandum, but also of representatives of countries benefiting from the resources of the International Fund for Mutual Aid.

c) So far as the application of the plan is concerned, recourse to existing organisations such as the International Bank for Reconstruction and Development and certain organs of the United Nations might be considered to avoid the creation of an international administrative organ, which would duplicate the work of those already functioning to the general satisfaction.

d) The political authority alone would be competent to fix the amount of the contribution from each state. There might be alternative methods of procedure, according to whether the state concerned accepted financial supervision or not. If it refused, the contribution would be arrived at by applying the progressive rate of the levy to the figure of military expenditure declared for the first year. If it accepted, the contribution would be fixed on the figure of military expenditure for the current financial year as verified by the International Secretariat. The only choice open to the political authority, voting according to a procedure to be defined, would be between the figure determined by the International Secretariat and, in case of rejection, the contribution of a lump sum.

The proposals contained in this memorandum could be studied immediately by the Sub-Committee of the Disarmament Commission of the U.N., if the Four Powers represented here gave the necessary instructions to that effect to their respective delegates.

d. *Proposal by the Soviet Delegation on the Reduction of Armaments and Prohibition of Atomic Weapons, July 21, 1955.*[34]

I

To lessen tension in the relations between States, to consolidate mutual confidence between them and to remove the threat of a new war, the Heads of Government of the Soviet Union, the United States of America, the United Kingdom,

[34] *Ibid.*, pp. 55-56.

and France recognise the need to strive to achieve the earliest possible conclusion of an International Convention on the reduction of armaments and the prohibition of atomic weapons.

As a result of the exchange of opinions on the reduction of armaments and the prohibition of atomic weapons they have agreed on the following:

1. The level of the armed forces of the USA, the USSR, and China shall be established at from 1 to 1.5 million men for each; that of the United Kingdom and France, at 650,000 men for each, while the level provided for China as well as other questions bearing on the armed forces of China shall be the subject of consideration in which the Government of the People's Republic of China is to participate.

The level of the armed forces of all other States shall not exceed 150,000 to 200,000 men and shall be agreed upon at an appropriate international conference.

2. After the armed forces and conventional armaments have been reduced to the extent of 75 per cent of the agreed reductions, a complete prohibition of atomic and hydrogen weapons shall come into effect. The elimination of such weapons from the armaments of States and their destruction shall be completed in the course of the reduction of armaments, covering the final 25 per cent of the agreed reductions. All atomic materials shall thereafter be used exclusively for peaceful purposes.

3. Simultaneously with the initiation of measures to effect the reduction of armaments and armed forces, and before the entry into force of the agreement on the complete prohibition of atomic and hydrogen weapons, the Four Powers shall solemnly pledge themselves not to use nuclear weapons which they shall regard as prohibited to them. Exceptions to this rule may be permitted for purposes of defence against aggression, when a decision to that effect is taken by the Security Council.

4. As one of the first measures for the execution of the programme for the reduction of armaments and the prohibition of atomic weapons, States possessing atomic and hydrogen weapons pledge themselves to discontinue tests of these weapons.

5. Effective international control shall be established over the implementation of measures for the reduction of armaments and the prohibition of atomic weapons.

6. The Heads of Government of the Four Powers have

instructed the Foreign Ministers to endeavour to reach necessary agreement on the still unsettled aspects of the abovementioned Convention, which is to be considered in the United Nations.

II

At the same time, the Heads of Government of the Soviet Union, the United States of America, the United Kingdom and France, fully determined not to permit the use of atomic and hydrogen weapons, which are weapons of mass destruction of people, and to deliver nations from the threat of a destructive atomic war, solemnly declare, that:

Pending the conclusion of the International Convention on the reduction of armaments and the prohibition of atomic weapons, the Soviet Union, the United States of America, the United Kingdom and France undertake not to be the first to use atomic and hydrogen weapons against any country and they call upon all other states to join this Declaration.

5. *East-West Contacts.*

Statement by the President, July 22, 1955.[35]

According to the adopted agenda, today we meet to discuss methods of normalizing and increasing the contacts between our nations in many fields. I am heartened by the deep interest in this question, which interest implies a common purpose to understand each other better. Unfortunately there exist unnecessary restrictions on the flow between us of ideas, of things and of people.

Like other questions we have considered during the past four days, this one cannot be considered independently or in isolation. All are related by their direct importance to the general objective of lessening world fears and tensions.

To help achieve the goal of peace based on justice and right and mutual understanding, there are certain concrete steps that could be taken:

(1) To lower the barriers which now impede the interchange of information and ideas between our peoples.

(2) To lower the barriers which now impede the opportunities of people to travel anywhere in the world for peaceful, friendly purposes, so that all will have a chance to know each other face-to-face.

[35] *Ibid.*, pp. 63-64.

(3) To create conditions which will encourage nations to increase the exchange of peaceful goods throughout the world.

Success in these endeavors should improve the conditions of life for all our citizens and elsewhere in the world. By helping eliminate poverty and ignorance, we can take another step in progress toward peace.

Restrictions on communications of all kinds, including radio and travel, existing in extreme form in some places, have operated as causes of mutual distrust. In America, the fervent belief in freedom of thought, of expression, and of movement is a vital part of our heritage. Yet during these past ten years even we have felt compelled, in the protection of our own interests, to place some restrictions upon the movement of persons and communications across our national frontiers.

This conference has the opportunity, I believe, to initiate concrete steps to permit the breaking down of both mild and severe barriers to mutual understanding and trust.

Now I should like to turn to the question of trade. I assume that each of us here is dedicated to the improvement of the conditions of life of our own citizens. Trade in peaceful goods is an important factor in achieving this goal. If trade is to reach its maximum capability in this regard, it must be both voluminous and world-wide.

The United Nations has properly been concerned in making available to the people of the under-developed areas modern technology and managerial abilities, as well as capital and credit. My country not only supports these efforts, but has undertaken parallel projects outside the United Nations.

In this connection the new atomic science possesses a tremendous potential for helping raise the standards of living and providing greater opportunity for all the world. World-wide interest in overcoming poverty and ignorance is growing by leaps and bounds, and each of the great nations should do its utmost to assist in this development. As a result new desires, new requirements, new aspirations are emerging almost everywhere as man climbs the upward path of his destiny. Most encouraging of all is the evidence that after centuries of fatalism and resignation, the hopeless of the world are beginning to hope.

But regardless of the results achieved through the United Nations effort or the individual efforts of helpful nations, trade remains the indispensable arterial system of a flourishing world prosperity.

If we could create conditions in which unnecessary restrictions on trade would be progressively eliminated and under which where there would be free and friendly exchange of ideas and of people, we should have done much to chart the paths toward the objectives we commonly seek.

By working together toward all these goals, we can do much to transform this century of recurring conflict into a century of enduring and invigorating peace. This, I assure you, the United States of America devoutly desires—as I know all of us do.

6. *Closing Statement by the President, July 23, 1955.*[36]

I welcome and warmly reciprocate the spirit of friendliness and good intent that have characterized the statements of the two preceding speakers.[37] But I do hope that my silence respecting certain of the statements made by the immediately preceding speaker will not by any means be interpreted as acquiescence on my part—far from it.

But it has seemed to me that in the closing minutes of this conference there is no necessity for me to announce to this conference and to the world the United States position on the important questions we have discussed. These I hope and believe have already been made clear. Therefore, it has not seemed particularly fitting once more to recite them in detail. Rather I content myself with some reflections on our work of the past week and an expression of some hopes for the future.

This has been an historic meeting. It has been on the whole a good week. But only history will tell the true worth and real values of our session together. The follow-through from this beginning by our respective Governments will be decisive in the measure of this Conference.

We have talked over plainly a number of the most difficult and perplexing questions affecting our several peoples and indeed the peoples of the entire world.

We did not come here to reach final solutions. We came to see if we might together find the path that would lead to solutions and would brighten the prospects of world peace.

In this final hour of our assembly, it is my judgment that the prospects of a lasting peace with justice, well-being, and

[36] *Ibid.*, pp. 80-81.
[37] Not printed.

broader freedom, are brighter. The dangers of the overwhelming tragedy of modern war are less.

The work of our Foreign Ministers as they strive to implement our directives will be of great importance, perhaps of even more than what we have done here. Theirs is the task, reflecting the substantive policies of their Governments, to reach agreement on courses of action which we here could discuss only in broad terms. I know we all wish them well.

I trust we will all support the necessary adjustments which they may find our Governments must make if we are to resolve our differences in these matters.

If our peoples, in the months and years ahead, broaden their knowledge and their understanding of each other, as we, during this week, have broadened our knowledge of each other, further agreement between our Governments may be facilitated. May this occur in a spirit of justice. May it result in improved well-being, greater freedom, and less of fear or suffering or distress for mankind. May it be marked by more of good will among men. These days will then indeed be ever remembered.

I came to Geneva because I believe mankind longs for freedom from war and rumors of war. I came here because of my lasting faith in the decent instincts and good sense of the people who populate this world of ours. I shall return home tonight with these convictions unshaken, and with the prayer that the hope of mankind will one day be realized.

7. *Directive of the Heads of Government of the Four Powers to the Foreign Ministers, July 23, 1955.*[38]

The Heads of Government of France, the United Kingdom, the U.S.S.R. and the U.S.A., guided by the desire to contribute to the relaxation of international tension and to the consolidation of confidence between states, instruct their Foreign Ministers to continue the consideration of the following questions with regard to which an exchange of views has taken place at the Geneva Conference, and to propose effective means for their solution, taking account of the close link between the reunification of Germany and the problems of European security, and the fact that the successful settlement of each of these problems would serve the interests of consolidating peace.

[38] *The Geneva Conference, etc.,* pp. 67-68.

1. *European Security and Germany.* For the purpose of establishing European security with due regard to the legitimate interests of all nations and their inherent right to individual and collective self-defence, the Ministers are instructed to consider various proposals to this end, including the following: A security pact for Europe or for a part of Europe, including provisions for the assumption by member nations of an obligation not to resort to force and to deny assistance to an aggressor; limitation, control, and inspection in regard to armed forces and armaments; establishment between East and West of a zone in which the disposition of armed forces will be subject to mutual agreement; and also to consider other possible proposals pertaining to the solution of this problem.

The Heads of Government, recognizing their common responsibility for the settlement of the German question and the re-unification of Germany, have agreed that the settlement of the German question and the re-unification of Germany by means of free elections shall be carried out in conformity with the national interests of the German people and the interests of European security. The Foreign Ministers will make whatever arrangements they may consider desirable for the participation of, or for consultation with, other interested parties.

2. *Disarmament*

The Four Heads of Government,

Desirous of removing the threat of war and lessening the burden of armaments,

Convinced of the necessity, for secure peace and for the welfare of mankind, of achieving a system for the control and reduction of all armaments and armed forces under effective safeguards,

Recognizing that achievements in this field would release vast material resources to be devoted to the peaceful economic development of nations, for raising their well-being, as well as for assistance to underdeveloped countries,

Agree:

(1) for these purposes to work together to develop an acceptable system for disarmament through the Sub-Committee of the United Nations Disarmament Commission;

(2) to instruct their representatives in the Sub-Committee in the discharge of their mandate from the United Nations to

take account in their work of the views and proposals advanced by the Heads of Government at this Conference;

(3) to propose that the next meeting of the Sub-Committee be held on August 29, 1955, at New York;

(4) to instruct the Foreign Ministers to take note of the proceedings in the Disarmament Commission, to take account of the views and proposals advanced by the Heads of Government at this Conference and to consider whether the four Governments can take any further useful initiative in the field of disarmament.

3. *Development of Contacts between East and West*

The Foreign Ministers should by means of experts study measures, including those possible in organs and agencies of the United Nations, which could (a) bring about a progressive elimination of barriers which interfere with free communications and peaceful trade between people and (b) bring about such freer contacts and exchanges as are to the mutual advantage of the countries and peoples concerned.

4. The Foreign Ministers of the Four Powers will meet at Geneva during October to initiate their consideration of these questions and to determine the organisation of their work.

8. *Appraising the Conference at the "Summit." Radio-Television Address by the President, July 25, 1955.*[39]

GOOD EVENING FRIENDS:

Secretary Dulles and I, with our associates, went to the Big Four Conference at Geneva resolved to represent as accurately as we could the aspirations of the American people for peace and the principles upon which this country believes that peace should be based.

In this task we had the bipartisan, indeed almost the unanimous, support of the Congress. This fact greatly strengthened our hand throughout the negotiations. Our grateful thanks go out to all your Senators and your Congressmen in the United States Congress. Aside from this, we had, during the past week, thousands of telegrams of encouragement and support from you as individuals. Along with these came

[39] *Ibid.*, pp. 83-87.

similar telegrams from great organizations, church organizations, business and great labor organizations.

All of these combined served to make us feel that possibly we were faithfully representing the views that you would have us represent. Now peace—the pursuit of peace—involves many perplexing questions. For example:

Justice to all nations, great and small;

Freedom and security for all these nations;

The prosperity of their several economies and a rising standard of living in the world;

Finally, opportunity for all of us to live in peace and in security.

Now, naturally, in the study of such questions as these, we don't proceed recklessly. We must go prudently and cautiously —both in reaching conclusions and in subsequent action. We cannot afford to be negligent or complacent. But, we must be hopeful. We must have faith in ourselves and in the justice of our cause. If we don't do this, we will allow our own pessimism and our own lack of faith to defeat the noblest purposes that we can pursue.

Now, because of the vital significance of all these subjects, they will be exhaustively surveyed by our government over a period of many weeks. Tonight the most that I can give to you are a few personal impressions and opinions that may have some interest for you and certainly have some bearing on the outcome and on the progress of those negotiations.

Of course, an interesting subject that could be taken up, had I the time, would be the personalities of the several delegations, the relationship or apparent relationships of one to the other—the principal considerations that seem to motivate them. These would all have a bearing on this problem. But I forego them and take up instead just two general opinions in which I am sure every American shares:

The first of these, that we must never be deluded into believing that one week of friendly, even fruitful, negotiation can wholly eliminate a problem arising out of the wide gulf that separates, so far, East and West. A gulf as wide and deep as the difference between individual liberty and regimentation, as wide and deep as the gulf that lies between the concept of man made in the image of his God and the concept of man as a mere instrument of the State. Now, if we think of those things we are apt to be possibly discouraged.

But I was also profoundly impressed with the need for all of us to avoid discouragement merely because our own proposals, our own approaches, and our own beliefs are not always immediately accepted by the other side.

On the night I left for Geneva, I appeared before the television to explain to you what we were seeking. I told you that we were going primarily to attempt to change the spirit in which these great negotiations and conferences were held. A transcript was made of that talk, and I should like now to read you one paragraph from it.

This is what I said with respect to our purpose: "We realize that one ingredient has been missing from all past conferences. This is an honest intent to conciliate, to understand, to be tolerant, to try to see the other fellow's viewpoint as well as we see our own. I say to you if we can change the spirit in which these conferences are conducted, we will have taken the greatest step toward peace, toward future prosperity and tranquility that has ever been taken in all the history of mankind."

During last week in formal conferences, and in personal visits, these purposes have been pursued. So now there exists a better understanding, a closer unity among the nations of NATO.

There seems to be a growing realization by all that nuclear warfare, pursued to the ultimate, could be practically race suicide.

There is a realization that negotiations can be conducted without propaganda and threats and invective.

Finally, there is a sharp realization by the world that the United States will go to any length consistent with our concepts of decency and justice and right to attain peace. For this purpose, we will work cooperatively with the Soviets and any other people as long as there is sincerity of purpose and a genuine desire to go ahead.

In the course of carrying on these discussions there were a number of specific proposals, some of which were items on the official agenda. That agenda contained German reunification and European security, disarmament and increased contacts of all kinds between the East and the West.

Most of these conference meetings were given wide publicity and even some of the specific suggestions made in those conferences likewise were publicized. In any event, I can assure you of one thing:

There were no secret agreements made, either understood agreements or written ones. Everything is put before you on the record.

Outside of these conference meetings there were numerous

unofficial meetings—conversations with important members of the other delegations and, of course, very specifically with the Soviet delegation.

In these conversations a number of subjects were discussed and among them the Secretary of State and I specifically brought up, more than once, American convictions and American beliefs and American concern about such questions as the satellites of Eastern Europe and the activities of international Communism. We made crystal clear what were American beliefs about such matters as these.

Now to take up for a moment the items on the official agenda.

Probably no question caused us as much trouble as that of German reunification and European security. At first we thought that these could be dealt with separately, but the American delegation concluded that they had to be dealt with as one subject. We held that Germany should be reunited under a government freely chosen by themselves, and under conditions that would provide security both for nations of the East and for nations of the West—in fact in a framework that provided European security.

In the matter of disarmament, the American government believes that an effective disarmament system can be reached only if at its base there is an effective reciprocal inspection and overall supervision system, one in which we can have confidence and each side can know that the other side is carrying out his commitments. Now because of this belief, we joined with the French and the British in making several proposals. Some were global, some were local, some were sort of budgetary in character. But all were in furtherance of this one single objective, that is, to make inspection the basis of disarmament proposals.

One proposal suggested aerial photography, as between the Soviets and ourselves by unarmed peaceful planes, and to make this inspection just as thorough as this kind of reconnaissance can do. The principal purpose, of course, is to convince every one of Western sincerity in seeking peace. But another idea was this: if we could go ahead and establish this kind of an inspection as initiation of an inspection system we could possibly develop it into a broader one, and eventually build on it an effective and durable disarmament system.

In the matter of increasing contacts, many items were discussed. We talked about a freer flow of news across the curtains of all kinds. We talked about the circulation of books and particularly we talked about peaceful trade. But the subject that took most of our attention in this regard was the possibility of increased visits by the citizens of one country into the territory of another, doing this in such a way as to give each the fullest possible opportunity to learn about the people of the other nation. In this particular subject there was the greatest possible degree of agreement. As a matter of fact, it was agreement often repeated and enthusiastically supported by the words of the members of each side.

As a matter of fact, each side assured the other earnestly and often that it intended to pursue a new spirit of conciliation and cooperation in its contacts with the other. Now, of course, we are profoundly hopeful that these assurances will be faithfully carried out.

One evidence as to these assurances will, of course, be available soon in the language and the terminology in which we will find speeches and diplomatic exchanges couched. But the acid test should begin next October because then the next meeting occurs. It will be a meeting of the Foreign Ministers. Its principal purpose will be to take the conclusions of this conference as to the subjects to be discussed there and the general proceedings to be observed in translating those generalities that we talked about into actual, specific agreements. Then is when real conciliation and some giving on each side will be definitely necessary.

Now, for myself, I do not belittle the obstacles lying ahead on the road to a secure and just peace. By no means do I underestimate the long and exhausting work that will be necessary before real results are achieved. I do not blink the fact that all of us must continue to sacrifice for what we believe to be best for the safety of ourselves and for the preservation of the things in which we believe.

But I do know that the people of the world want peace. Moreover, every other individual who was at Geneva likewise felt this longing of mankind. So, there is great pressure to advance constructively, not merely to reenact the dreary performances, the negative performances of the past.

We, all of us, individually and as a people now have possibly the most difficult assignment of our nation's history. Likewise, we have the most shining opportunity ever possessed by Americans. May these truths inspire, never dismay us.

I believe that only with prayerful patience, intelligence,

courage and tolerance, never forgetting vigilance and prudence, can we keep alive the spark ignited at Geneva. But if we are successful in this, then we will make constantly brighter the lamp that will one day guide us to our goal—a just and lasting peace.

Thank you. Good night to each of you.

B. The Geneva Meeting of Foreign Ministers, October 27-November 16, 1955.[1]

1. *Opening Statements.*

a. *Statement by the Minister of Foreign Affairs of France (Pinay), October 27, 1955.*[2]

The rule of rotation confers on the French representative the honour of presiding today over the first session of the Meeting of Foreign Ministers which is being held in accordance with the decisions taken by the Conference of the four Heads of Government last July.

I fully appreciate that honour and I am aware of all the responsibility which it entails.

But I am also convinced that, with your help, this responsibility will become a most pleasant duty.

I should like first to thank the United Nations for again offering us its generous hospitality with all the advantages of its highly perfected technical equipment.

Having done so, I should like to restrict this opening speech to a few general remarks on the nature of our task and the conditions in which it can be successful.

In the first place, I think we must be fully aware of our responsibilities. At no time, and on no pretext, must we allow that awareness to become dulled.

The Conference held in Geneva last July aroused tremendous hopes throughout the world.

For the first time—and that is perhaps in itself an important historical fact—the Heads of Government, responsible for the fate of hundreds of millions of men and women, solemnly declared it to be their joint aim to put an end to

[1] Following consultations through diplomatic channels the governments of the Four Powers agreed on August 11, 1955 that their Foreign Ministers would convene at Geneva on October 27, 1955. (Department of State Press Release 487, dated August 11, 1955.)

[2] *The Geneva Meeting of Foreign Ministers, October 27-November 16, 1955* (Department of State Publication 6156), pp. 14-17.

any recourse to arms in international relations, and their common determination to establish the firm foundations of a lasting peace.

But they did not confine themselves to the definition of that aim and the statement of that determination.

They also drafted the directive which is the basis of our work here today and which provides the broad outline of our search for workable solutions.

They have given us the task of carrying that search a step further and reaching positive results. In the fulfilment of that task we have no right to disappoint our peoples.

We must no longer be content to raise our peoples' hopes by the pious wishes of statesmen.

Henceforth we must bring about the realisation of the hopes which have just been born by a clear and determined effort of will.

How can this be done?

It seems to me that it will be a help if we observe certain simple rules.

The Heads of Government have drawn up a restricted programme which can be stated in terms of a series of definite questions.

To these definite questions we must provide definite—that is to say, clear and concrete—answers.

Too often, in the past, exchanges of view between the representatives of our Governments have been transformed into platforms from which each has appealed to his partner's public. Too often our discussions have been nothing but an interminable sequence of alternating monologues.

We should from the outset make every effort to avoid the all-too-natural and easy temptation to make long speeches. A conference is not a succession of uninterrupted monologues in which each is content with presenting his own point of view while turning a deaf ear to that of the others. It must be a series of give-and-take dialogues, in the course of which a human contact is established and maintained, thus making it possible to put oneself in the other man's place and to understand him.

There can be no real progress without mutual understanding.

Let us therefore try to regain this spirit of dialogue which we have to some extent lost. Obviously it is not a question of settling everything here and now. The scope of the task outlined for us is vast, given the importance of the problems we have to study, but it is sufficiently limited to remove any possibility of our going astray.

The time factor must play a part in our deliberations. In certain circumstances it can be an ally. In others, it can be an enemy. We must not as a matter of course rely on this factor to provide the solution to problems which can and must be settled now by the responsible powers.

The problem of disarmament, by its very complexity, will require a long-term effort. In this field we can doubtless reach agreement only on a certain number of preliminary measures which could be grouped in a first plan capable of rapid and practical implementation.

It is clear, on the other hand, that on item I of the agenda —German unity and security—there is no obstacle to an immediate decision on the terms of a plan designed to link the realisation of German unity with the devising of a system of security. Without such a decision no further progress would be possible. This does not mean that once such a decision is taken, we cannot proceed methodically towards its progressive realisation, taking all legitimate interests into account.

Another essential point:

For everyone to be assured of real security, we must bring about conditions which will ensure a more lasting peace for everyone, taking into account hard facts and the legitimate interests of all.

To be realistic we must take into consideration all aspects of reality and not—voluntarily or involuntarily—close our eyes to any of them. Taking account to everyone's legitimate interests obviously means respecting the meaning of those interests in the way that each has freely understood them.

Peace cannot be attained by attempts at dissociation. Peaceful coexistence completely rules out any manoeuvre likely to destroy the very basis of the partner's existence.

So far as we are concerned, that is the spirit in which we have come here. We do not ourselves accept the political philosophy of the Soviet Union. But we would not dream of denying to the Soviet peoples or to any other people, the right to such a philosophy. Nor would we dream of using diplomacy as a weapon for fighting that philosophy. Our hope is that a rapprochement between the two halves of the world, at present divided, may lead progressively to a lessening of these differences.

That is why the French Government attaches importance to the item on our agenda dealing with contacts between East and West.

So long as the division of the world continues, the security of Western Europe will remain indissolubly linked with the organisation for western security, and, in such circumstances, it would be an illusion to speak of a united Europe so far as security is concerned.

On the other hand, by varying, multiplying and strengthening economic, cultural and human contacts between the two parts of Europe, it should be possible progressively to build a united Europe, since such contacts would themselves create a new atmosphere.

This is perhaps a distant ideal. But it is on the basis of this ideal and with this ideal in view that the French Government has already defined and directed its policy, within the limits imposed upon it by the present division of Europe. For we still hope that our western European ideal of co-operation may be extended to the whole of Europe.

We are here to negotiate—that is to say, as equal partners, to seek solutions which will respect the basic interests of each. While we for our part are not prepared to allow the essential elements of our defence and security to become matters for negotiation, we are resolved to go as far as possible in seeking reasonable measures to meet the needs, the interests and the legitimate anxieties of the Soviet Union.

In these negotiations, our responsibilities impose one final duty upon us: a refusal to be gulled by false solutions, that is to say by those which somewhat clumsily conceal the absence of any solution, or those which are based on unacknowledged misunderstandings. So much is at stake that every demand of intellectual and moral integrity must be scrupulously respected. Such integrity, if used in the service of the cause to which we are devoted, will, I am sure, make it possible for us to obtain positive results.

May I, in conclusion, refer to the great personality of President Eisenhower. In this very room, scarcely three months ago, we were admiring his infectious vitality. After his cruel attack he is happily now well on the way to recovery. I am sure I shall be interpreting faithfully the feelings of us all if I propose that, at the outset of our work, we send him a message expressing our deep friendship and warmest good wishes.

Gentlemen, I declare the Meeting of Foreign Ministers open.

b. *Statement by the Foreign Secretary of the United Kingdom (Macmillan), October 27, 1955.*[3]

I am very glad to have the opportunity of saying a few words before we proceed to the work of the Conference.

The sudden illness of President Eisenhower, to which you, Mr. Chairman, have referred, was a cause of deepest regret in every part of Great Britain and of the British Commonwealth and Empire. When the news came, we felt it as a personal blow, just as if the President had been one of us. For we all of us think of the President in his dual role, our great leader in victory and our constant friend in the difficult years that have followed. There is no figure better known and more loved in my country. Not only my Government but all our people would wish to be associated with the message which you propose this Conference should send.

I do not think it is necessary to add to any of the more general observations that you have made, Mr. Chairman. I fully associate myself with their main tenour. The Conference in Geneva in July last set new hopes moving in the world. For us, who take up the work entrusted to us by the Heads of Governments, the next few weeks present both an inspiration and a challenge. We must bring to our task sympathy and understanding. We must not be disturbed by temporary set-backs or thrown out of our path by obstacles, however difficult.

At the same time, we must be realists. We must recognise that there are considerable gaps between the positions hitherto taken by the Western Powers and by the Union of Socialist Soviet Republics [*sic*]. We believe that these can be bridged, and we are determined to make every effort to achieve success.

The Government and people of Great Britain, speaking not only for themselves but for all those who recognise allegiance to the Commonwealth and Empire, are anxious for peace. There is no sacrifice that they would not make in the cause of peace; except that of principles which they regard as vital to their faith, or loyalty to the causes for which they have given so much.

[3] *Ibid.*, pp. 17-18.

c. *Statement by the Foreign Minister of the Soviet Union (Molotov), October 27, 1955.*[4]

Mr. Chairman, Gentlemen:

This Meeting has been called in accordance with the decision of the Heads of Government of the Four Powers. Its task is to discuss the matters provided for in the Directives agreed upon at the Geneva Conference.

The important historic significance of the Geneva Conference of the Heads of Government, held in July, is now recognized by everybody. It has served to ease international tension, particularly in the relations between the great powers. It has reflected the desire of peoples to put an end to the so-called "cold war." It has still further strengthened the peoples' will to ensure a firm and lasting peace. It has also paved the way for further joint consideration and settlement of urgent international problems in a spirit of mutual understanding and respect for the interests of the parties concerned, and in accordance with the task of ensuring peace among nations.

The Soviet Government is highly appreciative of these positive results achieved by the Conference of the Heads of Government and of the important contribution made to the success of the conference by President Eisenhower, Prime Minister Eden, and Premier Faure.

At one time statements were made which reflected a desire to obscure the positive results of the Geneva Conference. This must also be taken into consideration at the present time. It indicates the existence of considerable difficulties in achieving the objectives set by the Geneva Conference. It is our view, however, that the desire to consolidate the results achieved there and to proceed on that basis is common to us all.

The work of our Meeting will be closely watched in all parts of the world. Millions of people are expecting that as a result of this Meeting further progress will be made to improve co-operation among states, to further ease international tension and to consolidate universal peace.

All this places definite responsibilities upon us, the participants in this Meeting.

Since the Geneva Conference, the Government of the USSR has taken a number of new measures to further the

[4] *Ibid.*, pp. 18-23.

relaxation of tension in international relations. These steps have met with approval throughout the world.

The first thing to be mentioned is the decision to reduce the Soviet armed forces by 640,000 men.[5] Thus, the Soviet Union has given a practical demonstration of its readiness to promote actively the cessation of the armaments race and of its further desire to reduce international tension. The Governments of Poland, Czechoslovakia, Rumania, Hungary, Bulgaria and Albania are also known to have reduced their armed forces.[6]

The Soviet Union recently decided to relinquish its naval base at Porkkala-Udd on Finnish territory before the appointed time.[7] This was done despite the fact that the Peace Treaty with Finland provides for the continuation of the Soviet naval base until 1997. Thus, this year has seen the liquidation of both the Soviet naval bases on the territories of other States—the naval base at Port Arthur,[8] on Chinese territory, and the naval base on Finnish territory. The Soviet Union no longer has any military bases beyond its frontiers. These steps of the Soviet Government have contributed to the further strengthening of friendly ties with the said countries. They have received wide and favourable response as an example of the solving of the problem of military bases of the great powers on foreign territories—the urgent problem in international life.

Since the Geneva Conference the Soviet Union has established diplomatic relations with the German Federal Republic.[9] A Treaty on the relations between the USSR and the German Democratic Republic has been concluded and has entered into force.[10] Normal relations between the Soviet Union and both States existing on the territory of Germany

[5] The Soviet government announced on August 13, 1955 that it would reduce its armed forces by 640,000 men before December 15, 1955.

[6] The Soviet satellite states, following the example of the Soviet Union, also announced troop reductions as follows: Czechoslovakia 34,000 (August 24), Rumania 40,000 (August 30), Poland 47,000 (September 3), Albania 9,000 (September), Hungary 20,000 (September 7), Bulgaria 18,000 (September 20). All troop reductions were scheduled to be carried out before the end of December 1955.

[7] The Soviet Union and Finland signed an agreement on September 19, 1955 calling for the return of the Porkkala naval base, a Soviet held enclave on Finnish territory, which had been leased to Russia for fifty years under the terms of the 1947 peace treaty. At the same time the two governments signed a protocol extending their Treaty of Friendship, Cooperation and Mutual Assistance (originally signed on April 6, 1948) for another 20 years.

[8] *Documents on American Foreign Relations, 1954,* p. 328.

[9] See above, p. 108.

[10] See above, pp. 108-111.

undoubtedly will serve to reduce international tension in the centre of Europe and will have a positive influence on the settlement of the German problem.

In taking all these steps and in developing the Soviet Union's ties and co-operation both with Eastern and Western States, the Soviet Government is guided by the need to back up words with deeds in international affairs and, instead of being balked by unsettled problems, to move forward step by step and prepare the ground for the settlement of other matters of a more difficult nature.

The measures taken by the Soviet Union have made it obvious that there are still great opportunities for the further easing of international tension, provided, of course, that all states and, particularly, the great powers, act in the spirit of Geneva. Unfortunately, these opportunities are far from being utilized by all concerned.

The task of our Meeting is to continue the good work started at the Geneva Conference of the Heads of Government. Our principal objectives are thus defined.

The Heads of Government instructed us to discuss the following questions: 1) European security and Germany; 2) Disarmament; 3) The development of contacts between East and West.

The great importance of the question of *European security and Germany* was pointed out unanimously by the Heads of Government of the Four Powers—by the Chairman of the Council of Ministers of the USSR, N. A. Bulganin, President D. Eisenhower of the USA, Prime Minister A. Eden of the UK, and Premier E. Faure of France. The reason for this is obvious. Both the First and the Second World Wars began in Europe. These wars, unleashed by militarist Germany, brought the nations of Europe untold disaster and destruction the consequences of which are still felt to this day. Particulary great were the privations borne by the peoples of the Soviet Union as well as the peoples of Poland, Yugoslavia, Czechoslovakia, France, Belgium and the other countries of Europe which had been attacked by German militarism. We also know that as a result of these wars, the German people had to make great sacrifices to pay dearly for the adventurous war policy promoted by the aggressive militarist circles of Germany.

In view of this lesson of history and the need to establish certain guarantees of a peaceful and tranquil existence for the European States, we should make every effort to solve successfully the problem of ensuring security in Europe, which is of vital concern to all European peoples.

At the Geneva Conference in July the Soviet Government put forward its proposals on this problem. There can be no doubt that appropriate agreement on this matter would best help to consolidate peace and European security. The Soviet Government proposed that an all-European Treaty for Collective Security in Europe be concluded by all the interested European states and the United States of America.[11] The Heads of Government decided to refer our draft Treaty to the Foreign Ministers for their consideration. When this question comes up for discussion, the Soviet Delegation will put forward its arguments in support of the said proposals.

But it should be pointed out here and now that the principle obstacle to security in Europe is the existence of military groupings. The creation of such groupings was started by the North Atlantic bloc. These groupings set some countries against others and stimulate the armaments race. They increase the danger of a new war.

The Soviet Union is for the liquidation of military groupings. If for some reason this cannot be done immediately, we propose that it be done gradually, but that the paving of the way for the abolition of all military blocks and groupings should be started immediately. All measures designed to reduce international tension and strengthen confidence among nations, answer these purposes.

It is in connection with the problem of European security, which is the principal one for the peoples of Europe, that we are to consider the problem of Germany which is subordinate to it. The Soviet Union favours, as heretofore, the settlement of the German problem in the interests of European security and the reunification of Germany on peaceful and democratic principles. We assume that in solving the German problem reliable guarantees should be set up, so that German militarism will not arise again and threaten the peace and tranquillity of the European peoples. This is the only settlement of the problem of Germany's reunification that would be in the interests of the peoples of Europe and of the German people themselves.

It follows that consideration of the German problem inevitably raises the question as to which course a united Germany will follow—that of converting Germany into a militaristic state integrated, moreover, in the military groupings of

[11] See above, pp. 210-211

the Western powers—or that of a peace-loving and democratic state not participating in any military blocs but cooperating with other states in strengthening peace.

Now that Western Germany is being remilitarized in accordance with the Paris Agreements and is already included in the military groupings of the Western powers, new obstacles have arisen in the settlement of the German problem. Under these complicated conditions the necessary solution can be reached only gradually, through a reduction of international tension in Europe, through the creation of a reliable system of collective security, as the result of a rapprochement and a better cooperation between the two parts of Germany.

Recently the view has been expressed that both European security and the settlement of the German problem should be brought about by stages. This view should not be rejected if it serves to achieve genuine European security and to reestablish Germany's unity along peaceful and democratic lines. These purposes would not be met, however, through such a settlement of the German problem by which, under the guise of Germany's unification by stages, militarism would in fact be resurrected throughout Germany by stages. The resurgence of German militarism cannot be accepted, either at once or by stages.

On the other hand, under present conditions when there exist two German states with different social systems, the settlement of the German problem cannot be sought to the detriment of the interests of any one part of Germany, to the detriment of the social achievements of the workers of the German Democratic Republic, which are of the utmost importance to the German people as a whole. It would be quite unrealistic to try to bring about the unification of Germany through a mechanical merger of its two parts.

Moreover, we must realize that the settlement of the German problem is primarily the affair of the Germans themselves. Our task is to assist them in that respect, rather than to impose upon them any plans of our own.

A most important problem before our meeting, the positive settlement of which is awaited by all peoples, is the problem of *disarmament*. The peoples are right in regarding the present armaments race as one of the principal reasons for the existing tension and lack of confidence in relations between states. The armament race is deflecting enormous strength and resources from peaceful construction and is burdening nations more and more with taxes and soaring prices. That is a fact which no one should underestimate. It is in the interests of all peoples that the funds now used for the armaments race be switched to the improvement of public welfare and used for assisting underdeveloped countries and regions.

Our main task in considering the problem of disarmament is to find ways and means to stop the armaments race, to reduce inflated national armed forces—armies, navies, and air forces—to prohibit atomic weapons and to relieve mankind of the danger of atomic war. This can be achieved only by a substantial reduction of armaments, first of all by the great powers, and by taking steps to prohibit atomic weapons, so that this great achievement of the human mind and of technical progress—the discovery of ways to tap atomic energy—may be used for peaceful purposes only. It stands to reason that strict international control and an effective system of inspection are required in carrying out measures to reduce armaments and ban atomic weapons. It would be unconvincing, however, to talk about control and inspection and at the same time to continue the armaments race, to pile up atomic and hydrogen bombs and to inflate military budgets.

As you know, on May 10 of this year the Soviet Government submitted its detailed proposals concerning the reduction of armaments, the prohibition of atomic weapons, and the elimination of the danger of a new war.[12] In its subsequent statements the Soviet Government took into account such considerations of the Western powers as were directed towards the same goal of bringing about disarmament. In fact a wide measure of agreement has now been reached between the USSR, the USA, the UK, and France on a number of important points pertaining to disarmament—on the levels of armaments and armed forces, on the procedure and time-table for the prohibition of atomic weapons, on certain important aspects of international control in this field. It should also be noted, that the correspondence between President Eisenhower and Marshal Bulganin, Chairman of the Council of Ministers of the USSR, helps further to clarify the positions of the parties as regards certain important aspects of the disarmament problem.[13]

The problem of disarmament requires practical steps and

[12] See below, pp. 417-430.
[13] See below, pp. 441-448.

decisions. The Soviet Delegation is willing to consider any proposal that would contribute to the termination of the armaments race and to the solution of the problem of disarmament.

At this meeting the Soviet Government also attaches great importance to a discussion of the problem of *contacts* between East and West which would contribute toward international cooperation and toward better mutual understanding.

We realize that the development of contacts between the East and West can be successful only if it rests on a firm economic basis and on unhindered expansion of international trade. This is hampered at present by such factors as discrimination in international trade, disruption of normal relations in the field of credits, and other artificial obstacles to international cooperation.

It would also be desirable to agree upon measures to be taken for strengthening international ties in the field of culture, science, and technology[,] for the development of tourism and for furthering the exchange of experience in industry, agriculture and commerce. We think that there are considerable opportunities for strengthening these international ties.

In conclusion allow me to express my hope that our meeting will proceed in the same spirit of mutual understanding and willingness to cooperate that prevailed at the Geneva Conference of the Heads of Government and served to reduce international tension and to consolidate peace. In proceeding along this path we shall achieve positive results which will meet the aspirations of our peoples.

d. *Statement by the Secretary of State (Dulles), October 27, 1955.*[14]

We meet here charged with a heavy load of responsibility.

Last July the Heads of our Governments declared here their desire for a stable peace and reduction of tensions. The Four were able to agree on three issues which must be resolved in pursuit of these ends.

At the same time the "Summit" conference clearly brought out deep differences as to the proper road and means to achieve these objectives.

[14] *The Geneva Meeting of Foreign Ministers, etc.*, pp. 24-25.

The problem is this: Each of our Governments recognizes that the present situation is not a satisfactory basis for a secure peace. At the same time each has a concern that any changes should not impair its security. This is only natural.

The existing tension and distrust have deep roots that cannot easily be eradicated. But we have reached a critical point where we must either move forward in a series of common actions which will restore confidence or else the future might be not merely like the past, but worse still, a deterioration of the past.

The three topics on our agenda illustrate the nature of this problem.

Taking first the problem of Germany, all recognize that the division of Germany is a grave injustice and a source of instability. We have all agreed that Germany should be reunified by free elections. Yet to achieve German reunification at this stage requires that we each be satisfied that this step will not impair our security. Recognizing this necessity, the United States is prepared to join in assurances related to German unity, which will preclude any revival of German militarism. These, we believe, take proper account of all legitimate security interests, including those of the Soviet Union and should permit of proceeding promptly to achieve the reunification now long over-due.

The second item, disarmament, poses a similar problem. All recognize that present levels of armaments are a heavy burden on the various nations and should be reduced, not merely as a measure of economy, but because armaments designed for security may in fact lead to war. But no one of us can be expected to reduce our military capability materially except in step with similar reductions by others. Hence progress clearly depends, not merely on agreeing to reduce, but also on assurance that the agreed reductions will actually take place. Otherwise none will feel that it can safely carry out the agreed reductions. That is why the United States, the United Kingdom, and France have placed such heavy emphasis on an adequate inspection and control system as a prerequisite to genuine disarmament. Meanwhile, President Eisenhower's proposal for exchange of blueprints and aerial inspection could create an atmosphere conducive to progress in this field.

And touching on the third item of contacts, we all agree that greater contact between us could serve to promote mutual understanding. But in this field also we cannot expect, all at once, far-reaching action which will ignore all security considerations. We must tackle first those areas which on the one hand do not seriously involve the security of either side and which on the other hand assure reciprocal benefits.

The United States comes to this meeting dedicated to exploring patiently and sincerely all possible approaches to realistic solutions of these problems. We hope this spirit will be reciprocated. We shall have various proposals on these matters which seek to meet legitimate Soviet concerns. Our proposals aim to make possible the necessary changes in present conditions on a basis which does not impair the security of any other and indeed would greatly enhance that security by the removal of the existing sources of instability and tension. We hope that the Soviet Union will give these proposals the serious and sympathetic consideration which we believe they deserve.

The hope which I have expressed is the hope of President Eisenhower, whose thoughts are much with us, and I deeply appreciate your thought of him. Even since his illness he has twice discussed with me fully the problems which confront us here and he yesterday made a statement about our work, a copy of which I should like to circulate as a conference document.[15]

We here shall, I know, all be conscious of the fact that, as President Eisenhower says, in the statement of yesterday to which I alluded, the developments at Geneva will go far to demonstrate whether the "spirit of Geneva" marks a genuine change and will actually be productive of the peaceful progress for which the whole world longs.

2. *European Security.*

a. *Tripartite Proposal on the Reunification of Germany and Security, Submitted by the French Delegation, October 27, 1955.*[16]

(Excerpt)

At the Geneva Conference, the Heads of Government recognised, in their directive to the Foreign Ministers, the common responsibility of the Four Powers for the reunification of Germany by means of free elections in conformity with the

[15] Not printed. For text see *The Geneva Meeting of Foreign Ministers, etc.,* p. 11.
[16] *Ibid.,* pp. 27-33.

national interests of the German people and the interests of European security.

France, the United Kingdom and the United States of America have striven unceasingly for the reunification of Germany in freedom in order to promote real stability in Europe. Last year they put forward, in the Eden Plan,[17] proposals which offer the German nation the means to recover its unity in accordance with the rights of peoples and liberty of the individual. They renew these proposals in the paper attached hereto.[18]

Free elections leading to the formation of a single Government for the whole of Germany are the right way of ensuring full participation of the German people in the solution of the German problem, which the Soviet Government says it also desires. If agreement in principle is reached during the present Conference, it should be possible to settle without delay questions concerning the electoral law and the supervision of the elections, which could take place as early as 1956.

Without German unity, any system of European security would be an illusion. The division of Germany can only perpetuate friction and insecurity as well as grave injustice. France, the United Kingdom and the United States of America are not prepared to enter into a system of European security which, as in the Soviet proposals put forward at Geneva, does not end the division of Germany.

At the Geneva Conference the Soviet Government expressed concern about the policy and associations of a reunified German Government. The Soviet Union appears to fear that a unified Germany, established by free elections and free to choose its associates in collective defence, would constitute a threat to the security of the Soviet Union and Eastern Europe. The fact is that the North Atlantic Treaty Organisation and the Western European Union are strictly defensive organisations. Far from constituting a threat to peace, they contribute to the security not only of their members but of all states. This is evident from the various limitations and restrictions which the members of the Western European Union have assumed and from the restraint on individual action which the NATO system imposes on its

[17] *Documents on American Foreign Relations, 1954,* pp. 201-204.

[18] Not printed. The text with minor variations in language is identical with the Eden Plan submitted in January 1954.

members. If a reunified Germany elects to associate itself with these organisations, the inherent obligations of restraint and control would enhance rather than detract from Soviet security.

Nevertheless, to remove any possible grounds for Soviet refusal to reunify Germany promptly, France, the United Kingdom and the United States of America are prepared to take further steps to meet the concern expressed by the Soviet Government. They accordingly propose the conclusion of a treaty in the terms set forth below, concurrently with the conclusion of an agreement to reunify Germany under the Eden Plan. This treaty would comprise undertakings to refrain from the use of force and to withhold aid from an aggressor, provisions for the limitation and control of forces and armaments, and the obligation to react against aggression. The treaty would enter into force only in conjunction with the reunification of Germany. It would be carried out by stages. Its signature would be concurrent with the signature of the agreement on the Eden Plan. The final stage would become effective when a reunified Germany decides to enter NATO and the Western European Union.

France, the United Kingdom and the United States of America are convinced that these proposals could lead to an agreement satisfactory to both sides. If the Soviet Union's concern over immediate German reunification is primarily security, these proposals should constitute an acceptable basis for negotiation since they provide a system of controls in which the Soviet Union would directly participate, and reciprocal assurances from which the Soviet Union would directly benefit. Such a settlement, by creating confidence in an area vital for world security, would facilitate the solution of even wider problems.

OUTLINE OF TERMS OF TREATY OF ASSURANCE ON THE REUNIFICATION OF GERMANY

The treaty, which would be concluded concurrently with an agreement on the reunification of Germany under the Eden Plan, would cover the following subjects:

1. —*Renunciation of the Use of Force*—

Each party would undertake to settle, by peaceful means, any international dispute in which it might be involved, and to refrain from the use of force in any manner inconsistent with the purposes of the United Nations.

2. —*Withholding Support from Aggressors*—

Each party would agree to withhold assistance, military or economic, to any aggressor, and any party could bring the aggression to the attention of the United Nations, and seek such measures as are necessary to maintain or to restore international peace and security.

3. —*Limitation of Forces and Armaments*—

In a zone comprising areas of comparable size and depth and importance on both sides of the line of demarcation between a reunified Germany and the Eastern European countries, levels for armed forces would be specified so as to establish a military balance which would contribute to European security and help to relieve the burden of armaments. There would be appropriate provisions for the maintenance of this balance. In parts of the zone which lie closest to the line of demarcation, there might be special measures relating to the disposition of military forces and installations.

4. —*Inspection and Control*—

The parties would provide information on an agreed progressive basis on their armed forces in the zone. There would be agreement on progressive procedures of mutual inspection to verify such data and to warn against any preparation for surprise attack.

5. —*Special Warning System*—

In order to provide added depth to the surveillance system on both sides and thus give further protection against surprise attack, provision could be made to establish:

a) in the western part of the zone mentioned in paragraph 3, a radar warning system operated by the Soviet Union and the other eastern members of the treaty, and

b) a like system in the eastern part of that zone operated by the NATO members of the treaty.

6. —*Consultation*—

There would be suitable provision for consultation among the parties to implement the treaty.

7. —*Individual and Collective Self-Defence*—

It would be provided that nothing in the treaty would impair or conflict with the right of individual and collective self-defence recognised by the United Nations Charter and Treaties under it. No party would continue to station forces in the territory of any other party without the latter's consent, and upon request of the party concerned any party would withdraw its forces within a stated period, unless these forces are present in the territory concerned under collective defence arrangements.

8. —*Obligation to React Against Aggression*—

Each party would agree that armed attack in Europe by any party, which is also a NATO member, against any party which is not a NATO member, or vice-versa, would endanger the peace and security which is the object of this treaty, and that all the parties would then take appropriate action to meet that common danger.

9. —*Entry into Force by Stages*—

The provisions would come into effect progressively at stages to be agreed.

b. *Soviet Proposal of a General European Treaty on Collective Security in Europe, October 28, 1955.*

[The proposal is identical with the Soviet proposal introduced at the Geneva Conference of Heads of Government on July 20, 1955.] [19]

c. *Soviet Draft Treaty on Security in Europe, October 31, 1955.*[20]

Inspired by the desire to strengthen peace and recognizing the necessity to contribute in every possible way to reducing international tension and establishing confidence in relations between states,

Guided by the peaceful purposes and principles of the United Nations,

The Governments ______________________________

____

have agreed to conclude the present Treaty.

[19] See above, pp. 210-211.
[20] *The Geneva Meeting of Foreign Ministers, etc.*, pp. 79-80.

The States-parties to the Treaty solemnly declare that they assume the following obligations:

ARTICLE 1

The contracting parties undertake not to use armed force against one another and also to refrain from having recourse to the threat of force in their relations with each other and to settle any dispute that may arise among them by peaceful means.

ARTICLE 2

In the event that any one or several States-parties to the Treaty is subjected to an armed attack in Europe by any state or group of states, the other States-parties to the Treaty shall immediately render the state or states so attacked all such assistance, including military assistance, as may be deemed necessary for the purpose of re-establishing and maintaining international peace and security in Europe.

ARTICLE 3

The States-parties to the Treaty undertake to refrain from rendering under any pretext any direct or indirect assistance to the attacking state in Europe.

ARTICLE 4

The States-parties to the Treaty shall consult one another whenever, in the view of any one of them, there arises a threat of an armed attack in Europe against one or more of the States-parties to the Treaty, in order to take effective steps to remove any such threat. They shall immediately conduct the necessary consultations whenever agreed steps may be required for the reestablishment of peace, in the event of an attack on any State-party to the Treaty.

ARTICLE 5

The signatory states shall establish, by common consent, a special body (or bodies) for the purpose of holding the above-mentioned consultations and also for taking such other steps to assure security as may be found necessary in connection with the fulfilment by the states of their obligations under the present Treaty.

ARTICLE 6

The States-parties to the Treaty agree that obligations under the present Treaty shall not infringe upon the obligations assumed by them under existing treaties and agreements.

ARTICLE 7

The assumption by states of obligations under the present Treaty shall not prejudice the right of the States-parties to the Treaty to individual or collective self-defense in the event of an armed attack, as provided for in Article 51 of the United Nations Charter.

ARTICLE 8

The Treaty is of a provisional character and shall remain in effect until replaced by another, more extensive Treaty on European security which shall replace the existing treaties and agreements.

d. *Statement by the Secretary of State (Dulles) Appraising the Progress of Discussions on European Security, November 2, 1955.*[21]

Mr. Chairman, I feel that the discussions which we have had on one-half of Item 1, namely, the question of security, has brought about a considerable rapprochement of our positions. I am encouraged to think if we could make comparable progress on the other half of Item 1 that we would have fulfilled the expectations which the world placed in this conference.

As I have examined, in parallel columns, the proposals which were put forward by the Western Powers on the first working day of the conference, Document No. 7,[22] and compared them with the proposals and propositions which Mr. Molotov advanced last Monday,[23] I found that there was a very considerable parallelism in our thinking. I do not mean to suggest that our form of relations is alike or that important differences do not subsist but that there does seem to be a large measure of similarity in the approach. For example, Article 1 of the Western security proposal dealing with renunciation of force has its counterpart in Article 1 of the suggested security treaty which the Soviet Union put forward on Monday.

The principle that there should be no help given to an

[21] *Ibid.*, pp. 85-87.
[22] See above, pp. 247-249.
[23] See above, pp. 249-251.

aggressor appears in Article 2 of the Western proposal and in Article 3 of the draft Soviet treaty.

The idea that there should be a substantial zone within which special measures would be taken appears in Article 3 of the Western proposal and in the first proposition which Mr. Molotov outlined in his presentation on Monday.

The idea that within this zone there should be agreed limits of forces appeared in Article 3 of the Western proposal and in the second of the propositions which Mr. Molotov outlined in his presentation of Monday.

The idea that within this zone there should be reciprocal inspections to verify the agreed limitations appeared in Article 4 of the Western proposal and in the fourth proposition which Mr. Molotov outlined in his presentation of Monday.

Another special measure which the Western Powers suggested—that is, overlapping radar—does not have any counterpart in the Soviet proposals but this is a detailed proposal not touching on the substance.

The concept of consultation appeared in Article 6 of the Western proposals and appears in Articles 4 and 5 of the Soviet draft treaty.

Recognition of the inherent right of collective self-defense is found in Article 7 of the proposed Western treaty and in Article 7 of the draft Soviet treaty.

The concept that foreign forces, not forming part of agreed collective security, should be withdrawn on demand appears in Article 7 of the Western proposals and perhaps, although this is somewhat ambiguous, may be found within the context of the third of the propositions which Mr. Molotov made in his exposition of Monday when he speaks about the exercise of sovereignty.

The concept that there should be reaction against aggression appears in Article 8 of the Western Powers proposal and is also found in Article 2 of the draft Soviet treaty.

As I have said, the expression of these concepts is not always identical and there are sometimes quite important differences in the manner of expression. But, broadly speaking, we have, I think, achieved a quite remarkable degree of parallel thinking with respect to the concept of European security. When I say "parallel thinking" I am not using that word in the geometric term, which means two lines which never meet. I think there is reason to hope that these parallel lines may meet, and may meet shorter than infinity.

So where are we? It seems to me that we have reached a

point where as a result of constructive thinking on both sides we can see a realizable vision of security in Europe through means of a treaty which would conform to the Directive which the Heads of Government have given us.

We have, however, made no progress at all with reference to the other half of the first item, namely, the reunification of Germany, and I would like to endorse all that Mr. Macmillan has said with reference to the importance, if not the urgency, of the Soviet Union now making its proposals with respect to the reunification of Germany, the proposals that Mr. Molotov has indicated some days ago he has ready, but which so far he has not submitted. It is the view of the delegation of the United States that security proposals of the kind that we are considering could, indeed, provide security and the assurance of a durable peace in Europe if they were predicated, as the Directive indicates they should be, upon the reunification of Germany. We do not believe that any proposals, however, resourceful or ingenious, however buttressed, could provide durable peace for Europe if they were predicated upon the unnatural division of one of the great nations and one of the great peoples of Europe. That, I think, was surely the view of the Heads of our Governments, and is the view that is embodied in the Directive under which we are operating and which binds us.

I recall the statement by Premier Bulganin, his opening statement to the Summit Conference, in which he said, and I quote, "The reunification of Germany as a peace-loving and democratic state would be of paramount importance both to the peace of Europe and for the German nation itself." [24] In other words, Marshal Bulganin recognized that the thing which was of "paramount" importance was not a security treaty but the reunification of Germany. That, he said, was of "paramount importance" for the peace of Europe and that, I suppose, is why the Heads of Government in their Directive, having first taken account, as they put it, of the close link between the reunification of Germany and the problems of European security, agreed that "the reunification of Germany by means of free elections shall be carried out."

In conclusion, let me say that I think we have made progress, good progress, in our discussion of the problem of European security. But I am convinced of this, that it is not possible to make any further progress until we know the views of the Soviet Union with respect to the closely linked prob-

[24] See above, p. 204.

lem which we are directed, as part of the same subject, to consider, namely, "the reunification of Germany by means of free elections."

So I repeat the plea of Mr. Macmillan that Mr. Molotov should give us his ideas on that subject. And I am confident that if we can bring our ideas on that subject as close together as we have brought our ideas together in relation to the problem of European security, then, indeed, we will have made this conference successful.

e. *Soviet Proposal Concerning Basic Principles of a European Security Treaty, November 9, 1955.*

[The proposal is identical with the text of a proposal introduced by the Soviet delegation at the Geneva Conference of Heads of Government on July 21, 1955.][25]

f. *Soviet Proposal of a Summary Statement of the Four Foreign Ministers on Agreed Positions on the Question of European Security, November 15, 1955.*[26]

The Foreign Ministers of the USSR, the USA, the United Kingdom, and France state, that, though, as a result of an exchange of opinions held on the first item of the agenda—European security and Germany—the necessary degree of agreement has not yet been achieved, nevertheless a concurrence of the positions with regard to a number of important questions pertaining to European security has been revealed, namely:

1. All members of the Meeting have expressed themselves in favour of stipulating in a treaty on European security that parties to the treaty renounce the use of force in their mutual relations.

2. An agreement has been reached that obligations under the treaty on European security should provide for joint measures for the purpose of resisting possible aggression in Europe.

3. An agreement has also been reached that states-parties to the treaty should not render assistance to an aggressor.

4. There has been recognized the necessity for establishing a zone between East and West, on the territory of which

[25] See above, pp. 212-213.
[26] *The Geneva Meeting of Foreign Ministers, etc.*, pp. 174-175.

measures would be taken to establish the maximum levels of the armed forces of the respective states, with the institution of an appropriate inspection.

5. There has been recognized the necessity for mutual consultations of the parties to the treaty for the purpose of ensuring the fulfilment by the states of the obligations assumed by them under the treaty on European security.

6. There is also a complete accord that the obligations under the treaty on European security should not affect the inalienable right of states to individual or collective self-defense.

At the same time all the members of the Meeting note that no agreement has yet been reached on such basic questions as the guaranteeing of European security on the basis of strengthening cooperation between states and also the settlement of the German problem and the re-establishment of German unity.

All members of the Meeting have manifested a desire to continue their efforts directed towards the achievement of such an agreement.

g. *Comments by the Secretary of State (Dulles) on the Soviet Proposal of a Summary Statement, November 16, 1955.*[27]

Mr. Chairman, yesterday the Soviet Delegation introduced a proposal whereby the Foreign Ministers would express their view that the concurrence of position on a number of important questions pertaining to European security had been made discernible, and the paper then lists some six areas of agreement. I neither ignore the fact that a certain parallelism has developed in our thinking on this subject, nor do I minimize the importance of that fact. Indeed, I think I myself was perhaps the first to call attention to it in a statement which I made here analyzing on a sort of parallel-column basis the elements which were common to the proposals by the Western powers and the second set of proposals put in by the Soviet Union.[28] I would, however, have to point out that that statement was made before the position of the Soviet Union with respect to the reunification of Germany had been fully exposed.[29] The differences which there

[27] *Ibid.*, pp. 175-176.
[28] See above, pp. 251-254.
[29] See below, pp. 259-263.

emerged as to our views on security, particularly in relation to Germany, NATO, and the Brussels Treaty indicated that on fundamentals there is still a very considerable measure of disagreement as far as security is concerned.

I do feel that the exchange of opinions which we have had here indicates that if the insecurity due to the division of Germany could be eliminated, other aspects of security could perhaps be resolved. But I am afraid that this Soviet paper would give somewhat of a false impression, because it does not adequately develop the strong feeling of the Western powers that with the division of Germany there cannot be security, and also the strong feelings of the Western powers as to the value both for themselves and for others of such organizations as the North Atlantic Treaty Organization and the Brussels Organization.

Furthermore, I fear that it would be difficult—perhaps impossible—in the time that is available to us to agree on a precise wording of the points where a certain concurrence of positions—to use the Soviet phrase—has been developed. These matters are highly technical, every word used has an import which has to be weighed, and to agree upon the precise formulation, even where we are in general accord, would be a task of some delicacy, taking time and study by our experts.

I think the record on this matter is clear. It does have in it elements from which I think we can draw some satisfaction. But I am inclined to think that it is better to let the record speak for itself rather than to attempt a summarization of the record which, for both of the reasons I have indicated, would, I think, be difficult to agree upon.

3. *Germany.*

a. *Tripartite Proposal on the Reunification of Germany and Security, Submitted by the French Delegation, October 27, 1955.*[30]

b. *Soviet Proposal on the Establishment of an All-German Council, November 2, 1955.*[31]

Guided by the desire to further the development of full cooperation between the German Democratic Republic and the German Federal Republic and the creation of conditions for the settlement of the German problem and for the re-

[30] See above, pp. 245-249.

[31] *The Geneva Meeting of Foreign Ministers, etc.*, pp. 98-99.

unification of Germany by means of free elections in conformity with the national interests of the German people and the interests of European security, the Foreign Ministers of the U.S.S.R., the U.S.A., the United Kingdom and France declare the following:

Under present conditions when the German people are deprived of the possibility of living in a united state, the need to bring about cooperation between the G.D.R. and the G.F.R. which would facilitate the settlement of the problem of Germany's national reunification, is becoming ever more urgent. That purpose would be met by the establishment by agreement between the German Democratic Republic and the German Federal Republic of an all-German body to coordinate their efforts in the political, economic and cultural life of the German people and also to cooperate with other states in the consolidation of peace.

Such a representative body of the German people could be an All-German Council to be established on the basis of the following principles:

1. An All-German Council shall be formed, composed of the representatives of the parliaments of the German Democratic Republic and the German Federal Republic, as a consultative body to discuss matters, in the solution of which the German Democratic Republic and the German Federal Republic are interested.

2. Mixed committees shall be set up under the All-German Council, composed of representatives of the governments of the German Democratic Republic and the German Federal Republic, on matters relating to economic and cultural ties between the two German states, Germany currency and intra-German financial transactions, customs, post and telegraph, communications, etc.

3. The All-German Council shall bring about accord on the numerical strength, armaments, and disposition of units required to ensure the defence of the frontiers and territories of the German Democratic Republic and the German Federal Republic.

4. The All-German Council shall bring about accord on matters relating to the participation of the German Democratic Republic and the German Federal Republic in measures designed to consolidate European security and shall consider by mutual agreement questions pertaining to the establishment of prerequisites for the unification of Germany, as a peaceful and democratic state.

The Foreign Ministers of the USSR, the USA, the United Kingdom and France express the hope that the German Democratic Republic and the German Federal Republic will make the necessary efforts to achieve agreement on the establishment of the All-German Council.

c. *Tripartite Proposal on the Reunification of Germany by Free Elections, Submitted by the United States Delegation, November 4, 1955.*[32]

On the joint initiative of the Governments of France, the United Kingdom, the United States and the Federal Republic of Germany, the Foreign Ministers of France, the United Kingdom and the U.S. submit the following proposal as the first step in order to carry out the reunification of Germany in freedom in accordance with the Plan presented by the Three Powers on October 28:[33]

Draft Decision of the Conference

In conformity with the common responsibility of their governments for the settlement of the German question and the reunification of Germany and in compliance with the Directive of their Heads of Government that the settlement of the German question and the reunification of Germany by means of free elections shall be carried out in conformity with the national interests of the German people and the interests of European security, the Foreign Ministers of France, the U.K., the USSR, and the U.S. have agreed as follows:

1. Free and secret elections shall be held throughout Germany during September 1956, for the selection of representatives for an all-German National Assembly to draft a constitution and to form a government thereunder for a reunified Germany.

2. Each of the Four Powers will designate a representative to a Commission to prepare, in consultation with German experts, the electoral law for such elections, including effective provisions for safeguards and supervision to insure the freedom of such elections.

3. The Commission shall undertake its functions promptly and shall submit its report to the Four Powers by January 1956.

[32] *Ibid.,* pp. 136-137.
[33] See above, pp. 245-249.

d. *Statement by the Minister of Foreign Affairs of the Soviet Union (Molotov) on Problems Related to Germany, November 8, 1955.*[34]

(Excerpts)

Mr. Chairman, Gentlemen:

At the preceding meeting of November 4 Mr. Dulles introduced on behalf of the delegations of the United States of America, the United Kingdom, and France proposals concerning the German problem which pertain to the conduct of all-German elections. The Soviet Delegation examined these proposals carefully and studied them. Today we have also heard the statements of Mr. Pinay and Mr. Macmillan in defense of the proposals of the Three Powers.[35] In this connection the Soviet Delegation considers it necessary to state the following.

Mr. Dulles' proposal states that it is introduced "in accordance with a plan presented by the Three Western Powers on October 28." This is also confirmed by the entire content of the said proposal. Consequently, the proposal of November 4 of the three delegations is not anything new as compared with the proposal of October 28. The very proposals of October 28 of the Three Powers show that their purpose is to remilitarize not only West Germany but also East Germany, and to bring not only West Germany but also all of Germany into the North Atlantic bloc, which is directed against the Soviet Union and not against the USSR alone. There is no need to prove that the Soviet Union cannot sympathize with such an objective and cannot contribute to its achievement at all. The peoples of the Soviet Union know German militarism too well to contribute to its revival with their own hands. They know that the revival of German militarism is incompatible with the maintenance of the peace and security of the peoples of Europe.

* * *

The question of all-German elections is not merely a question of a change of government. Such elections in Germany decide the destiny of the country, the question as to whether a united Germany will develop as a peaceful

[34] *The Geneva Meeting of Foreign Ministers, etc.,* pp. 145-152.
[35] Not printed.

democratic state or will become a militaristic state and will again be a menace to its neighbors.

The proposal is made here to accept the plan of all-German elections as a means of uniting Germany. On the one hand, this plan, as was shown previously, ignores the conditions actually existing in Germany, since the question of holding such elections has not yet matured. On the other hand, even if we agreed to such an artificial plan we could not put it into practice without the agreement of the Germans themselves, who live in the German Democratic Republic and the German Federal Republic. Finally, such a mechanical merger of the two parts of Germany by means of so-called "Free Elections" which would, moreover, be held, as is provided for in the "Eden Plan," in the presence of foreign troops, could lead to the violation of the vital interests of the working masses of the German Democratic Republic, to which one cannot agree.

Naturally, plants and factories, land and natural resources, must not be taken away from the working masses of the GDR. From this it is evident that an attempt to carry out the so-called "Eden Plan" would involve serious complications inside Germany which none of us, of course, wishes to happen.

From this it follows that only full cognizance of the fact that there exist on the territory of Germany two different German states and that the reunification of Germany cannot be brought about other than by mutual agreement of these states: it is only by this means that the right solution of the German question can be found.

It is well known that in the relations between the two parts of Germany there is no mutual confidence, which is necessary for the reestablishment of Germany's unity. The representatives of one part of Germany, namely, of the German Federal Republic, do not even want to meet with the representatives of the other part of Germany, the German Democratic Republic. In these circumstances the task of the Four Powers is to facilitate by all means the establishment of such confidence, to contribute to the rapprochement of the two German states and to the establishment of cooperation between them. At the same time one cannot think that the Germans of Eastern and Western Germany are interested in the unification of Germany in a lesser degree than are the Americans, French, British or Russians.

* * *

The ways to reestablish German unity on a peaceful and democratic basis can and should be found, though, under the present conditions, these ways cannot be recognized as short and simple. Time, patience and endurance will be needed. Such a way, in our opinion, would be the creation of an all-German Council which could at the beginning coordinate the appropriate actions of the GDR and the GFR in the field of political, economic and cultural life insofar as they affect all-German interests as well as action concerning the strengthening of peace and security in Europe. There are many common questions in the field of trade, movement between West and East Germany, etc., on which an agreed decision will be of advantage to all the Germans. The agreed decision on such questions would contribute to the development of full cooperation between the GFR and the GDR and to the creation of conditions for the settlement of the German question and for the reunification of Germany by means of free elections, in accordance with the national interests of the German people and of European security.

This all leads us to the conclusion that the further consideration of the German question will be beneficial to the cause only when Germans themselves find a common language and take into their own hands preparations for the solution of this question. The discussion at this Meeting has shown once again that there is no other way for the solution of the German problem.

The representatives of the Western powers have not yet expressed their attitude to the proposal on the creation of an all-German Council. One cannot disregard the fact that this proposal takes into account the existing conditions in Germany and actually leads to rapprochement and to the creation of prerequisites for the unification of Germany, without encroaching upon the interests of either of the German states and without interfering with the social systems which at present exist in the GDR and in the GFR.

* * *

It was asserted here, in particular by Mr. Macmillan,[36] that the Soviet Union has changed its position on the German question by comparison with the Berlin meeting of January 1954, when the Soviet Government deemed it possible to agree to general elections in Germany.[37]

[36] Not printed.

[37] *Foreign Ministers Meeting: Berlin Discussions, January 25- February 18, 1954* (Department of State Publication 5399).

It is true that at that time we considered it possible, under certain conditions, to agree to all-German elections, but our proposals were disregarded. Since that time nearly two years have elapsed and the situation has seriously changed—the Paris Agreements have entered into force, Western Germany has set itself against Eastern Germany and carried out many announced and unannounced measures for remilitarization, has joined military blocs, NATO included, and put itself under the joint military command of the Western Powers' grouping. How can anyone disregard all that has happened during these two years? How can anyone under these conditions speak of all-German elections?

It should be recalled that in the course of the discussion of the question of the Paris Agreements statements were made to the effect that after the ratification of these agreements it would be possible to speak with the Soviet Union on the German question from "positions of strength."

Now that the implementation of the Paris Agreements has come into full swing, it has become clear that attempts of such a kind cannot have any success either as regards the German question or any other question. One cannot fail to recall something else; we repeatedly pointed out that the Paris Agreements would be detrimental to the possibility of reuniting Germany and would raise unsurmountable obstacles in this respect. Nevertheless, no heed was taken.

* * *

. . . the principal point in the proposal by the Three Powers is neither German reunification nor all-German elections. In the proposal by the Three Powers both problems are subordinated to the major objective stated in their document of October 28 which says that the treaty's "final stage would become effective when a reunified Germany decides to enter NATO and the Western European Union." Thus this plan is a means of remilitarizing and including in the Western military groupings not only Western Germany but the whole of Germany.

All this convinces us that the proposals by the Three Western Powers on the German question have nothing to do with ensuring European security.

* * *

Our proposals take into account the interests of European states and the national interests of the German people. They are based on due consideration for the actual situation. They do not promise any easy solution of the complicated international problems and of the German question in particular, but such a solution in these circumstances unfortunately does not exist.

Our proposal to set up an All-German Council opens up the possibility of really bringing the two German states closer together. We are convinced that were such an all-German body to appear for the first time after the Second World War, it would play a historic role in the creation of external and internal prerequisites for German reunification.

e. *Comments by the Secretary of State (Dulles) on the Soviet Position on Germany, November 9, 1955.*[38]

(Excerpts)

Yesterday, Mr. Molotov, just returned from Moscow, made a statement on behalf of the Soviet Union. It had such grave implications that I asked that we should suspend our meeting until today so as to be able to give his statement deliberate thought. I am now in a position to express the views of my Government.

My first observation is that the Soviet position if persisted in will perpetuate conditions which put in jeopardy the peace of Europe. My second observation is that it strikes a crippling blow at the possibility of developing relations of confidence with the Soviet Union. I ask your permission, Mr. Chairman, to deal with these two points in order.

I.

The Soviet Union says in the most categorical manner that the security of Europe is best assured by a continued division of Germany at least until Germany can be unified under conditions which would Sovietize the whole of Germany. Mr. Molotov extolled the governmental regime which the Soviet has established in the German zone, the so-called "German Democratic Republic," and said it has "a great future ahead of it because it is moving along the main road of progress and because it has strong and loyal friends." It is, he said, "impossible to accept" a reunification of Germany which might jeopardize that "great future" for this Sovietized segment of Germany.

[38] *The Geneva Meeting of Foreign Ministers, etc.*, pp. 154-159.

But, Mr. Chairman, the Directive which brought us here, and which ought to guide us here, did not ask us to judge of the relative merits of social systems as between that of the Federal Republic of Germany and that of the so-called "German Democratic Republic." It told us to reunite Germany in the "national interest." Thus, the German people themselves will determine under what system they want to live.

The problem which our Heads of Government did direct us to study was how to assure European security and German reunification, two problems which the four Heads of Government agreed were closely linked.

* * *

And because our Directive specifically requires us to take account of the close link between the reunification of Germany and the problems of European security, the Western powers[,] loyally complying with the Directive, proposed a security system based upon a reunified Germany. The proposals which we made embody greater assurances than have ever before been contrived to preserve the peace. There would be not only solemn undertakings to abstain from aggression, to withhold help to an aggressor, and, in effect, to guarantee against aggression, but there would be physical and material safeguards, consisting of a level of forces to be agreed upon and actual inspections to ensure that these levels were maintained. There would be ample and dependable safeguards, in which the Soviet Union, Poland, and Czechoslovakia would take part, against re-creation of a menacing military force. There would be novel and effective provisions to ensure against any possibility of surprise attack.

These provisions, based on a reunified Germany, would give Europe a security which it has not known for hundreds of years. Indeed, the merit of the proposals we made were so obvious that the Soviet Union itself, after studying them, introduced supplementary security proposals of its own which were closely modeled on ours. However, the Soviet proposals in this respect, as indeed every proposal that the Soviet Union has made, are predicated upon the continued division of Germany.

As President Eisenhower said again and again last July, "European security and the reunification of Germany are inseparable." It is not possible to have European security without the reunification of Germany.

I recall that Mr. Molotov speaking on October 31, 1939,

after the outbreak of the Second World War, referred to the relations between Germany and the other Western European States during the preceding two decades, and to what he called the "German efforts to break the fetters of the Versailles Treaty." "This it is," he said, "that in the long run led to the present war in Europe."

The Versailles Treaty did impose certain fetters upon Germany. But nothing that the Versailles Treaty did compares with the cruelty and injustice of dividing the German people by the separation from Germany of the Soviet Zone comprising 17,000,000 Germans. The anguish of this is demonstrated by the fact that 2,704,680 Germans at the cost of great sacrifice and risks, fled from the Soviet Zone into West Germany. During the last month of October there were 32,874 refugees.

The situation, thus dramatized, cannot be indefinitely perpetuated without grave risk.

Yet, it is to perpetuate this very risk that the Soviet Union finds itself compelled to reject the far-reaching and solid security proposals which I referred to. Surely, better statesmanship than that can be found.

We urge upon the Soviet Government that it should not perpetuate the injustice of a divided Germany with the menace which it carries to European security. Can we not learn from the lesson of Versailles? We make that plea, and we shall go on making it, in the hope, and, indeed, in the expectation that before it is too late wisdom will prevail.

II.

I turn now to the effect of the Soviet action upon international relations generally.

* * *

The Government of the United States believes that the refusal of the Government of the Soviet Union even to discuss seriously the reunification of Germany involves a grave breach of the agreement of the Heads of Government. The effect of this is bound to affect adversely the overall relations of the Soviet Union with other countries, including the United States.

I would be less than frank if I did not say that so far as the United States is concerned, what has happened here has largely shattered such confidence as was born at the Summit Conference at Geneva.

There can, of course, be peace and a limited degree of working relations as between nations which have no confidence that agreements between them—even though made at the highest level—will be honored. However, relations under those conditions are bound to be difficult and restricted.

Let me illustrate what I say by referring to what remains to be discussed at this Conference. We are directed to go on to discuss here the problem of disarmament and the development of contacts between the East and the West. But I am bound to say that I fear that these discussions will profit us little when we feel that we cannot make agreements between us which are dependable.

III.

Mr. Chairman, the peoples of all the world were heartened by the agreement of the Heads of Government reached here last July.

* * *

It is not the desire or the intention of the United States, so far as we can control it, to revert to the conditions which existed prior to the meeting of the Heads of Government last July. It is our purpose to continue to strive by all the means in our power for a just and durable peace. But I do deplore the set-back to European security and the damage to the spirit of Geneva which has been inflicted by the Soviet Union.

When the issues are as great as those here at stake, we shall not easily be discouraged. It is still our hope that the Soviet Union, if not now, then soon, may give loyal substance to the agreement of the Heads of Government that Germany shall be reunified by free elections.

When that day comes, European security can be assured, and the spirit of Geneva will have borne a major part of the good fruit which it seemed to offer to the world.

4. *Disarmament.*

a. *Soviet Proposal on the Reduction of Armaments and the Prohibition of Atomic Weapons, November 10, 1955.*[39]

(Excerpts)

[Article I of the Soviet proposal corresponds to the text of points 1-5 of Article I of the Soviet proposal submitted at the

[39] *Ibid.*, pp. 184-186.

Geneva Conference of Heads of Government on July 21, 1955. See above, pp. 220-221.]

II

The Foreign Ministers of the Four Powers have recognized the need to strive to achieve the necessary agreement on the still unsolved questions of the above-mentioned Convention, subject to consideration by the United Nations Organization.

Being guided by the desire to reduce international tension, to strengthen confidence among states and to put an end to the armaments race, the Foreign Ministers have agreed that it is necessary in this connection to consider first of all the following provisions [*the provisions in the following?*]:

a) In the proposal of the USSR of May 10 of this year on the reduction of armaments, the prohibition of atomic weapons and the elimination of the threat of a new war;[40]

b) In the proposal by the President of the United States of July 21 on aerial photography and exchange of military information;[41]

c) In the proposals by the Government of the United Kingdom on disarmament submitted on July 21 and August 29;[42] and

d) In the proposal by the Government of France on the financial control over disarmament and on the conversion of the resources thus released for peaceful purposes.[43]

[Article III of the Soviet proposal corresponds to the text of Article II of the Soviet proposal submitted at the Geneva Conference of Heads of Government on July 21, 1955. See above, p. 222.]

b. *Tripartite Proposal on Disarmament, Submitted by the United Kingdom Delegation, November 10, 1955.*[44]

The Four Ministers of Foreign Affairs

1. *Note* that their representatives on the sub-committee of the United Nations Disarmament Commission, in the pursuit of their efforts to establish a satisfactory system of disarmament, have followed the directive given by the four Heads of Government at Geneva on July 27, 1955;

[40] See below, pp. 417-430.
[41] See above, pp. 213-216.
[42] See above, pp. 216-217.
[43] See above, pp. 217-220.
[44] *The Geneva Meeting of Foreign Ministers, etc.*, pp. 199-201.

2. *Take note* of the work the sub-committee has accomplished in the spirit of the conference of the Heads of Government during its meetings in New York from August 29 to October 7, 1955, and express their appreciation to the sub-committee for its efforts;[45]
3. *Express* their agreement on the following:
   (a) the renunciation of the use of nuclear weapons and all other weapons in any manner inconsistent with the Charter of the United Nations;
   (b) the need to arrive at limitations and reductions of armaments and of armed forces;
   (c) the need to devote to the peaceful economic development of nations, for raising their well-being, as well as for assistance to less developed countries, the material resources that would be released by agreements in the disarmament field;
   (d) the fact that an effective system of inspection and control is the keystone of any disarmament program, and, consequently, the need to establish an organ responsible for the inspection and control of agreed measures of disarmament under effective safe-guards;
   (e) the fact that there are possibilities beyond the reach of international control for evading this control and for organizing the clandestine manufacture of atomic and hydrogen weapons even if there is a formal agreement on international control;
   (f) the need for continued scientific search by each state, with appropriate consultation between governments, for methods which might be derived from evolving scientific knowledge that would make possible a thoroughly effective inspection and control system of nuclear weapons as part of a disarmament program covering all kinds of armaments;

4. *Declare* their intent to continue to seek agreements on a comprehensive program for disarmament which will promote international peace and security with the least diversion for armament of the world's human and economic resources;

5. *Recognize* that inspection, control, limitation and reduction of armaments can best be achieved in an atmosphere which is free of fear and suspicion;

6. *Propose* accordingly that, as a contribution to such an atmosphere and as a prelude to a general disarmament programme, the States concerned:—

[45] See below, pp. 432-441.

(a) should agree promptly to put into early operation, in order to help prevent a surprise attack:

(i) a plan for exchange of military blueprints and aerial inspection on the basis of the proposal of the President of the United States of July 21, 1955; and

(ii) a plan for establishing control posts at key points, as suggested in the proposals of the Chairman of the Council of Ministers of the U.S.S.R. of July 21, 1955;[46]

(b) should also agree:

(i) to arrange for the exchange and publication of information regarding military expenditures and budgets, as suggested in the proposals made by the Prime Minister of France on July 22, 1955;[47] and

(ii) to study how best to gain practical experience regarding the problems of inspection and control, as suggested by the Prime Minister of the United Kingdom on July 21, 1955.

7. *Direct* their representatives on the United Nations Disarmament Commission to request that its sub-committee be reconvened at an early date and continue to seek an acceptable solution to the problem of disarmament.

c. *Soviet Proposal of a Statement by the Four Foreign Ministers on the Problem of Disarmament, November 15, 1955.*[48]

Being guided by the desire to contribute to the reduction of international tension, the strengthening of mutual confidence among states, the elimination of the threat of war and the reduction of the burden of armaments, the Foreign Ministers of the Soviet Union, the United States of America, the United Kingdom, and the French Republic, are convinced, as before, of the necessity of continuing to seek an agreement for a vast program of disarmament which would contribute to international peace and to security, with the minimum diversion of the human and economic resources of the world to the needs of armament.

Their discussions have shown that there is agreement in this purpose and that on certain important points concern-

[46] Not printed.
[47] See above, pp. 217-220.
[48] *The Geneva Meeting of Foreign Ministers, etc.*, pp. 225-226.

ing the reduction of armaments and the prohibition of atomic weapons, including the necessity for establishing effective control, the positions of the Four Powers have come closer together. As regards questions concerning which no agreement has yet been reached, the Ministers have agreed that the Four Powers should jointly with other states concerned continue efforts to eliminate differences and thus work out an acceptable system of disarmament which would include a reduction of all armaments and armed forces under effective guarantees.

At the same time the Ministers have agreed that a study of the methods of control over the fulfillment by states of disarmament obligations, a study which is being conducted at present in various countries, should aim to facilitate the settlement of the disarmament problem.

The Ministers have agreed that in this connection it is necessary, first of all, to continue discussion in accordance with the Directive of the Heads of Government, [of] those clauses which are contained:

(a) In the proposals of the USSR of May 10 and July 21 of this year on the problems of reducing armaments, forbidding atomic weapons, and eliminating the threat of a new war;
(b) In the proposal of the President of the USA on July 21 concerning aerial photographs and the exchange of military information;
(c) In the proposals of the Government of the United Kingdom on the problem of disarmament, introduced on July 21 and August 29, and
(d) In the proposal of the Government of France concerning financial control over disarmament and concerning the conversion of the resources thus released to peaceful purposes.

The Ministers likewise state that there has been complete unanimity to the effect that the Four Powers, in accordance with the statements of the heads of their governments, in their mutual relations will refrain from the use of armed force and will strive to solve peacefully the differences which exist or which may arise among them.

d. *Tripartite Proposal of a Statement of the Four Foreign Ministers on Disarmament, November 16, 1955.*[49]

Guided by the desire to contribute to lessening international tension, strengthening confidence between states and reducing the burden of armaments,

The Foreign Ministers of the Soviet Union, the United States of America, the United Kingdom and the French Republic remain convinced of the need to continue to seek agreement on a comprehensive program for disarmament which will promote international peace and security with the least diversion for armament of the world's human and economic resources.

Their discussions showed that, while there was agreement on this objective, it was not yet possible to reach agreement on effective methods and safeguards for achieving it.

The Ministers will transmit the record of these discussions to their representatives on the United Nations Disarmament Sub-Committee. They believe that their exchange of views has been useful in clarifying their respective positions and should assist the Sub-Committee in its efforts to reach agreement, as their representatives continue to carry out the directive of the heads of government, taking into account the proposals made at the July conference.

In the meantime the Ministers agree that the studies of methods of control which are now proceeding in different countries should be designed to facilitate a settlement of the disarmament problem.

The Ministers further reaffirmed the obligation of their governments to refrain from the use of force in any manner inconsistent with the Charter of the United Nations.

5. *Development of East-West Contacts.*

a. *Soviet Proposal, October 31, 1955.*[50]

The Directive of the Heads of Government of the U.S.S.R., the U.S.A., the United Kingdom and France on the development of contacts between East and West point[s] out the necessity to study "measures, including possible measures in organs and agencies of the United Nations, which could (a)

[49] *Ibid.*, p. 227.
[50] *Ibid.*, pp. 239-240.

bring about a progressive elimination of barriers that interfere with free communications and peaceful trade between peoples and (b) bring about such free contacts and exchanges as are to the mutual advantage of the countries and peoples concerned."

In accordance with the above, the Foreign Ministers of the Four Powers, guided by the desire to promote the strengthening of peaceful co-operation among states, have agreed on the following:

1. It is recognized that measures should be taken to facilitate the development of international trade with a view to eliminating existing obstacles and restrictions in international trade between East and West and to applying the principle of the most-favored-nation treatment in the fields of trade and navigation.

2. The Four Powers will do their utmost to facilitate the free passage of merchant ships of all countries through straits and canals of international importance and to remove existing restrictions on sea communications with certain states.

3. Measures shall be taken to broaden international scientific and technical relations, particularly in the field of the peaceful uses of atomic energy (technology, agriculture, medicine, etc.) through holding conferences with the participation of the respective specialists, etc. Appropriate steps shall be taken by the representatives of the Four Powers in international organisations dealing with international co-operation in the field of science and technology.

As an immediate measure, to consider it desirable to convene an international conference in 1956 on the use of atomic energy in the field of public health.

4. The Four Powers declare themselves in favour of the participation in international specialized agencies (ILO, UNESCO, WHO, ITU, etc.) of all states desiring to cooperate in the work of these organisations.

5. The following measures shall also be encouraged, including possible measures in organs and agencies of the United Nations which could facilitate the strengthening of contacts between East and West in the sphere of industry, agriculture, cultural relations and in the development of tourism:

(a) Mutual exchange of delegations and reciprocal visits of representatives of industry, agriculture and trade for the purpose of exchanging experience and learning of the achievements of the respective countries in these fields[;]

(b) Expansion of cultural relations between countries for the purpose of developing broader intercourse among men of science and culture and of exchanging cultural values with a view to the desirability of concluding appropriate agreements between countries on cultural co-operation;

(c) Expansion of the mutual exchange of publications (books, magazines, newspapers, etc.) between institutions of scientific research, libraries, scientific and cultural associations, social organisations and individuals;

(d) Measures for a broader development of international tourism and sports relations between nations;

(e) Measures for the elimination of existing artificial barriers in the field of immigration and other regulations which hamper the expansion of the above-mentioned contacts between states.

b. *Statement by the Secretary of State (Dulles), October 31, 1955.*[51]

The Heads of Government meeting here last July directed us to study measures, including those possible in the United Nations, for the progressive elimination of barriers interfering with free communication and peaceful trade and for the establishment of freer contacts and exchanges which are of advantage to both East and West.

The reductions of barriers and greater human contacts that we seek are not merely ends in themselves. They are designed to help to assure that the peace we seek is not passive, but a curative and creative force which enables men and nations better to realize those individual and national aspirations which conform to moral law.

The United States approaches hopefully, even though guardedly, a study of measures to eliminate barriers to free communications and peaceful trade. We know that, in an atmosphere of tension, communications are not readily made free, nor trade made normal. But we must break at some point a vicious circle in which lack of freedom in communications and the absence of normal trade relations and personal contacts lead to further misunderstanding between peoples and increased tension.

We have already begun discussion of one of the fundamental causes of international tension, the division of Germany, and we shall go on to discuss the world's vast arma-

[51] *Ibid.*, pp. 240-245.

ments. However, as agreed between the Four Ministers at New York, we are willing, simultaneously with our own consideration of European Security and Germany, and Disarmament, to proceed through a committee of experts with a study of the elimination of barriers to free communications and trade and the establishment of freer contacts.

Upon conclusion of their study, these experts should, I assume, report back to the Four Ministers, so that we may consider the results of their study, both upon the individual topics and in the aggregate, and so that we may be in a position likewise to coordinate our observations, proposals and conclusions under item III of our agenda with the results of our work on the other items.

In this matter of "contacts" the United States Delegation will ask that specific measures be considered with the faith and optimism that were brought here last July by the President of the United States. When I saw President Eisenhower in Denver, just before leaving for Geneva, he re-affirmed his high hopes for progress at this conference, not only with respect to the reunification of Germany within the framework of European security and disarmament, but also in the development of contacts between our peoples.

Contacts between peoples is not a new thing for the United States. It is part of our heritage. Our nation itself is composed of people from every land who have brought with them new ideas and have made valuable contributions enriching our society.

We are naturally a friendly people who like to know and be known. We have long wanted to learn more about the Soviet Union and its peoples and we have hoped that they would come to know us, and what we say and think and do. There is a solid basis for good will between us. It is a fact of history which should be remembered now that our peoples have never fought each other.

So we did not understand it when the rulers of the Soviet Union sought to seal off their people from outside contacts. But when this happened and strains developed, the United States, in its turn, placed restrictions on exchanges with the USSR. But these restrictions were solely in response to the actions initiated by the Soviet Government in this period.

Recently, we have noted that the attitude of the Soviet Government may be changing. We welcome this development. It provides a basis of hope for accomplishment in this item of our agenda.

II

The subject of contacts can be divided into three parts: (1) freedom for exchanges of information and ideas; (2) freedom for exchanges of persons and travel; (3) development of trade between East and West.

Information

In the field of exchanges of information, we immediately encounter basic obstacles.

There is an all-embracing Soviet censorship of press and radio. There is systematic jamming of radio broadcasts from other countries. We hope that steps will be initiated at this conference looking to the removal of these obstacles.

In addition to the removal of obstacles, the United States will encourage specific projects in this field, such as an exchange of radio broadcasts between the United States and the Soviet Union. For example, there might, as a beginning, be a monthly exchange of commentaries on world developments as seen from Soviet and Western points of view. In the United States, radio broadcasting is not controlled by the government and our government cannot bind American broadcasting companies to any particular course of action. However, our major radio companies tell us that they are prepared to provide regular radio time in the United States for Soviet broadcasts if this is compatible with our national policy. The United States Government would welcome this, provided that reciprocal privileges are granted to the United States on the Soviet radio. Through such an exchange, the peoples of both our countries would have the benefit of free discussion, criticism and debate on outstanding issues of the day.

A concrete step promoting a mutually useful exchange of information and ideas was taken by the United States on September 9th of this year. The United States proposed to the Soviet Government that it permit the renewed circulation in the Soviet Union of an official Russian-language magazine entitled *Amerika*.[52] We are prepared to permit the comparable circulation of an official Soviet magazine in the United States.

We wish also to advance proposals for the distribution of

[52] In a Note delivered to the U.S. Embassy in Moscow on December 16, 1955 the Soviet Government gave its consent to the distribution of 50,000 copies of "an American monthly illustrated magazine in the Russian language." See *Department of State Bulletin,* v. 34 (January 2, 1956), pp. 18-19.

American films in the Soviet Union and for the establishment, on a reciprocal basis, of information centers in the respective capitals.

Travel

In the field of exchanges of persons and travel, another basic obstacle is immediately encountered. The arbitrary rate of exchange of the ruble makes all travel in the Soviet Union excessively expensive for foreigners. The ruble rate also has an adverse effect on many aspects of the exchange of information and the development of trade. It is important that steps should be taken to eliminate this obstacle.

The United States has played an active role in recent months in effecting exchanges of persons with the Soviet Union. A group of Soviet agriculturalists toured the United States and a group of American farmers visited the Soviet Union. Groups of Soviet construction experts and newspapermen are now travelling widely throughout our country. Two outstanding Soviet musical artists have been invited to make concert tours in the United States, one of which has already begun. These visitors will bear witness to the wide range of facilities and opportunities which they enjoy in the United States in line with the purposes of their visits.

We shall continue to consider such proposals favorably to the extent to which they accrue to the mutual advantage of both countries and contribute to and reflect a spirit of real cooperation.

It is to be hoped that, in general, visits between the United States and the Soviet Union will gradually become more normal occurrences in the future. Americans are fond of travel and many people from other countries visit us each year. In 1954 almost one million Americans went abroad. Four hundred and fifty thousand foreign travelers entered the United States.

In the general area of travel, the United States has specific proposals to advance. Among them is a proposal for an agreement in principle on reciprocal civil aviation rights, which Great Britain and France as well as the United States desire to support. If accepted, this would mean insofar as the United States is concerned that Soviet commercial airplanes, for example, might land at Idlewild, the international airport near New York, and United States airplanes might similarly land at the airport serving Moscow. We also hope that the controls which now are imposed on the movements of foreigners in the Soviet Union will be reduced. The United States is prepared to reduce, on a basis of reciprocity, the controls which we imposed on Soviet citizens as a result of the restrictions in the USSR.

Due to the lack of adequate protection afforded to American citizens in the Soviet bloc countries, the United States Government imposed passport restrictions in 1952 on the travel of Americans to the countries of Eastern Europe. These are being removed today. Hereafter, American passports will be valid for the Soviet Union and all the countries of Eastern Europe with which the United States maintains relations.

Trade

The third aspect of contacts relates to *peaceful* trade. So far as *strategic* trade is concerned, I support fully the observations which Mr. Macmillan and M. Pinay have already made.[53] Strategic trade is a matter of *security* concern and is clearly outside the purview of Item III of the Directive, which speaks of "peaceful trade." The restrictions which govern strategic trade are a consequence, not a cause, of tensions, and involve only a very narrow portion of the wide area of potential trade.

To a trading nation such as the United States, peaceful foreign trade is most important. However, it is conducted by the United States primarily as a matter of individual enterprise in response to commercial motivation.

United States exporters and importers buy and sell a tremendous range of diverse things. Judging from our limited knowledge of the present conditions of life within the Soviet bloc, there would seem to be a great number of United States materials and products, as well as those of other Western countries, which could fill immediate needs.

The state of trade, however, stands in marked contrast to this appraisal. Although the Western countries continue to offer Eastern Europe ready access to an enormous area of potential trade, the level of trade between them is still low as compared with pre-war years and is only a very small proportion of total world trade and of the trade of most Western countries.

Plainly the reason for the continued low level of East-West trade has been an unwillingness or lack of interest on the part of the Soviet Union. While talking generalities about

[53] Not printed.

trade, the Soviet Government has continued to confine its international trade even in the case of peaceful goods, within strict controls and the rigidities of bilateral, barter trade, arrangements. It has pursued a policy of economic nationalism and regionalism which ignores the benefits of free exchanges. In contrast, the Western nations have sought to widen the multilateral base of their trade and to increase the extent to which each of them shares in the international division of labor. Trade in peaceful goods between the members of the non-Communist world has risen to an unprecedented level. The same opportunities have been and are now offered by the Western nations to the Soviet bloc countries.

The general question of Soviet interest in peaceful international trade can only be answered in specific terms. Is the Soviet Union now prepared to expand its exports sufficiently to make possible a much higher level of trade with the West? If so, what goods will be available? If the USSR believes that serious obstacles to peaceful trade exist on the Western side, we want to know what they are.

Before coming here to Geneva, I consulted with the heads of the appropriate departments of my Government and arranged for progressively simplifying certain of our operating procedures concerning exports to the Soviet bloc countries, so that the pathway to commercial enterprise might become smoother.

These measures can facilitate trade, but they cannot produce trade where commercial incentive is lacking or where Western interest in trade is not reciprocated in Eastern Europe. The discussions here, it is hoped, will disclose the specific steps which can be taken to increase the peaceful trade between the West and Eastern Europe. We shall await with sympathetic interest the suggestions which the representatives of the Soviet Union may make upon this subject.

We agreed at New York that detailed discussion at Geneva of East-West contacts would be left to our experts. As the United States expert, I have appointed Mr. William H. Jackson. He is serving not merely at my request but at the personal request of President Eisenhower.

I hope that the experts may begin their important task without delay. I would suggest that they make a careful study of specific projects in the field of improved contacts and prepare recommendations concerning their implementation, including procedures which could be developed through the organs and agencies of the United Nations.

We shall eagerly await the results of the experts' work, which contains so much of hope and promise for a better and more peaceful world.

c. *Tripartite Proposal, Submitted by the French Delegation, October 31, 1955.*[54]

The Foreign Ministers of Great Britain, France, and the United States, mindful of the Directive issued at Geneva by the Heads of Government, express their desire to explore, together with the Foreign Minister of the Soviet Union, measures designed to bring about a progressive elimination of barriers which interfere with free communications and with peaceful trade between peoples and to bring about such freer contacts and exchanges as are to the mutual advantage of the countries and peoples concerned.

The three Ministers wish to point out that their Governments have consistently favored free communication of information and ideas, free exchange of persons, and the development of peaceful trade, as constructive means of promoting an atmosphere of confidence among states and a better understanding among peoples. Their Governments have always sought to foster free expression of thought, to promote the free development of individual conscience, and to encourage, through a free competition of ideas, the development of objective opinion. The three Western Governments are confident that a constructive development of contacts with the Soviet Union together with the progressive resolution of those substantive issues which constitute the true causes of international tension, can contribute to the establishment of the durable peace desired by all mankind.

It is the view of the Western Powers that the four Governments must contribute actively to the establishment of a better understanding between the peoples of the West and the peoples of Eastern Europe. It is hoped that future contacts will expand in such a way as to correspond to the natural desire of men to understand each other and to search for that which unites them. For their own part the three Foreign Ministers are convinced that this work of mutual understanding, which must eventually lead to peaceful changes enlarging the area of those freedoms which mankind holds dear, will receive the moral approbation of the peoples of Eastern Europe as well as the peoples of the West.

[54] *The Geneva Meeting of Foreign Ministers, etc.*, pp. 245-248.

Accordingly the Western Powers consider that it is essential, in agreement with the Soviet Union, to determine forthwith the areas in which it appears most appropriate to proceed with exchanges that are to the mutual advantage of the peoples of Eastern Europe and the West.

It is with this intention that the three Western Governments submit a program of action. Cognizant of the fact that the evolution of free societies has produced individual traditions and processes, it is understood that arrangements made by the Three Western countries aimed at the implementation of this program would be in accord with their national traditions and procedures. The program of the Western Governments comprehends the following concrete propositions.

1. Freer exchange of information and ideas should be facilitated. All censorship should be progressively eliminated. The obstacles which hamper the flow of full factual information and varied comment between the peoples of the West and those of the Soviet Union, should be removed.

2. Arrangements should be made for the four Powers to open information centers, on a basis of reciprocity, in each other's capitals where these do not already exist. Everyone should be allowed full use of these centers without hindrance or discouragement from their own government.

3. The four Powers, where they do not already do so should permit the publication and facilitate the distribution to public institutions and private individuals in each other's countries of official periodicals printed in English, French or Russian.

4. Exchanges of books, periodicals and newspapers between the principal libraries, universities and professional and scientific bodies in the Soviet Union and the three Western countries should be encouraged. Such books, periodicals and newspapers should also be available for general and unimpeded public sale in the Soviet Union on the one hand and the three Western countries on the other.

5. There should be a substantial increase in the exchange of government publications and full lists, catalogs and indexes of such publications should be made available by Governments where they do not already do so.

6. The film producers of the three Western countries are ready to make films available to the Soviet Union at normal commercial prices and on normal commercial terms. Soviet films are already accepted in the West on these terms.

7. There should be exchanges of exhibitions between the Soviet Union and the three Western countries.

8. The systematic jamming of broadcasts of news and information is a practice to be deplored. It is incompatible with the Directive from the Four Heads of Government and should be discontinued.

9. The Soviet Union and the Western Powers should consider the desirability of exchanging monthly uncensored broadcasts on world developments. This could take the form of half hours for the Soviet Union on the Western broadcasting systems with reciprocal arrangements for the Western Powers on the Soviet system.

10. The censorship of outgoing press despatches and the denial to journalists of access to normal sources of information are serious barriers to the free circulation of ideas. The four Governments, where appropriate should take immediate steps to remove such barriers.

11. Private tourism should be increased. This will require more liberal procedures as regards travel restrictions and other administrative practices. Above all it will require reasonable rates of currency exchange.

12. There should be further exchanges of persons in the professional, cultural, scientific and technical fields. Exchanges should be arranged on the basis of principles approved by the governments concerned.

13. Meetings of outstanding scientists and scholars of the four countries at reputable international congresses should be facilitated.

14. There should be cultural and sporting exchanges on a reciprocal basis, drawing on the best each has to offer under the auspices of the principal cultural institutions and sporting organizations on both sides.

15. A beginning should be made with exchanges of students[,] particularly those engaged in language and other area studies. It should be possible for the students to share fully and freely the student life of the country they visit.

16. Restrictions on the ability of the members of the diplomatic missions of the four governments to travel in each other's countries should be removed on a basis of reciprocity.

17. Agreement should be reached in principle for reciprocal exchanges of direct air transport services between cities of the Soviet Union and cities of the three Western countries.

So far as trade is concerned, the Western Powers sincerely desire to see an improvement in commercial relations between the countries of Eastern Europe and themselves, leading to an increase in mutual trade in peaceful goods. To this end they have made freely available to the countries of

Eastern Europe a wide area of trade with respect both to exports and imports. That only small advantage has so far been taken of these opportunities is, in their view, basically a reflection of policies and conditions within the countries of Eastern Europe. While they feel, therefore, that the major initiative in securing an increase in East-West trade must be taken by the countries of Eastern Europe, they are, for their part, prepared to consider sympathetically any proposals which seem likely to lend [*lead?*] to a mutually beneficial development of peaceful trade.

In particular the Western Powers would urge the Soviet Government to make it less difficult for Western private traders to engage in and to develop opportunities for East-West trade to the advantage of both sides.

If the Four Powers can agree on the above propositions a great step forward will have been made towards better understanding between nations. This might in due course serve as the foundation for a further expansion of contacts on a broader international basis.

d. *French Proposal of a Draft Four-Power Declaration, November 14, 1955.*[55]

In conformity with the Directive of the Heads of Governments of the U.S.A., the French Republic, the United Kingdom and the U.S.S.R., the Foreign Ministers of the Four Powers instructed their experts to "study measures, including those possible in organs and agencies of the United Nations, which could:—

(a) bring about a progressive elimination of barriers which interfere with free communications and peaceful trade between peoples,

and

(b) bring about such freer contacts and exchanges as are to the mutual advantage of the countries and peoples concerned."

A. Mindful of the Directive and conscious of the importance of the problems which were entrusted for study to the Committee of Experts, the Foreign Ministers of the Four Powers have agreed to propose to their respective Governments:—

[55] *Ibid.*, pp. 266-267.

—to create conditions favorable to greater exchanges of peaceful goods so that traders and trading organisations could respond more fully to the economic incentives inherent in existing opportunities for such exchanges.

—to eliminate gradually the barriers to the free communication of ideas and information, in particular those in the fields of publication, press and radio broadcasting.

—to endeavour to put an end to the difficulties which hamper the free movement of persons (restrictions on the freedom of movement of individuals, artificial exchange rates).

B. In expectation that measures will be taken to eliminate these various obstacles, the Foreign Ministers of the Four Powers believe that it would be desirable to facilitate and increase East-West contacts in the following fields:—

(a) cultural exchanges, in particular;
exchanges of films and exhibitions;
exchanges of books, periodicals and newspapers;
exchanges of official publications;
broadcasting exchanges.

(b) scientific and technical exchanges;
participation of outstanding scholars in international congresses.

(c) exchanges of students.

(d) sporting exchanges.

(e) development of tourism, both on a collective and an individual basis.

Having agreed in principle to the increase of East-West contacts in these various fields, the Government of the U.S.S.R. and each of the three Western Governments shall in each individual case settle the details of these exchanges by bilateral agreement. These exchanges should take place to the mutual advantage of the different countries in as objective and efficient way as possible. They will take place under the auspices of the most representative organisations.

C. The Ministers of Foreign Affairs of the Four Powers recommend that each of the interested governments should take into consideration certain concrete measures likely to facilitate future contacts between the Soviet Union and the three Western countries:

—The opening of Reading Rooms in their respective capitals;

—Unrestricted distribution of official magazines published by their respective Embassies in the language of the country concerned;
—Suppression, on a basis of reciprocity, of restrictions on diplomatic missions;
—Grant of facilities to journalists for access to normal sources of information with freedom from censorship;
—Protection of copyright;
—Protection of industrial property (including patents);
—Grant of reciprocal facilities for commercial representatives to visit or reside in their countries;
—More generous publication of statistics and trade data;
—More equitable arrangements for the insurance of freight;
—Early establishment of direct air links between the Soviet Union and Western countries.

D. In accordance with the Directive of the Four Heads of Government, the Foreign Ministers of the Four Powers declare that it would be desirable to take account of the contribution which could be made by the organs and agencies of the United Nations in putting into effect the measures envisaged by the present conference.

e. *Soviet Proposal of a Draft Four-Power Declaration, November 15, 1955.*[56]

Guided by the interests of strengthening peace, the creation of an atmosphere of confidence and the development of cooperation between peoples, the Foreign Ministers, in accordance with the directives of the Heads of Government of the USSR, the USA, the United Kingdom, and the French Republic have studied the "measures, including those possible in organs and agencies of the United Nations, which could (a) bring about a progressive elimination of barriers which interfere with free communications and peaceful trade between people and (b) bring about such freer contacts and exchanges as are to the mutual advantage of the countries and peoples concerned."

A. Proceeding from the directive, and, fully cognizant of the importance of the problems the study of which was entrusted to the Committee of Experts, the Foreign Ministers of the Four Powers have agreed to propose to their respective Governments:

[56] *Ibid.*, pp. 269-270.

To create conditions favorable to the development of world trade and, with these objectives in view, to adopt measures directed toward the removal of existing barriers and restrictions in the realm of trade between East and West in such a way that businessmen and commercial organizations could, on a wider scale, take advantage of the opportunities offered to them for exchanges between East and West.

To do all that lies within their power to adopt measures for assisting the free passage of merchant vessels of all countries through straits and canals of international importance and for the removal of restrictions now existing in sea communications with certain states.

To assist in the exchange of books, newspapers, scientific journals, documentary and other films, and also radio broadcasts, in accordance with agreements which may be of a bilateral or a multilateral nature.

B. The Foreign Ministers of the Four Powers assume that it is desirable to facilitate and extend relations between East and West in the following fields:

a) Cultural intercourse, particularly in the publishing business, and the exchange of cultural delegations, exhibitions, etc.

b) Scientific and technical exchanges; the participation of scholars in international congresses.

c) Visits of promoters of industry, agriculture, and commerce.

d) Exchanges between trade-union, scientific, technical, and artistic organizations.

e) The exchange of professors and students and lecturers.

f) The exchange of athletes and athletic teams.

g) The development of tourism, both on a collective as well as an individual basis.

For purposes of further developing existing contacts, the Four Governments can, if necessary, determine the methods of these exchanges. The exchanges should take place to the mutual advantage of the countries signatory to the arrangement and on an objective and practical basis.

C. The Foreign Ministers of the Four Powers consider that there are a number of concrete questions relating to the development of contacts between East and West which should be examined forthwith by the countries concerned, taking into account their respective interests and legal regulations.

D. In accordance with the directive of the Heads of Government, the Foreign Ministers of the Four Powers declare that when applying measures provided for by the present Meeting it would be desirable to take into account the contribution which the organs and institutions of the United Nations could offer, in accordance with the principles of the Charter of the UN.

The four Ministers recommend participation in the specialized international organizations (ILO, UNESCO, WHO, ITU, and others) for all states desirous of cooperating in these organizations.

f. *Statement by the Secretary of State (Dulles), November 15, 1955.*[57]

Mr. Chairman:

Yesterday, the French Delegation submitted a proposal which, after study, the United States was ready to accept had it been accepted by the Soviet Delegation.[58] Apparently, however, that French proposal is now rejected by the Soviet Delegation. The Soviet Delegation has now submitted a proposed draft statement by the Four Powers, which I have studied during the brief recess we have had.[59] I regret to be forced to the conclusion that this present Soviet proposal does not adequately meet the Directive under which we are acting, primarily in that it contains nothing, or practically nothing, designed to permit of an exchange of ideas and of information.

It will be recalled that President Eisenhower in his statement here on July 22 on this topic put first of all the importance, as he put it—and I quote: "First to lower the barriers which now impede the interchange of information and ideas between peoples." [60] The Soviet proposal does not seem to make any effort at all to meet the views of the Western powers with respect to the importance of free communication in the realm of information and ideas.

In view of the rejection by the Soviet Union of the French proposal, I have compared the present Soviet proposal with that which the three Western powers introduced on October 31st through the medium of the French Delegation:[61]

Item 1 of that proposal contemplated a freer exchange of

[57] *Ibid.*, pp. 270-272.
[58] See above, pp. 282-284.
[59] See above, pp. 284-286.
[60] See above, p. 222.
[61] See above, pp. 279-282.

information and ideas and a progressive elimination of censorship. That is rejected.

Item 2 proposed to have information centers on a basis of reciprocity which the people could freely use. That is rejected.

Item 3 proposed to permit the publication and facilitate the distribution of official periodicals. That is rejected.

Item 4 dealt with exchange of books. It is accepted insofar as it relates to the exchange. But the vital part, which dealt with making these books available for public sale, is rejected.

Item 5, with reference to the exchange of government publications and full lists, catalogues, and indices, also seems to be rejected.

Item 6, dealing with exchange of films at normal commercial prices and on normal terms, seems to be rejected subject to the possibility that there might hereafter be an agreement on this topic.

Item 8, dealing with the reduction of jamming of news and information broadcasts, is rejected.

Item 9, with reference to exchanging uncensored broadcasts, appears also to be rejected, although it is suggested that there might hereafter be an agreement covering broadcast exchanges.

Item 10, dealing with the elimination of the censorship of outgoing press dispatches and access by journalists to normal sources of information, is rejected.

Item 11 relates to tourism. There is a reference in the Soviet paper to tourism, but the Soviet Union rejects any suggestion that there should, to facilitate this, be reasonable rates of currency exchange.

Item 16, dealing with the restriction on the travel by members of the diplomatic missions on a basis of reciprocity, also is rejected.

Item 17, dealing with reciprocal exchanges of direct air transport services[,] is rejected.

In other words, of our 17 concrete proposals only five seem to be partially accepted. I emphasize that all of those which relate to a freer exchange of ideas, news, uncensored information have been rejected. The Soviet Union seems to have picked out of our proposal only four or five suggestions which it deems to its interest, and to have rejected all the others, without any spirit of give and take, and with a complete omission of anything of substance in the realm of exchange of ideas.

I pointed out in my remarks yesterday[62] that we consider that peace is not solidly based unless the peoples of the different countries can have access to what other peoples believe and, I think, that to base peace upon the power of government to dictate what peoples shall think about each other is, in our opinion, a very dangerous condition. And because the Soviet paper would perpetuate what we deem to be a very great danger to peace and good understanding between peoples, and because it does not seem to us to comply with the Directive which guides us, we do not find it acceptable.

6. *Final Communiqués.*

a. *Quadripartite Communiqué, November 16, 1955.*[63]

In compliance with the Directive issued by the four Heads of Government after their meeting in Geneva in July, the Foreign Ministers of the French Republic, the United Kingdom, the Union of Soviet Socialist Republics and the United States of America met in Geneva from October 27 to November 16, 1955. They had a frank and comprehensive discussion of the three items entrusted to them in the Directive, namely: 1. European Security and Germany, 2. Disarmament, and 3. Development of Contacts between East and West.

The Foreign Ministers agreed to report the result of their discussions to their respective Heads of Government and to recommend that the future course of the discussions of the Foreign Ministers should be settled through diplomatic channels.

b. *Tripartite Declaration on Germany and European Security, November 16, 1955.*[64]

At Geneva, the Foreign Ministers of France, the United Kingdom and the United States of America tried to reach agreement with the Soviet Foreign Minister on what the Four Heads of Government in July agreed were the closely linked problems of German Reunification and European Security. To this end they made a proposal for the Reunification of Germany by free elections in 1956 and for a Treaty of Assurance giving the Soviet Union far-reaching safeguards against aggression when Germany was reunified.

[62] *The Geneva Meeting of Foreign Ministers, etc.,* p. 261.
[63] *Ibid.,* p. 305.
[64] *Ibid.,* pp. 305-306.

Marshal Bulganin in July had agreed that the Reunification of Germany was the common responsibility of the Four Powers and should be carried out by means of Free Elections. The Soviet Foreign Minister, however, despite the Directive of the Heads of Government, made it plain that the Soviet Government refused to agree to the Reunification of Germany since that would lead to the liquidation of the East German regime. He made counterproposals which would have involved the continued division of Germany as well as the eventual dissolution of the Western security system. It is for this reason that the negotiations have failed.

The Foreign Ministers of France, the United Kingdom and the United States of America are aware that this result must bring a sense of cruel disappointment to the German people, East and West of the zonal border which now unjustly divides them. However, the three Foreign Ministers believe that the Soviet Government will come to recognize that its own self-interest will be served by ending the injustice of a divided Germany. They believe that the Soviet Government will realize that so long as it persists in withholding unity from the German people, thus perpetuating the division of Europe, there can be no solid security in Europe, nor indeed in the world.

The three Western Powers will themselves not cease their efforts to end the injustice and wrong now being done by dividing the German people and will continue to stand ready to contribute to the security which can be enjoyed by all only when Germany is reunified.

7. *Report to the Nation: Radio-Television Address by the Secretary of State (Dulles), November 18, 1955.*[65]

(Excerpts)

For the last three weeks the British, the French and ourselves have been negotiating with the Russians at Geneva. I got back yesterday and reported fully to the President in a talk which began last evening and was resumed this morning. Now I am reporting to you, the American people.

As I expect most of you know, this Geneva meeting did not reach any agreements. As a result, many questions are in the air.

* * *

[65] *Ibid.*, pp. 1-9.

(1) Does this second Geneva Conference end the so-called "spirit of Geneva"?

The answer to that question depends upon what is meant by the "spirit of Geneva." Some felt that the spirit of Geneva was some magic elixir which would of itself solve all of the great problems of the world. Obviously, it was not that. Any such view was doomed to disillusionment.

That was never the view of the President nor myself. We constantly warned against that view. President Eisenhower, before he went to Geneva, said that that Conference would be a beginning and not an end. At Geneva he said that the value of the Conference could only be judged by what happened afterwards. And after he returned he told the American people that the acid test of the Summit Conference would begin when the Foreign Ministers met.

That testing, so far as it has gone, has shown that the Soviet leaders would like to have at least the appearance of cooperative relations with the Western nations. But it has shown that they are not yet willing to create the indispensable conditions for a secure peace. Also they have seriously set back the growth of any confidence the free world can justifiably place in Soviet promises. They did this by refusing to negotiate for the reunification of Germany, to which they had agreed in July.

However, they seem not to want to revert to the earlier reliance on threats and invective. In that respect the spirit of Geneva still survives.

(2) Has the outcome of the second Conference at Geneva increased the risk of general war?

President Eisenhower said that he believed that the Summit Conference made it less likely that there would be open war between our countries. Nothing that happened at the Foreign Ministers Conference requires a change in that estimate. So that aspect of the Geneva spirit also remains.

(3) Do the events of the last three weeks mean that the cold war will be resumed in its full vigor?

The phrase "cold war" is a loose one.

Of course, there are sharp differences between the objectives of the Soviet Government and our own. We believe in justice for all and in the right of nations to be free and the right of individuals to exercise their God-given capacity to think and to believe in accordance with the dictates of their mind and conscience. We shall not cease to pursue these objectives or ever seek a so-called peace which compromises them.

However, these great purposes which have been characteristic of our nation from its beginning can be and will be pursued by us without resort to violence or without resort to the use of hatred and perversion of truth which are characteristic of war. It is our purpose to continue to seek friendship and understanding with the Russian people as a whole and to use truth as the instrument of our national policy.

The "cold war" in the sense of peaceful competition will inevitably go on. The spirit of Geneva could not and did not change that fact. Moreover, we must assume that the Soviet Union will continue its efforts by means short of war to make its system prevail as it has done in the past. We can, however, hope that this competition will not entail all the same hostility and animosity which so defiled the relations between us in the past.

(4) Will the United States now have radically to revise its programs for defense and mutual security?

The answer to this is "no." We have not lowered our guard on the basis of Soviet promises and did not do so because of the Summit Conference. Our security programs, which are bi-partisan in character, are designed to meet the peril as long as it may continue. We are on what we call a long haul basis. Our military strength must be based on the capability of the Soviet bloc and cannot vary with their smiles or frowns. We will reduce our own military strength only as the Soviets demonstrably reduce their own. Hence the outcome of the Geneva Conference does not require us to alter the general scope of our programs. Their general order of magnitude can remain as planned.

Our steady policies have proved their worth. We believe in holding fast and reinforcing that which has proved good.

(5) Does this last Geneva Conference mean an end to future negotiation with the Soviet Union?

It need not be an end and neither the President nor I believe that it will be an end. It would of course be foolish to attempt new negotiations if everything remains as it was when this last Conference came to an end.

We know, however, that conditions will change because change is the law of life.

At this Geneva Conference the Soviet Union had to face up concretely to the cost of achieving the larger results which it says it wants in terms of European security, disarmament, and increased contacts between East and West.

On this occasion no positive results were achieved. But I recall that President Eisenhower, after returning from Geneva, said that he was "profoundly impressed with the need for all of us to avoid discouragement merely because our own proposals, our own approaches, and our own beliefs are not always immediately accepted by the other side." And he pointed to the difficulty of bridging the wide and deep gulf between individual liberty and regimentation and between the concept of man made in the image of God, and the concept of man as the mere instrument of the State.

That gulf has created obstacles so great that they could not be overcome at this recent Geneva Conference.

That does not mean that our efforts at that Conference were wasted. The proposals we advanced were basically sound and respected the legitimate interest of all. When solutions come, they will have to take into account the principles which we sought to apply.

The Soviets pride themselves on being realists. They have shown in the past that they will adapt their policies to facts and realities once they recognize them. We believe that the free nations, by maintaining and strengthening their unity, can make it apparent to the Soviet Union that solutions such as we proposed are in its real interest and will benefit them more than the local and temporary advantages to which they now seem to attach overriding importance.

Of course the Soviets will not change their policies if they believe that the free world is going to fall apart. That is why continuation of the present partnership of the independent nations is indispensable to a peaceful solution of present problems.

It is vital that all free nations, including ourselves, clearly understand this basic truth.

I am happy to be able to make a good report about this partnership.

In Paris, before the Geneva Conference, we had a useful session of the NATO Council.[66] It was attended by virtually all of the Foreign Ministers of the 15 member countries. It served further to cement the unity represented by the Council.

While in Europe I also consulted with leaders of the movement to develop still further the unity of Europe. This move-

[66] Not printed.

ment is again becoming vigorous. In my talks, I made clear that the initiative for further steps toward European integration must come from the Europeans themselves but that the United States stands ready and eager to help to realize this great idea.

I went to Spain, Italy and Yugoslavia.[67] In each place I had a full and helpful discussion of the international scene. The result was, I think, to create better understanding and firmer ties of friendship.

Finally, a most important fact is that at the Geneva Conference there were the closest personal and working relations between the British Foreign Minister, Mr. Macmillan[,] and the French Foreign Minister, Mr. Pinay, and myself. We also worked closely with the representatives of the Federal Republic of Germany in matters that concerned it.

This spirit of fellowship, which fortified our common effort in a common cause, is one of the important products of the Geneva Conference.

The statement which I make to you tonight follows extended conference with President Eisenhower. He authorizes me to say that he fully shares the evaluation which I have made of the Geneva Conference and of its impact upon our national policies. That evaluation stems from the President's ruling and life purpose for a fair, just and durable peace for the world, a purpose which I share and which, with him, I strive to implement.

And now, in closing, let me read from my verbatim notes of our conference at Gettysburg this morning. As I was leaving, the President turned to me and said:

"I know that no setback, no obstacle to progress will ever deter this government and our people from the great effort to establish a just and durable peace. Success may be long in coming, but there is no temporal force so capable of helping achieve it as the strength, the might, the spirit of 165 million free Americans. In striving toward this shining goal, this country will never admit defeat."

[67] See above, pp. 165-166.

CHAPTER FOUR

THE FAR EAST AND SOUTHEAST ASIA

A. The Formosa Crisis.

1. *Message from the President to Congress on the Defense of Formosa, January 24, 1955.*[1]

To the Congress of the United States:

The most important objective of our Nation's foreign policy is to safeguard the security of the United States by establishing and preserving a just and honorable peace. In the Western Pacific a situation is developing in the Formosa Straits that seriously imperils the peace and our security.

Since the end of Japanese hostilities in 1945, Formosa and the Pescadores have been in the friendly hands of our loyal ally, the Republic of China. We have recognized that it was important that these islands should remain in friendly hands. In unfriendly hands, Formosa and the Pescadores would seriously dislocate the existing, even if unstable, balance of moral, economic, and military forces upon which the peace of the Pacific depends. It would create a breach in the island chain of the Western Pacific that constitutes, for the United States and other free nations, the geographical backbone of their security structure in that ocean. In addition, this breach would interrupt north-south communications between other important elements of that barrier, and damage the economic life of countries friendly to us.

The United States and the friendly Government of the Republic of China, and indeed all the free nations, have a common interest that Formosa and the Pescadores should not fall into the control of aggressive Communist forces.

Influenced by such considerations, our Government was prompt, when the Communists committed armed aggression in Korea in June 1950, to direct our Seventh Fleet to defend Formosa from possible invasion from the Communist mainland.[2]

These considerations are still valid. The Seventh Fleet continues under Presidential directive to carry out that de-

[1] House Document 76, 84th Cong., 1st Sess., transmitted January 24, 1955.
[2] *Documents on American Foreign Relations, 1950,* pp. 444-445.

fensive mission. We also provide military and economic support to the Chinese Nationalist Government and we cooperate in every proper and feasible way with that Government in order to promote its security and stability. All of these military and related activities will be continued.

In addition, there was signed last December a Mutual Defense Treaty between this Government and the Republic of China, covering Formosa and the neighboring Pescadores. It is a treaty of purely defensive character. That treaty is now before the Senate of the United States.[3]

Meanwhile Communist China has pursued a series of provocative political and military actions, establishing a pattern of aggressive purpose. That purpose, they proclaim, is the conquest of Formosa.

In September 1954 the Chinese Communists opened up heavy artillery fire upon Quemoy Island, one of the natural approaches to Formosa, which had for several years been under the uncontested control of the Republic of China. Then came air attacks of mounting intensity against other free China islands, notably those in the vicinity of the Tachen group to the north of Formosa. One small island (Ichiang) was seized last week by air and amphibious operations after a gallant few fought bravely for days against overwhelming odds. There have been recent heavy air attacks and artillery fire against the main Tachen Islands themselves.[4]

The Chinese Communists themselves assert that these attacks are a prelude to the conquest of Formosa. For example, after the fall of Ichiang, the Peiping radio said that it showed a—"determined will to fight for the liberation of Taiwan [Formosa]. Our people will use all their strength to fulfill that task."

Clearly, this existing and developing situation poses a serious danger to the security of our country and of the entire Pacific area and indeed to the peace of the world. We believe that the situation is one for appropriate action of the United Nations under its charter, for the purpose of ending the present hostilities in that area. We would welcome assumption of such jurisdiction by that body.

Meanwhile, the situation has become sufficiently critical to impel me, without awaiting action by the United Nations, to

[3] *Ibid., 1954,* pp. 360-364.

[4] The evacuation of the Tachen Islands with the assistance of U.S. Naval and Air forces was completed on February 11, 1955. See Department of State Press Release 82, dated February 11, 1955.

ask the Congress to participate now, by specific resolution, in measures designed to improve the prospects for peace. These measures would contemplate the use of the Armed Forces of the United States if necessary to assure the security of Formosa and the Pescadores.

The actions that the United States must be ready to undertake are of various kinds. For example, we must be ready to assist the Republic of China to redeploy and consolidate its forces if it should so desire. Some of these forces are scattered throughout the smaller offshore islands as a result of historical rather than military reasons directly related to defending Formosa. Because of the air situation in the area, withdrawals for the purpose of redeployment of Chinese Nationalist forces would be impractical without assistance of the Armed Forces of the United States.

Moreover, we must be alert to any concentration or employment of Chinese Communist forces obviously undertaken to facilitate attack upon Formosa, and be prepared to take appropriate military action.

I do not suggest that the United States enlarge its defensive obligations beyond Formosa and the Pescadores as provided by the treaty now awaiting ratification. But, unhappily, the danger of armed attack directed against that area compels us to take into account closely related localities and actions which, under current conditions, might determine the failure or the success of such an attack. The authority that may be accorded by the Congress would be used only in situations which are recognizable as parts of, or definite preliminaries to, an attack against the main positions of Formosa and the Pescadores.

Authority for some of the actions which might be required would be inherent in the authority of the Commander in Chief. Until Congress can act I would not hesitate, so far as my constitutional powers extend, to take whatever emergency action might be forced upon us in order to protect the rights and security of the United States.

However, a suitable congressional resolution would clearly and publicly establish the authority of the President as Commander in Chief to employ the Armed Forces of this Nation promptly and effectively for the purposes indicated if in his judgment it became necessary. It would make clear the unified and serious intentions of our Government, our Congress, and our people. Thus it will reduce the possibility that the Chinese Communists, misjudging our firm purpose and national unity, might be disposed to challenge the position of the United States, and precipitate a major crisis which even they would neither anticipate nor desire.

In the interest of peace, therefore, the United States must remove any doubt regarding our readiness to fight, if necessary, to preserve the vital stake of the free world in a free Formosa, and to engage in whatever operations may be required to carry out that purpose.

To make this plain requires not only Presidential action but also congressional action. In a situation such as now confronts us, and under modern conditions of warfare, it would not be prudent to await the emergency before coming to the Congress. Then it might be too late. Already the warning signals are flying.

I believe that the threatening aspects of the present situation, if resolutely faced, may be temporary in character. Consequently, I recommend that the resolution expire as soon as the President is able to report to the Congress that the peace and security of the area are reasonably assured by international conditions, resulting from United Nations action or otherwise.

Again I say that we would welcome action by the United Nations which might, in fact, bring an end to the active hostilities in the area. This critical situation has been created by the choice of the Chinese Communists, not by us. Their offensive military intent has been flaunted to the whole world by words and by deeds. Just as they created the situation, so they can end it if they so choose.

What we are now seeking is primarily to clarify present policy and to unite in its application. We are not establishing a new policy. Consequently, my recommendations do not call for an increase in the Armed Forces of the United States or any acceleration in military procurement or levels of defense production. If any unforeseen emergency arises requiring any change, I will communicate with the Congress. I hope, however, that the effect of an appropriate congressional resolution will be to calm the situation rather than to create further conflict.

One final point: The action I request is, of course, no substitute for the treaty with the Republic of China which we have signed and which I have transmitted to the Senate. Indeed, present circumstances make it more than ever important that this basic agreement should be promptly brought into force, as a solemn evidence of our determination to stand fast in the agreed treaty area and to thwart all attacks directed against it. If delay should make us appear indecisive in this basic respect, the pressures and dangers would surely mount.

Our purpose is peace. That cause will be served if, with your help, we demonstrate our unity and our determination. In all that we do we shall remain faithful to our obligations as a member of the United Nations to be ready to settle our international disputes by peaceful means in such a manner that international peace and security, and justice, are not endangered.

For the reasons outlined in this message, I respectfully request that the Congress take appropriate action to carry out the recommendations contained herein.

DWIGHT D. EISENHOWER.

THE WHITE HOUSE, *January 24, 1955.*

2. *Joint [Congressional] Resolution on the Defense of Formosa, Adopted by the House of Representatives, January 25, 1955 and the Senate, January 28, 1955.*[5]

Whereas the primary purpose of the United States, in its relations with all other nations, is to develop and sustain a just and enduring peace for all; and

Whereas certain territories in the West Pacific under the jurisdiction of the Republic of China are now under armed attack, and threats and declarations have been and are being made by the Chinese Communists that such armed attack is in aid of and in preparation for armed attack on Formosa and the Pescadores,

Whereas such armed attack if continued would gravely endanger the peace and security of the West Pacific Area and particularly of Formosa and the Pescadores; and

Whereas the secure possession by friendly governments of the Western Pacific Island chain, of which Formosa is a part, is essential to the vital interests of the United States and all friendly nations in or bordering upon the Pacific Ocean; and

Whereas the President of the United States on January 6, 1955, submitted to the Senate for its advice and consent to ratification a Mutual Defense Treaty between the United States of America and the Republic of China, which recognizes that an armed attack in the West Pacific area directed

[5] Public Law 4, 84th Cong., 1st Sess. (January 29, 1955). The vote in the House was 409-3, in the Senate 85-3.

against territories, therein described, in the region of Formosa and the Pescadores, would be dangerous to the peace and safety of the parties to the treaty:[6] Therefore be it

Resolved by the Senate and House of Representatives of the United States of America in Congress assembled, That the President of the United States be and he hereby is authorized to employ the Armed Forces of the United States as he deems necessary for the specific purpose of securing and protecting Formosa and the Pescadores against armed attack, this authority to include the securing and protection of such related positions and territories of that area now in friendly hands and the taking of such other measures as he judges to be required or appropriate in assuring the defense of Formosa and the Pescadores.

This resolution shall expire when the President shall determine that the peace and security of the area is reasonably assured by international conditions created by action of the United Nations or otherwise, and shall so report to the Congress.

3. *Mutual Defense Treaty with the Republic of China: Statement by the Secretary of State (Dulles) before the Senate Foreign Relations Committee, February 7, 1955.*[7]

A mutual defense treaty has been signed by the Republic of China and the United States and is now before the Senate for its advice and consent to ratification.

Before discussing the text of the treaty, let me outline the basic considerations which underlie it

The United States has been developing a pattern of mutual security with other friendly and free nations of the Western Pacific. In 1952 security treaties were concluded with the Philippines, with Australia and New Zealand, and with Japan.[8] In 1953 a security treaty was signed with the Republic of Korea,[9] and in 1954 the Manila Pact was signed.[10]

The considerations which impelled the making of these treaties equally impelled the making of a security treaty with the Republic of China. The territory it occupies comprises an important link in the so-called "island chain" that bounds the

[6] *Department of State Bulletin,* v. 32 (January 24, 1955), p. 150.
[7] *Ibid.* (February 21, 1955), pp. 287-290.
[8] *Documents on American Foreign Relations, 1951,* pp. 262-267. The treaties were signed in 1951 and entered into force in 1952.
[9] *Ibid., 1953,* pp. 312-313.
[10] *Ibid., 1954,* pp. 319-323.

western rim of the Pacific. Also the Government of that Republic is strongly anti-Communist and an ally of proved loyalty.

Under these circumstances the omission of the Republic of China began to take on significance. It was suggested that the reason for this omission was that the United States desired to keep open the possibility of trading Taiwan [Formosa] and the Pescadores to Communist China as part of a general settlement in the area.

Such ignoble suggestions were damaging to the morale and prestige of the Republic of China and they reflected on the integrity and honor of the United States itself.

The appearance of discrimination against the Republic of China could not be continued without prejudice to moral and political standards that we need to maintain.

The Republic of China had proposed a security treaty in December of 1953. I then felt that a treaty was in principle desirable but that careful study would be required because of the existence of special factors. These primarily grew out of the fact that hostilities continued between the Republic of China and the Chinese Communist regime, which has *de facto* control of the Chinese mainland.

Such studies took place, and there were exchanges of views through diplomatic channels. In September 1954 I visited Taiwan [Formosa], following the Manila Pact conference, and talked with President Chiang Kai-shek about the treaty and the special problems involved.

Following my return to the United States, it was decided to proceed actively and, to this end, in October 1954, I asked Walter S. Robertson, Assistant Secretary of State for Far Eastern Affairs, to go to Taiwan [Formosa] for further consultation with the Chinese authorities. Subsequent negotiations were conducted at Washington, principally with His Excellency Yeh Kung-ch'ao, Chinese Minister for Foreign Affairs. The Foreign Minister and I initialed the treaty on November 23, 1954, and signed it here in Washington on December 2, 1954.[11]

In these matters, there has been close cooperation on a bipartisan basis with the Foreign Relations Committee and particularly the present chairman, the former chairman, and the members of the Far Eastern Subcommittee. This cooperation has related not merely to the matters of principle involved but also to the terms of the treaty itself.

[11] *Ibid.*, pp. 360-362.

I should like now to describe those terms.

The treaty consists of a preamble and 10 substantive articles. The preamble is substantially similar to that of our treaty with the Philippines and other treaties in the Pacific area.

Article I is substantially identical with the first article of the Philippine and ANZUS pacts. It says that the parties will settle their international disputes by peaceful means and in accordance with their obligations under the Charter of the United Nations, and that they will refrain in their international relations from the threat or use of force in any way inconsistent with the purposes of the United Nations.

Article II incorporates in the treaty the principle of the Vandenberg resolution [S. Res. 239, 80th Cong.].[12] The parties pledge themselves, by self-help and mutual aid, to maintain and develop their capacity to resist armed attack. The increasing need for capacity to resist internal subversion as well as external attack, which was reflected in the Manila Pact, is also reflected in this article II of the China treaty. It speaks of "communist subversive activities directed from without against their territorial integrity and political stability."

Article III is similar to the corresponding article of the Southeast Asia Collective Defense Treaty in pledging the parties to strengthen their free institutions and cooperate to promote economic progress and social well-being.

Consultation regarding implementation of the treaty is provided for under article IV.

Article V, substantially identical with article IV of the Philippine treaty and article IV of the ANZUS pact, says that each party recognizes that an armed attack in the West Pacific area against the territories of either party would be dangerous to itself and that each party would act to meet the common danger in accordance with its constitutional processes. Like the other treaties, and in identical language, this article provides for reporting immediately to the Security Council all measures taken to deal with an attack, and for terminating all such measures when the Security Council has taken the necessary action.

Article VI specifies the territories mentioned in articles II and V to be—"in respect of the Republic of China, Taiwan and the Pescadores; and in respect of the United States of America the island territories in the West Pacific under its

[12] *Documents on American Foreign Relations, 1948,* pp. 583-584.

jurisdiction." It also provides that articles II and V will be applicable to "such other territories as may be determined by mutual agreement." It is our view that an agreement to extend the coverage of the China defense treaty to additional territories would in practical terms amount to an amendment of the treaty and should be submitted to the Senate for its advice and consent.

Article VII grants to the United States the right to dispose such land, air, and sea forces in and about Taiwan [Formosa] and the Pescadores as may be required for their defense, as determined by mutual agreement. It does not make such disposition automatic or mandatory. A similar provision is found in article IV of the Korean treaty.

Article VIII, substantially identical with article VI of the Philippine and the ANZUS treaties, makes it clear that the obligations of the parties under the treaty do not affect in any way their obligations under the Charter of the United Nations, and recognizes the primary responsibility of the United Nations in maintaining international peace and security.

Article IX requires that the treaty be ratified by constitutional process before it shall come into force.

Article X provides that the treaty shall remain in force indefinitely but that either country may terminate it one year after giving notice. Substantially identical provisions are found in our treaties with Korea and the Philippines.

To summarize—what the treaty would accomplish is this:

It would give the Chinese Communists notice, beyond any possibility of misinterpretation, that the United States would regard an armed attack directed against Taiwan [Formosa] and the Pescadores as a danger to its own peace and safety and would act to meet the danger—such action to be in accordance with our constitutional processes.

It would provide firm reassurance to the Republic of China and to the world that Taiwan [Formosa] and the Pescadores are not a subject for barter as part of some Far Eastern "deal" with the Chinese Communists.

Taken in conjunction with the treaties which have already been concluded by the United States and to which I have referred above, this treaty rounds out the Western Pacific security system. It would be theoretically preferable if that rounding out were accomplished by a multilateral regional pact. This may come as a future development. However, that is not practical at the present time, and, in the meantime, we need to act within the limits of the practical.

After the treaty was signed, there took place an exchange of notes, dated December 10, 1954, between the Chinese Minister for Foreign Affairs and myself.[13] These were designed to insure that our two Governments will act in harmony and concert in relation to the present troubled state of affairs in that area. It was agreed that offensive military operations by either party from the territories held by the Republic of China would be undertaken only as a matter of joint agreement. This is obviously a reasonable and prudent understanding, because unilateral action of an offensive character by one party might throw heavy burdens upon the other party. Therefore, neither will act in disregard of the other.

It is furthermore agreed that military elements which are a product of joint effort and contribution will not be removed from the treaty area to a degree which would substantially diminish its defensibility unless by mutual agreement. This means, for example, that, if the United States has granted supplies and equipment for the forces on Formosa or has aided in the training, support, and equipment of armed forces, the resultant strength will not be removed from Formosa to other areas without our consent. Otherwise, the United States might be required continuously to replace what we had designed for the defense of Formosa.

The understandings thus expressed are important and reasonable in the light of the existing situation. They are the kind of arrangements which are proper as between friends and allies facing a common danger. They do not in any way impugn the sovereign equality of the parties.

Since this treaty was submitted to the Senate, the Congress has enacted Public Law 4[14] authorizing the President to use the armed forces of the United States in relation to Formosa and the Pescadores. The President's request for that authority arose out of Chinese Communist activities which in turn seemed to bear some relationship to the decisions of the United States which would be solemnized by this treaty and by the Manila Pact, which was approved by the Senate last week.

Relative quiet had prevailed off the China coast since 1949 until on September 3, 1954, the Chinese Communists opened

[13] *Documents on American Foreign Relations, 1954*, pp. 363-364.
[14] See above, pp. 298-299.

heavy artillery fire on Quemoy Island. That was just 3 days before the opening of the Manila conference which concluded the Manila Pact. Then when it was known that the United States intended to negotiate this Treaty of Mutual Defense with the Republic of China, the Chinese Communists stepped up their anti-American activities. They announced their condemnation to imprisonment of United States flyers. Indeed, that announcement coincided to the very day with the initialing of the security treaty by the Foreign Minister of the Republic of China and myself. Subsequently, Chinese Communist military activities in the Formosa Straits have been greatly intensified as part of what Communist propaganda proclaims to be their intention to exert their full force to conquer Formosa.

On January 24, the Chinese Communist Premier and Foreign Minister said, "The Chinese people must liberate Taiwan [Formosa] and the United States must . . . withdraw all its armed forces from Taiwan [Formosa] and the Taiwan [Formosa] Straits." [15]

The armed hostilities in the area seemed so likely to endanger the maintenance of international peace and security that on January 28, 1955, the representative of New Zealand brought the situation to the attention of the U.N. Security Council;[16] and on January 31, 1955, the Council invited a representative of the Chinese Communist regime to participate in the discussion of this item.[17] On February 3, 1955, the Chinese Communist Premier and Foreign Minister rejected that invitation.[18] In so doing, he referred to this defensive treaty as "aggression" and again demanded that the United States "withdraw all its armed forces from Taiwan [Formosa] and the Taiwan [Formosa] Straits."

I doubt that the Chinese Communists really intend to wage war against the United States unless the United States abandons this treaty with all that that abandonment would imply. However, I do not doubt that the Chinese Communists are probing our resolution. They no doubt hope that we want peace so ardently that we will retreat in the face of their threats.

It is true that we want peace and that we want it ardently.

[15] The quotation is from a statement by the Premier of Communist China (Chou En-lai) transmitted by the Peiping radio and monitored in London. For text see *New York Times* January 25, 1955.
[16] United Nations Document S/3354, dated January 28, 1955.
[17] The vote was 9-1 (U.S.S.R.) -1 (China).
[18] United Nations Document S/3358, dated February 3, 1955.

However, we do not want it at the price of our security or of our honor. Indeed experience shows that those who try in that way to buy peace in fact only increase the ultimate danger of war. They encourage the aggressors to make ever-mounting demands, so that in the end there is no alternative to fighting.

Under the circumstances which the Chinese Communists themselves have deliberately created, failure to conclude this treaty would have the gravest consequences. It would at once endanger the entire non-Communist position in the Western Pacific and Southeast Asia. It would stimulate the aggressive activities of international communism everywhere and would grievously hurt the interests of free peoples everywhere, including the interests of our own United States.

Such a course is to my mind unthinkable. In the face of Communist probing deeds and blustering words, the United States should remain calm, but it should remain firm in its purpose. It is at least possible that the enactment of Public Law 4 and the ratification of this treaty will together create a situation in which the present warlike mood of the Chinese Communists may subside.

The congressional authority to the President and the treaty ratification are two complementary acts. Under the circumstances that the Chinese Communists have created, neither, alone, is enough.

Therefore, I now urge the prompt consent of the Senate to the ratification of the mutual defense treaty with the Republic of China.[19]

B. Negotiations for the Release of United Nations Command Personnel: The Hammarskjold Mission.

Report by the United Nations Secretary General (Hammarskjold), September 9, 1955.[1]

1. The General Assembly, by resolution 906 (IX) of 10 December 1954, requested the Secretary-General to seek the release, in accordance with the Korean Armistice Agreement, of eleven United Nations Command personnel and all other captured personnel of the United Nations Command still

[19] The Senate gave its advice and consent on February 9, 1955 by a vote of 64-6. The President ratified the treaty on February 11, 1955. Notifications were exchanged with the Republic of China on March 3, 1955.

[1] United Nations Document A/2954, dated September 9, 1955.

detained.[2] It further requested the Secretary-General to make, by the means most appropriate in his judgment, continuing and unremitting efforts to this end and to report progress to all Members on or before 31 December 1954.

2. On 31 December 1954, I submitted a report[3] informing Members that, following an exchange of communications with the Prime Minister of the State Council and Minister for Foreign Affairs of the People's Republic of China and a meeting in Stockholm with General Keng Piao, Ambassador of the People's Republic of China, arrangements were made for the Secretary-General to visit Peking.

3. As stated in my annual report to the General Assembly on the work of the Organization,[4] my visit to Peking was made necessary because of the need to establish a direct contact with the Central People's Government of the People's Republic of China, since this Government was not represented in any organs of the United Nations. The visit, aimed primarily at clarifying the substantive and legal aspects of the matter, established this direct contact on a personal basis. It thus provided possibilities to pursue the discussion concerning the problem raised by the detention of the United Nations personnel referred to in the General Assembly resolution.

4. After my return from Peking I continued, within the framework of the contact thus established, an exchange of views with Mr. Chou En-lai, Prime Minister and Minister for Foreign Affairs of the People's Republic of China. The contact was maintained mainly through a series of communications transmitted by the Swedish Embassy in Peking. I received valuable assistance also from representatives of the Governments of other Member States.

5. A renewed personal contact with a representative of the Central People's Government of the People's Republic of China, Ambassador Keng Piao, was made by me in Stockholm on 23 April 1955.

6. By a letter to me, given to the Swedish Ambassador in Peking in the early afternoon of 29 May 1955 [New York time], Mr. Chou En-lai announced that an investigation of the cases of four detained fliers had been completed and that it had been decided that they should be deported immedi-

[2] *Documents on American Foreign Relations, 1954,* p. 359.
[3] United Nations Document A/2891, dated December 31, 1954.
[4] United Nations General Assembly *Official Records, Tenth Session,* Supplement No. 1, pp. 13-14.

ately from the territory of the People's Republic of China.[5] The four men arrived in Hong Kong on 31 May 1955.[6]

7. By an oral message to me, given to the Swedish Ambassador in Peking at 1 o'clock in the morning, 1 August 1955 [New York time], and transmitted by him, Mr. Chou En-lai announced that the Central People's Government of the People's Republic of China had decided to release as soon as feasible the eleven American fliers who had been detained and imprisoned, and that an announcement to that effect would be made in Peking at 10 a.m. on 1 August 1955 (New York time). The eleven men arrived in Hong Kong on 4 August 1955.[7]

8. Mr. Chou En-lai has expressed his hope that the contact established will be continued. In reply I have stated that this hope is shared by me.

C. Bilateral Negotiations between the United States and Communist China.

1. *State Department Announcement on United States Representations to Secure the Release of Americans Held Captive by Communist China, March 1, 1955.*[1]

(Excerpt)

While United Nations Secretary General Hammarskjold continues his efforts to secure the release of American military personnel of the United Nations Command imprisoned in Communist China, a continuing effort is also being made by the United States Government to secure the release of other detained and imprisoned Americans. Yesterday the United States Consul General at Geneva met with a Chinese Communist representative to renew United States demands for release of these American citizens from their unwarranted detention. The Communist representative, however, reiterated the Communist position that no Americans are being unjustly detained.

This was the eleventh in a series of meetings held at Geneva since last June on this subject. During this period 18 Americans who had been imprisoned or otherwise detained

[5] For a text of the verdict of the "Military Tribunal of the Supreme Court of the People's Republic of China" see *New York Times,* May 31, 1955.
[6] The flyers released were 1st Lieut. Lyle W. Cameron, Capt. Harold Fischer, 1st. Lieut. Roland W. Parks and Lt. Col. Edwin L. Heller.
[7] *Department of State Bulletin,* v. 33 (August 15, 1955), p. 262.
[1] Department of State Press Release 112, dated March 1, 1955.

have left Communist China, including Dr. Malcolm Bersohn and Mrs. W. A. Rickett who were released on the Hong Kong border on February 27.

Twenty-six American civilians, including John T. Downey and Richard G. Fecteau, remain in jail; three are under house arrest, and twelve others are still denied exit permits.

2. *State Department Announcement Concerning the Possibility of Direct Negotiations with Communist China on the Problem of Formosa, April 23, 1955.*[2]

The Department of State has received press reports concerning the statement of Chou En-lai at the Bandung Conference.[3] The United States always welcomes any efforts, if sincere, to bring peace to the world. In the Formosa region we have an ally in the free Republic of China and of course the United States would insist on free China participating as an equal in any discussions concerning the area.

If Communist China is sincere there are a number of obvious steps it could take to clear the air considerably and give evidence before the world of its good intentions. One of these would be to place in effect in the area an immediate cease-fire. It could also immediately release the American airmen and others whom it unjustly holds. Another could be the acceptance of the outstanding invitation by the Security Council of the United Nations to participate in discussions to end hostilities in the Formosa region.

[2] Department of State Press Release 226, dated April 23, 1955.

[3] The Prime Minister of Communist China (Chou En-lai), speaking before the Political Committee of the Asian-African Conference at Bandung, on April 23, 1955 said, among other things: "As to the relations between China and the United States, the Chinese people do not want to have war with the United States. We are willing to settle international disputes by peaceful means. If those of you here would like to facilitate the settlement of disputes between the United States and China by peaceful means, it would be most beneficial to the relaxation of tension in the Far East and also to the postponement and prevention of a world war."

3. *News Conference Statement by the Secretary of State (Dulles) on the Possibility of Negotiating with Communist China on the Problem of Formosa, April 26, 1955.*[4]

(Excerpts)

I feel that developments of the last ten days may in retrospect seem of decisive importance both in Europe and in Asia.

The Bandung conference, as we had hoped, seems to have exerted a restraint on the Chinese Communists. I had always felt that it would be salutary if the Chinese Communists were confronted with the opinion of the free nations of Asia. That opinion was powerfully expressed in favor of peace and against direct and indirect aggression. There seems now a chance that the Communist Chinese may be deterred from pursuing the course of violence which has characterized their action in relation to Korea, to Tibet, to Indochina and, more recently, in relation to the Taiwan [Formosa] Straits.

The Chinese Communists found no backing for their announced program of seizing Taiwan [Formosa] by force. On the contrary, they felt it useful in the last hours of the Bandung conference to propose to negotiate a peaceful settlement. Whether or not that was a sincere proposal remains to be seen. Perhaps the Chinese Communists were merely playing a propaganda game. But we intend to try to find out. In doing so we shall not, of course, depart from the path of fidelity and honor toward our ally, the Republic of China.

* * *

[In response to questions with respect to apparent conditions for negotiations implied by the State Department announcement of April 23, 1955,[5] issued in the Secretary's absence and without his concurrence, Mr. Dulles answered in part as follows:[6]]

There are two paragraphs in the State Department release, as I recall. The first paragraph said in substance that we would not discuss a disposal of the area in the absence of the Chinese Nationalists. That stands as a pre-condition. We are

[4] Department of State Press Release 230, dated April 26, 1955.
[5] See above, p. 308.
[6] Department of State Press Release 231, dated April 26, 1955.

not going to deal with the rights of the Chinese Nationalists, and their claims, in their absence.

Now, the other paragraph mentions certain things which it said would clear the air and be evidence of sincerity. Those are not stated as conditions precedent. It is said that it would be helpful if the Chinese Communists would release our flyers, etc. Those things were not stated as conditions, and were never intended to be conditions. They are very much like what the President and I often said in relation to the rulers of the Soviet Union—that it would be very helpful evidence of their sincerity if they would do certain things such as signing the Austrian Treaty. That was one of the things mentioned two years ago by the President in his Chance-for-Peace address. Nevertheless, that was never regarded as an indispensable prerequisite to talking with the Soviet Union. Actually, before any Austrian Treaty, I did meet with the Soviet Union at Berlin.

* * *

The first thing, it seems to me, that requires to be determined is whether we must prepare for war in that area or whether there is apt to be a cease-fire in the area. One cannot very well settle matters under the threat of a gun. So far there has been nothing but war threats in the area. There has been and there is still continuing a very large buildup, particularly of Chinese Communist air capabilities, in the Formosa Straits area. There has been until quite recently a very violent propaganda campaign to the effect that they were going to take Formosa by force and that the islands, such as Tachen, were useful to carry out their program of force. As I say, you do not negotiate—at least, the United States does not negotiate—with a pistol aimed at its head.

The first thing is to find out whether there is a possibility of a cease-fire in the area. That is a matter which can be discussed perhaps bilaterally, or at the United Nations, or possibly under other circumstances.

But I regard a cease-fire as the indispensable prerequisite to anything further. When you get into further matters then the interests of the Chinese Nationalists would naturally come to play a very large part.

* * *

4. *Joint Communiqué on Continuing Talks between Representatives of the United States and Communist China on the Ambassadorial Level, Issued simultaneously at Washington and Peiping, July 25, 1955.*[7]

As a result of communication between the United States and the People's Republic of China through the diplomatic channels of the United Kingdom, it has been agreed that the talks held in the last year between consular representatives of both sides at Geneva should be conducted on ambassadorial level in order to aid in settling the matter of repatriation of civilians who desire to return to their respective countries and to facilitate further discussions and settlement of certain other practical matters now at issue between both sides. The first meeting of ambassadorial representatives of both sides will take place on August 1, 1955 at Geneva.

5. *News Conference Statement by the Secretary of State (Dulles) on Talks between Representatives of the United States and Communist China, July 26, 1955.*[8]

Last April at the Bandung conference Mr. Chou En-lai suggested that there should be bilateral talks with the United States. He said, "The Chinese people do not want to have war with the United States. We are willing to settle international disputes by peaceful means."

Immediately [on April 23, 1955] the Department of State responded by stating that "the United States always welcomes any efforts, if sincere, to bring peace to the world." [9] Then at my subsequent press conference [April 26, 1955] I referred to Mr. Chou En-lai's statement and said, "Whether or not that was a sincere proposal remains to be seen. Perhaps the Chinese Communists are merely playing a propaganda game. But we intend to try to find out. In doing so we shall not, of course, depart from the path of fidelity and honor to our ally, the Republic of China." [10]

Developments since then indicate the possibility of obtaining beneficial results from a continuance of the talks which have been going on at Geneva for the past year and their restoration to the original ambassadorial level.

[7] Department of State Press Release 451, dated July 25, 1955.
[8] *Department of State Bulletin,* v. 33 (August 8, 1955), pp. 220-221.
[9] See above, p. 308.
[10] See above, p. 309.

Four out of the 15 United Nations prisoners of war have been released.[11] A few more United States civilians have been released. These results, though meager, are something. Chinese Communist warlike activities, such as had been displayed in relation to I-chiang and Tachen,[12] have not been resumed and there has been something approximating a *de facto* cease-fire in the Taiwan [Formosa] area. The former belligerent Communist propaganda about Taiwan and against the United States has recently been somewhat subdued.

In addition, various governments which have diplomatic relations with the People's Republic of China have indicated their own belief in the desire of the Chinese Communists to pursue a peaceful path.

Under these circumstances the United States proposed on July 11 to Mr. Chou En-lai that the talks that had been going on at Geneva, recently at the consular level, should be somewhat raised in level and enlarged in scope. This proposal was made through the intermediary of the United Kingdom, which represents the interests of the United States in Communist China. There was prompt acceptance of this proposal and, after the date was agreed to, a mutually agreed communiqué with reference to it was arrived at and simultaneously issued in Peiping and in Washington yesterday morning.

It was made clear that the offer of the United States did not imply any diplomatic recognition whatsoever. It was also made clear that we were not prepared in any way in these talks to make arrangements which would prejudice the rights of our ally, the Republic of China.

The United States will be represented at Geneva on August 1 by our Ambassador to Czechoslovakia, U. Alexis Johnson. It was Ambassador Johnson who represented the United States in the Geneva talks with the Chinese Communists when these talks first began a year ago. Prior to that, as a Departmental officer, he devoted himself largely to the Korean Armistice negotiations.

The United States is concerned with getting back the American civilians still detained in Communist China. In this connection we are prepared to discuss with the Chinese Communists the status of the few Chinese students in the United States who desire to return to Communist China and who the

[11] See above, pp. 306-307

[12] See above, p. 295.

Chinese Communists claim, without foundation, are prevented.

We also want to reinforce the efforts of the United Nations to get back the Americans who as members of the United Nations Command in Korea became prisoners of war and are still held by the Chinese Communists.

As to other practical matters which might be considered, the United States would like to be sure of precautions taken against a repetition of such incidents as involved the shooting down of the Cathay airliner with loss of American lives and injury to American civilians.[13]

Of course, the basic thing is that which I pointed out in my press conference of April 26, namely, "whether we must prepare for war in that area or whether there is apt to be a cease-fire in the area."

The United States believes that whatever may be the differences which now divide countries, these differences should not be settled by recourse to force where this would be apt to provoke international war. The United States has itself consistently acted on that belief. Wherever we give any military assistance, it is under the explicit condition that it will not be used for aggressive purposes. There is no doubt but what East Germany is part of Germany, but Chancellor Adenauer has given solemn assurance that he will not use force to unite his country. There is no doubt that North Korea is a part of Korea, but the security treaty which we made with the Republic of Korea makes clear that the United States will not extend its protection other than to areas which we recognize as having been lawfully brought under the jurisdiction of the Republic of Korea, and we do not believe that aggressive force is such a lawful means. There is no doubt but that North Viet-Nam is part of Viet-Nam, but we stated in connection with the Indochina armistice that we were opposed to any renewal of aggression to bring about the unification of Viet-Nam.

Both the Republic of China and the Chinese People's Republic claim that the area held by the other is part of China. But in connection with the mutual security treaty which the United States made with the Republic of China, it was agreed that the Republic of China would not use force except as a matter of joint agreement, subject to action of an emergency

[13] *Department of State Bulletin,* v. 31 (August 2, 1954), p. 165; (August 9, 1954), pp. 196-197; and (August 16, 1954), pp. 241-242.

character which was clearly an exercise of the inherent right of self-defense.[14]

We believe that the principle of nonrecourse to force is valid not merely for the United States and its allies but that it is valid for all.

We shall hope to find out in the forthcoming talks whether the Chinese Communists accept the concept of a cease-fire in accordance with the United Nations principle of avoiding any use or threat of force which could disturb the peace of nations.

No doubt the Chinese Communists will have matters of their own to bring up. We shall listen to hear what they are, and if they directly involve the United States and Communist China we will be disposed to discuss them with a view to arriving at a peaceful settlement.

As President Eisenhower said last night,[15] "The United States will go to any length consistent with our concepts of decency and justice and right to attain peace. For this purpose we will work cooperatively with the Soviets and any other people as long as there is sincerity of purpose and a genuine desire to go ahead."

That is the principle which will govern the continuation of our talks with the Chinese Communists at Geneva.

6. *News Conference Comments by the Secretary of State (Dulles) on the Renunciation of Force in the Formosa Straits, August 2, 1955.*[16]

(Excerpts)

* * *

I think that the treaty arrangements which we have with the Republic of China make it quite clear that it is in our mutual contemplation that force shall not be used. The whole character of that treaty is defensive. That is underlined throughout the treaty itself and in the concurrent understandings that were arrived at in that connection; so while the United States would not feel that it was in a position to act as in any sense an agent for the Republic of China, nevertheless I do think that the whole pattern that has been woven there by the United States is in itself evidence that we

[14] *Documents on American Foreign Relations, 1954,* pp. 363-364.

[15] See above, p. 229.

[16] Department of State Press Release 470, dated August 2, 1955.

accept for ourselves, and in our alliances seek to make it a principle of those alliances, that force shall not be used to achieve national ambitions. That is the same principle which we invoke and which we hope will guide the Chinese Communists, and we naturally accept it for ourselves. As you probably know, all of the agreements under which we give military assistance to various countries are very explicit in their provisions that the equipment shall not be used for any aggressive purpose.

* * *

What we hope to arrive at by progressive steps is a situation where the Chinese Communists will have renounced the use of force to achieve their ambitions. That is the thing I have been emphasizing and driving at for months, because if they are not willing to do that, if they want to use force to achieve their ambitions, that will almost surely start up a war the limits of which could not be defined in advance. How that is brought about I don't know. That is a matter of policy for the Chinese Communists. I don't know how they will choose to make that clear, if indeed they do make it clear. I already have said that the speech of Chou En-lai of last Friday went further in that direction than anything that he has yet said.[17] I hope that out of what is taking place either at Geneva or outside of Geneva, and the whole trend of world events, will create a situation so that we can feel that we are not under the threat of war from the situation in that area. I said in my press conference of April 26, you may remember, that the United States was not willing to negotiate with a pistol at its head;[18] that the first thing to do is to find out whether there was a threat of war there, because if that

[17] The reference is to a foreign policy report delivered by the Prime Minister of Communist China before the National People's Congress in Peiping on July 30, 1955. In his address, Chou En-lai reiterated his contention that since there was no war between the United States and China, the question of cease-fire did not arise. He asserted that "conditions permitting the . . . liberation of Taiwan [Formosa] will continue to increase. If possible the Chinese [Communist] Government is willing to enter into negotiations with the responsible local authorities of Taiwan [Formosa] to map out concrete steps for . . . peaceful liberation." Speaking of the forthcoming ambassadorial talks with the United States, Chou En-lai said, among other things, that "provided both sides are sincerely desirous of negotiation and conciliation it should be possible . . . to reach, first of all, a reasonable settlement of the question of the return of civilians to their respective countries. [And] to make preparations for negotiations . . . for relaxing and eliminating the tension in the Taiwan [Formosa] area." For fuller excerpts from Chou En-lai's address see *New York Times,* July 31, 1955.

[18] See above, p. 310.

was the case then, as far as the United States is concerned, it would be quite impossible to negotiate these practical matters.

I pointed out last week that a number of things had happened which indicated that the pistol had been laid down and that it made it possible to try to clear up now some of these practical matters between us.[19] But the important thing is that the pistol should be permanently discarded and we hope that the trend of events will bring reassurance on that point.

* * *

7. *Ambassadorial Talks at Geneva.*

a. *Agreed Announcement by the Ambassadors of the United States (Johnson) and Communist China (Wang) Concerning the Return of Civilians to their Respective Countries, September 10, 1955.*[20]

The Ambassadors of the United States of America and the People's Republic of China have agreed to announce measures which their respective governments have adopted concerning the return of civilians to their respective countries.

With respect to Chinese in the United States, Ambassador U. Alexis Johnson, on behalf of the United States, has informed Ambassador Wang Ping-nan that:

1. The United States recognizes that Chinese in the United States who desire to return to the People's Republic of China are entitled to do so and declares that it has adopted and will further adopt appropriate measures so that they can expeditiously exercise their right to return.

2. The Government of the Republic of India will be invited to assist in the return to the People's Republic of China of those who desire to do so as follows:

A. If any Chinese in the United States believes that contrary to the declared policy of the United States he is encountering obstruction in departure, he may so inform the Embassy of the Republic of India in the United States and request it to make representations on his behalf to the United States Government. If desired by the People's Republic of China, the Government of the Republic of India may also investigate the facts in any such case.

B. If any Chinese in the United States who desires to

[19] See above, pp. 311-314.

[20] *Department of State Bulletin,* v. 33 (September 19, 1955), p. 456.

return to the People's Republic of China has difficulty in paying his return expenses, the Government of the Republic of India may render him financial assistance needed to permit his return.

3. The United States Government will give wide publicity to the foregoing arrangements and the Embassy of the Republic of India in the United States may also do so.

With respect to Americans in the People's Republic of China, Ambassador Wang Ping-nan, on behalf of the People's Republic of China, has informed Ambassador U. Alexis Johnson that:

1. The People's Republic of China recognizes that Americans in the People's Republic of China who desire to return to the United States are entitled to do so, and declares that it has adopted and will further adopt appropriate measures so that they can expeditiously exercise their right to return.

2. The Government of the United Kingdom will be invited to assist in the return to the United States of those Americans who desire to do so as follows:

A. If any American in the People's Republic of China believes that contrary to the declared policy of the People's Republic of China he is encountering obstruction in departure, he may so inform the Office of the Chargé d'Affaires of the United Kingdom in the People's Republic of China and request it to make representations on his behalf to the Government of the People's Republic of China. If desired by the United States, the Government of the United Kingdom may also investigate the facts in any such case.

B. If any American in the People's Republic of China who desires to return to the United States has difficulty in paying his return expenses, the Government of the United Kingdom may render him financial assistance needed to permit his return.

3. The Government of the People's Republic of China will give wide publicity to the foregoing arrangements and the Office of the Chargé d'Affaires of the United Kingdom in the People's Republic of China may also do so.

b. *Statement Issued by the United States Delegation, September 14, 1955.*[21]

At today's meeting Ambassador [U. Alexis] Johnson indicated it would be premature to discuss other practical

[21] *Ibid.* (September 26, 1955), p. 489.

matters at issue before carrying out the agreed announcement of last Saturday[22] regarding the return of civilians who wish to return to their countries.

Only full implementation of the agreed announcement can resolve the problem of the return of American civilians. In that announcement the People's Republic of China said "it will further adopt appropriate measures" so that American civilians can "expeditiously" exercise their rights to return.

The faithful carrying out of the terms of that announcement should be the continued task of the Geneva meetings and should provide a basis for proceeding to the discussion of other practical matters at issue.

c. *United States Statement and Proposal on Renunciation of Force, October 8, 1955.*[23]

One of the practical matters for discussion between us is that each of us should renounce the use of force to achieve our policies when they conflict. The United States and the PRC [People's Republic of China] confront each other with policies which are in certain respects incompatible. This fact need not, however, mean armed conflict, and the most important single thing we can do is first of all to be sure that it will not lead to armed conflict.

Then and only then can other matters causing tension between the parties in the Taiwan area and the Far East be hopefully discussed.

It is not suggested that either of us should renounce any policy objectives which we consider we are legitimately entitled to achieve, but only that we renounce the use of force to implement these policies.

Neither of us wants to negotiate under the threat of force. The free discussion of differences, and their fair and equitable solution, become impossible under the overhanging threat that force may be resorted to when one party does not agree with the other.

The United States as a member of the United Nations has agreed to refrain in its international relations from the threat or use of force. This has been its policy for many years and is its guiding principle of conduct in the Far East, as throughout the world.

The use of force to achieve national objectives does not

[22] See above, pp. 316-317.
[23] *Department of State Bulletin*, v. 34 (January 30, 1956), pp. 166-167.

accord with accepted standards of conduct under international law.

The Covenant of the League of Nations, the Kellogg-Briand Treaties, and the Charter of the United Nations reflect the universal view of the civilized community of nations that the use of force as an instrument of national policy violates international law, constitutes a threat to international peace, and prejudices the interests of the entire world community.

There are in the world today many situations which tempt those who have force to use it to achieve what they believe to be legitimate policy objectives. Many countries are abnormally divided or contain what some consider to be abnormal intrusions. Nevertheless, the responsible governments of the world have in each of these cases renounced the use of force to achieve what they believe to be legitimate and even urgent goals.

It is an essential foundation and preliminary to the success of the discussions under Item 2 that it first be made clear that the parties to these discussions renounce the use of force to make the policies of either prevail over those of the other. That particularly applies to the Taiwan area.

The acceptance of this principle does not involve third parties, or the justice or injustice of conflicting claims. It only involves recognizing and agreeing to abide by accepted standards of international conduct.

We ask, therefore, as a first matter for discussion under Item 2, a declaration that your side will not resort to the use of force in the Taiwan area except defensively. The United States would be prepared to make a corresponding declaration. These declarations will make it appropriate for us to pass on to the discussion of other matters with a better hope of coming to constructive conclusions.

d. *Chinese Communist Draft Declaration on Renunciation of Force, October 27, 1955.*[24]

1. Ambassador Wang Ping-nan on behalf of the Government of the People's Republic of China and Ambassador U. Alexis Johnson on behalf of the Government of the United States of America jointly declare that,

2. In accordance with Article 2, Paragraph 3, of the

[24] *Ibid.*, p. 167.

Charter of the United Nations, "All members shall settle their international disputes by peaceful means in such a manner that international peace and security, and justice, are not endangered"; and

3. In accordance with Article 2, Paragraph 4 of the Charter of the United Nations, "All members shall refrain in their international relations from the threat or use of force against the territorial integrity or political independence of any state, or in any other manner inconsistent with the purposes of the United Nations";

4. The People's Republic of China and the United States of America agree that they should settle disputes between their two countries by peaceful means without resorting to the threat or use of force.

5. In order to realize their common desire, the People's Republic of China and the United States of America decide to hold a conference of Foreign Ministers to settle through negotiations the question of relaxing and eliminating the tension in Taiwan area.

e. *United States Draft Declaration on Renunciation of Force, November 10, 1955.*[25]

1. The Ambassador of the United States of America and the Ambassador of the People's Republic of China during the course of the discussions of practical matters at issue have expressed the determination that the differences between the two sides shall not lead to armed conflict.

2. They recognize that the use of force to achieve national objectives does not accord with the principles and purposes of the United Nations Charter or with generally accepted standards of international conduct.

3. They furthermore recognize that the renunciation of the threat or use of force is essential to the just settlement of disputes or situations which might lead to a breach of the peace.

4. Therefore, without prejudice to the pursuit by each side of its policies by peaceful means they have agreed to announce the following declarations:

5. Ambassador Wang Ping-nan informed Ambassador U. Alexis Johnson that:

6. In general, and with particular reference to the Taiwan

[25] *Ibid.*

area, the People's Republic of China renounces the use of force, except in individual and collective self-defense.

7. Ambassador U. Alexis Johnson informed Ambassador Wang Ping-nan that:

8. In general, and with particular reference to the Taiwan area, the United States renounces the use of force, except in individual and collective self-defense.

f. *Chinese Communist Draft Counterproposal for an Agreed Announcement, December 1, 1955.*[26]

1. Ambassador Wang Ping-nan, on behalf of the Government of the People's Republic of China, and Ambassador U. Alexis Johnson on behalf of the Government of the United States of America, agree to announce:

2. The People's Republic of China and the United States of America are determined that they should settle disputes between their two countries through peaceful negotiations without resorting to the threat or use of force;

3. The two Ambassadors should continue their talks to seek practical and feasible means for the realization of this common desire.

g. *State Department Announcement on the Failure of Communist China to Implement the Agreed Announcement, December 16, 1955.*[27]

The Chinese Communists on December 15 issued a statement defending their continued detention of United States civilians in China.[28] At the same time they accused the United States of not complying with the Agreed Announcement of September 10 regarding the repatriation of civilians to Communist China.

Because the Communist statement contains many errors, this statement is being made. The facts show that the United States has scrupulously complied with its agreement and that Chinese in the United States are now and have at all times since the announcement been free to leave.

Unfortunately the same is not true with respect to the Chinese Communist performance of its agreement to permit United States civilians to "expeditiously" return to the

[26] *Ibid.*
[27] Department of State Press Release 699, dated December 16, 1955.
[28] Not printed. The Chinese Communist statement was issued by Ambassador Wang at Geneva.

United States. Of the 19 United States citizens in Communist China who were being prevented from returning on September 10, the date of the Chinese Communist agreement, only 5 have been released.[29]

United States Ambassador Johnson has repeatedly protested to Communist Ambassador Wang in the Geneva talks, the failure of the Communists to permit United States citizens to leave China. He has also protested the cruel and inhuman treatment of those concerning whom facts are available.

The answer to these protests has been the public statement by the Communists charging that the United States has not permitted Chinese to leave the United States.

In the Agreed Announcement of September 10, the Chinese Communist Ambassador declared:

"The People's Republic of China recognizes that Americans in the People's Republic of China who desire to return to the United States are entitled to do so, and declares that it has adopted and will further adopt appropriate measures so that they can expeditiously exercise their right to return."

This declaration is simple, clear, and positive. It says that any United States citizen has the right to leave China, and that the Communists have taken or will take the necessary steps so that those who wish may leave "expeditiously." No distinction is made as between those in prison and those out of prison. All United States citizens who wish to leave should have been out of Communist China long before this. The continued holding of these United States citizens by the Communists is a violation of their Agreed Announcement, for which the United States must continue to protest.

As for the Communist charge that the United States is preventing Chinese from leaving the United States, it is sufficient to point out that not a single Chinese has been refused exit. If anyone knows of any Chinese who wishes to leave and who claims he is being prevented, he should communicate at once with the Department of State or the Indian Embassy at Washington, which the United States has agreed may render assistance. The Indian Embassy has made no representation that any Chinese is being prevented from leaving.

It is unfortunate that the Chinese Communists have seen fit to make a public announcement containing charges which are without foundation. This cannot conceal the fact that United States citizens continue to be held in prison by the

[29] See above, pp. 316-317.

Communists in violation of their public announcement of September 10. It is to be hoped that these United States citizens will be permitted promptly to leave Communist prisons and return to their homes.

D. The Manila Pact.

Communiqué on the Meeting of the Council of the Southeast Asia Collective Defense Treaty, Bangkok, February 25, 1955.[1]

The Foreign Ministers of Australia, New Zealand, Pakistan, the Philippines, Thailand, the United Kingdom, and the United States and the Representative of France have completed the First Meeting of the Council established by the Southeast Asia Collective Defense Treaty.[2] The Treaty entered into force on February 19, 1955, following the deposit of the instruments of ratification with the Government of the Republic of the Philippines. The Council has held six sessions in Bangkok from February 23 to February 25 under the Chairmanship of H. R. H. Prince Wan Waithayakon, Foreign Minister of the Government of Thailand.

The Council met in circumstances which give increasing urgency to the objectives of the Treaty. The Members of the Council declared the dedication of their Governments to the purposes and principles set forth in the Charter of the United Nations, and in particular, they asserted their hatred of war and their determination to take all possible measures to preserve and strengthen peace. They reiterated that such military arrangements as they may make will be purely defensive, in accordance with their international obligations, and will never be used for purposes of aggression.

The Council reaffirmed the aim of their Governments, as set forth in the Pacific Charter: to uphold the principle of equal rights and self-determination of peoples; to promote self-government and to secure the independence of all countries whose peoples desire it and are able to undertake its responsibilities; to continue to cooperate in the economic, social, and welfare fields in order to promote higher living standards, economic progress, and social well-being in this region; and to prevent or counter by appropriate means any attempt in the Treaty area to subvert their freedom or to destroy their sovereignty or territorial integrity.

[1] *Department of State Bulletin,* v. 32 (March 7, 1955), pp. 371-373.
[2] *Documents on American Foreign Relations, 1954,* pp. 319-323.

Upholding the principle of non-interference in the internal affairs of other states, the Council stressed the paramount need for the maintenance in peace of the integrity and authority of freely constituted governments in the area and of the right of peoples to determine their own destiny without external interference. They, therefore, condemned not only warlike action but also those subtle forms of aggression by which freedom and self-government are undermined and men's minds subverted.

This Meeting has provided the Members of the Council with an opportunity for bringing about closer ties among their own governments in achieving their common objectives and purposes under the Treaty. They believe that the Manila Treaty is already exerting a positive influence for the maintenance of peace in Southeast Asia and the Southwest Pacific, and that the solidarity of the member nations, shown at the present meeting, will serve as an increasingly powerful deterrent against aggression. The Council recognized the continuing dangers to peace and security in the Treaty area and agreed that these threats make it imperative that the member governments take steps to strengthen the common defense.

It was recognized that subversion and infiltration constitute a serious threat to the peace and security of the area and that this demands special efforts in all aspects of the national life. The Council discussed specific attempts by elements directed from outside to subvert free institutions and governments in the Treaty area. The Council viewed these subversive activities with grave concern and was determined to help the peoples of the area to resist them. There was agreement on the need for cooperation among the member governments to assist one another in combatting the subversive activities of international Communism. The Council decided to arrange for continuing consultation and mutual assistance and to make it possible for each member government to draw upon the experience of the others in dealing with this danger. In this connection the Council received a valuable report on the Philippine experience in combatting internal dissidence, and noted the statement of the United Kingdom Delegation on the improved situation in Malaya.

The Council agreed upon the importance of implementing Article III of the Treaty which provides:

"The Parties undertake to strengthen their free institutions and to cooperate with one another in the further development of economic measures, including technical assistance, designed both to promote economic progress and social well-being and to further the individual and collective efforts of governments toward these ends."

Arrangements were made for economic experts designated by member governments to meet periodically wherever appropriate and convenient on matters within the scope of this Article.

The members of the Council recognized that while certain economic matters such as trade, the international payments, development, investment, and sound economic progress involved a wider geographic area and desirably included cooperation with many friendly states as well as with the member states, nevertheless special economic questions arise out of the Treaty commitments of the member governments and may involve individual and cooperative steps which member states could take to resolve these questions. The economic experts designated will advise Council representatives on these measures. The first meeting of the economic experts will take place at an early date.

The Council noted with interest the statement by the United States Delegation about the peaceful uses of atomic energy. The Council is deeply conscious of the potential contributions of atomic energy to the health and standards of living of the peoples of the member nations and welcomed the proposed discussions relating to further cooperation and assistance in the atomic energy programs directed toward achieving these benefits.

Realizing the importance to the security of Southeast Asia and the Southwest Pacific of the States of Cambodia, Laos, and of the free territory under the jurisdiction of the State of Viet Nam, the Council reaffirmed the determination of the member governments to support these three States in maintaining their freedom and independence as set forth in the Protocol to the Treaty. The Council was informed of assistance which had been extended to the three States and expressed the hope that member governments would offer further assistance.

Having thus exchanged views, the members of the Council made the following arrangements to help carry out the provisions of the Treaty:

Operation of the Council

The governments will be represented on the Council by their Foreign Ministers or their designated representatives. The Council will meet at least once each year and more often when deemed necessary. It will usually meet in the Treaty area. Decisions of the Council will be taken by unanimous agreement.

Designation of Council Representatives

In order to assure close and continuing cooperation when the Council is not in session, the Council has agreed to designate Council representatives who will have their seat in Bangkok. The Council representatives will maintain continuing consultation on matters relating to the Treaty and will perform such special tasks as the Council may, from time to time, direct. They may make agreed recommendations to the Council or, when the Council is not in session, to the member governments with respect to implementation of the Treaty. Through the Council representatives the member governments may raise matters relating to the Treaty and agree on the steps to be taken in carrying out its provisions.

The Council representatives may request the member governments to designate specially qualified personnel to assist them in specific tasks. Working groups composed of such personnel may meet wherever appropriate and convenient.

The Council representatives will ensure appropriate exchange of information and close coordination of planning among such groups as may from time to time be working on projects under the Treaty. They will also make arrangements for a Secretariat to assist them, the personnel of the Secretariat being made available by the representatives on a contributed basis.

The Council directed that the Council representatives begin operations as soon as possible and that one of their first tasks should be to arrange meetings of specially qualified personnel designated by member governments to assist the Council representatives in considering means of strengthening cooperation in combatting subversion and infiltration.

The Council also requested the Council representatives to explore the opportunities for increasing cultural and technical cooperation among the member governments and to submit recommendations to the next meeting of the Council.

Military Advisers to the Council

Each of the governments agreed to designate a Military Adviser to its member of the Council.

The Military Advisers will make recommendations to the Council on military cooperation under the Treaty.

They will meet periodically as required, will formulate their own rules of procedure and any necessary organizational arrangements.

The Military Advisers at this Council meeting met on February 24 and 25. They exchanged views concerning the military aspects of the Defense Treaty and as a result of these discussions their staff planners will meet in Manila in April 1955 to initiate plans for the implementation of certain military aspects of the Treaty. Shortly thereafter the Military Advisers will again convene in Bangkok.

Peace and Security of the Area

Although they represent diverse nations and peoples, the members of the Council were unanimous in the belief that this meeting has enabled them to understand and appreciate the problems facing the governments of the countries covered by the Treaty in the common effort to ensure peace and security under the Treaty. The progress achieved at this first Council meeting provides solid hope for closer cooperation among the member governments for the good of the region as a whole. The members of the Council are united in their conviction that the common efforts of their governments are contributing positively to the peace and security of the area, both for the member governments and for other free nations in the region. The Council expressed the hope that these free nations will associate themselves in the near future with the work to be undertaken under the Treaty.

E. Japan.

Joint Statement on Discussions Held between the Foreign Minister of Japan (Shigemitsu) and the Secretary of State (Dulles), Washington, August 31, 1955.[1]

Mamoru Shigemitsu, Deputy Prime Minister and Foreign Minister of Japan, has concluded three days of discussions with Secretary of State John Foster Dulles and other high United States officials.

The Foreign Minister was accompanied among others by Ichiro Kono, Minister of Agriculture and Forestry; Nobusuke Kishi, Secretary-General of the Japan Democratic Party; Ambassador to the United States Sadao Iguchi; Ambassador Toshikazu Kase, Japan's Permanent Observer to the United

[1] *Department of State Bulletin,* v. 33 (September 2, 1955), pp. 419-420.

Nations; and Takizo Matsumoto, Deputy Chief Cabinet Secretary.

American officials in addition to the Secretary of State who met with the Foreign Minister and members of his party included: Under Secretary of State Herbert Hoover, Jr.; Deputy Secretary of Defense Reuben B. Robertson, Jr.; Chairman of the Joint Chiefs of Staff Admiral Arthur W. Radford; Mr. John Hollister, Director of the International Cooperation Administration; Deputy Under Secretary of State Robert Murphy; Assistant Secretary of Defense Gordon Gray; Ambassador to Japan John M. Allison; and Acting Assistant Secretary of State for Far Eastern Affairs William J. Sebald.

A free and frank exchange of views from the global viewpoint was held concerning more recent international developments, notably the implications of the "Summit" meeting at Geneva,[2] the present United Nations discussions on disarmament, and the impending Conference of Foreign Ministers at Geneva.[3] The Far Eastern situation was also discussed. Secretary Dulles explained the policy of the United States to support freedom firmly while exploring patiently every avenue which may lead to the enhancement of general peace. Foreign Minister Shigemitsu drew on his experience in the Soviet Union and China in interpreting his nation's policies. The Secretary of State and the Foreign Minister concurred in the view that while the immediate danger of major war had perhaps receded there still remain elements of uncertainty in the situation, particularly in the Far East, and that the continued solidarity of the free world is needed to maintain improved prospects of peace.

The Foreign Minister expressed Japan's resolve to maintain cooperation with the United States and the free world as the cornerstone of its foreign policy. In this connection the Secretary of State and the Foreign Minister, recognizing the desirability of closer cooperation between their countries for the purpose of securing stability and enduring peace in the Far East, agreed that consultations between their Governments should continue on various problems of mutual concern.

The basic problems of Japanese security were discussed. The Foreign Minister indicated that Japan's defense strength has now reached a considerable level and expressed the firm determination that the policy of progressive increase will be

[2] See above, pp. 171-232.
[3] See above, pp. 232-293.

continued within the limit of Japan's capacity. He explained the plans for increasing Japan's defense capabilities recently formulated by the Japanese defense authorities. It was agreed that these plans should be studied in the course of the continuing consultations in Tokyo on United States-Japanese defense relationships and should be reviewed from time to time in the light of strategic requirements.

It was agreed that efforts should be made, whenever practicable on a cooperative basis, to establish conditions such that Japan could, as rapidly as possible, assume primary responsibility for the defense of its homeland and be able to contribute to the preservation of international peace and security in the Western Pacific. It was also agreed that when such conditions are brought about it would be appropriate to replace the present Security Treaty[4] with one of greater mutuality.

With the conclusion of such a treaty as an objective, it was further agreed that consultations would take place in Tokyo between Japanese and United States representatives on defense problems and that in such consultations consideration will be given to the establishment of schedules for the progressive withdrawal of United States ground forces as Japan's own defense capacity increases and taking into account the related situation in Asia.

On the problem of Japan's financial contribution to the support of United States forces in Japan, there was agreement on the desirability of establishing a general formula for progressive reduction over the next several years.

The Foreign Minister emphasized Japan's need to expand its trade with other countries particularly in Asia and expressed appreciation for the help of the United States in assisting Japan to become a full member of the General Agreement on Tariffs and Trade.[5]

Secretary Dulles expressed current thinking about assistance for the economic development of the free nations of Asia pursuant to United States legislation. It was recognized that the measures planned would facilitate Japan's efforts to improve its economic position and attain a higher standard of living. The Secretary stressed the contribution to economic development which could be made by foreign private investment both in Japan and in other countries of the area.

The Foreign Minister requested the early release of war

[4] *Documents on American Foreign Relations, 1951,* pp. 266-267.
[5] See above, p. 68.

criminals under United States jurisdiction. The Secretary of State described the complexity of the problem and indicated that the question of the release of the war criminals will be kept under continuous and urgent examination.

It was agreed that no major obstacles remain to settlement for economic assistance rendered to Japan during the occupation and that utmost efforts will be made to bring the negotiations in Tokyo on this subject between the two Governments to an early conclusion.

Throughout these talks the representatives of the United States and Japan recognized that Japan, as a major power in Asia, should play an active role in friendly cooperation with other Asian nations in contributing to stability and peace in Asia. They agreed that in view of Japan's efforts to establish internal stability, reconstruct the national economy and strengthen its defense capacity, there is a firmer basis for continuing cooperation between the United States and Japan. Foreign Minister Shigemitsu and Secretary of State Dulles confirmed anew the determination of their Governments to expand this relationship further so that they together and with others may pursue their work for the consolidation of world peace and freedom.

F. The Colombo Plan.

Communiqué on the Seventh Meeting of the Consultative Committee for Economic Development in South and South-East Asia, Singapore, October 21, 1955.[1]

The Consultative Committee, representing the member Governments of the Colombo Plan for Co-operative Development in South and South-East Asia, has met from 17th to 21st October at Singapore.

2. As at previous meetings of the Consultative Committee, opportunity was taken to review progress under the Colombo Plan during the past year, to define the task which lies ahead and in the renewal of personal contacts to share experience in the solution of common problems. The Ministers had received a draft report prepared by the officials at their preliminary meeting. After full consideration and discussion they reached agreement on the text of the Fourth Annual Report of the Consultative Committee and approved its publication in the capitals of member countries not before 22nd November, 1955.

[1] *Department of State Bulletin,* v. 33 (December 12, 1955), pp. 994-995.

3. During the fourth year of the Colombo Plan most countries of the Area maintained and a few surpassed their previous rate of economic progress. In general there were noticeable increases in national income and output, particularly in industrial and mineral production and power generation. Some projects adopted at the outset of the Plan have now not only been completed but are beginning to bear fruit. Favourable world economic conditions have created an increased demand for the products of the Area and made it easier for developing countries to obtain the capital equipment they need. But the prices of some commodities, such as rice, have fallen and countries dependent on the export of these commodities have had special difficulties.

4. Member Governments in the Area aimed in 1954-55 at devoting to development in the public sector not less than the equivalent of some £752 million as compared with some £542 million in 1953-54, and they hope to achieve an even higher expenditure in 1955-1956. The bulk of this outlay is of course provided by the countries in the Area themselves. Over two-fifths of it is directed to agriculture, one quarter to transport and one quarter to social welfare.

5. The substantial amounts of capital made available by contributing Governments, the International Bank for Reconstruction and Development and by other institutions has been of appreciable and increasingly effective assistance to the countries of the Colombo Plan area in furthering their development programmes. Such capital has special value as it represents foreign exchange which can stimulate a much larger amount of domestic investment.

6. It was recognised that external private capital is an essential supplement to the activities of Governments. Factors which may deter the flow of such investment were considered, and note was taken of the special steps being taken to encourage it by many member Governments in the Area.

7. The discussions in the Consultative Committee showed that, despite wide differences between their situations, certain problems are common to most countries in the Area. Prominent amongst these is the vital need for ever greater food production, to feed 10 million additional people a year in the Area and also to improve existing standards of life. Large increases in food production have been achieved in many countries, but they are not yet large enough and further increases may require proportionately greater effort.

8. Prominent also is the need for greater technical skills

which, at least as much as finance, are the key to economic progress and social welfare. Under the various technical assistance schemes nearly 7,200 places have been found for trainees outside their own countries, of which some 2,200 places where found in the past year. Similarly some 1,200 experts were provided during the year to the countries of South and South-East Asia, bringing the total to 3,700. The Consultative Committee recognised that this type of contribution is of great significance. They also considered means of extending the scope, increasing the volume and improving the operation of the technical assistance programmes.

9. The task ahead is described in the attached extract from the Annual Report.[2] It poses the problems to be faced, indicates some of the lines on which solutions may be found, and describes a situation which offers a challenge to all member Governments in their efforts to secure the onward progress of South and South-East Asia to greater prosperity, stability and peace.

10. In 1950 it was agreed that the Colombo Plan should run until 30th June, 1957. This date no longer has any special significance and it was generally agreed that the development programmes of the countries of South and South-East Asia would have to be continued for many years to come. The Consultative Committee decided that the Plan should continue until 30th June, 1961, and that the future of the Plan should be considered by the Committee at the 1959 meeting.

11. Finally, the Consultative Committee accepted the kind invitation of the Minister for External Affairs of the Government of New Zealand to meet next year in New Zealand.

G. The Bandung Conference of Asian-African Countries.

Final Communiqué, Bandung, April 24, 1955.[1]

The Asian-African Conference, convened upon the invitation of the Prime Ministers of Burma, Ceylon, India, Indonesia and Pakistan met in Bandung from the 18th to the 24th April, 1955. In addition to the sponsoring countries the following 24 countries participated in the conference:

1. Afghanistan
2. Cambodia
3. People's Republic of China

[2] Not printed. See *ibid.*, pp. 995-997.
[1] *Report on Indonesia,* v. 6, No. 9 (June 1955), pp. 28-31.

4. Egypt
5. Ethiopia
6. Gold Coast
7. Iran
8. Iraq
9. Japan
10. Jordan
11. Laos
12. Lebanon
13. Liberia
14. Libya
15. Nepal
16. Philippines
17. Saudi Arabia
18. Sudan
19. Syria
20. Thailand
21. Turkey
22. Democratic Republic of Vietnam
23. State of Vietnam
24. Yemen

The Asian-African Conference considered problems of common interest and concern to countries of Asia and Africa and discussed ways and means by which their people could achieve fuller economic, cultural and political cooperation.

A. *Economic Cooperation*

1. The Asian-African Conference recognized the urgency of promoting economic development in the Asian-African region. There was general desire for economic cooperation among the participating countries on the basis of mutual interest and respect for national sovereignty. The proposals with regard to economic cooperation within the participating countries do not preclude either the desirability or the need for cooperation with countries outside the region, including the investment of foreign capital. It was further recognized that the assistance being received by certain participating countries from outside the region, through international or under bilateral arrangements, had made a valuable contribution to the implementation of their development programmes.

2. The participating countries agreed to provide technical assistance to one another, to the maximum extent practicable, in the form of: experts, trainees, pilot projects and equipment for demonstration purposes; exchange of know-how and establishment of national, and where possible, regional training and research institutes for imparting technical knowledge and skills in cooperation with the existing international agencies.

3. The Asian-African Conference recommended: the early establishment of the Special United Nations Fund for Economic Development; the allocation by the International Bank for Reconstruction and Development of a greater part of its resources to Asian-African countries; the early estab-

lishment of the International Finance Corporation which should include in its activities the undertaking of equity investment, and encouragement to the promotion of joint ventures among Asian-African countries in so far as this will promote their common interest.

4. The Asian-African Conference recognized the vital need for stabilizing commodity trade in the region. The principle of enlarging the scope of multilateral trade and payments was accepted. However, it was recognized that some countries would have to take recourse to bilateral trade arrangements in view of their prevailing economic conditions.

5. The Asian-African Conference recommended that collective action be taken by participating countries for stabilizing the international prices of and demand for primary commodities through bilateral and multilateral arrangements, and that as far as practicable and desirable, they should adopt a unified approach on the subject in the United Nations Permanent Advisory Commission on International Commodity Trade and other international forums.

6. The Asian-African Conference further recommended that: Asian-African countries should diversify their export trade by processing their raw material, wherever economically feasible, before export; intraregional trade fairs should be promoted and encouragement given to the exchange of trade delegations and groups of businessmen; exchange of information and of samples should be encouraged with a view to promoting intraregional trade and normal facilities should be provided for transit trade of landlocked countries.

7. The Asian-African Conference attached considerable importance to Shipping and expressed concern that shipping lines reviewed from time to time their freight rates, often to the detriment of participating countries. It recommended a study of this problem, and collective action thereafter, to induce the shipping lines to adopt a more reasonable attitude. It was suggested that a study of railway freight of transit trade may be made.

8. The Asian-African Conference agreed that encouragement should be given to the establishment of national and regional banks and insurance companies.

9. The Asian-African Conference felt that exchange of information on matters relating to oil, such as remittance of profits and taxation, might eventually lead to the formulation of common policies.

10. The Asian-African Conference emphasized the par-

ticular significance of the development of nuclear energy for peaceful purposes, for the Asian-African countries. The Conference welcomed the initiative of the Powers principally concerned in offering to make available information regarding the use of atomic energy for peaceful purposes; urged the speedy establishment of the International Atomic Energy Agency which should provide for adequate representation of the Asian-African countries on the executive authority of the Agency; and recommended to the Asian and African Governments to take full advantage of the training and other facilities in the peaceful uses of atomic energy offered by the countries sponsoring such programmes.

11. The Asian-African Conference agreed to the appointment of Liaison Officers in participating countries, to be nominated by their respective national Governments, for the exchange of information and ideas on matters of mutual interest. It recommended that fuller use should be made of the existing international organizations, and participating countries who were not members of such international organizations, but were eligible, should secure membership.

12. The Asian-African Conference recommended that there should be prior consultation of participating countries in international forums with a view, as far as possible, to furthering their mutual economic interest. It is, however, not intended to form a regional bloc.

B. *Cultural Cooperation*

1. The Asian-African Conference was convinced that among the most powerful means of promoting understanding among nations is the development of cultural cooperation. Asia and Africa have been the cradle of great religions and civilizations which have enriched other cultures and civilizations while themselves being enriched in the process. Thus the cultures of Asia and Africa are based on spiritual and universal foundations. Unfortunately contacts among Asian and African countries were interrupted during the past centuries. The peoples of Asia and Africa are now animated by a keen and sincere desire to renew their old cultural contacts and develop new ones in the context of the modern world. All participating Governments at the Conference reiterated their determination to work for closer cultural cooperation.

2. The Asian-African Conference took note of the fact that the existence of colonialism in many parts of Asia and Africa in whatever form it may be not only prevents cultural

cooperation but also suppresses the national cultures of the people. Some colonial powers have denied to their dependent peoples basic rights in the sphere of education and culture which hampers the development of their personality and also prevents cultural intercourse with other Asian and African peoples. This is particularly true in the case of Tunisia, Algeria and Morocco, where the basic right of the people to study their own language and culture has been suppressed. Similar discrimination has been practised against African and coloured people in some parts of the Continent of Africa. The Conference felt that these policies amount to a denial of the fundamental rights in the sphere of education and culture in some parts of Asia and Africa by this and other forms of cultural suppression.

In particular, the Conference condemned racialism as a means of cultural suppression.

3. It was not from any sense of exclusiveness or rivalry with other groups of nations and other civilisations and cultures that the Conference viewed the development of cultural cooperation among Asian and African countries. True to the age-old tradition of tolerance and universality, the Conference believed that Asian and African cultural cooperation should be developed in the larger context of world cooperation.

Side by side with the development of Asian-African cultural cooperation the countries of Asia and Africa desire to develop cultural contacts with others. This would enrich their own culture and would also help in the promotion of world peace and understanding.

4. There are many countries in Asia and Africa which have not yet been able to develop their educational, scientific and technical institutions. The Conference recommended that countries in Asia and Africa which are more fortunately placed in this respect should give facilities for the admission of students and trainees from such countries to their institutions. Such facilities should also be made available to the Asian and African people in Africa to whom opportunities for acquiring higher education are at present denied.

5. The Asian-African Conference felt that the promotion of cultural cooperation among countries of Asia and Africa should be directed towards:

(I) the acquisition of knowledge of each other's country;
(II) mutual cultural exchange, and
(III) exchange of information.

6. The Asian-African Conference was of opinion that at this stage the best results in cultural cooperation would be achieved by pursuing bilateral arrangements to implement its recommendations and by each country taking action on its own, wherever possible and feasible.

C. *Human Rights and Self-determination*

1. The Asian-African Conference declared its full support of the fundamental principles of Human Rights as set forth in the Charter of the United Nations and took note of the Universal Declaration of Human Rights as a common standard of achievement for all peoples and all nations.

The Conference declared its full support of the principles of self-determination of peoples and nations as set forth in the Charter of the United Nations and took note of the United Nations resolutions on the rights of peoples and nations to self-determination, which is a pre-requisite of the full enjoyment of all fundamental Human Rights.

2. The Asian-African Conference deplored the policies and practices of racial segregation and discrimination which form the basis of government and human relations in large regions of Africa and in other parts of the world. Such conduct is not only a gross violation of human rights, but also a denial of the fundamental values of civilisation and the dignity of man.

The Conference extended its warm sympathy and support for the courageous stand taken by the victims of racial discrimination, especially by the peoples of African and Indian and Pakistani origin in South Africa; applauded all those who sustain their cause, re-affirmed the determination of Asian-African peoples to eradicate every trace of racialism that might exist in their own countries; and pledged to use its full moral influence to guard against the danger of falling victims to the same evil in their struggle to eradicate it.

D. *Problems of Dependent Peoples*

1. The Asian-African Conference discussed the problems of dependent peoples and colonialism and the evils arising from the subjection of peoples to alien subjugation, domination and exploitation.

The Conference is agreed:

(a) in declaring that colonialism in all its manifestations is an evil which should speedily be brought to an end;
(b) in affirming that the subjection of peoples to alien subjugation, domination and exploitation constitutes a denial

of fundamental human rights, is contrary to the Charter of the United Nations and is an impediment to the promotion of world peace and cooperation;
(c) in declaring its support of the cause of freedom and independence for all such people, and
(d) In calling upon the powers concerned to grant freedom and independence to such peoples.

2. In view of the unsettled situation in North Africa and of the persisting denial to the peoples of North Africa of their right to self-determination, the Asian-African Conference declared its support of the rights of the people of Algeria, Morocco and Tunisia to self-determination and independence and urged the French Government to bring about a peaceful settlement of the issue without delay.

E. *Other Problems*

1. In view of the existing tension in the Middle East, caused by the situation in Palestine and of the danger of that tension to world peace, the Asian-African Conference declared its support of the rights of the Arab people of Palestine and called for the implementation of the United Nations Resolutions on Palestine and the achievement of the peaceful settlement of the Palestine question.

2. The Asian-African Conference, in the context of its expressed attitude on the abolition of colonialism, supported the position of Indonesia in the case of West Irian based on the relevant agreements between Indonesia and the Netherlands.

The Asian-African Conference urged the Netherlands Government to reopen negotiations as soon as possible, to implement their obligations under the above-mentioned agreements and expressed the earnest hope that the United Nations would assist the parties concerned in finding a peaceful solution to the dispute.

3. The Asian-African Conference supported the position of Yemen in the case of Aden and the Southern parts of Yemen known as the Protectorates and urged the parties concerned to arrive at a peaceful settlement of the dispute.

F. *Promotion of World Peace and Cooperation*

1. The Asian-African Conference, taking note of the fact that several States have still not been admitted to the United Nations, considered that for effective cooperation for world peace, membership in the United Nations should be univer-

sal, called on the Security Council to support the admission of all those States which are qualified for membership in terms of the Charter. In the opinion of the Asian-African Conference, the following among participating countries, viz: Cambodia, Ceylon, Japan, Jordan, Libya, Nepal, a unified Vietnam were so qualified.

The Conference considered that the representation of the countries of the Asian-African region on the Security Council, in relation to the principle of equitable geographical distribution, was inadequate. It expressed the view that as regards the distribution of the non-permanent seats, the Asian-African countries which, under the arrangement arrived at in London in 1946, are precluded from being elected, should be enabled to serve on the Security Council, so that they might make a more effective contribution to the maintenance of international peace and security.

2. The Asian-African Conference having considered the dangerous situation of international tension existing and the risks confronting the whole human race from the outbreak of global war in which the destructive power of all types of armaments, including nuclear and thermo-nuclear weapons, would be employed, invited the attention of all nations to the terrible consequences that would follow if such a war were to break out.

The Conference considered that disarmament and the prohibition of the production, experimentation and use of nuclear and thermo-nuclear weapons of war are imperative to save mankind and civilisation from the fear and prospect of wholesale destruction. It considered that the nations of Asia and Africa assembled here have a duty towards humanity and civilisation to proclaim their support for disarmament and for the prohibition of these weapons and to appeal to nations principally concerned and to world opinion, to bring about such disarmament and prohibition.

The Conference considered that effective international control should be established and maintained to implement such disarmament and prohibition and that speedy and determined efforts should be made to this end.

Pending the total prohibition of the manufacture of nuclear and thermo-nuclear weapons, this Conference appealed to all the powers concerned to reach agreement to suspend experiments with such weapons.

The Conference declared that universal disarmament is an absolute necessity for the preservation of peace and requested the United Nations to continue its efforts and appealed to all concerned speedily to bring about the regulation, limitation, control and reduction of all armed forces and armaments, including the prohibition of the production, experimentation and use of all weapons of mass destruction, and to establish effective international control to this end.

G. *Declaration on the Promotion of World Peace and Cooperation*

The Asian-African Conference gave anxious thought to the question of world peace and cooperation. It viewed with deep concern the present state of international tension with its danger of an atomic world war. The problem of peace is correlative with the problem of international security. In this connection, all States should cooperate, especially through the United Nations, in bringing about the reduction of armaments and the elimination of nuclear weapons under effective international control. In this way, international peace can be promoted and nuclear energy may be used exclusively for peaceful purposes. This would help answer the needs particularly of Asia and Africa, for what they urgently require are social progress and better standards of life in larger freedom. Freedom and peace are interdependent. The right of self-determination must be enjoyed by all peoples, and freedom and independence must be granted, with the least possible delay, to those who are still dependent peoples. Indeed, all nations should have the right freely to choose their own political and economic systems and their own way of life, in conformity with the purposes and principles of the Charter of the United Nations.

Free from mistrust and fear, and with confidence and goodwill towards each other, nations should practise tolerance and live together in peace with one another as good neighbours and develop friendly cooperation on the basis of the following principles:

1. Respect for fundamental human rights and for the purposes and principles of the Charter of the United Nations.
2. Respect for the sovereignty and territorial integrity of all nations.
3. Recognition of the equality of all races and of the equality of all nations large and small.
4. Abstention from intervention or interference in the internal affairs of another country.
5. Respect for the right of each nation to defend itself singly

or collectively, in conformity with the Charter of the United Nations.

6. (a) Abstention from the use of arrangements of collective defence to serve the particular interests of any of the big powers. (b) Abstention by any country from exerting pressures on other countries.
7. Refraining from acts or threats of aggression or the use of force against the territorial integrity or political independence of any country.
8. Settlement of all international disputes by peaceful means, such as negotiation, conciliation, arbitration or judicial settlement as well as other peaceful means of the parties' own choice, in conformity with the Charter of the United Nations.
9. Promotion of mutual interests and cooperation.
10. Respect for justice and international obligations.

The Asian-African Conference declared its conviction that friendly cooperation in accordance with these principles would effectively contribute to the maintenance and promotion of international peace and security, while cooperation in the economic, social and cultural fields would help bring about the common prosperity and well-being of all.

The Asian-African Conference recommended that the five sponsoring countries consider the convening of the next meeting of the Conference, in consultation with the participating countries.

CHAPTER FIVE

THE NEAR AND MIDDLE EAST AND AFRICA

A. The Baghdad Pact.

1. *Pact of Mutual Cooperation between Iraq and Turkey, Signed at Baghdad, February 24, 1955.*[1]

Whereas the friendly and brotherly relations existing between Iraq and Turkey are in constant progress, and in order to complement the contents of the Treaty of friendship and good neighbourhood concluded between His Majesty the King of Iraq and His Excellency The President of the Turkish Republic signed in Ankara on the 29th of March, 1946, which recognized the fact that peace and security between the two countries is an integral part of the peace and security of all the Nations of the world and in particular the Nations of the Middle East, and that it is the basis for their foreign policies;

Whereas Article 11 of the Treaty of Joint Defence and Economic Co-operation between the Arab League states provides that no provision of that Treaty shall in any way affect, or is designed to affect any of the rights and obligations accruing to the contracting parties from the United Nations Charter;

And having realised the great responsibilities borne by them in their capacity as members of the United Nations concerned with the maintenance of peace and security in the Middle East region which necessitate taking the required measures in accordance with Article 51 of the United Nations Charter;

They have been fully convinced of the necessity of concluding a pact fulfilling these aims and for that purpose have appointed as their Plenipotentiaries:

His Majesty King Faisal II
King of Iraq
His Excellency Al Farik Nuri As-Said
Prime Minister

[1] *The Middle East Journal,* v. 9, No. 2 (Spring 1955), pp. 177-178.

His Excellency Burhanuddin Bash-Ayan
Acting Minister for Foreign Affairs

His Excellency Celal Bayar
President of the Turkish Republic
His Excellency Adnan Menderes
Prime Minister
His Excellency Professor Fuat Köprülü
Minister for Foreign Affairs

who have communicated their full powers, found to be in good and due form, have agreed as follows:

ARTICLE I

Consistent with Article 51 of the United Nations Charter the High Contracting Parties will co-operate for their security and defence. Such measures as they agree to take to give effect to this co-operation may form the subject of special agreements with each other.

ARTICLE II

In order to ensure the realisation and effect application of the co-operation provided for in Article I above, the competent authorities of the High Contracting Parties will determine the measures to be taken as soon as the present Pact enters into force. These measures will become operative as soon as they have been approved by the Governments of the High Contracting Parties.

ARTICLE III

The High Contracting Parties undertake to refrain from any interference whatsoever in each other's internal affairs. They will settle any dispute between themselves in a peaceful way in accordance with the United Nations Charter.

ARTICLE IV

The High Contracting Parties declare that the dispositions of the present Pact are not in contradiction with any of the international obligations contracted by either of them with any third state or states. They do not derogate from, and cannot be interpreted as derogating from, the said international obligations. The High Contracting Parties undertake not to enter into any international obligation incompatible with the present Pact.

ARTICLE V

This pact shall be open for accession to any member of the Arab League or any other state actively concerned with the security and peace in this region and which is fully recognized by both of the High Contracting Parties.[2] Accession shall come into force from the date of which the instrument of accession of the state concerned is deposited with the Ministry of Foreign Affairs of Iraq.

Any acceding State Party to the present Pact may conclude special agreements, in accordance with Article I, with one or more states parties to the present Pact. The competent authority of any acceding State may determine measures in accordance with Article 2. These measures will become operative as soon as they have been approved by the Governments of the Parties concerned.

ARTICLE VI

A Permanent Council at Ministerial level will be set up to function within the framework of the purposes of this Pact when at least four Powers become parties to the Pact.

The Council will draw up its own rules of procedure.

ARTICLE VII

This Pact remains in force for a period of five years renewable for other five year periods. Any Contracting Party may withdraw from the Pact by notifying the other Parties in writing of its desire to do so, six months before the expiration of any of the above-mentioned periods, in which case the Pact remains valid for the other Parties.

ARTICLE VIII

This Pact shall be ratified by the Contracting Parties and ratifications shall be exchanged at Ankara as soon as possible. Thereafter it shall come into force from the date of the exchange of ratifications.

IN WITNESS whereof, the said Plenipotentiaries have signed the present Pact in Arabic, Turkish and English all three texts being equally authentic except in the case of doubt when the English text shall prevail.

DONE in duplicate at Baghdad this second day of Rajab 1374 Hijri corresponding to the twenty-fourth day of February 1955.

[2] The United Kingdom adhered to the Pact on April 5, 1955, Pakistan on September 23, 1955 and Iran on October 19, 1955.

2. *Communiqué, Baghdad Pact Council Meeting, Baghdad, November 22, 1955.*[3]

The inaugural meeting of the Baghdad Pact Powers, Iran, Iraq, Pakistan, Turkey and the United Kingdom, was held in Baghdad on November 21 and 22 under the chairmanship of the Prime Minister of Iraq, Al Sayyed Nuri Al-Said. Iran was represented by the Prime Minister Hussein Ala; Pakistan by the Prime Minister Choudhury Mohammed Ali; Turkey by the Prime Minister Adnan Menderes; and the United Kingdom by the Foreign Secretary, the Right Honorable Mr. Harold Macmillan.

2. The U.S. Government, having accepted the invitation of the Baghdad Pact Powers to take part in their proceedings in the capacity of observers, was represented on the Council by the U.S. Ambassador at Baghdad and on the military committee by a United States Service Representative [Adm. John H. Cassady].

The Council welcomed the intention expressed by the U.S. Government to establish permanent political and military liaison with the Council and to have an observer present at the organizational meeting of the economic committee.[4]

3. The Government of Iraq emphasized that, as laid down in the preamble and in paragraph 4 of the Baghdad Pact, the responsibilities of Iraq under the pact and as a member of the Council are in full accord with her obligations under the treaty of joint defence and economic cooperation between the Arab League States. The other member powers were glad to note this.

4. The Council decided that the Baghdad Pact, the special agreement concluded under the Pact between Iraq and the United Kingdom,[5] and the instruments of accession of the Powers who have joined the Pact, should be registered by the Government of Iraq with the United Nations.

5. The 5 governments in council reaffirmed their intention as provided in the Pact and consistently with Article 51 of the

[3] *Department of State Bulletin,* v. 34 (January 2, 1956), pp. 16-18.

[4] The United States, though not a member of the Pact, expressed willingness to establish military and political liaison with it. It designated the American Ambassador to Iraq (Gallman) as its political liaison officer and the American Army Attaché in Baghdad (Tucker) as its military liaison officer with the Baghdad Pact Organization. See Department of State Press Release 660, dated November 19, 1955.

[5] On April 4, 1955 the United Kingdom and Iraq signed a new agreement replacing the Anglo-Iraqi treaty of June 30, 1930.

United Nations Charter to work in full partnership with united purpose for peace and security in the Middle East, to defend their territories against aggression or subversion, and to promote the welfare and prosperity of the peoples in that region.

6. The 5 governments in council reviewed the critical world situation particularly in the light of the Geneva Conference and resolved in consequence to maintain constant contact and even closer cooperation in the face of any threat to their common interests.

7. The five governments set up a permanent Council as provided for in Article 6 of the Pact. The Council will be deemed to be in continuous session. Ministerial meetings will take place at least once a year. Iraq as host country will provide the first chairmanship until the end of 1956, and the chairmanship will be held thereafter in alphabetical order of the other powers for a period of 1 year. If, however, additional meetings were to be held elsewhere than in the capital of the regular chairman, the host country will be asked to provide the chairman for that meeting.

8. The permanent seat of the organization and its dependent bodies shall be in Baghdad.

9. Each government will appoint a deputy representative to the Council with Ambassadorial rank.

10. The Council, through their permanent deputies in Baghdad, shall meet at any time to discuss any matters of political, economic and military interest to the 5 governments.

11. The Council agreed that a permanent secretariat for the Baghdad Pact organization should be established in Baghdad.

12. The Council established a permanent military committee responsible and subordinate to the Council and charged with carrying out such directive as may be entrusted to it. The representatives of the 5 governments on the military committee will be their Chiefs of Staff or their deputies.

13. The military committee at its first meetings laid the foundations of a military organization to ensure the security of the region. In this connection the Council noted that the Governments of Iraq and of the United Kingdom have concluded a special agreement under the pact on the 4th of April, 1955. By this agreement Iraq assumed full responsibility for her own defence, and took over the command and the guarding of all defence installations in Iraq. Withdrawal of United

Kingdom forces for the bases at Habbaniya and Shaiba is proceeding according to plan and as stipulated in the special agreement between Iraq and the United Kingdom. The Council further noted that the United Kingdom is affording Iraq help in building up her armed forces and maintaining them in a state of readiness for the defence of Iraq.

14. The Council took note with appreciation of the generous and valuable help extended to each of them by the United States Government in the form of free aid in the provision of arms and other military equipment to enable them to strengthen their defence against aggression, and of the support and encouragement of the U.S. Government in their efforts to cooperate for peace.

15. An economic committee was set up to develop and strengthen the economic and financial resources of the region. In particular the economic committee will consider ways and means of sharing experience in the field of development; and how a regional approach to some of the problems involved would be a common benefit, including discussion on a regional basis with the World Bank, the World Health Organization, UNICEF and other specialized agencies.

16. In this connection the Council viewed with satisfaction the practical progress already made in this field. They noted, for example, that the United Kingdom has decided to assist Iraq by making available gold to constitute a reserve of 5 million pounds during the next 2 years, and by other forms of financial cooperation.

17. The Council noted the statement of the U.K. representative that his government is ready to use their experience in the field of atomic energy to assist other countries of the pact with their own atomic energy projects for the peaceful application of the science; and particularly that they were ready to assist Baghdad Pact countries in the application of atomic techniques with special reference to local and regional problems. The Council welcomed this offer and directed the economic committee to consider its practical application.

18. The 5 governments expressed their gratification for the extensive economic assistance which has been freely accorded by the Government of the United States.

19. The Council decided to meet again in special session in Tehran during the first half of April, 1956. They directed the military committee and the economic committee to report progress at that session.

B. The Arab-Israeli Dispute.

1. *Resolution of the United Nations Security Council, Adopted March 29, 1955.*[1]

Recalling its resolutions of 15 July 1948, 11 August 1949, 17 November 1950, 18 May 1951 and 25 November 1953;

Having heard the report of the Chief of Staff of the Truce Supervision Organization and statements by the Representatives of Egypt and Israel;

Noting that the Egyptian-Israeli Mixed Armistice Commission on 6 March 1955 determined that a "prearranged and planned attack ordered by Israeli authorities" was "committed by Israeli regular army forces against the Egyptian regular army force" in the Gaza Strip on February 28th, 1955;

Condemns this attack as a violation of the cease-fire provisions of the Security Council resolution of 15 July 1948 and as inconsistent with the obligations of the parties under the General Armistice Agreement between Egypt and Israel and under the Charter;

Calls again upon Israel to take all necessary measures to prevent such actions;

Expresses its conviction that the maintenance of the General Armistice Agreement is threatened by any deliberate violation of that Agreement by one of the parties to it, and that no progress towards the return of permanent peace in Palestine can be made unless the parties comply strictly with their obligations under the General Armistice Agreement and the cease-fire provisions of its resolution of July 15, 1948.

2. *Resolution of the United Nations Security Council, Adopted March 30, 1955.*[2]

The Security Council,

Taking note of those sections of the report by the Chief of Staff of the Truce Supervision Organization which deal with the general conditions on the Armistice Demarcation Line between Egypt and Israel, and the causes of the present tension;

Anxious that all possible steps shall be taken to preserve

[1] United Nations Document S/3378, dated March 29, 1955. The resolution, sponsored jointly by the U.S., U.K. and France was adopted unanimously.
[2] United Nations Document S/3379, dated March 30, 1955. The resolution, sponsored jointly by the U.S., U.K. and France, was adopted unanimously.

security in this area, within the framework of the General Armistice Agreement between Egypt and Israel;

Requests the Chief of Staff to continue his consultations with the Governments of Egypt and Israel with a view to the introduction of practical measures to that end;

Notes that the Chief of Staff has already made certain concrete proposals to this effect;

Calls upon the Governments of Egypt and Israel to cooperate with the Chief of Staff with regard to his proposals, bearing in mind that, in the opinion of the Chief of Staff, infiltration can be reduced to an occasional nuisance if an agreement were effected between the parties on the lines he has proposed;

Requests the Chief of Staff to keep the Council informed of the progress of his discussions.

3. *The Middle East: Address by the Secretary of State (Dulles) before the Council on Foreign Relations, New York, August 26, 1955.*[3]

One of the first things I did as Secretary of State was to go to the Middle East. I wanted to see for myself that area so rich in culture and religious tradition, yet now so torn by strife and bitterness. So, in the spring of 1953, I visited Egypt, Israel, Jordan, Syria, Lebanon, Iraq, and Saudi Arabia. Upon my return I spoke of the impressions gathered on that trip and of the hopes which I held as a result of talks with leaders and people there.[4]

Some of those hopes have become realities. At that time the Suez Base was a center of controversy and of potential strife. Now, as a result of patient effort, in a spirit of conciliation, the problem of the Suez Base has been successfully resolved.

Another problem which was then concerning many of the leaders in the Middle East was that of the security of the area. It was clear that effective defense depended upon collective measures and that such measures, to be dependable, needed to be a natural drawing together of those who felt a sense of common destiny in the face of what could be a common danger. Here, too, there has been some encouraging progress.

A third problem which called for attention was the need for water to irrigate land. I mentioned in my report the

[3] Department of State Press Release 517, dated August 26, 1955.
[4] *Department of State Bulletin,* v. 28 (June 15, 1953), pp. 831-835.

possibility that the rivers flowing through the Jordan Valley might be used to make this valley a source of livelihood rather than dispute. Since then Ambassador Eric Johnston has held talks with the governments of countries through which the River Jordan runs. They have shown an encouraging willingness to accept the principle of coordinated arrangements for the use of the waters. Plans for the development of the valley are well advanced. Ambassador Johnston is now on his fourth visit to the countries concerned in an effort to eliminate the small margins of difference which still exist.

A beginning has been made, as you see, in doing away with the obstacles that stand in the way of the aspirations of the Middle Eastern peoples. It is my hope—and that is the hope of which I would now speak—that the time has come when it is useful to think in terms of further steps toward stability, tranquillity, and progress in the Middle East.

The Arab-Israel Problem

What are the principal remaining problems? They are those which were unresolved by the armistices of 1949 which ended the fighting between Israelis and Arabs. Before taking up these problems specifically, I would first pay high tribute to what the United Nations has done to preserve tranquillity and to serve humanity in the area. Despite these indispensable efforts, three problems remain that conspicuously require to be solved.

The first is the tragic plight of the 900,000 refugees who formerly lived in the territory that is now occupied by Israel.

The second is the pall of fear that hangs over the Arab and Israel people alike. The Arab countries fear that Israel will seek by violent means to expand at their expense. The Israelis fear that the Arabs will gradually marshal superior forces to be used to drive them into the sea, and they suffer from the economic measures now taken against them.

The third is the lack of fixed permanent boundaries between Israel and its Arab neighbors.

There are other important problems. But if these three principal problems could be dealt with, then the way would be paved for the solution of others.

These three problems seem capable of solution, and surely there is need.

Border clashes take an almost weekly toll of human lives and inflame an already dangerous mood of hatred. The sufferings of the Arab refugees are drawn out almost beyond the point of endurance. The fears which are at work, on each side, lead to a heavy burden of armament, which constitutes a serious drag on economic and social progress. Responsible leaders are finding it hard to turn their full attention and energies to the positive task of creating conditions of healthy growth.

Serious as the present situation is, there is a danger that, unless it improves, it will get worse. One ill leads to another, and cause and effect are hard to sort out. The atmosphere, if it worsens, could becloud clear judgments, making appear attractive what would in fact be reckless.

Both sides suffer greatly from the present situation, and both are anxious for what they would regard as a just and equitable solution. But neither has been able to find that way.

This may be a situation where mutual friends could serve the common good. This is particularly true since the area may not, itself, possess all of the ingredients needed for the full and early building of a condition of security and well-being.

The United States, as a friend of both Israelis and Arabs, has given the situation deep and anxious thought and has come to certain conclusions, the expression of which may help men of good will within the area to fresh constructive efforts. I speak in this matter with the authority of President Eisenhower.

Proposed Loan to Israel

To end the plight of the 900,000 refugees requires that these uprooted people should, through resettlement and, to such an extent as may be feasible, repatriation, be enabled to resume a life of dignity and self-respect. To this end, there is need to create more arable land where refugees can find permanent homes and gain their own livelihood through their own work. Fortunately, there are practical projects for water development which can make this possible.

All this requires money.

Compensation is due from Israel to the refugees. However, it may be that Israel cannot, unaided, now make adequate compensation. If so, there might be an international loan to enable Israel to pay the compensation which is due and which would enable many of the refugees to find for themselves a better way of life.

President Eisenhower would recommend substantial participation by the United States in such a loan for such a purpose. Also he would recommend that the United States contribute to the realization of water development and irrigation projects which would, directly or indirectly, facilitate the resettlement of the refugees.

These projects would, of course, do much more than aid in the resettlement of refugees. They would enable the people throughout the area to enjoy a better life. Furthermore, a solution to the refugee problem would help in eliminating the problem of recurrent incidents which have plagued and embittered the settlements on both sides of the borders.

Collective Security Measures

The second principal problem which I mentioned is that of fear. The nature of this fear is such that it is hardly within the capacity of the countries of the area, acting alone, to replace the fear with a sense of security. There, as in many other areas, security can be assured only by collective measures which commit decisive power to the deterring of aggression.

President Eisenhower has authorized me to say that, given a solution of the other related problems, he would recommend that the United States join in formal treaty engagements to prevent or thwart any effort by either side to alter by force the boundaries between Israel and its Arab neighbors. I hope that other countries would be willing to join in such a security guaranty, and that it would be sponsored by the United Nations.

By such collective security measures the area could be relieved of the acute fears which both sides now profess. The families located near the boundaries could relax from the strain of feeling that violent death may suddenly strike them; the peoples of the area whose standards of living are already too low would no longer have to carry the burden of what threatens to become an armaments race if indeed it does not become a war; the political leadership of the area could devote itself to constructive tasks.

Problem of Boundaries

If there is to be a guaranty of borders, it would be normal that there should be prior agreement upon what the borders are. That is the third major problem. The existing lines separating Israel and the Arab states were fixed by the Armistice Agreements of 1949. They were not designed to be permanent frontiers in every respect; in part, at least, they reflected the status of the fighting at the moment.

The task of drawing permanent boundaries is admittedly one of difficulty. There is no single and sure guide, for each of two conflicting claims may seem to have merit. The difficulty is increased by the fact that even territory which is barren has acquired a sentimental significance. Surely the overall advantages of the measures here outlined would outweigh vastly any net disadvantages of the adjustments needed to convert armistice lines of danger into boundary lines of safety. In spite of conflicting claims and sentiments, I believe it is possible to find a way of reconciling the vital interests of all the parties. The United States would be willing to help in the search for a solution if the parties to the dispute should desire.

If agreement can be reached on these basic problems of refugees, fear, and boundaries, it should prove possible to find solutions for other questions, largely economic, which presently fan the flames of hostility and resentment.

It should also be possible to reach agreement on the status of Jerusalem. The United States would give its support to a United Nations review of this problem.

I have not attempted to enumerate all the issues on which it would be desirable to have a settlement; nor have I tried to outline in detail the form which a settlement of any of the elements might take. I have tried to show that possibilities exist for an immeasurable improvement and that the possibilities do not require any nation taking action which would be against its interests whether those interests be measured in terms of material strength or in terms of national prestige and honor. I have also, I trust, made clear that the Government of the United States is disposed to enlarge those possibilities by contributions of its own, if this be desired by those concerned.

Both sides in this strife have a noble past, a heritage of rich contributions to civilization; both have fostered progress in science and the arts. Each side is predominantly representative of one of the world's great religions. Both sides desire to achieve a good life for their people and to share, and contribute to, the advancements of this century.

At a time when a great effort is being made to ease the tension which has long prevailed between the Soviet and Western worlds, can we not hope that a similar spirit should prevail in the Middle East? That is our plea. The spirit of conciliation and of the good neighbor brings rich rewards to the people and to the nations. If doing that involves some burdens, they are burdens which the United States would share, just as we would share the satisfaction which would result to all peoples if happiness, contentment, and good will could drive hatred and misery away from peoples whom we hold in high respect and honor.

4. *Resolution of the United Nations Security Council, Adopted September 8, 1955.*[5]

The Security Council,

Recalling its resolution of 30 March 1955,[6]

Having received the report of the Chief of Staff of the Truce Supervision Organization,[7]

Noting with grave concern the discontinuance of the talks initiated by the Chief of Staff in accordance with the abovementioned resolution,

Deploring the recent outbreak of violence in the area along the Armistice Demarcation Line established between Egypt and Israel on 24 February 1949,

1. Notes with approval the acceptance by both parties of the appeal of the Chief of Staff for an unconditional cease-fire;

2. Calls upon both parties forthwith to take all steps necessary to bring about order and tranquility in the area, and in particular to desist from further acts of violence and to continue the cease-fire in full force and effect;

3. Endorses the view of the Chief of Staff that the armed forces of both parties should be clearly and effectively separated by measures such as those which he has proposed;

4. Declares that freedom of movement must be afforded to United Nations Observers in the area to enable them to fulfill their functions;

5. Calls upon both parties to appoint representatives to meet with the Chief of Staff and to co-operate fully with him to these ends; and

6. Requests the Chief of Staff to report to the Security Council on the action taken to carry out this Resolution.

[5] United Nations Document S/3432, dated September 8, 1955. The resolution, sponsored jointly by the U.S., U.K. and France, was adopted unanimously.

[6] See above, pp. 348-349.

[7] United Nations Document S/3430, dated September 6, 1955.

5. *Joint Anglo-American Statement on the Sale of Arms to Countries in the Middle East, New York, September 27, 1955.*[8]

The United States Secretary of State and British Foreign Secretary discussed together reports relating to their arms supply policies in the Middle East.

They wish to state that the United States and British Governments have for some time been in close consultation with each other as well as with other governments in relation to this matter and that there has been, and continues to be, complete harmony of views between their two governments.

Both governments base their policies on the desire, on the one hand, to enable the various countries to provide for internal security and for their defense, and on the other, to avoid an arms race which would inevitably increase the tensions in the area. They will continue, and hope other governments will continue, to be guided by these principles.

6. *News Conference Statement by the Secretary of State (Dulles) on Soviet Shipments of Arms to Arab Countries, October 4, 1955.*[9]

At my press conference the last of August [August 30] I was asked about possible Soviet bloc shipments of arms to Arab countries. I made two observations. The first was that the Arab countries were independent governments and free to do whatever they wished in the matter. My second observation was that from the standpoint of the U.S. relations with the Soviet Union, such delivery of arms would not contribute to relaxing tensions.

Those two observations stand today. I might add this:

It is difficult to be critical of countries which, feeling themselves endangered, seek the arms which they sincerely believe they need for defense. On the other hand, I doubt very much that, under the conditions which prevail in the area, it is possible for any country to get security through an arms race. Also it is not easy or pleasant to speculate on the probable motives of the Soviet bloc leaders.

[8] *Department of State Bulletin,* v. 33 (October 10, 1955), p. 560.

[9] Department of State Press Release 588, dated October 4, 1955. The question of Soviet bloc shipments of arms to Arab countries arose as a result of the confirmation by the Premier of Egypt (Nasser) on September 27, 1955 of the conclusion of a trade agreement with Czechoslovakia whereby Egypt would receive armaments in return for cotton and wool.

In my talk about this matter of August 26, I spoke of the fear which dominated the area and said that I felt that it could be dissipated only by collective measures designed to deter aggression by anyone.[10] I proposed a security guarantee sponsored by the United Nations. That, I said, would relieve the acute fears which both sides now profess.

It is still my hope that such a solution may be found.

7. *State Department Announcement on Israeli-Arab Hostilities, November 5, 1955.*[11]

During recent weeks, especially during the last few days, the United States has noted, with deep concern, the increasing tempo of hostilities between Israel and Egypt. According to our information there have been violations of the General Armistice Agreement by both Israel and Egypt which have led to bloodshed and loss of life. The United States deplores resort to force for the settlement of disputes. The Secretary General of the United Nations and General Burns have put forward proposals to Israel and Egypt which are designed to ease the present situation along their common border. The United States strongly supports the United Nations' efforts to achieve settlement by peaceful means, especially the current proposals of General Burns, who is the Chief of Staff of the United Nations Truce Supervision Organization.

Recent reports have also been received that United Nations Observers who are under General Burns' direction have been prevented from carrying out their assigned functions. The United States continues to believe that these United Nations Observers should have full liberty to perform their peaceful functions.

Assistant Secretary Allen informed the Ambassadors of Israel and Egypt of the attitude of the United States and asked for information with respect to their Governments' intentions regarding these matters.

8. *Statement by the President on Hostilities in the Near East, Denver, November 9, 1955.*[12]

All Americans have been following with deep concern the latest developments in the Near East. The recent outbreak

[10] See above, pp. 349-354.
[11] Department of State Press Release 638, dated November 5, 1955.
[12] *Department of State Bulletin,* v. 33 (November 21, 1955), p. 845.

of hostilities has led to a sharp increase in tensions. These events inevitably retard our search for world peace. Insecurity in one region is bound to affect the world as a whole.

While we continue willing to consider requests for arms needed for legitimate self-defense, we do not intend to contribute to an arms competition in the Near East because we do not think such a race would be in the true interest of any of the participants. The policy which we believed would best promote the interests and the security of the peoples of the area was expressed in the Tripartite Declaration of May 25, 1950.[13] This still remains our policy.

I stated last year that our goal in the Near East as elsewhere is a just peace. Nothing has taken place since which invalidates our fundamental policies, policies based on friendship for all of the peoples of the area.

We believe that true security must be based upon a just and reasonable settlement. The Secretary of State outlined on August 26th[14] the economic and security contributions which this country was prepared to make toward such a solution. On that occasion I authorized Mr. Dulles to state that, given a solution of the other related problems, I would recommend that the United States join in formal treaty engagements to prevent or thwart any effort by either side to alter by force the boundaries between Israel and its Arab neighbors.

Recent developments have made it all the more imperative that a settlement be found. The United States will continue to play its full part and will support firmly the United Nations, which has already contributed so markedly to minimize violence in the area. I hope that other nations of the world will cooperate in this endeavor, thereby contributing significantly to world peace.

9. *Letter from the President to Rabbi Silver, November 15, 1955.*[15]

I am glad to comply with your request to send a message to the meeting which you are addressing this evening, as I know of your great concern about the recent developments in the Near East which disturb all of us.

A threat to peace in the Near East is a threat to world peace. As I said the other day,[16] while we continue willing

[13] *Documents on American Foreign Relations, 1950,* pp. 659-662.
[14] See above, pp. 349-354.
[15] *Department of State Bulletin,* v. 33 (November 28, 1955), p. 895.
[16] See also the preceding document.

to consider requests for arms needed for legitimate self-defense, we do not intend to contribute to an arms competition in the Near East. We will continue to be guided by the policies of the Tripartite Declaration of May 25, 1950. We believe this policy best promotes the interest and security of the peoples of the area.

We believe the true and lasting security in the area must be based upon a just and reasonable settlement. It seems to me that current problems are capable of resolution by peaceful means. There is no reason why a settlement of these problems cannot be found, and when realized I would be prepared to recommend that the United States join in formal treaty engagements to prevent or thwart any effort by either side to alter by force the boundaries upon which Israel and its immediate neighbors agree.

The need for a peaceful settlement becomes daily more imperative. The United States will play its full part in working toward such a settlement and will support firmly the United Nations in its efforts to prevent violence in the area. By firm friendship towards Israel and all other Nations in the Near East, we shall continue to contribute to the peace of the world.

DWIGHT D. EISENHOWER

C. Egypt.

United States Assistance in the Construction of the High Aswan Dam; Communiqué on Discussions between the Minister of Finance of Egypt (Kaissouni) and the Acting Secretary of State (Hoover), Washington, December 17, 1955.[1]

Mr. Abdel Moneim El Kaissouni, Egyptian Minister of Finance, met yesterday with Acting Secretary of State Herbert Hoover, Jr., British Ambassador Sir Roger Makins and World Bank President Eugene Black for final talks before his departure for Cairo.

During their stay in Washington, Mr. Kaissouni and his colleagues have been carrying on discussions with the management of the World Bank and representatives of the United States and United Kingdom Governments concerning possible assistance in the execution of the High Aswan Dam project.

[1] *Department of State Bulletin,* v. 33 (December 26, 1955), pp. 1050-1051.

The United States and British Governments assured the Egyptian Government through Mr. Kaissouni of their support in this project, which would be of inestimable importance in the development of the Egyptian economy and in the improvement of the welfare of the Egyptian people. Such assistance would take the form of grants from the United States and the United Kingdom toward defraying foreign exchange costs of the first stages of the work. This phase, involving the Coffer Dam, foundations for the main dam, and auxiliary work will take from four to five years. Further, assurance has been given to Mr. Kaissouni that the Governments of the United States and the United Kingdom would, subject to legislative authority, be prepared to consider sympathetically in the light of then existing circumstances further support toward financing the later stages to supplement World Bank financing.

Mr. Kaissouni plans to leave Washington for Egypt today, and it is understood that he will report to his Government on his talks here. Final understandings with the British and American Governments and the World Bank will await Mr. Kaissouni's consultation with the Egyptian Government.

D. French North Africa.

1. *Tunisia.*

News Conference Statement by the Secretary of State (Dulles), August 10, 1955.[1]

It is a source of much satisfaction to the United States that France and Tunisia have agreed upon conventions which provide a new framework for close cooperation between the French and Tunisian communities.[2] It is significant that agreement on these conventions was reached through negotiations on a basis of equality between the parties directly concerned. France and Tunisia may take real satisfaction and pride in the achievement of this agreement.

The manner in which the agreement was reached, the impressive majorities by which both Houses of the French Parliament approved the conventions, and the extensive support they have received in Tunisia indicate a common realization of the need for continued cooperation.

[1] Department of State Press Release 484, dated August 10, 1955.

[2] An agreement between the French and Tunisian governments ordering the relations between them was signed on June 3, 1955 and ratified by the French National Assembly on July 9, 1955.

The Franco-Tunisian negotiations demonstrate that mutually satisfactory progress can be made on such difficult problems if they are dealt with in time by the parties concerned with determination, realism, and good will.

2. *Algeria.*

a. *Statement by the United States Representative to the United Nations (Lodge) on Inscribing the Algerian Item on the Agenda of the General Assembly, September 22, 1955.*[3]

We believe the Assembly should bear in mind certain relevant factors as it decides whether to inscribe on its agenda the item entitled "The Question of Algeria."

Remembering that a vote on the inscription of an item is without prejudice to the ultimate question of the Assembly's competence, we must in this particular case take into account the following:

Unlike Morocco and Tunisia, which are French protectorates, Algeria under French law is administratively an integral part of the French Republic. We have noted in the explanatory memorandum[4] which has been submitted by the members that have proposed the item respecting Algeria that it is stated that "there is an imperative need for negotiations between the Government of France and the true representatives of the Algerian people" and that consideration of the Algerian question by the General Assembly would facilitate a solution by making the need for negotiation evident. We have noted further that reference is made to the right of the people of Algeria to independence as well as to the concern of the international community in a prompt solution of the Algerian problem, a concern to which the French Government is claimed to have failed to respond. This memorandum indicates clearly that what is sought by the sponsors of the item is the sanction of the General Assembly to a course of action intended to bring about fundamental changes in the composition of the French Republic. It is the considered conclusion of the U.S. Government that the proposed item, viewed in the context of the action proposed to be sought in the General Assembly, falls within the provisions of article 2, paragraph 7 of the United Nations Charter.

[3] *Department of State Bulletin,* v. 33 (October 3, 1955), p. 546.
[4] Not printed.

For these reasons, the United States will vote against including this item in the Assembly's agenda.[5]

b. *Statement by the United States Representative to the United Nations (Lodge) on the Decision of the General Assembly to Strike the Algerian Item from its Agenda, November 25, 1955.*[6]

The United States supported the motion of the distinguished representative from India [V. K. Krishna Menon] because we believe that in the circumstances it was wise and constructive.[7] Our reasons for opposing inscription were stated both in the General Committee[8] and in the plenary and are in the record. For the future, the United States hopes that all of us will bear in mind the grave implications of this organization in taking up questions where the action sought would conflict with the provisions of article 2, paragraph 7, of the charter.

This action today is another example of the spirit of accommodation and compromise—perhaps comity is a good word—which is essential to the proper functioning of the United Nations and to the achievement of its fundamental purposes.

We cannot, of course, close our eyes to the realities of certain situations and the differences of opinion as to what should be done about them. But this must not make us forget that the United Nations was conceived in the first place as a center for harmonizing the actions of its members.

The particular action we have just taken was made possible by wise statesmanship. Having restored the conditions necessary for full French participation in our work, we may now look forward to a continuation of such statesmanship, statesmanship for which the presence and the wise counsel of France are indispensable.

[5] The vote on inscription in the General [Steering] Committee was 5 (Egypt, Mexico, Poland, Thailand and the U.S.S.R.-8 (France, Haiti, Luxembourg, New Zealand, Norway, U.K., U.S., Assembly President)-2 (China, Ethiopia). The General Assembly, reversing the vote of the General Committee on September 30, decided by a vote of 28-27 to debate the Algerian question. Thereupon the French delegation withdrew from the Assembly.

[6] *Department of State Bulletin*, v. 33 (December 12, 1955), p. 992.

[7] The Indian proposal read: "The General Assembly decides not to consider further the item entitled 'The question of Algeria' and is therefore no longer seized of this item on the agenda of the tenth session." It was adopted by the General Assembly without objection on November 25, 1955 as resolution 909 (X).

[8] See above, p. 360.

The motion we have just approved has led us out of a most difficult situation fraught with danger for the United Nations. The United States was therefore glad to join in its approval.

3. *Morocco.*

a. *State Department Announcement on the Reinstatement of the Sultan (Mohammed V) as Sovereign of Morocco, November 18, 1955.*[9]

The U.S. Government welcomes the return of Mohammed V to Morocco and on this anniversary of his accession to the throne wishes to extend warm and friendly greetings to him and the people of Morocco.

His Majesty's return marks a significant step in the development of cooperation between Morocco and France.[10] While there are many problems yet to be worked out, the degree of concession and the friendly spirit which are demonstrated by both French and Moroccans augur well for success in working out mutually satisfactory arrangements. It is earnestly hoped that such arrangements will lead to the peace and prosperity of the Moroccan community.

b. *Statement by the United States Representative to the United Nations (Lodge) in Plenary Session of the General Assembly, November 28, 1955.*[11]

The constructive events which have taken place in connection with the Moroccan situation since it was last considered by the General Assembly give great satisfaction to the United States. It is clear now that the General Assembly last year acted wisely in adopting a resolution which, after noting reports that negotiations between France and Morocco would be initiated, expressed confidence that a satisfactory solution would be achieved.[12] The discussions held to date between France and Morocco prove that our confidence was well placed.

I wish to take this opportunity on behalf of the United

[9] Department of State Press Release 657, dated November 18, 1955.

[10] In accordance with a decision of the French Council of Ministers, Sidi Mohammed ben Yussef, who was deposed as Sultan of Morocco in 1953, was reinstated as *de jure* sovereign of Morocco at a ceremony in Paris on November 6, 1955.

[11] *Department of State Bulletin,* v. 33 (December 19, 1955), pp. 1040-1041.

[12] *Documents on American Foreign Relations, 1954,* p. 404.

States Government and the American people to express again our best wishes to His Majesty, the Sultan Mohammed V, and to the Moroccan people. His Majesty's return to Morocco was an important step toward the solution of the Moroccan problem on a basis agreed upon by France and Morocco. It is but another demonstration of the fact that mutually satisfactory progress can be made on the most difficult problems if they are dealt with in time by the parties concerned and if they are approached with determination, realism, optimism, and good will.

This year has also witnessed the signing of conventions which provide a new framework for close cooperation between France and Tunisia. Agreement on those conventions was reached through negotiations on a basis of equality between the parties directly concerned. It is this type of negotiation which the United States has always favored.

The United States believes that the similarly peaceful and progressive development of free political institutions capable of fulfilling the aspirations of the Moroccan people will benefit both France and Morocco. It would accord with the traditional sympathy of the people of the United States for those who aspire to self-government.

The Foreign Minister of France and the Sultan of Morocco announced on November 6 the basis on which the two Governments have agreed to undertake negotiations which we hope will result in more lasting bonds of amity between the two countries. It is therefore incumbent upon us in the General Assembly to do everything we can to contribute to an atmosphere in which the parties directly concerned can work out the problems outstanding between them. Their solution requires the utmost good will, patience, and restraint on both sides. That is why the United States strongly hopes that the recent disorders within the Moroccan community will cease.

The United States believes that the best way to encourage progress on this question is to demonstrate our faith in the common purpose of the two Governments directly concerned. We hope that everything will be done to make as harmonious as possible the pending negotiations which have as their goal the orderly political development and the social and economic advancement of the Moroccan people.

We hope that these negotiations will strengthen the links of friendship between the peoples of France and Morocco. The progress already made toward a more constructive relationship is evidence that this approach has commended itself to both France and Morocco as the only approach which can lead to a just and harmonious settlement of remaining differences, a settlement consistent with the spirit of the charter.

The sincere good wishes of the United States go out to the people of France and Morocco as they turn to the important negotiations which will, we are certain, lead to the achievement of their common purpose. We believe that the 31-power resolution which is before the committee is consistent with this approach. We shall therefore support it.

c. *General Assembly Resolution 911 (X), Adopted December 3, 1955.*[13]

The General Assembly,

Having considered the question of Morocco,

Noting that negotiations between France and Morocco will be initiated regarding this question,

Expressing confidence that a satisfactory solution of the question of Morocco will be achieved,

Decides to postpone further consideration of this item.

[13] United Nations General Assembly *Official Records, Tenth Session,* Supplement No. 19, pp. 3-4. The resolution was adopted by a vote of 51-0 with Australia, Belgium, Luxembourg, the Netherlands and the U.K. abstaining.

CHAPTER SIX

THE WESTERN HEMISPHERE

A. Inter-American Relations.

1. *Stepping up United States Aid to the Inter-American Highway.*

a. *Statement by the Vice President (Nixon), Panama, February 26, 1955.*[1]

The present program for United States participation in the construction of the Pan American Highway is inadequate, uneconomical, and completely unrealistic. For 15 years our Government has been publicly committed in its foreign policy to support and aid in the construction of the highway. At the present rate appropriations are being made, it will take—unless an accelerated program for completion is adopted—from 15 years to a quarter of a century to complete it. Neither the taxpayers of the United States nor those of the other countries concerned are receiving the full benefit of what is in concept and will be in fruition a magnificent program.

There is no question about United States policy with regard to the highway. We are publicly committed to aid in its completion. Dribbling out the funds as we are presently doing is penny wise and pound foolish. Such a program not only costs substantially more in dollars, but it delays inexcusably the great benefits both we and our neighbors to the South would derive from the completed highway. To put it simply, the less we spend each year on this program, the more it will cost in the long run.

Reducing the annual appropriation for the highway does not save the U.S. taxpayer's money. It increases the total bill he will eventually have to pay. Since the United States is committed to contribute its share of the cost of the highway eventually, we should move up the completion date and appropriate as much as can be economically expended consistent with the capacity of the other contributing countries each year. In conversations with the officials in each of the coun-

[1] *Department of State Bulletin*, v. 32 (April 11, 1955), pp. 596-597.

tries I have visited and with the United States Government officials who are familiar with this program, I have been advised that it would be possible to finish the highway in as little as 4 years if an accelerated program were adopted. This should be our objective. The sooner the highway is completed, the sooner it can begin to pay for itself.

Each of the Chiefs of State of the countries I have visited and each of our Ambassadors have emphasized that the Inter-American Highway, once completed, would make a greater contribution to the overall welfare of these individual nations than any other single thing the United States could do.

There are several reasons why the highway assumes such an important position in the area.

(1) It is of importance economically because it will open up huge sections of these countries which have hitherto been inaccessible. The very process of developing these regions will inevitably bring a great demand for U.S. machinery, equipment, and other products with an obvious benefit to U.S. industry. A healthy economy in Central America and Panama is of as great an interest to us as it is to those countries themselves. A contributing factor to such economic progress will be a substantial increase in income from tourists proceeding from the United States.

(2) The highway, once completed, would have an inestimable value in promoting political stability. Many of the tensions and misunderstandings which existed in the past have been due to completely inadequate communications which have prevented the free movement of persons and goods and the full exchange of points of view. Through an improved mutual understanding and increased economic activity many of the conditions which communism has exploited in Central America in the past would be eliminated.

(3) Strategically the last war showed the urgent need for means of transporting material quantities of foodstuffs and supplies to the area which would be independent of sea transport. We were fortunate in that the problem became no more serious. But we have no assurance that the absence of overland communication from the U.S. to the Canal Zone would not be disastrous if, despite all our efforts, another war should come. Furthermore, we cannot count on an indefinite period of time in which to remedy this situation.

For those at all familiar with the problem there can be no question of the compelling reasons for pushing the highway to an early completion. In our own interest and in that of

Central America and Panama, it is essential that the job be done with all possible speed.

b. *Letter from the President to the Vice-President (Nixon), April 1, 1955.*[2]

DEAR MR. VICE PRESIDENT: For some time I have had under consideration the desirability of accelerating the completion of the Inter-American Highway which extends from the United States to the Canal Zone via the Central American countries.

The early completion of the Inter-American Highway in close cooperation with the affected countries is a clearly established objective of United States policy.

Although this project has been under construction sporadically since 1934 and the Congress has appropriated funds in the amount of $53,723,000 to date for its completion, the incompleted state of the project prevents realization of maximum benefits.

Recently I have sought the advice of interested agencies of the Government and I am convinced that for economic and political reasons now is the appropriate time to speed completion of the Inter-American Highway. I believe this would be the most significant single action which the United States can take in Central America and Panama to bring about the most mutually advantageous results.

Among the considerations which make me feel that an accelerated construction program on the highway is essential are these:

1. A completed highway will provide a very important contribution to the economic development of the countries through which it passes.
2. There will be an opportunity for increased trade and improved political relations among these countries and the United States.
3. The resultant increase in tourist traffic would not only improve cultural relations but also serve as a very important element in the development of their economies through earnings of foreign exchange.
4. The existence of such an all-weather highway would be of substantial security importance, both in providing overland

[2] *Ibid.*, pp. 595-596.

contact and communication as far southward as the Panama Canal, and in bringing an important physical link between these countries in our common defense of the Western Hemisphere against aggression from without and subversion from within.

The stabilizing effect of these factors will tend to bar any possible return of communism which was so recently and successfully defeated in this area.

It is estimated that the amount needed to complete the Inter-American Highway in a three-year period is $112,470,000, of which $74,980,000 would be the share of the United States, leaving $37,490,000 as the combined share of the several cooperating countries on the usual 2:1 matching basis.

In the Federal-Aid Highway Acts of 1952 and 1954 Congress authorized the expenditure of $56,000,000 for this project. Funds actually appropriated against these authorizations have totaled $6,750,000, leaving a balance of $49,250,000 yet to be appropriated. Of this amount $5,750,000 is currently included in budget estimates now pending before the Congress. In order to accelerate the highway work sufficiently to permit its completion within the next three years, an additional authorization of $25,730,000 will be needed. It will also be necessary to increase our 1956 appropriation request from $5,750,000 to $74,980,000.

In the near future I shall transmit to the Congress the necessary budget request to carry out this program, and I trust that the Congress will give this proposal for accelerated completion of the Inter-American Highway its most favorable consideration.

Sincerely,
DWIGHT D. EISENHOWER

2. *Treaty of Mutual Understanding and Cooperation with Panama: Statement by the Assistant Secretary of State for Inter-American Affairs (Holland) before the Senate Foreign Relations Committee, July 15, 1955.*[3]

The Treaty of Mutual Understanding and Cooperation between the United States and Panama and the accompanying Memorandum of Understandings Reached, both of which

[3] *Department of State Bulletin,* v. 33 (August 1, 1955), pp. 185-188. The treaty was ratified by Panama on March 15, 1955. The Senate gave its advice and consent on July 29, 1955 and the Treaty was ratified by the President on August 17, 1955.

were signed at Panama City on January 25, 1955,[4] resulted from negotiations which were begun in September 1953 at the request of Panama.

The last revision of our treaty relations with Panama relating to the construction and operation of the Panama Canal took the form of the General Treaty of March 2, 1936. While that treaty satisfied certain Panamanian aspirations which had grown up over the years since the original treaty of 1903, it failed to satisfy Panama's desire that its commerce share more fully in the benefits to be derived from the market in the Canal Zone and from ships transitting the Canal. However, local prosperity resulting from United States wartime expenditures in that region diminished the importance accorded these matters during the war and the immediate postwar period. As United States expenditures progressively tapered off in the postwar period and Panama began to encounter greater economic problems, these requests for greater commercial advantages were revived. Panama also took the position that it would be equitable to accord her a greater direct benefit from the Canal enterprise, in the form of increased annuity payments.

Shortly after taking office in 1952, President José Antonio Remón Cantera announced his intention to seek United States agreement to a review of treaty relations pertaining to the Canal. In the spring of 1953 the United States agreed to embark upon such discussions, which were begun in Washington in September 1953,[5] on the basis of a list of requests presented by Panama. At this same time President Remón made a State visit to Washington, at the conclusion of which Presidents Eisenhower and Remón issued a joint statement setting forth the principles which were to guide the subsequent negotiations.[6] The discussions continued in Washington until August 1954, at which time the Panamanian delegation returned to Panama to consult with their Government with regard to the positions expressed by the United States on the various Panamanian requests. President Eisenhower then informed President Remón by letter of those matters on which the United States was prepared to take affirmative action and listed certain requests on the part of the United States which, taken together, formed the basis on which the United States was willing to formulate agreements. The

[4] For the text of the treaty and of an accompanying memorandum see *ibid.*, v. 32 (February 7, 1955), pp. 237-244.
[5] *Ibid.*, v. 29 (September 28, 1953), p. 418.
[6] *Ibid.* (October 12, 1953), p. 487.

Panamanian President indicated that his Government was disposed to proceed to the drafting of agreements on the basis of President Eisenhower's communication, and drafting negotiations were begun in Panama in September. Final texts were agreed to in December, and the signing of the official texts took place in Panama January 25, 1955.

These negotiations, in all phases, were carried on in close consultation with the Department of Defense and the Governor of the Panama Canal Zone, as well as other agencies of the Government which were interested in certain of the matters under consideration. The agreements which are now before the Senate are supported by all the executive agencies whose respective areas of responsibility are touched upon by provisions of the agreements.

Development of Panamanian Economy

In a general way, I would say to the committee that our consideration of the Panamanian proposals was based on most careful analysis and study of each individual problem. We adopted the general principle, in considering these proposals, that it was to the interest of the United States to assist Panama to develop its economy so that Panama will be less dependent on the Canal as such as a major source of income, so long as any arrangements in this regard would not conflict with the essential interests of the United States and those of individuals resident in the Zone. It was possible to take a number of steps of this nature in the hope of building greater economic and political stability in this area so vital to us. On the other hand, Panama made a number of requests which, if accepted, might have weakened the jurisdictional position of the United States in the Canal Zone, or might have accorded Panama a special position in economic relations with the United States or required the United States to assume financial obligations in matters for which the United States was not prepared to accept responsibility. The United States could not favorably consider these requests.

The United States, for its part, obtained certain concessions which are beneficial to the United States in the discharge of its responsibilities in the Canal Zone.

A detailed analysis of the provisions of the agreements will be found in the memorandum of the Secretary of State to the President dated May 5, 1955, which was transmitted to the Senate as an enclosure to the President's letter of May 9,

1955.[7] In view of the Secretary's explanation of the provisions of the agreements set forth in his memorandum, it would be repetitious for me to go into the background of each provision in this presentation. These agreements cover such a wide range of subject matter, however, that I think it might be helpful to review with you some of their more important provisions.

Increased Annuity to Panama

Article I of the treaty provides for an increase in the annuity paid to Panama for our rights in the Canal Zone from the present $430,000 to $1,930,000. Panama's request for an increased annuity became the key issue in the negotiations. A mutually satisfactory resolution of this issue was indispensable to the successful conclusion of the negotiations and to bringing about greater harmony in relations between the two countries. It was felt that while no legal obligation existed an increase in the annuity was justified, bearing in mind the rights, powers, and privileges granted to the United States in the Zone and their strategic and commercial value to the United States. The offer of an increased annuity was made conditional upon Panama's accepting language, inserted in the preamble and in article I, designed to safeguard the rights and jurisdictional position of the United States in the Zone. This language provides express recognition that the provisions of the 1903 Convention, the 1936 General Treaty, and the present treaty may be modified only by mutual consent; and both parties recognize the absence of any obligation on the part of either party to alter the amount of the annuity.

Article II of the treaty enables the Republic of Panama to levy income taxes on Panamanian citizens employed by Canal Zone agencies, irrespective of their place of residence, and citizens of third countries so employed who reside in territory under the jurisdiction of Panama. United States citizens and members of the Armed Forces (irrespective of nationality) who are employed by Canal Zone agencies are exempt from Panamanian income tax regardless of their place of residence.

Panama has been precluded from such taxation by article X of the 1903 Convention. Our agreement to such taxation expresses a principle which is recognized in United States tax legislation that a government may impose taxes on its citizens wherever resident and on noncitizens who actually reside

[7] S. Exec. F, 84th Cong., 1st Sess.

within its jurisdiction. Panama's request for permission to tax these categories of Canal Zone employees was agreed to since the present situation with respect to their taxation is considered inequitable and to serve no real interest of the United States. It is provided that any such tax imposed by Panama shall be on a nondiscriminatory basis.

Under article V of the treaty the United States agrees, subject to enactment of legislation by the United States Congress, to transfer to Panama certain lands, with improvements thereon, in territory under Panamanian jurisdiction and in the Canal Zone when and as determined by the United States to be no longer needed for United States Government purposes. This agreement accords with our policy of not retaining properties within Panamanian jurisdiction past the time when they are in fact required for Canal purposes. The lands and improvements to which this article refers, as well as the conditions governing the transfers, are set forth in item 2 of the Memorandum of Understandings Reached.

In article VIII of the treaty Panama agrees to reserve an area of some 19,000 acres in the Rio Hato region for the exclusive use of the United States Armed Forces for Maneuvers and military training for a period of 15 years, without cost to the United States, subject to extension as may be agreed by the two Governments. Panama also has agreed in the memorandum to lease to the United States for 99 years, for a nominal consideration, two parcels of land contiguous to the United States Embassy residence and to preserve permanently the area in front of the Embassy office building as a park.

In article IX Panama waives its right under article XIX of the 1903 Convention to free transportation over the Panama Railroad for persons in its service, and in article X Panama waives certain rights under the 1903 Convention in order to enable the United States in its discretion to prohibit or restrict certain specified bus and truck traffic on a possible new strategic highway across the Isthmus within the Zone, in the event of the discontinuance of the Panama Railroad and the construction of the road.

Several of the provisions in both the treaty and the memorandum were negotiated for the purpose of affording Panama greater commercial opportunities in the Canal Zone subject, where deemed necessary, to appropriate competitive safeguards. I refer in this connection to article XII of the treaty and items 3, 4, 6, 7, 8, 9, and 10 of the United States undertakings in the memorandum. Subject to specified conditions and qualifications, we propose to exempt Panamanian products from the Buy American Act when purchased for use in the Zone; to withdraw from the business of selling supplies to ships in the Zone, with certain exceptions; to withdraw service and commissary privileges and free import privileges from non-United States citizen Zone employees resident in Panama; to afford the economy of Panama full opportunity to compete for purchases by Canal Zone agencies; to import merchandise for resale in the Zone from either United States or Panamanian sources insofar as feasible; and to withdraw from certain manufacturing and processing activities in the Zone. The conditions to which these items are subject are those deemed necessary for the protection of the essential interests of this Government and of the residents of the Zone.

Panamanian Labor

Item 1 of the United States undertakings in the memorandum embodies certain agreements reached with respect to the employment of Panamanian labor in the Zone. It was considered to be in the interest of the United States, not only in its relations with Panama but also in regard to its position throughout Latin America, to eliminate any appearance of discrimination in the treatment of such labor. Such a policy is in accord with the exchange of notes dated March 2, 1936, ancillary to the 1936 General Treaty and with the joint statement issued October 1, 1953, by the Presidents of the United States and Panama. Accordingly we have agreed, subject to the enactment of the necessary legislation by the Congress, to the establishment of a single basic wage level for all employees in a given category regardless of citizenship, with certain increments to be added to the pay of a United States citizen employee; to uniform application of the Civil Service Retirement Act to all United States and Panamanian citizen employees of this Government in the Zone; to equality of opportunity for Panamanian citizens for employment in all United States Government positions in the Zone for which they are qualified except where security considerations require the employment of United States citizens only; and admission of Panamanian citizens to participation in job training programs.

The executive branch considers that these agreements mark a step forward in our relations with Panama and that their approval is in the national interest.

I, and other representatives of the interested executive agencies, will be happy to respond to any questions the committee may wish to ask regarding the agreements.

3. *Action by the Organization of American States in the Conflict between Costa Rica and Nicaragua.*

a. *Resolution of the Council of the Organization of American States, Adopted January 12, 1955.*[8]

THE COUNCIL OF THE ORGANIZATION OF AMERICAN STATES, ACTING PROVISIONALLY AS ORGAN OF CONSULTATION,

Taking into account the petition and the information that the Government of Costa Rica has just presented, requesting military assistance, and

Considering that yesterday a Committee was appointed to conduct an on-the-spot investigation of the facts pertaining to the situation described by the Government of Costa Rica,

Resolves:

1. To request the Chairman of the Council to communicate by cable with the Investigating Committee, requesting it to submit, on an urgent basis, as soon as it arrives in Costa Rica, a preliminary report on the situation existing in the territory of that Republic, in order to enable the Council to reach the decision that should be adopted in accordance with the Inter-American Treaty of Reciprocal Assistance.

2. To request the American governments that they take the necessary measures to prevent the use of their territories for any military action against the government of another State.

3. To request the governments that are in a position to do so that they place at the disposal of the Investigating Committee aircraft to make, in the name of the Committee and under its supervision, pacific observation flights over the regions affected by the present situation, with prior notification by the Chairman of the Council to the governments whose territories are traversed.

[8] *Department of State Bulletin,* v. 32 (January 24, 1955), p. 132.

b. *Resolution of the Council of the Organization of American States, Adopted January 16, 1955.*[9]

THE COUNCIL OF THE ORGANIZATION OF AMERICAN STATES, ACTING PROVISIONALLY AS ORGAN OF CONSULTATION,

Taking into account the petition presented by the Delegation of Costa Rica; and considering the reports received from the Investigating Committee, the Council, acting provisionally as Organ of Consultation, according to which the Government of Costa Rica does not have the necessary aircraft or arms to defend itself against attacks by foreign aircraft of the type that is now being received by the revolutionary forces;

Noting that the Government of Costa Rica is negotiating the purchase of aircraft, and

Bearing in mind the statement of the Delegation of the United States to the effect that if the Council so requested, it would comply with the request received from the Government of Costa Rica for the purchase of aircraft,

Resolves:

To request the Governments of the Member States of the Organization to expedite the order for the purchase of aircraft that Costa Rica may have placed with them.[10]

c. *Report of the Special Committee of the Council of the Organization of American States, August 26, 1955.*[11]

Resolution III, approved on February 24, 1955,[12] by the Council of the Organization, Acting Provisionally as Organ of Consultation, established this Special Committee for the purpose of offering its cooperation to the Representatives of the Governments of Costa Rica and Nicaragua in carrying out the pertinent provisions of Resolution II approved on that date, especially with regard to the preparation of the bilateral agreement called for by the Pact of Amity between these two Republics and the establishment of the Commission of Investigation and Conciliation contemplated in the American Treaty on Pacific Settlement.

[9] *Department of State Bulletin,* v. 32 (January 31, 1955), pp. 182-183.
[10] In response to the resolution, which was passed unanimously, the United States sold four P-51 airplanes to Costa Rica. The planes were delivered to Costa Rican authorities at San José on January 17, 1955.
[11] *Department of State Bulletin,* v. 33 (October 3, 1955), pp. 546-548.
[12] Not printed.

This Special Committee was composed of the Representative of Uruguay who was elected Chairman of the Committee, and the Representatives of Argentina, Brazil, Chile, Ecuador, El Salvador, Mexico, Paraguay, and the United States. The Committee, installed on February 28 last, has been meeting regularly since then in order to fulfill the high purposes of the responsibility entrusted to it. Immediately after the resolutions of February 24 had been approved by the Council, the Presidents of Costa Rica and Nicaragua each sent a message to the Chairman of the Council in which they acknowledged the effectiveness of the action taken by the Council of the Organization of American States, and reaffirmed their determination to settle their differences in a friendly manner. At the same time, the attitude of Ambassadors Fernando Fournier and Guillermo Sevilla Sacasa, the Representatives of Costa Rica and Nicaragua, respectively, their encouraging statements, and the spirit of cordiality demonstrated whenever the Committee met with them, showed a splendid desire to reach the best understanding possible, in accordance with the recommendations of the Council acting provisionally as Organ of Consultation. The Committee has noted with pleasure the cordial meeting of May 7, 1955, between the Foreign Ministers of Costa Rica and Nicaragua held at their common border on the occasion of the opening of the section of the Pan American Highway that unites these two Republics.

The Commission on Investigation and Conciliation referred to in Resolutions II and III of February 24, has been established, thanks to the diligent efforts of both governments. This Commission is composed of Mr. John C. Dreier, Chairman, and Messrs. Alberto Domínguez Cámpora, Mario A. Esquivel, Mario de Pimentel Brandão, and Oscar Sevilla Sacasa. Also, at meetings of the Special Committee the Costa Rican and Nicaraguan Representatives stated that several other problems of concern to both governments either had been, or were being, satisfactorily settled. Insofar as concerns the bilateral agreement mentioned in the Pact of Amity entered into by Costa Rica and Nicaragua on September 21, 1949, for the signing of which a cordial appeal was made in Resolution II approved by the Council, Acting Provisionally as Organ of Consultation, the Chairman of this Special Committee had occasion, at the meeting of August 4, to report to the aforesaid Organ that the two preliminary steps in the negotiations for the signing of this important document had been taken. These were: (1) the presentation on May 27 to the Government of Nicaragua by the Government of Costa Rica of a draft containing the basic provisions for the agreement; and (2) the transmittal on August 2 by the Government of Nicaragua to the Government of Costa Rica of its observations on this draft. In the oral report that by decision of the Special Committee, its Chairman presented to the Council, Acting Provisionally as Organ of Consultation, at the meeting of August 4, the Committee expressed its satisfaction with all these evidences of friendship and good will and the concrete measures that had been taken by both governments. At the same meeting and in the afternoon meeting held on that day, the Representatives of both parties provided additional information concerning the most important aspects of the draft. After taking into consideration the additional information provided by the Representatives of Costa Rica and Nicaragua and the views expressed by other Members of the Council, it was decided:

1. That the Special Committee shall meet, as soon as its Chairman deems it convenient, to draft a report covering the course of the bilateral negotiations between Costa Rica and Nicaragua for the purpose of preparing the bilateral agreement provided for in Resolutions II and III of February 24, 1955.

2. That the Special Committee, in the light of the views expressed at today's meetings, submit an opinion as to the advisability of canceling arrangements for the consultation.

Insofar as the first point of the above-cited decision of the Council is concerned, the additional information indicated the progress made up to August 4 in the direct negotiations that were being carried out between Costa Rica and Nicaragua for the purpose of preparing the bilateral agreement. The negotiations have continued to be carried out most diligently since then, and even now, Ambassadors Fernando Fournier and Guillermo Sevilla Sacasa, the Representatives of Costa Rica and Nicaragua respectively, are, in a spirit of true cooperation, doing everything within their power to expedite the signing of the agreement.

With regard to the advisability of canceling the Meeting of Consultation, the Committee has kept uppermost in its mind the views expressed at the meetings of August 4, Resolution II (6) of February 24, and the understanding on the basis of which Resolution II (6) was drafted and approved. These facts show that the Council is duly qualified to decide whenever it so desires, to cancel the Meeting of Consultation in the light of the development of the situation, within a reasonable length of time. In view of the decision taken by the Council on August 4, and taking as a basis the aforementioned facts, this Special Committee has come to the conclusion that the Meeting of Consultation referred to in the resolution approved by the Council of the Organization on January 11 should now be canceled.

To fulfill the high purposes of the February 24 resolutions, and in view of the opinions expressed at meetings of both the Council and the Special Committee, a final measure that could be adopted at the same time that the Meeting of Consultation is canceled would be to authorize the Committee to continue to offer both Parties all the cooperation they desire until the negotiations now being carried on are concluded. This Committee would subsequently report to the governments, through the Council of the Organization, with respect to the results of its work.

In view of these considerations, this Special Committee has the honor to submit the following draft resolution:[13]

THE COUNCIL OF THE ORGANIZATION OF AMERICAN STATES ACTING PROVISIONALLY AS ORGAN OF CONSULTATION

HAVING SEEN the report of the Special Committee of the Council Acting Provisionally as Organ of Consultation, presented today,

RESOLVES:

1. To cancel the Meeting of Consultation of Ministers of Foreign Affairs that was convoked, in accordance with the Inter-American Treaty of Reciprocal Assistance, by the January 11, 1955 resolution of the Council of the Organization.

2. To terminate the provisional activities of the Council as Organ of Consultation.

3. To retain the Special Committee while the negotiations for the signing of the bilateral agreement provided for in the present Pact of Amity and in Resolution II approved by this Council on February 24, 1955, are in course, so as to enable it to continue to cooperate with the Representatives of Costa Rica and Nicaragua whenever they require such cooperation. The Special Committee shall duly report on this

[13] The resolution was adopted by the Council of the Organization of American States on September 8, 1955.

matter to the governments, through the Council of the Organization.

4. To state that it is pleased that the Commission on Investigation and Conciliation has been established by Costa Rica and Nicaragua, and to repeat that it is confident the two Parties will utilize the services of the aforesaid Commission, in accordance with the treaties in force between them.

August 26, 1955.

JOSÉ A. MORA
Ambassador of Uruguay
Chairman of the Committee

HÉCTOR DAVID CASTRO
Ambassador,
Representative of El Salvador

JOSÉ R. CHIRIBOGA V.
Ambassador,
Representative of Ecuador

GUILLERMO ENCISO VELLOSO
Ambassador,
Representative of Paraguay

JORGE ISMAEL SARAVIA
Ambassador,
Representative of Argentina

JOHN C. DREIER
Ambassador,
Representative of the United States

FERNANDO LOBO
Ambassador,
Representative of Brazil

ALBERTO SEPÚLVEDA CONTRERAS
Ambassador,
Representative of Chile

ANDRÉS FENOCHIO
Representative of Mexico

B. Canada.

1. *Agreement on Distant Early Warning System.*

a. *Canadian Note, May 5, 1955.*[1]

WASHINGTON, D.C.
May 5, 1955

No. 306

SIR,

I have the honour to refer to my Note No. 791 of November 16, 1954,[2] regarding the joint establishment by Canada and the United States of America of a comprehensive warning and control system against air attack. My Note read in part as follows:

[1] *Department of State Bulletin,* v. 33 (July 4, 1955), p. 22.
[2] Not printed. For joint U.S.-Canadian statement see *Documents on American Foreign Relations, 1954,* pp. 430-431.

"The Canadian Government has now considered a proposal put forward through the Permanent Joint Board on Defense that the construction of the Distant Early Warning element of the over-all joint Canada-United States warning system should be the responsibility of the United States Government. The Canadian Government concurs in this proposal subject to the conclusion at an early date of an agreement as to the terms which shall govern the work. At the same time, however, the Canadian Government wishes to state its intention to participate in the project, the nature and extent of such participation to be determined in the near future."

I am instructed by my Government to inform you that its participation during the construction phase of the project will consist of giving assistance to the United States authorities in organizing and using Canadian resources, and to helping by making available the facilities of the armed forces and other agencies of the Canadian Government when appropriate. I am also instructed to state that the Canadian Government intends to participate effectively in the operation and maintenance phase of the project, the character of such participation to be determined on the basis of studies to be carried out during the construction phase.

My Government now proposes that the annexed conditions[3] should govern the establishment by the United States of a distant early warning system in Canadian territory. If these conditions are acceptable to your Government, I suggest that this Note and your reply should constitute an agreement effective from the date of your reply.

Accept, Sir, the renewed assurances of my highest consideration.

A. D. P. HEENEY.
[Canadian Ambassador to the U.S.]

b. *United States Reply, May 5, 1955.*[4]

MAY 5, 1955

EXCELLENCY:

I have the honor to acknowledge your Note No. 306 of May 5, 1955. You refer to the construction by the United States of the Distant Early Warning element of a compre-

[3] Not printed. The conditions cover a number of technical and legal issues connected with the construction and maintenance of the Distance Early Warning System. See *Department of State Bulletin*, v. 33 (July 4, 1955), pp. 22-25.
[4] *Ibid.*

hensive warning and control system, being established jointly by the United States and Canada, and annex a statement of conditions to govern the establishment of this line in Canadian territory which were developed in discussion between representatives of the two Governments.

The United States Government notes the intentions of your Government with regard to participation in the construction, operation and maintenance of the project and both concurs in the conditions annexed to your Note and confirms that your Note and this reply shall constitute an agreement of our two Governments effective today.

Accept, Excellency, the renewed assurances of my highest consideration.

For the Secretary of State:
ROBERT MURPHY

2. *Economic Relations.*

Communiqué on the Meeting of the United States-Canadian Committee on Trade and Economic Affairs, Ottawa, September 26, 1955.[5]

1. The joint United States-Canadian Committee on Trade and Economic Affairs, which met in Washington in March 1954,[6] held its second meeting in Ottawa today.

The United States was represented by:

Hon. John Foster Dulles,
Secretary of State
Hon. George M. Humphrey,
Secretary of the Treasury
Hon. Ezra Taft Benson,
Secretary of Agriculture
Hon. Sinclair Weeks,
Secretary of Commerce

Canada was represented by:

Rt. Hon. C. D. Howe, M.P.,
Minister of Trade and Commerce, and Defence Production
Rt. Hon. J. G. Gardiner, M.P.,
Minister of Agriculture
Hon. L. B. Pearson, M.P.,
Secretary of State for External Affairs

[5] *Ibid.* (October 10, 1955), pp. 576-577.
[6] *Documents on American Foreign Relations, 1954,* pp. 420-424.

Hon. W. E. Harris, M.P.,
Minister of Finance

2. In addition to the members of the Joint Committee, His Excellency Douglas Stuart, United States Ambassador to Canada, and His Excellency A. D. P. Heeney, Canadian Ambassador to the United States, participated in the discussions.

3. This Committee was established by the United States and Canadian Governments to provide an opportunity for Cabinet members of both countries concerned with economic and trade matters to meet together periodically and review developments of common interest. Its existence symbolizes the close and friendly relations existing between the two countries and is evidence of the interest which each country has in a great number and variety of economic questions affecting the other. Its meetings supplement and reinforce the daily exchanges which take place between official representatives and between private citizens of the two countries.

4. At today's meeting the exchanges of views dealt mainly with general commercial policies and prospects, with progress being achieved in dealing with broad international trade and payments problems, and with policies relating to trade in agricultural products.

5. The Committee emphasized the importance of encouraging a large and growing volume of mutually beneficial trade between the United States and Canada. They discussed the difficulties which were experienced from time to time in this connection. They shared the view that this trade would develop most satisfactorily as part of a wide-spread system of freer trade and payments. Such a multilateral pattern of trade would also best serve to sustain relations between the United States and Canada, and between each of them and the many countries with which they are associated throughout the world, on a wholesome and durable basis. The Committee recognized that policies and practices which promoted these purposes were important to the national well-being and security of the two countries.

6. The Committee noted that, with the high rates of employment and economic activity which had prevailed in most parts of the world, the level of international trade had generally been well maintained during the past year. While some progress had been made in removing restrictions and reducing discrimination in many countries, there remained, however, a need for further advances in this field.

7. It was realized that difficult, although, it is hoped, temporary problems existed as a result of the accumulation of large quantities of some agricultural products in several countries. These problems, if not handled carefully, could adversely affect the trade in such products and might also have damaging consequences for international trade generally. The members of the Committee were able to acquaint one another with their views on these matters. It was agreed that, in dealing with these problems, there should be closer consultation in an effort to avoid interference with normal commercial marketings.

8. It was recalled that the initiative for the creation of this Committee had come from conversations between President Eisenhower and Prime Minister St. Laurent in 1953,[7] reflecting the keen desire which both have always shown to improve understanding and strengthen relations between the two countries. At the meeting today the Canadian members expressed their deep sympathy with President Eisenhower in his illness and their hopes that he would soon be restored to full health.

[7] *Ibid., 1953,* p. 405.

CHAPTER SEVEN

THE UNITED NATIONS

A. Tenth Anniversary of the Signing of the United Nations Charter.

***Closing Address by the President (van Kleffens) of the Commemorative Meetings Held at San Francisco, June 20-26, 1955.*[1]**

(Excerpt)

* * *

All Members participants in the commemorative meeting of the United Nations assembled in San Francisco on the tenth anniversary of the Organization have reaffirmed their common determination to save succeeding generations from the scourge of war. The ten years since 26 June 1945 have given new meaning and urgency to this universal aspiration of the peoples, for they know that another war fought with the weapons now at their disposal would bring untold calamities to mankind. Their aim is peace based, in accordance with the explicit text of the Charter, on security, justice, and good neighbourliness.

They proclaim again their common dedication to the purposes and principles formulated in the United Nations Charter. They recognize that the hope of enduring peace rests upon how well the nations carry out these purposes and uphold these principles in their relations with each other.

They have reaffirmed their determination to make new efforts to settle international disputes, as the Charter calls upon them to do, by peaceful means in such a manner that international peace and security, and justice, are not endangered, and to live together in peace and amity.

They have pledged themselves equally to press forward in the search for agreement on a disarmament plan that can provide a greater measure of security to the nations and re-

[1] *Tenth Anniversary of the Signing of the United Nations Charter, Proceedings of the Commemorative Meetings,* United Nations, New York, 1955, p. 299. The statement by Mr. van Kleffens was made in response to requests that he as President sum up the sense of the proceedings of the Commemorative Meetings.

move the threat of atomic destruction from the world. They declare their belief in the determination of the nations to direct the creative resources, thus freed from the burden of armaments, to the improvement of the lives of peoples everywhere.

The difficulties before us are as evident as the dangers and disappointments of the past. But we have the Charter for our guide, the Charter which prescribes that the United Nations shall be used as a center for harmonizing the actions of the Member States.

B. Review of the U.N. Charter.

1. *Statement by United States Representative to the General Assembly (Bell) in Plenary Session, November 17, 1955.*[1]

The proposal to call a general conference to review the charter of the United Nations is the only item on our agenda placed there directly by the charter itself. It is a matter of fundamental concern to us all.

The United States recalls the circumstances in which the framers of the charter at the San Francisco conference in 1945 drew up the provisions of article 109, which places the matter of a review conference on our agenda. Some of the provisions of the charter were accepted at that time in a spirit of generous compromise despite serious misgivings. A number of the smaller member states accepted the charter in its present form on the assumption that after a period of trial they would have an opportunity to reexamine and reassess its provisions. Article 109 was therefore drafted to provide for the automatic placement of the question of a review conference on the agenda of the Tenth Session of the General Assembly. The spirit prevalent at San Francisco resulted in the phrasing of the question in positive terms, and article 109 therefore speaks of inclusion in the agenda of "the proposal to call such a conference." The United States sincerely supported inclusion of article 109 in the charter and considers it a matter of simple fulfillment of an obligation to lend our full support to the calling of a charter review conference.

Governments and peoples of member states in many parts of the world have already contributed much in thought, discussion, and preparatory studies to the problems that

[1] *Department of State Bulletin*, v. 33 (December 5, 1955), pp. 948-951.

might be dealt with at such a conference. The fact that the question of holding a review conference was to come before this Assembly has served as a focus for constructive research and planning.

Within the United States public and official interest in effective implementation by the United Nations of its principles and purposes led to the establishment of a subcommittee of the Senate Foreign Relations Committee to advise the Senate and the President with respect to policy on charter review. Over a 2-year period the committee conducted hearings on this subject throughout our land. In Washington, Akron, Milwaukee, Greensboro, and Louisville, in Des Moines, Minneapolis, and Atlanta, in San Francisco, Denver, and Miami, the committee heard testimony. In every region of the country it consulted public officials and representatives from the widest range of business and professional groups, of labor and agricultural associations, of churches and religious organizations, and of private organizations concerned with national and international affairs. It heard a representative group of experts in their individual capacities and interested private citizens from every walk of life. Concurrently, the committee published thorough staff studies on various aspects of the question.[2]

Private groups engaged in scholarly research and in the public discussion of national affairs have contributed their views on the question of charter review. They have begun highly useful activities in the advancement and dissemination of ideas and information relating to the task. The Brookings Institution has conducted over the past 4 years an extensive research project. The Brookings studies deal with the history of the charter; the organization, functions, and procedures of the United Nations; the role of the organization in the maintenance of peace and security, and in the promotion of the general welfare; regional security arrangements; and major proposals for changes in the United Nations system.[3] The Carnegie Endowment for International Peace has conducted a survey of national policies and attitudes with respect

[2] *Review of the United Nations Charter: Compilation of Staff Studies Prepared for the Use of the Subcommittee on the United Nations Charter of the* [Senate] *Committee on Foreign Relations,* U.S. Senate. S. Doc. 164, 83d Cong., Washington 1955, 365 pp.

[3] Leland M. Goodrich and Anne P. Simmons, *The United Nations and the Maintenance of International Peace and Security* (Washington: Brookings Institution, 1955) and Francis O. Wilcox and Carl M. Marcy, *Proposals for Changes in the United Nations* (Washington: Brookings Institution, 1955).

to the United Nations on a worldwide scale and is publishing a comprehensive series of more than 20 volumes embodying its findings.[4] Institutes of public affairs, universities, learned societies, and professional associations on their own initiative have conducted public forums and discussions of problems relating to charter review. The position of the United States Government on this question, then, is the product of long and careful study and of extensive consultation with the citizenry it represents.

The United Nations Secretariat, too, has also laid much groundwork for a profitable and careful appraisal of United Nations operations. As directed by the Eighth General Assembly, it has undertaken preparatory studies of practices as they have evolved under the charter. Four volumes of its *Repertory of Practice of United Nations Organs* have already been published. I am glad to take this opportunity to express the appreciation of the United States for the Secretariat's contribution to our common task. In our view, the Secretariat should carry forward this important work.

The United States believes that a review conference should be held. The United Nations has become a new and vital force in world affairs. Now a period of trial has elapsed and a body of valuable experience has been built up. Much good can come from a collective scrutiny at the proper time of the role, accomplishments, shortcomings, and potentialities of this great instrument. We do not conceive of the task as merely the narrow consideration of specific verbal changes. Neither do we conceive of the task as one of rewriting the charter or changing the basic character of the organization.

Article 109 directs our attention to *review* rather than to *revision* of the charter. A review of the charter could usefully determine whether or not improvements in the United Nations machinery are desirable and feasible. We believe it would be valuable to examine procedures and operations within the charter framework as well as to review the charter itself. We need, it seems to us, to take time out from the urgencies of specific problems before us at a regular session to study, reflect, and consult on the United Nations system as a whole. We need to consider the machinery, evolution, and potentialities of the United Nations not in the short range as they relate to items on our agenda but in the long range as they relate to the effectiveness of the organization in the achievement of its basic purposes. The charter has, to the

[4] None of these were published before the end of 1955.

credit of the founders of the United Nations, proved its practicality and workability to a remarkable degree. It has, in such advances as the Uniting for Peace resolution, proved its flexibility under changing circumstances. But, as the Secretary of State has reminded us, "Few would contend that it is a perfect instrument, not susceptible to improvement."

Secretary Dulles has called to our attention at this session the epochal developments in the atomic and disarmament fields. These developments would seem to justify the reexamination of a charter drafted when the possibilities of atomic warfare were not known as they are today.

Not only have there been new developments in the momentous years since the charter was signed, but some of the expectations and assumptions upon which the charter was based have not been fulfilled. Certain powers in the charter have never been utilized. Other provisions have operated in a way that was not anticipated. In these respects, too, new comparisons between charter goals and available powers and machinery for their fulfillment deserve our mature consideration.

Another pressing reason for such a conference would be, in the view of the United States, to reconsider the method prescribed by the charter for the admission of new members. If, however, as we hope, it now becomes possible to admit a number of states as new members, a conference to review the charter would enable these new members to share with us their wisdom in the improvement of the instrument that defines their obligations.

Good may also come, we believe, from our studying and consulting together on the purposes of the charter in the light of experience and conditions in the world today. At the conference at San Francisco in 1945, deliberations on the fundamentals of peace and justice under a regime of law resulted in a consensus of unprecedented breadth. By its focus on fundamentals, a conference of the kind envisaged in the charter, if held at the proper time, might likewise serve to broaden that consensus. It might serve to strengthen the ties between us and to emphasize the depth of our common needs and purposes.

The United Nations, a decade of experience has shown, derives its greatest strength from the support and understanding of the peoples of the world. The organization occupies a unique position in relation to the moral force of world opinion. It is, in the words of the late Senator Vandenberg, "the town meeting of the world." It is our belief that a conference to review the charter could greatly strengthen that public understanding. We believe, as well, that the weight of informed public opinion based upon such a conference might prove to be a constructive influence in the achievement of agreement to recommended improvements.

If a conference to review the charter is to be successful in broadening our areas of agreement and understanding, if it is to result in improving and strengthening United Nations machinery and processes, two prerequisites would seem to be essential.

In the first place, the conference should be held under favorable international circumstances. Dangers and tensions continue to exist today. If optimum results are to be achieved from charter review, there is need for a more favorable political climate.

In the second place, adequate time must be allowed for the completion of careful and thorough preparatory work. The problems confronting a charter review conference will be Herculean. Patience, wisdom, and statesmanship will be required in making the fullest prior preparations and studies, if we are not to do harm to the United Nations and to relations among states.

The resolution before us, cosponsored by Canada, Ecuador, Iraq, Thailand, the United Kingdom, and the United States,[5] makes adequate provision, we believe, for both of these prerequisites. It recognizes that a review conference such as contemplated in article 109 of the charter should be held under auspicious international circumstances; it decides that such a conference shall be held; and it establishes a broadly representative committee to report to the Twelfth Session of the General Assembly with recommendations relating to the time and place of the conference and to its organization and procedures. The committee as proposed will have the task of laying the procedural and organizational groundwork for a successful conference. It will have the further duty of feeling the pulse of international developments to find the propitious time when the conference will be most productive in improving the charter and broadening the consensus among us. Adoption of this resolution by the General Assembly would, in our view, constitute a decision in principle to hold a review conference and contemplates parallel action in the

[5] Not printed. A revised version of the draft resolution was adopted by the General Assembly. See below, pp. 390-391.

Security Council at an early date, as provided in the charter.

The farseeing men who drafted the charter at San Francisco had no illusions that it was an immutable document. The provisions for amendment were obviously put into it for a purpose. The charter and the procedures under it have served remarkably well. We recognize to the full that there are dangers in any attempt at revision, but we do not see such dangers in a review to determine whether there are any changes that could usefully be made in the charter or in the procedures that have developed under it. This Tenth General Assembly offers an opportunity with the least possible difficulty of instituting the review process. We urge that the Assembly seize this opportunity.

We commend this action to your consideration as the fulfillment of the expectations of our founders and of the peoples of the world and as a milestone in the forward movement of the United Nations.

2. *General Assembly Resolution 992 (X), Adopted November 21, 1955.*[6]

The General Assembly,

Mindful that paragraph 3 of Article 109 of the Charter of the United Nations provides that if a General Conference of the Members of the United Nations for the purpose of reviewing the Charter has not been held before the tenth annual session of the General Assembly, such a conference shall be held if so decided by a majority vote of the Members of the General Assembly and by a vote of any seven members of the Security Council,

Believing that it is desirable to review the Charter in the light of experience gained in its operation,

Recognizing that such a review should be conducted under auspicious international circumstances,

1. *Decides* that a General Conference to review the Charter shall be held at an appropriate time;

2. *Further decides* to appoint a Committee consisting of all the Members of the United Nations to consider, in consultation with the Secretary-General, the question of fixing a time and place for the Conference, and its organization and procedures;

[6] United Nations General Assembly *Official Records, Tenth Session,* Supplement No. 19, p. 49. The resolution was adopted by a vote of 43-6 (Soviet bloc, Syria)-9 (Afghanistan, Denmark, Iceland, India, Norway, Saudi Arabia, Sweden, Yemen, Yugoslavia).

3. *Requests* the Committee to report with its recommendations to the General Assembly at its twelfth session;

4. *Requests* the Secretary-General to complete the publication programme undertaken pursuant to General Assembly resolution 796 (VIII) of 23 November 1953[7] and to continue, prior to the twelfth session of the General Assembly, to prepare and circulate supplements, as appropriate, to the *Repertory of Practice of United Nations Organs;*

5. *Transmits* the present resolution to the Security Council.

C. Admission of New Members.

1. *General Assembly Resolution 918 (X), Adopted December 8, 1955.*[1]

The General Assembly

Having noted the general sentiment which has been expressed on numerous occasions in favour of the widest possible membership of the United Nations,

Having received the preliminary report[2] of the Committee of Good Offices established by the General Assembly resolution 718 (VIII) of 23 October 1953,[3]

Taking into account the statements about the admission of new members made by permanent members of the Security Council in the general debate of the present session of the General Assembly,

Believing that a broader representation in the membership of the United Nations will enable the organization to play a more effective role in the current international situation,

1. *Expresses appreciation* of the work and efforts of the Committee of Good Offices;

2. *Requests* the Security Council to consider, in the light of the general opinion in favour of the widest possible membership of the United Nations, the pending applications for membership of all those eighteen countries about which no problem of unification arises;

3. *Requests further* that the Security Council make its report on these applications to the General Assembly during the present session.

[7] *Documents on American Foreign Relations, 1953,* p. 449.

[1] United Nations General Assembly *Official Records, Tenth Session,* Supplement No. 19, p. 8. The resolution was adopted by a vote of 52-2 (China, Cuba)-5 (Belgium, France, Greece, Israel, U.S.).

[2] United Nations Document A/2973, dated September 19, 1955.

[3] *Documents on American Foreign Relations, 1953,* pp. 418-419.

2. *General Assembly Resolution 995 (X), Adopted December 14, 1955.*[4]

The General Assembly,

Having received the recommendations of the Security Council of 14 December 1955[5] that the following countries should be admitted to membership in the United Nations: Albania, Jordan, Ireland, Portugal, Hungary, Italy, Austria, Romania, Bulgaria, Finland, Ceylon, Nepal, Libya, Cambodia, Laos and Spain,

Having considered the application for membership of each of these countries,

Decides to admit the above-mentioned sixteen countries to membership in the United Nations.

3. *State Department Announcement by the Acting Chief of the News Division (White) to Newspaper Correspondents, December 15, 1955.*[6]

The United States is greatly pleased that despite continued Soviet obstruction over the past 9 years, including the casting of 44 vetoes on admission of new members, 12 free nations have at long last taken their rightful place in the United Nations.

These countries have a great contribution to make to this world body and should increase considerably the vitality and usefulness of the organization.

One glaring injustice remains. As Ambassador [John M.] Allison informed the Japanese Foreign Minister early today, we are extremely sorry that the Soviet Union has once again seen fit to veto Japan's admission to the United Nations. Japan's just claim to membership, which the United States has consistently and actively supported, has again been frustrated by the Soviet Union. The cynical action of the Soviet Union was in defiance of the recognition by the overwhelming majority of the present members of the United Nations that Japan is fully eligible for membership under the charter. It is clear that the Soviet Union in vetoing Japan has sought

[4] United Nations General Assembly *Official Records, Tenth Session,* Supplement No. 19, p. 50.

[5] United Nations Document A/3099, dated December 14, 1955. The Security Council met on December 14, 1955 to consider a Soviet draft resolution recommending the admission of 16 countries to the United Nations. The resolution was adopted by a vote of 8-0-3.

[6] *Department of State Bulletin,* v. 33 (December 26, 1955), pp. 1071-1072.

only to preserve for itself a bargaining pawn. We think the opinion of the world will know how to appraise this self-serving tactic.

Ambassador Lodge made every effort yesterday to bring about the seating of Japan, and the United States will continue to urge upon the United Nations the admission of Japan, which, like the other free nations already admitted, has a considerable contribution to make to the effectiveness of the organization.[7] Indeed, it is not too late to hope that the Soviet Union will yield to the tremendous pressure of world opinion and withdraw its veto of Japan. There is still time to do this if the Soviet Union will but recognize the injustice of Japan's exclusion.

D. Miscellaneous General Assembly Resolutions.

1. *Advisory Services in the Field of Human Rights: General Assembly Resolution 926 (X), Adopted December 14, 1955.*[1]

The General Assembly,

Considering that by Articles 55 and 56 of the United Nations Charter the States Members of the United Nations have pledged themselves to promote universal respect for, and observance of, human rights and fundamental freedoms for all without distinction as to race, sex, language or religion,

Recognizing that technical assistance, by the international interchange of technical knowledge through international co-operation, represents one of the means by which it is possible to promote the human rights objectives of the United Nations as set forth in the Charter and in the Universal Declaration of Human Rights,

Recalling General Assembly resolution 729 (VIII) of 23 October 1953 authorizing the Secretary-General to render at the request of Member States, services which do not fall

[7] At the Security Council meeting of December 14, 1955 at which the admission of 16 countries to the United Nations was recommended, the U.S. Representative to the U.N. (Lodge) proposed an amendment to the Soviet draft resolution, recommending the admission of Japan. The amendment was vetoed by the Soviet Union. Mr. Lodge then submitted a draft resolution providing that the Security Council should recommend to the General Assembly that it admit Japan to the United Nations at its eleventh regular session. The draft resolution was vetoed by the Soviet Union at the Security Council meeting of December 15, 1955.

[1] United Nations General Assembly *Official Records, Tenth Session,* Supplement No. 19, pp. 13-14. Adopted by a vote of 51-0-5 (Australia, France, New Zealand, Sweden, U.K.).

within the scope of existing technical assistance programmes, in order to assist those States in promoting and safeguarding the rights of women,

Recalling General Assembly resolution 730 (VIII) of 23 October 1953 authorizing the Secretary-General to render, at the request of any Member State, technical advice and other services which do not fall within the scope of existing technical assistance programmes, in order to assist the Government of that State within its territory in the eradication of discrimination or in the protection of minorities, or both,

Recalling General Assembly resolution 839 (IX) of 17 December 1954 authorizing the Secretary-General to render, at the request of Member States, services which do not fall within the scope and objectives of existing technical assistance programmes, in order to assist those States in promoting freedom of information, and Economic and Social Council resolution 574A (XIX) of 26 May 1955 requesting the Secretary-General to take steps to put into operation a programme to promote freedom of information by providing such services as experts, fellowships and seminars,

Taking account of the arrangements previously established by the General Assembly concerning the regular technical assistance programme and the advisory services of the United Nations in its resolutions 200 (III) of 4 December 1948, 246 (III) of 4 December 1948, 305 (IV) of 16 November 1949, 418 (V) of 1 December 1950, 518 (VI) of 12 January 1952 and 723 (VIII) of 23 October 1953,

Considering that the specialized agencies, within their competence and by virtue of their regular programmes of technical assistance, are already rendering important services to their members with a view to ensuring the effective observance of human rights,

1. *Decides* to consolidate the technical assistance programmes already approved by the General Assembly (relating to the promotion and safeguarding of the rights of women, the eradication of discrimination and the protection of minorities and the promotion of freedom of information) with the broad programme of assistance in the field of human rights proposed in the present resolution, the entire programme to be known as "advisory services in the field of human rights";

2. *Authorizes* the Secretary-General:

(a) Subject to the directions of the Economic and Social Council, to make provision at the request of Governments, and with the co-operation of the specialized agencies where appropriate and without duplication of their existing activities, for the following forms of assistance with respect to the field of human rights:

(i) Advisory services of experts;
(ii) Fellowships and scholarships;
(iii) Seminars;

(b) To take the programme authorized by the present resolution into account in preparing the budgetary estimates of the United Nations;

3. *Requests* the Secretary-General to undertake the assistance provided for in paragraph 2 (a) above, in agreement with the Governments concerned, on the basis of requests received from Governments and in accordance with the following policies:

(a) The kind of service to be rendered to each country under paragraph 2 (a) (i) shall be determined by the Governments concerned;

(b) The selection of the persons under paragraph 2 (a) (ii) shall be made by the Secretary-General on the basis of proposals received from Governments;

(c) The amount of assistance and the conditions under which it is to be rendered shall be decided by the Secretary-General with due regard to the greater needs of the underdeveloped areas, and in conformity with the principle that each requesting Government shall be expected to assume responsibility, as far as possible, for all or a considerable part of the expenses connected with the assistance furnished to it either by making a contribution in cash, or by providing supporting staff, services and payment of local costs for the purpose of carrying out the programme;

(d) The assistance shall be applicable to any subject in the field of human rights, in addition to the subjects covered by the relevant resolutions of the General Assembly, provided however that the subject shall be one for which adequate advisory assistance is not available through a specialized agency and which does not fall within the scope of existing technical assistance programmes;

4. *Requests* the Secretary-General to report regularly to the Economic and Social Council, to the Commission on Human Rights and, as appropriate, to the Commission on the Status of Women, on the measures which he takes in compliance with the terms of the present resolution;

5. *Recommends* that the specialized agencies continue to develop their technical assistance activities with a view to aiding Member States to further the effective observance of human rights;

6. *Invites* the specialized agencies to communicate to the Economic and Social Council, for transmission to the Commission on Human Rights, any observations which they may find appropriate on the above assistance and on any new measures of assistance which they may deem necessary with a view to assisting Member States in furthering the effective observance of human rights;

7. *Expresses the hope* that international and national non-governmental organizations, universities, philanthropic foundations and other private groups will supplement this United Nations programme with similar programmes designed to further research and studies, the exchange of information and assistance in the field of human rights;

8. *Requests* the Secretary-General to inform Member States of this new programme and of the procedures to be followed in obtaining assistance;

9. *Requests* the Economic and Social Council to submit to the General Assembly at its thirteenth session a report containing:

(a) An evaluation of the projects carried out under the programme of advisory services in human rights, with particular reference to the extent to which these projects have furthered the aims and purposes of the United Nations in the field of human rights;

(b) Recommendations concerning the future of the programme.

2. *Palestine Refugees: General Assembly Resolution 916 (X), Adopted December 3, 1955.*[2]

The General Assembly,

Recalling its resolutions 194 (III) of 11 December 1948, 302 (IV) of 8 December 1949, 393 (V) of 2 December 1950, 513 (VI) of 26 January 1952, 614 (VII) of 6 November 1952, 720 (VIII) of 27 November 1953 and 818 (IX) of 4 December 1954,

Noting the annual report[3] and the special report[4] of the

[2] *Ibid.*, pp. 7-8. Adopted by a vote of 38-0-17.
[3] *Ibid.*, Supplement No. 15.
[4] *Ibid.*, Supplement No. 15A.

Director of the United Nations Relief and Works Agency for Palestine Refugees in the Near East and the report[5] of the Advisory Commission of the Agency,

Having reviewed the budgets for relief and rehabilitation prepared by the Director of the Agency,

Noting that repatriation or compensation of the refugees, as provided for in paragraph 11 of resolution 194 (III), has not been effected, that no substantial progress has been made in the programme for reintegration of refugees endorsed in paragraph 2 or resolution 513 (VI) and that the situation of the refugees therefore continues to be a matter of grave concern,

1. *Directs* the United Nations Relief and Works Agency for Palestine Refugees in the Near East to pursue its programmes for the relief and rehabilitation of refugees, bearing in mind the limitations imposed upon it by the extent of the contributions for the fiscal year;

2. *Requests* the Agency to continue its consultation with the United Nations Conciliation Commission for Palestine in the best interest of their respective tasks, with particular reference to paragraph 11 of resolution 194 (III);

3. *Requests* the Governments of the area, without prejudice to paragraph 11 of resolution 194 (III), to make a determined effort, in co-operation with the Director of the Agency, to seek and carry out projects capable of supporting substantial numbers of refugees;

4. *Notes with gratification* that the Government of the Hashemite Kingdom of the Jordan and the Agency have made substantial progress toward resolving the difficulties which impede the granting of rations to all qualified refugee children in Jordan;

5. *Notes* the serious need of the other claimants for relief as described in the special report prepared by the Director pursuant to paragraph 6 of resolution 818 (IX), namely, the frontier villagers in Jordan, the non-refugee population of the Gaza strip, a number of the refugees in Egypt, and certain of the Bedouin;

6. *Appeals* to private organizations to give them increased assistance to the extent that local governments cannot do so;

7. *Urges* all Governments and individuals to support these private organizations with food, goods and services;

8. *Requests* the Negotiating Committee for Extra-Budgetary Funds, after the receipt of the budgets from the Direc-

[5] United Nations Document A/3017, dated November 7, 1955.

tor of the Agency, to seek such funds as may be required by the Agency;

9. *Appeals* to the Governments of Member and non-member States to make voluntary contributions to the extent necessary to carry through to fulfilment the Agency's programmes, and thanks the numerous religious, charitable and humanitarian organizations for their valuable and continuing work in assisting the refugees;

10. *Expresses its thanks* to the Director and the staff of the Agency for their continued faithful efforts to carry out their mandate, and requests the Governments of the area to continue to facilitate the work of the Agency and to ensure the protection of its personnel and property;

11. *Requests* the Director of the Agency to continue to submit the reports referred to in paragraph 21 of resolution 302 (IV) as well as the annual budgets.

3. *The Korean Question.*

a. *General Assembly Resolution 920 (X), Adopted October 25, 1955.*[6]

Recalling General Assembly resolutions 410 (V) of 1 December 1950, 701 (VII) of 11 March 1953, 725 (VIII) of 7 December 1953, and 828 (IX) of 14 December 1954,

Taking note of the report of the Agent General on the work of the United Nations Korean Reconstruction Agency for the period 1 September 1954 to 30 June 1955,[7] and of the comments thereon by the United Nations Commission for the Unification and Rehabilitation of Korea,[8]

Recognizing the particular importance of the Agency's programme for the relief and rehabilitation of the Republic of Korea,

1. *Commends* the Agent General of the United Nations Korean Reconstruction Agency for the excellent progress made by the Agency in pursuing its mission of assisting the Korean people to relieve the sufferings and to repair the devastation caused by aggression;

2. *Stresses* the desire that the approved programmes of the Agency be expeditiously implemented to the maximum extent possible within available funds;

[6] United Nations General Assembly *Official Records, Tenth Session,* Supplement No. 19, p. 9. Adopted by a vote of 47-0-8.

[7] *Ibid.,* Supplement No. 18.

[8] United Nations Document A/2982, dated September 23, 1955.

3. *Expresses* appreciation for the valuable and continuing assistance given to the Agency by United Nations specialized agencies and by voluntary non-governmental organizations.

b. *General Assembly Resolution 910* (X), *Adopted November 29, 1955.*[9]

A

REPORT OF THE UNITED NATIONS COMMISSION FOR THE UNIFICATION AND REHABILITATION OF KOREA

The General Assembly,

Having noted the report of the United Nations Commission for the Unification and Rehabilitation of Korea signed at Seoul, Korea, on 7 September 1955,[10]

Recalling that, in resolution 811 (IX) of 11 December 1954, in approving the report[11] of the fifteen Governments participating in the Geneva Korean Political Conference on behalf of the United Nations, the General Assembly expressed the hope that it would soon prove possible to make progress towards the achievement by peaceful means of a unified, independent and democratic Korea under a representative form of government and of full restoration of international peace and security in the area,

Noting that paragraph 62 of the Armistice Agreement of 27 July 1953[12] provides that the Agreement "shall remain in effect until expressly superseded either by mutually acceptable amendments and additions or by provision in an appropriate agreement for a peaceful settlement at a political level between both sides,"

1. *Reaffirms* its intention to continue to seek an early solution of the Korean question in accordance with the objectives of the United Nations;

2. *Urges* that continuing efforts be made to achieve these objectives;

3. *Requests* the Secretary-General to place the Korean question on the provisional agenda of the eleventh session of the General Assembly.

[9] United Nations General Assembly *Official Records, Tenth Session,* Supplement No. 19, p. 3. The vote on "A" was 44-0-11, on "B" 48-0-6.
[10] *Ibid.,* Supplement No. 13.
[11] United Nations Document A/2786, dated November 11, 1954.
[12] *Department of State Bulletin,* v. 29 (August 3, 1953), pp. 132-140.

B

PROBLEM OF EX-PRISONERS OF THE KOREAN WAR

The General Assembly,

Noting that, pending their final disposition, a number of ex-prisoners of the Korean war remain temporarily in India,

1. *Notes with appreciation* that the Governments of Argentina and Brazil have generously offered to resettle as many of the ex-prisoners as opt to settle in those countries and that, in respect of the offer of Brazil, consultations with regard to arrangements are taking place;

2. *Requests* the Governments of Member States able to do so, to assist in bringing about a full solution of this problem by accepting for resettlement those ex-prisoners not covered by the present offers;

3. *Requests* the Government of India to report to the General Assembly at its eleventh session on this problem.

CHAPTER EIGHT

DISARMAMENT AND THE PEACEFUL USES OF ATOMIC ENERGY

A. Disarmament.

1. *Meetings of the Subcommittee of the United Nations Disarmament Commission, London, February 25—May 18, 1955.*[1]

a. *Soviet Draft Resolution, February 25, 1955.*[2]

The Security Council (*General Assembly*),

Recognizes that the cessation of the armaments race would contribute to the relaxation of tension in international relations and the strengthening of world peace, and also to the reduction of the tax burden which that race imposes on the peoples;

Further recognizes that in order to save mankind from the threat of an annihilating atomic war, immediate steps must be taken to reach international agreement on the complete prohibition of atomic, hydrogen and other types of weapons of mass destruction;

Takes into account the demands made by wide circles of international public opinion with regard to the necessity for the destruction of stocks of atomic and hydrogen weapons in the possession of States;

Considers that the destruction of stocks of atomic and hydrogen weapons would contribute to the relaxation of international tension and the attainment of the fundamental goal —the complete and unconditional prohibition of atomic and hydrogen weapons;

The Security Council (*General Assembly*),

Decides:

1. To propose to all States, both Members and non-

[1] Pursuant to Resolution 808 (IX), adopted by the General Assembly of the United Nations on November 4, 1954 (*Documents on American Foreign Relations, 1954,* pp. 461-462), the Subcommittee of the U.N. Disarmament Commission, composed of representatives of the United States, France, Canada, the U. K. and the U.S.S.R. resumed closed discussions in London on February 25, 1955.

[2] *Department of State Bulletin,* v. 32 (May 30, 1955), pp. 892-893.

Members of the United Nations, that they should pledge themselves, as a first step towards the reduction of armaments and armed forces, not to increase their armaments and armed forces above the level of 1 January 1955 and not to increase their appropriations for military purposes above the level of the appropriations for these purposes in 1955,

2. To propose to all States which possess atomic and hydrogen weapons that they should destroy completely stocks of those weapons in their possession, and use atomic materials solely for peaceful purposes,

3. To institute international control over the observance of this decision.

b. *Joint Memorandum by the Four Western Delegations, March 4, 1955.*[3]

The four delegations ask the following question:

"Does the Soviet representative agree that the three proposals contained in the operative paragraph of his draft resolution of 25 February 1955 shall be carried out in the order and in the manner laid down in paragraphs 5, 6, and 7 of the French-United Kingdom memorandum of 11 June 1954,[4] accepted by the Soviet Union on 30 September 1954,[5] as the basis of a draft international disarmament convention?"

c. *Joint Draft Resolution by the Four Western Delegations, March 8, 1955.*[6]

The General Assembly (*Security Council*),

Recalling its resolution of November 4, 1954,[7] which was adopted unanimously,

Recalling further that in that resolution it concluded that a further effort should be made to reach agreement on comprehensive and co-ordinated proposals to be embodied in a draft international disarmament treaty,

Bearing in mind that the proposals for a disarmament programme submitted by France and the United Kingdom on June 11, 1954 were accepted by the U.S.S.R. according to its

[3] *Ibid.*, p. 892.
[4] *Documents on American Foreign Relations, 1954*, pp. 457-459.
[5] *Ibid.*, pp. 459-461.
[6] *Department of State Bulletin*, v. 32 (May 30, 1955), pp. 892-894.
[7] *Documents on American Foreign Relations, 1954*, pp. 461-462.

draft resolution of October 8, 1954,[8] as a basis for a draft international disarmament treaty,

1. *Considers* that all States possessing nuclear weapons should regard themselves as prohibited in accordance with the terms of the Charter of the United Nations from the use of such weapons except in defence against aggression;

2. *Recommends* that such a disarmament treaty should include an immediate and explicit acceptance of this prohibition by all signatory States, pending the total prohibition and elimination of nuclear weapons as proposed in the subsequent paragraphs of this resolution;

3. *Further recommends* that the obligations assumed by the Members of the United Nations to refrain in their international relations from the threat or use of force against the territorial integrity or political independence of any State should be accepted by all signatory States not Members of the United Nations;

4. *Considers* that such a disarmament treaty prepared by the Disarmament Commission and submitted by it to the Security Council to the General Assembly and to a World Disarmament Conference should include provisions covering the following:

(a) The total prohibition of the use and manufacture of nuclear weapons and weapons of mass destruction of every type, together with the conversion of existing stocks of nuclear weapons for peaceful purposes;

(b) Major reductions in all armed forces and conventional armaments;

(c) The establishment of a control organ with rights and powers and functions adequate to guarantee the effective observance of the agreed prohibitions and reductions;

5. *Further considers* that after the approval of the draft treaty by the World Disarmament Conference this instrument would be open to signature and adherence by all States. The treaty would enter into force immediately it had been ratified by those of the signatories who would be specified in the treaty;

6. *Decides* that the treaty should provide that the disarmament programme should be carried out as described below:

I. After the constitution and positioning of the control organ, which shall be carried out within a specified time, and

[8] *Ibid.*, pp. 459-461.

as soon as the control organ reports that it is able effectively to enforce them, the following measures shall enter into effect:

(a) Overall military manpower shall be limited to levels existing on December 31, 1954 or such other date as may be agreed at the World Disarmament Conference.
(b) Overall military expenditure, both atomic and non-atomic, shall be limited to amounts spent in the year ending 31 December 1954 or such other date as may be agreed at the World Disarmament Conference.

II. As soon as the control organ reports that it is able effectively to enforce them, the following measures shall enter into effect:

(a) One-half of the agreed reductions of conventional armaments and armed forces shall take effect;
(b) On completion of (a) the manufacture of all kinds of nuclear weapons and all other prohibited weapons shall cease.

III. As soon as the control organ reports that it is able effectively to enforce them, the following measures shall enter into effect:

(a) The second half of the agreed reductions of conventional armaments and armed forces shall take effect;
(b) On completion of (a):
  (i) The total prohibition and elimination of nuclear weapons and the conversion of existing stocks of nuclear materials for peaceful purposes shall be carried out;
  (ii) The total prohibition and elimination of all other prohibited weapons shall be carried out.

7. *Expresses* the hope that when all the measures enumerated above have been carried out the armaments and armed forces of the Powers will be further reduced to the levels strictly necessary for the maintenance of internal security and the fulfillment of the obligations of signatory States under the terms of the United Nations Charter;

8. *Decides* that the control organ shall remain in being to ensure that the reductions, prohibitions and eliminations are faithfully and permanently observed;

9. *Requests* the Commission to inform the General Assembly as soon as the preparation of the draft treaty has

progressed to a point where, in the judgment of the Commission, its programme is ready for submission to the World Disarmament Conference.

d. *Joint Declaration by the Four Western Delegations, March 11, 1955.*[9]

The Delegations of Canada, France, the United Kingdom and the United States of America wish to place on record their attitude towards the draft resolution introduced by the delegation of the USSR on 25 February. The Soviet proposal calls for the immediate destruction of stocks of nuclear weapons without halting the production of these weapons and with no provision for the reduction of military manpower and of conventional armaments. It makes only the barest reference to international control. Moreover, this programme would, in the words of the Soviet representative, "be carried out here and now without waiting for the examination of other questions"—in other words, without agreement on the other essential elements of the comprehensive disarmament programme which the Sub-Committee was instructed to work out.

As they have repeatedly stated in the Sub-Committee, the four Western Delegations are ready to discuss the proposals set forth in the Soviet draft resolution on the understanding that such proposals form an integral part of a phased disarmament programme. However, the Soviet Delegation has for its part made it clear that the Soviet Government has put forward these proposals on a completely different basis. In so doing it has abandoned the principle laid down in the resolution of the General Assembly which was co-sponsored by the Soviet Delegation and approved unanimously by the General Assembly on 4 November 1954. In these circumstances the Western Delegations feel obliged to declare that the Soviet draft resolution of 25 February is unacceptable.

The Soviet Delegation must be aware that the other Governments represented on the Sub-Committee, and with them the vast majority of the nations of the world, could not accept a resolution which deliberately violated two of the essential principles of any disarmament plan: the necessity of ensuring that it should be carried out by stages and that it should apply equally to all the elements of the military power of a State. Any disarmament plan, to be acceptable must be drawn

[9] *Department of State Bulletin,* v. 32 (May 30, 1955), p. 894.

up in such a way that each of its stages increases the security of all parties and not the security of only one of the parties at the expense of the others. It must provide for genuine and effective international control and inspection, fully competent to ensure its effective execution.

The Western Delegations therefore propose that the Sub-Committee should now proceed to a discussion of the comprehensive draft resolution [of March 8] sponsored by the Delegations of Canada, France, the United Kingdom and the United States. This draft resolution is based on the Franco-British plan of 11 June 1954, which was accepted by the Soviet Government on 30 September 1954 as the basis of a Disarmament Treaty.

The Soviet Delegation will have observed that the three elements of a disarmament programme which in its own draft resolution were singled out for prior execution are contained in this four-Power draft resolution. The Western Delegations would be willing to discuss the three elements of the Soviet proposal prior to a discussion of any of the other points in their own draft resolution. If, however, the Soviet Delegation insists that its proposals should be agreed and carried out before there can be any examination of other questions and phases of a disarmament programme, the Sub-Committee will unhappily be faced with the prospect of deadlock. In that event there could be no doubt with whom the responsibility for such a result must lie.

e. *Joint Draft Resolution by the Four Western Delegations, March 12, 1955.*[10]

The General Assembly (Security Council),

Recalling its unanimous resolution of 4 November 1954 referring to the need for a draft international disarmament convention to provide *inter alia* for major reduction of all armed forces and all conventional armaments;

Recalling that the Anglo-French proposals of 11 June 1954 on the phasing of a disarmament programme have been accepted as a basis for a draft international disarmament convention as stated in the draft resolution of the USSR of 8 October 1954;

Noting that the Anglo-French proposals provide for major reductions in all armed forces and conventional armaments;

Considers that the provisions in a draft disarmament con-

[10] *Ibid.*, pp. 894-895.

vention relating to reductions in armed forces and conventional armaments should be based on the following principles:

(a) There shall be major reductions in the armed forces of the United States, the USSR, France, China and the United Kingdom.
(b) There shall be an agreed level of armed forces to which all States in excess of it shall reduce, so that no State shall have armed forces strong enough to be a serious threat to international peace.
(c) The levels of all States' armed forces shall be established at fixed agreed limits or shall be calculated on the basis of simple agreed criteria, including demographic, geographic, economic and political factors, with the objective of reducing the possibility of aggression and avoiding a disequilibrium of power dangerous to international peace and security.
(d) No State shall be entitled to increase its armed forces above the levels existing at the entry into force of the disarmament convention, except that special arrangements will have to be made for certain specified States which will provide for levels of armed forces and armaments in accordance with the principles set out in paragraph (c) above.
(e) The agreed levels of armed forces shall apply not only to armies, navies and air forces, but also to all paramilitary forces and all internal security forces of a military type.
(f) No State shall retain or acquire any armaments and equipment in excess of those quantities agreed upon for the maintenance of the armed forces permitted under the Convention. The levels and types of such armaments and equipment shall be such as to prevent undue concentration of total permitted armed forces in a manner which might threaten international peace and security.

Requests the Disarmament Commission in its preparation of a draft international disarmament convention, in accordance with General Assembly resolution 502 (VI) of 11 January 1952,[11] to take full account of these principles.

[11] *Ibid.*, v. 26 (March 31, 1952), p. 507.

f. *Soviet Draft Resolution, March 18, 1955.*[12]

The General Assembly instructs the United Nations Disarmament Commission to prepare and submit for confirmation by the Security Council a draft international convention (treaty) designed to strengthen peace and increase international security and providing for the prohibition of atomic, hydrogen and other weapons of mass destruction and their elimination from the armaments of States, a substantial reduction in armaments and the establishment of international control over the implementation of these decisions on the basis of the French and United Kingdom proposals of 11 June 1954.

Accordingly, the convention (treaty) should contain the following basic provisions:

(1) The following measures shall be taken simultaneously:

(a) In the course of six months (or one year), States shall reduce their armaments, armed forces and budgetary appropriations for military requirements to the extent of 50 percent of the agreed norms. Armaments and armed forces shall be reduced from the strength of armaments and armed forces existing on 1 January 1955, and appropriations shall be reduced from the amount of appropriations for military requirements during 1955.

State parties to the convention (treaty) shall pledge themselves, as a first step towards the reduction of armaments and armed forces, not to increase their armaments and armed forces above the level of 1 January 1955 and not to increase their appropriations for military requirements above the level of the appropriations for these purposes in 1955.

In the case of the United States, the Union of Soviet Socialist Republics, France, China and the United Kingdom, a major reduction of armaments and armed forces is considered to be necessary; and with a view to the execution of further measures relating to general disarmament, it is also considered necessary to convene in 1955 a world conference on the general reduction of armaments and the prohibition of atomic weapons, to be attended by States both Members and non-Members of the United Nations.

In establishing the norms for the reduction of armaments

[12] *Ibid.*, v. 32 (May 30, 1955), pp. 895-896.

of States, simple agreed criteria, including demographic, geographic, economic and political factors shall be taken into account, with a view to the strengthening of world peace and international security and the diminution of the threat of aggression.

(b) For the purpose of supervising the fulfilment by States of the obligations in connection with the reduction of armaments and armed forces provided for in subparagraph (a), a temporary international control commission shall be established under the Security Council with the right to require States to provide the necessary information on the measures taken by them to reduce armaments and armed forces. The commission shall take the necessary steps to supervise the fulfilment by States of the obligations assumed by them in connection with the reduction of armaments, armed forces and appropriations for military requirements. States shall periodically supply the commission at established intervals with information concerning the implementation of the measures provided for in the convention (treaty).

(2) On completion of the measures referred to in paragraph (1), the following measures shall be taken simultaneously:

(a) In the course of six months (or one year), States shall reduce their armaments, armed forces and budgetary appropriations for military requirements by the remaining 50 per cent of the agreed norms from the strength of armaments and armed forces existing on 1 January 1955 and shall reduce their appropriations from the amount of appropriations for military requirements during 1955;

(b) A complete prohibition of atomic, hydrogen and other weapons of mass destruction shall be carried into effect, the production of such weapons shall be discontinued and they shall be entirely eliminated from the armaments of States; all existing atomic materials shall be used only for peaceful purposes.

The carrying out of these measures must be completed not later than the carrying out of the measures taken for the reduction of armaments and armed forces referred to in paragraph (2) (a), and the production of atomic and hydrogen weapons shall cease immediately, as soon as a start is made with the reduction of armaments, armed forces and appropriations for military requirements in respect of the remaining 50 per cent of the agreed norms. States shall institute a standing international organ for the supervision of the implementation of the convention (treaty) on the prohibition of atomic, hydrogen and other weapons of mass destruction, the discontinuance of the production of these weapons and their elimination from the armaments of States and the reduction of armaments, armed forces and appropriations for military requirements. This international organ shall have powers to exercise supervision, including inspection on a continuing basis, to the extent necessary to ensure implementation of the convention by all States.

In all States signatories to the convention, the international control organ shall have its own permanent staff of inspectors, having unrestricted access, within the limits of the supervisory functions they exercise, to all establishments subject to control.

Staff recruited to carry out the work of inspection shall be selected on an international basis.

(3) It is to be hoped that when all the measures enumerated above have been carried out, the armaments and armed forces of the Powers will be further reduced to the levels strictly necessary for the maintenance of internal security and the fulfillment of the obligations of signatory States under the terms of the United Nations Charter.

g. *Joint Anglo-French Memorandum, March 29, 1955.*[13]

The United Kingdom and France consider that there should be major reductions in the armed forces of the five permanent members of the Security Council. To this end they are each prepared to reduce their overall armed forces to a total of 650,000 men, as part of a general scheme of reductions which would provide that:

(1) There shall be a uniform ceiling for the three other permanent members of the Security Council which shall be fixed at a figure between one and one and a half million men.

(2) The forces permitted to other States shall in all cases be considerably lower than the levels established for the five permanent members of the Security Council.

(3) No State shall be entitled to increase its armed forces

[13] *Ibid.*, pp. 896-897.

above the levels existing at the entry into force of the disarmament convention, except that special arrangements will have to be made for certain specified States which will provide for levels of armed forces and armaments such as will reduce the possibility of aggression and avoid a disequilibrium of power dangerous to international peace and security.

h. *Amendments Submitted by the Four Western Delegations to the Four-Power Resolution of March 8, dated March 31, 1955.*[14]

Between the present paragraphs 6 and 7 insert a new paragraph 7, as follows, and renumber the succeeding paragraphs accordingly:

7. *Considers* that the disarmament treaty should establish time-limits applicable to the various limitations, reductions and prohibitions described in paragraph 6, subject to any extension of time which may be essential in any phase to permit States to complete these measures.

i. *Amendments Submitted by the Four Western Delegations to the Four-Power Resolution of March 8, dated April 1, 1955.*[15]

1. Paragraph 6 I (a) is amended by inserting before "overall" the words "Conventional armaments and."
2. Add to paragraph 6 a final sub-paragraph as follows: The measures mentioned in sub-paragraphs II and III above shall be accompanied by consequent reductions in overall military expenditures.

j. *Proposal on Nuclear Disarmament by the Four Western Delegations, April 18, 1955.*[16]

The delegations of Canada, France, the United Kingdom and the United States of America make the following proposal in relation to the destruction and prohibition of nuclear and other weapons of mass destruction and the conversion for peaceful purposes of all stocks of fissile material in the possession of any State.

[14] *Ibid.*, p. 897.
[15] *Ibid.*, p. 897.
[16] *Ibid.*, p. 897.

(1) A disarmament treaty shall include provision for the total prohibition of the use and manufacture of nuclear and other weapons of mass destruction and for the elimination of existing stocks; these measures shall be fitted in with reductions in armed forces and arms in such a way that no country's security will be endangered in the process;

(2) the elimination of nuclear and other weapons of mass destruction must be supervised by an effective system of international control;

(3) when all nuclear and other weapons of mass destruction have been eliminated and all stocks of such weapons destroyed, all States signatory to the Disarmament Treaty shall convert and devote their supplies of fissile material to peaceful purposes only;

(4) all States signatory to the Disarmament Treaty which produce fissile material or possess scientific knowledge or experience in the nuclear field shall contribute to the fullest extent to the promotion of the peaceful uses of nuclear energy by all suitable means, and in particular through the International Atomic Energy Agency;[17]

(5) to this end, the States signatory to the Disarmament Treaty:

(a) shall encourage and assist world-wide research and development, including full freedom to exchange information relating to industrial, medical and other peaceful uses of nuclear energy;
(b) shall make provision for nuclear materials to meet the need for research in and practical applications of nuclear energy for peaceful purposes, including the production of electric power;
(c) shall foster the interchange of scientific, medical and technical information in the field of the peaceful uses of nuclear energy;
(d) shall pay special regard to the needs of underdeveloped territories;
(e) shall seek to devote a proportion of the savings resulting from world-wide disarmament and from the elimination of nuclear weapons to assistance in this field.

[17] See below, p. 479.

k. *Joint Anglo-French Memorandum on the Prohibition and Elimination of Nuclear Weapons, April 19, 1955.*[18]

The Soviet representative has claimed that the disarmament programme put forward by the Western Powers in their draft resolution of 8 March is unco-ordinated and that the prohibition of atomic weapons and the conversion of stocks of such weapons to peaceful purposes should be carried out simultaneously with the second half of the agreed reductions in armed forces and conventional armaments.[19]

The delegations of France and the United Kingdom agree that it is desirable that the reductions in armed forces and conventional armaments should be better co-ordinated with the abolition of nuclear weapons. In order to reach agreement on this point they suggest that the Soviet delegation should agree that the production of nuclear weapons should cease at the earlier stage proposed in paragraph 6 II of the Western Powers' draft resolution of 8 March, instead of at the later stage suggested in the Soviet draft resolution of 19 March.[20] For their part they would be prepared to agree that the prohibition of the use of nuclear weapons and the process of eliminating all nuclear stocks should be carried out at the same time as the final quarter of the agreed reductions in armed forces and conventional armaments begins, i. e. when 75 per cent of those reductions have been completed.

This proposal would entail amending the Western draft resolution of 8 March in the following respects (new words underlined):

Paragraph 6 II to read:

As soon as the control organ reports that it is able effectively to enforce them, the following measures shall enter into effect:

(a) One-half of the agreed reductions of conventional armaments and armed forces shall take effect;

(b) On completion of (a), the manufacture of atomic, hydrogen and all other weapons of mass destruction shall cease.

Paragraph 6 III to read:

"As soon as the control organ reports that it is able effec-

[18] *Department of State Bulletin,* v. 32 (May 30, 1955), pp. 897-898.

[19] The remarks of the Soviet representative (Gromyko) are not printed.

[20] The reference is to the Soviet draft printed above, pp. 408-410.

tively to enforce them, the following measures shall enter into effect:

(a) the third quarter of the agreed reductions of conventional armaments and armed forces shall take effect;

(b) on completion of (a), a complete prohibition on the use of atomic, hydrogen and other weapons of mass destruction shall come into force. Simultaneously, the elimination of these weapons and the final quarter of the agreed reductions in armed forces and conventional armaments shall begin; and both processes shall be completed within the time-limit laid down in the Disarmament Treaty. All atomic materials shall then be used only for peaceful purposes."

Paragraph 6 III (b) (ii) to be deleted.

The Delegations of France and the United Kingdom wish to make it clear that this proposal is dependent on agreement being reached on two essential elements in the disarmament programme, namely, (a) drastic reductions in the armed forces and conventional armaments of the great Powers so that an equilibrium is attained as suggested in the Anglo-French memorandum of 29 March 1955, and (b) the institution of an effective system of control which would operate throughout the whole disarmament programme.

1. *Joint Draft Resolution on the Principles of Controls Submitted by the Four Western Delegations, April 21, 1955.*[21]

The General Assembly (*Security Council*),

Recalling its unanimously adopted resolution of 4 November 1954, referring to the need for a draft international disarmament treaty to provide *inter alia* for the establishment of a control organ with rights, powers and functions adequate to guarantee the effective observance of the major reductions in armed forces and conventional armaments and the total prohibition of the manufacture and use of nuclear weapons,

Recalling that the Anglo-French proposals of 11 June 1954 on the phasing of a disarmament programme have been accepted as a basis for a draft international disarmament

[21] *Department of State Bulletin,* v. 32 (May 30, 1955), pp. 898-900.

treaty as stated in the draft resolutions of the Union of Soviet Socialist Republics of 20 October 1954 and of 19 March 1955,

Recalling that the Anglo-French proposals provide that the control organ must be in position and able to carry out its tasks effectively before each phase of the disarmament programme begins, and consequently require its progressive development and expansion,

Recommends that the provisions of the draft disarmament treaty relating to the responsibilities, functions, powers and rights of the control organ should be based on the following principles:

A. The control organ shall have, to the extent necessary to ensure implementation of the treaty by all nations, full responsibility for supervising and guaranteeing effective observance of all the provisions of the disarmament treaty including:

(1) The limitations on levels of conventional armaments and overall military manpower, and on overall military expenditures including both atomic and non-atomic (paragraph 6 I (a) and (b) of the four-power draft resolution of 8 March 1955);
(2) The major reductions in armed forces and conventional armaments (paragraphs 6 II (a) and 6 III (a) of the four-power draft resolution of 8 March 1955);
(3) The total prohibition of manufacture and use, and the elimination of nuclear weapons and all other weapons of mass destruction, as well as conversion of existing stocks of nuclear materials to peaceful uses (paragraphs 6 II (b), 6 III (b) of the four-power draft resolution of 8 March 1955);
(4) The continued supervision of permitted atomic energy installations and facilities.

B. In order to enable it to carry out these responsibilities and functions, the control organ shall be accorded powers to be exercised in accordance with the terms of the disarmament treaty and which shall include the following:

(1) To determine, within the limits established by the disarmament treaty, the details of the methods and processes of supervising and guaranteeing the effective observance of the various phases of agreed limitations, reductions, and prohibitions, in order to ensure that the disarmament programme is carried out as rapidly as possible and with safety and equity for all;

(2) To supervise and verify the disclosures of information required at each stage of the disarmament programme laid down in the four-power draft resolution of 8 March 1955, with respect to all armaments and armed forces and related installations and facilities;

(3) To ensure that installations, facilities, equipment, and materials, including stocks of nuclear materials, are disposed of or utilized in accordance with the terms of the disarmament treaty;

(4) To organize and conduct field and aerial surveys in connexion with the above functions and for the purpose of determining whether all installations and facilities have been disclosed;

(5) To conduct such research as is necessary to keep itself in the forefront of nuclear knowledge and to enable it to be fully effective in eliminating the destructive uses of nuclear energy, so that such energy shall be used only for peaceful purposes;

(6) To report and provide information to the Security Council, the General Assembly and the signatory States and to make recommendations concerning appropriate action by them in the event of violation of the disarmament treaty;

(7) To take such measures provided for in the treaty as may be necessary to deal with violations of the disarmament treaty pending action by the Security Council, the General Assembly or the signatory States, and to call upon the party concerned and its agents to comply with such measures, without prejudice to the rights, claims or position of the party concerned.

C. In order to ensure that the international officials of the control organ are continuously in a position to fulfil their responsibilities, they will be granted the right:

(1) to be stationed permanently in the countries adhering to the disarmament agreement;

(2) of unrestricted access to, egress from and travel within the territory of participating States, and unrestricted access to all installations and facilities as required by them for the effective performance of their responsibilities and functions;

(3) of unrestricted use of communication facilities necessary for the discharge of their responsibilities;

(4) of inviolability of person, premises, property and archives.

D. The control organ shall remain in being to ensure that the reductions, prohibitions and eliminations are faithfully and permanently observed.

m. *Soviet Proposal on the Reduction of Armaments, the Prohibition of Atomic Weapons and the Elimination of the Threat of a New War, May 10, 1955.*[22]

The General Assembly,

Recognizing the heavy responsibility which rests with the United Nations for the maintenance of peace among the peoples, considers it its duty to draw the attention of all States to the situation which is at present developing in relations between States.

More than ever before, the peoples, which so recently experienced the Second World War with the heavy loss of life and the vast material destruction that war inflicted, are displaying an unflinching will for peace.

As a result of this deep desire of the peoples for peace, it has already proved possible to bring the bloodshed in Korea and Indo-China to an end and thereby to create more favourable conditions for the settlement of other outstanding international problems.

At the same time, the peoples are showing a legitimate concern for the fate of peace, with particular reference to the situation which is developing in Europe and Asia. This concern has found expression, in particular, in the resolutions adopted at the conference of Asian and African countries held recently in Bandung, which was of great importance in the struggle for peace, freedom and the independence of peoples.[23]

So far from improving, the situation in some areas of the world is at present deteriorating, and mutual distrust between States is becoming intensified. The absence of the necessary confidence in relations between States is the chief obstacle to the settlement of outstanding problems both in Europe and in Asia.

This applies pre-eminently to relations between the great Powers, which bear the primary responsibility for the maintenance of universal peace and the security of peoples.

[22] *Ibid.*, pp. 900-905.
[23] See above, pp. 332-341.

Despite the obligations assumed by the great Powers, together with the other States Members of the United Nations, to co-operate with a view to the maintenance of peace and international security, the relations between them do not correspond with these requirements. Mistrust in relations between the Powers led, after the end of the Second World War, to the rise of the threat of a new war still more terrible in its consequences.

As a result of this mistrust, particularly in the relations between the permanent members of the Security Council, the armaments race is assuming ever-increasing proportions, and land, naval and air forces are steadily increasing. The supreme achievements of science and technique are being used to produce the most destructive means for exterminating human beings. The armaments race has assumed particularly large proportions in the production of the highly dangerous atomic and hydrogen weapons.

Large numbers of foreign military bases are being established on the territory of other States, a fact which is causing legitimate anxiety to the States in whose vicinity these bases are being established. The creation of such bases is also increasingly endangering the security of the States on whose territory they are established. The existence of these bases, many of which are being used for the preparations for atomic war that are being carried out by certain Powers, is still further intensifying mistrust in relations between States and increasing international tension.

As a result of all this, the world has for many years been in a state of "cold war," and the military preparations of States are laying a constantly increasing burden on the shoulders of the peoples.

Despite the fact that as long ago as 1947 the General Assembly unanimously adopted a decision condemning all forms of propaganda "either designed or likely to provoke or encourage any threat to the peace, breach of the peace or act of aggression", propaganda for a new war is being openly carried on in a number of States. Calls to war, far from being brought to a stop, have become increasingly frequent in the press, on the radio and in public statements; and especially frequent, in recent times, have been calls for atomic war.

The former traditional economic and trade links between numerous States, developed over many years, have been broken, with all the resulting adverse consequences for international economic co-operation.

The situation that has arisen requires that immediate and effective action should be taken to relax international tension and to strengthen mutual confidence in relations between States. This can only be achieved if an end is put to the "cold war" and if the propaganda for a new war which is being carried on in certain States, with its accompanying incitement of enmity and hatred between peoples and its inflaming of certain peoples against others, is brought to a stop.

Continuance of the propaganda which is being carried on in certain countries with a view to fanning war hysteria, as also incitement to war, can only intensify international tension and mutual distrust between States, thereby intensifying the threat of a new world war.

On the other hand, the cessation of the "cold war" between States would help to bring about a relaxation of international tension, the creation of the necessary confidence in international relations, the removal of the threat of a new war and the establishment of conditions permitting a peaceful and tranquil life of the peoples. This, in turn, would create the requisite conditions for the execution of a broad disarmament programme, with the establishment of the necessary international control over its implementation.

To these ends, the General Assembly:

1. *Recommends* all States to take the necessary steps to ensure scrupulous compliance with the General Assembly resolution condemning all forms of propaganda for a new war, to put an end to all calls for war and for the kindling of hostility between peoples in the press, on the radio, in the cinema and in public statements. Failure to comply with this recommendation shall be regarded as a violation by a State of its international duty and of its obligations to the United Nations, namely, to abstain in its international relations from the threat or the use of force and not to permit violations of the territorial integrity or political independence of any State.

2. *Notes with satisfaction* the successes achieved in the talks between the interested States on the Korean question—which led to the termination of the war in Korea—and also on the question of the cessation of hostilities in Indo-China. Two dangerous hotbeds of war in the Far East were thereby eliminated.

As a result of negotiations between interested States it has also proved possible to settle the question of the conclusion of a Treaty of State with Austria, providing for the restoration of an independent Austria. The settlement of the Austrian question constitutes a new and important contribution to the consolidation of peace in Europe and promotes the creation of conditions for the successful settlement of other outstanding post-war problems.

All this testifies to the fact that the possibilities of settling outstanding international problems by means of negotiations between States in the interests of peace, freedom and the national independence of peoples have by no means been exhausted.

3. *Considers* that the reduction of international tension and the creation of the requisite confidence between States would be promoted if the Four Powers—the Soviet Union, the United States, the United Kingdom and France—would immediately withdraw their armies of occupation from the territory of Germany inside their national frontiers, with the exception of strictly limited contingents of forces left temporarily in German territory pending the conclusion of an agreement for their complete withdrawal. These ends would also be served by the formation of strictly limited contingents of local police forces in both parts of Germany and the establishment of joint control by the Four Powers over the execution of the relevant agreement.

The General Assembly will welcome any other steps which the Four Powers may take with a view to withdrawing their forces from German territory, and also with a view to facilitating the settlement of the German problem in the interest of European security and the national unification of Germany as a single peace-loving and democratic State.

4. *Considers it necessary* that the permanent members of the Security Council should reach agreement on the liquidation of foreign military bases on the territory of other States and inform the Security Council and the General Assembly of the results. Such an agreement would be of great importance for the reduction of international tension and the removal of mistrust in relations between States, and would help to create the necessary conditions for ending the armaments race.

5. *Invites States* having experience in the production of atomic materials and atomic energy to give extensive industrial and scientific and technical assistance to other countries in the field of the peaceful use of atomic energy, without subordinating such assistance to any demands of a political or military nature.

6. *Invites* the States concerned to settle outstanding questions in the Far East in accordance with the principles of sovereignty and territorial integrity, since the existing situation of tension in certain areas of the Far East is fraught with the danger of a new war and constitutes a serious threat to the maintenance of universal peace.

7. *Considers it necessary* that States, in their economic relations, should remove every form of discrimination impeding the development of broad economic co-operation between them, particularly in the field of trade. The rupture of the old-established former trade links between States is prejudicial to both private and State interests. The removal of such discrimination and the broad development of international trade relations based on the principle of mutual benefit will help to consolidate friendly relations between States and will promote the improvement of the well-being of peoples. Without the removal of these obstacles to the development of international trade no genuine relaxation of tension in international relations can be anticipated.

A further important means for the improvement of mutual understanding and the reconciliation of peoples is the development of international cultural relations, notably through the extensive interchange of delegations, through mutual visits by representatives of industry, agriculture, trade, science, culture and art and by student delegations, and through the development of tourism.

8. *Decides* to place on the agenda of its next session the question of the results achieved through the implementation by States of the provisions of this Declaration, having regard to the fact that the implementation of these provisions will correspond to the desire of the peoples for peace, will promote the creation of the necessary confidence between States and will thereby facilitate the carrying into effect of a broad disarmament programme, with the establishment of effective international control over its execution.

Concerning the Conclusion of an International Convention on the Reduction of Armaments and the Prohibition of Atomic Weapons

The General Assembly (Security Council),

Seeking to deliver mankind from a new and destructive war, to reduce the tension in relations between States, and to relieve the peoples of the heavy burden of taxation they bear as a result of the continuing armaments race,

Desirous of rendering possible the use of resources thus released to improve the well-being of the peoples and to afford extensive assistance to the economically under-developed countries,

Instructs the United Nations Disarmament Commission to draw up and submit for the approval of the Security Council a draft "international convention (treaty) on the question of the reduction of armaments and the prohibition of atomic, hydrogen and other weapons of mass destruction."

Such a convention, having as its purpose the strengthening of peace and international security, shall provide for:

(a) the complete prohibition of the use and production both of nuclear and of all other weapons of mass destruction, and the conversion of existing stocks of nuclear weapons for peaceful purposes;
(b) a major reduction in all armed forces and all conventional armaments;
(c) the establishment of a control organ with rights and powers and functions adequate to guarantee in the case of all States alike the effective observance of the agreed prohibitions and reductions.

Accordingly, the convention (treaty) shall contain the basic provisions set forth hereunder relating to the execution of measures for the reduction of the conventional armaments of States, the prohibition of atomic, hydrogen and other weapons of mass destruction and the procedure for the carrying out of these measures in two stages:

First Stage—Measures To Be Taken in 1956

The following measures shall be taken in 1956:

1. The States Parties to the convention (treaty) shall pledge themselves, as a first step towards the reduction of armaments and armed forces, not to increase their armed forces and conventional armaments above the level obtaining on 31 December 1954. They shall also pledge themselves not to increase their appropriations for armed forces and armaments, including atomic weapons, above the level of the expenditures effected for those purposes during the year ended 31 December 1954.

The above-mentioned measures shall be carried out within two months of the entry into force of the corresponding agreement.

The United States, the USSR, China, the United Kingdom

and France shall furnish the Disarmament Commission, within one month after the entry into force of the convention (treaty), with full official figures of their armed forces, conventional armaments and expenditures for military requirements.

2. An agreed level shall be established to which armed forces of all States in excess of that level shall be reduced, in order that no State may possess armed forces capable of constituting a serious threat to international peace. A substantial reduction shall be effected in the armed forces of the United States, the USSR, China, the United Kingdom and France. To these ends the above-mentioned five powers shall undertake to reduce the strength of their armed forces so that they do not exceed the following figures:

United States	1,000,000 to 1,500,000.
Union of Soviet Socialist Republics	1,000,000 to 1,500,000.
China	1,000,000 to 1,500,000.
United Kingdom	650,000.
France	650,000.

The five Powers shall pledge themselves also to reduce their conventional armaments correspondingly.

The above-mentioned five Powers shall in the course of one year effect a reduction in their armed forces and armaments by 50 per cent of the difference between the level of their armed forces and armaments obtaining on 31 December 1954 and the reduced level of the armed forces and armaments of each of these States established in accordance with the pledges made by them as set forth hereinabove.

Appropriations by States for armed forces and conventional armaments shall be reduced correspondingly.

3. There shall be convened, not later than during the first half of 1956, a world conference on the general reduction of armaments and the prohibition of atomic weapons, to be attended by States both Members and non-Members of the United Nations, with a view to determining the size of the reduction of the armaments and armed forces of the other States and to prohibiting atomic weapons.

The strength of the armed forces which other States shall be authorized to retain, shall in all cases be considerably lower than the levels established for the five permanent members of the Security Council.

The size of the reduction in the armaments of States, including those of the permanent members of the Security

Council, shall be established on the basis of simple agreed criteria, including demographic, geographic, economic and political factors, with a view to the strengthening of world peace and international security and the diminution of the threat of aggression.

4. As one of the first measures for the execution of the programme for the reduction of armaments and the prohibition of atomic weapons, States possessing atomic and hydrogen weapons shall pledge themselves to discontinue tests of these weapons.

With a view to supervision of the fulfilment by States of the afore-mentioned pledge, an international commission shall be set up which shall be required to report to the Security Council and the General Assembly.

5. Simultaneously with the initiation of measures to effect the first half of the agreed reduction of the armaments and armed forces of the five Powers to the prescribed levels and before the entry into force of the agreement on the complete prohibition of atomic weapons, States shall solemnly pledge themselves not to use nuclear weapons, which they shall regard as prohibited to them. Exceptions to this rule may be permitted for purposes of defence against aggression, when a decision to that effect is taken by the Security Council.

6. States possessing military, naval and air bases in the territories of other States shall pledge themselves to liquidate such bases.

The question of the bases to be liquidated during the first stage shall be dealt with by supplementary agreement.

The carrying out of these measures must promote the strengthening of the requisite confidence between States and facilitate the execution of the measures for the reduction of armaments and the prohibition of atomic weapons envisaged for the second stage.

Second Stage—Measures To Be Taken in 1957

The following measures shall be taken in 1957:

1. The production of atomic and hydrogen weapons shall be discontinued immediately, and budgetary appropriations of States for military requirements shall be reduced correspondingly.

2. The United States, the USSR, China, the United Kingdom and France shall, in the course of one year, reduce their armed forces and armaments by the remaining 50 per cent of the difference between the level of the armed forces and

armaments of each of these five States obtaining on 31 December 1954 and the reduced level of the armed forces and armaments of each of these States established in accordance with the pledges made by them under the convention. These States shall correspondingly reduce their appropriations for armed forces and conventional armaments.

During this stage, measures with a view to the reduction of the armaments and armed forces of other States to the extent established for them at the world conference shall also be completed.

3. After the reduction of armed forces and conventional armaments has been carried out to the extent of 75 per cent of the total reduction laid down in the convention, a complete prohibition on the use of atomic, hydrogen and other weapons of mass destruction shall come into effect. The elimination of such weapons from the armaments of States and their destruction shall begin simultaneously with the final 25 per cent of the agreed reductions of armed forces and conventional armaments; and both these processes shall be completed within the time-limits in 1957. All atomic materials shall thereafter be used exclusively for peaceful purposes.

States shall pledge themselves to promote extensive international co-operation in the peaceful uses of atomic energy. This co-operation shall include the free exchange of information concerning the use of atomic energy in industry, agriculture and medicine and in other branches of economic and scientific activity. In this connexion, special attention shall be given to assistance to economically under-developed countries. Such assistance shall not be subordinated to any demands of a political or military nature.

States shall endeavour to devote a portion of the savings achieved through world-wide disarmament and the elimination of nuclear weapons to the extensive use of atomic energy for peaceful purposes.

4. Measures for the liquidation of all foreign military, naval and air bases on the territories of other States shall be completed.

On the completion of all the measures enumerated above, it would be desirable that the Powers should further reduce their armaments and armed forces to the levels strictly necessary for the maintenance of internal security and the fulfilment of the obligations of signatory States under the terms of the United Nations Charter.

The question of the obligations of China, as one of the permanent members of the Security Council, under the convention on the reduction of armaments and the prohibition of atomic, hydrogen, and other weapons of mass destruction shall be the subject of consideration, in which the People's Republic of China shall participate.

Concerning International Control Over the Reduction of Armaments and the Prohibition of Atomic Weapons

The General Assembly,

Recognizing the great importance and the necessity of instituting effective international control over the fulfilment by States of their obligations under the convention on the reduction of armaments and armed forces and the prohibition of atomic and hydrogen weapons,

Notes that the requisite conditions for the institution of a control system which would enjoy the confidence of all States and would fully meet the requirements of international security do not at present exist.

It is impossible to disregard the fact that there exists at present considerable international tension and mistrust in relations between States. It is this that accounts for the fact that, in the conditions of mistrust among States which have come into being, barriers of every sort are being erected even in regard to the interchange of industrial, agricultural, scientific, cultural and other delegations. Such a situation renders difficult the attainment of agreement providing for States to grant access to their undertakings, particularly those engaged in military production, to foreign control officials who might carry out the inspection of such undertakings.

In the present circumstances, in which many States are displaying legitimate anxiety for their security, it can hardly be expected that they should trustingly provide other States with facilities for access to industrial and other resources of theirs which are vital to their security.

In so far as the necessary trust does not at the present time exist between States, a situation may arise in which the adoption of decisions on international control will in reality be reduced to a mere formality which does not achieve the objective. Such a possibility is the more inadmissible in that very great fears exist among peaceloving peoples, in present conditions, in connexion with the existence of atomic and hydrogen weapons, in regard to which the institution of international control is particularly difficult.

This danger is inherent in the very nature of atomic production. It is well known that the production of atomic energy for peaceful purposes can be used for the accumulation of stocks of explosive atomic materials, and for their accumulation in constantly increasing quantities. This means that States having establishments for the production of atomic energy can accumulate, in contravention of the relevant agreements, large quantities of explosive materials for the production of atomic weapons. The danger of this state of affairs is particularly clear in view of the fact that where the requisite quantities of explosive atomic materials exist production of actual atomic and hydrogen bombs is technically perfectly feasible and can be effected on a large scale.

Thus, even given the existence of a formal agreement on international control, opportunities, which cannot be covered by the international control system, exist for evading such control and for organizing the clandestine manufacture of atomic and hydrogen weapons. In these circumstances, the security of the States signatories to the international convention cannot be guaranteed, since it would be open to a potential aggressor to accumulate stocks of atomic and hydrogen weapons for a surprise atomic attack on peaceloving States.

Until an atmosphere of confidence has been created in relations between States, any agreement on the institution of international control can only serve to lull the vigilance of the peoples. It will create a false sense of security despite the actual existence of the threat of the production of atomic and hydrogen weapons and consequently also of the threat of surprise attack and the unleashing of an atomic war with all its appalling consequences for the peoples.

It must also be borne in mind that preparations for a new war, the danger of which has been vastly increased by the development of atomic and hydrogen weapons, inevitably necessitate the concentration of large military formations at certain points together with large quantities of conventional armaments—aircraft, artillery, tanks, warships and so forth. The concentration and movement of large formations of land, sea and air forces cannot be effected except through important communication centres, ports and airfields. Under conditions of modern military technique, the importance of such points in the preparation of an aggressive war has not diminished, but is on the contrary increasing.

In addition to atomic and hydrogen weapons, for all their destructive capacity, armies of many millions and vast quantities of conventional armaments, which are of decisive importance to the outcome of any major war, would inevitably be involved in military operations in the event of the outbreak of war.

All this must be taken into account in dealing with the problem of instituting international control over the fulfilment by States of their obligations under the convention on the reduction of armaments and the prohibition of atomic weapons.

The problem of instituting international control and of the rights and powers of the international control organ must therefore be considered in close connexion with the execution of the above-mentioned measures for the relaxation of international tension, the strengthening of trust between States and the carrying out of other measures relating to the reduction of armaments and the prohibition of atomic weapons.

In view of the foregoing,

the General Assembly institutes an international control organ having the following rights and powers:

1. *During the first stage* of execution of the measures for the reduction of armaments and the prohibition of atomic weapons,

(a) in order to prevent a surprise attack by one State upon another, the international control organ shall establish on the territory of all the States concerned, on a basis of reciprocity, control posts at large ports, at railway junctions, on main motor highways and in aerodromes. The function of these posts shall be to ensure that no dangerous concentration of military land forces or of air or naval forces takes place.

(b) The international control organ shall have the right to require from States any necessary information on the execution of measures for the reduction of armaments and armed forces.

(c) the control organ shall have unimpeded access to records relating to the budgetary appropriations of States for military purposes, including all decisions of their legislative and executive organs on the subject. States shall periodically, within specified time-limits, furnish the control organ with information on the execution of the measures provided for in the convention (treaty).

2. *During the second stage* of execution of measures for the reduction of armaments and the prohibition of atomic weapons:

The carrying out of the measures provided for in the Declaration set forth above and of the measures for the reduction of armaments and armed forces and the prohibition of atomic and hydrogen weapons envisaged for the first stage will create the requisite atmosphere of confidence between States, thereby ensuring the necessary conditions for the extension of the functions of the international control organ.

In these circumstances, the international control organ shall have the following rights and powers:

(a) To exercise supervision, including inspection on a continuing basis, to the extent necessary to ensure implementation of the convention by all States. In the discharge of these functions, the international control organ shall also have the right to require from States any necessary information on the execution of measures for the reduction of armaments and armed forces.

Staff recruited to carry out the work of inspection shall be selected on an international basis.

(b) To have in all States signatories to the convention its own permanent staff of inspectors, having unimpeded access at all times, within the limits of the supervisory functions they exercise, to all objects of control.

In order to prevent a surprise attack by one State upon another, the international control organ shall in particular have on the territory of all the States concerned, on a basis of reciprocity, control posts at large ports, at railway junctions, on main motor highways and in aerodromes.

(c) The control organ shall have unimpeded access to records relating to the budgetary appropriations of States for military purposes, including all decisions of their legislative and executive organs on the subject. States shall periodically, within specified time-limits, furnish the control organ with information on the execution of the measures provided for in the convention (treaty).

3. The control organ shall make recommendations to the Security Council on measures of prevention and suppression with regard to States infringing the convention on the reduction of armaments and the prohibition of atomic weapons.

4. The functions and powers of the permanent international control organ shall be defined on the basis of the foregoing principles, and appropriate instructions shall be prepared for this purpose.

n. *Comments by the United States Representative (Wadsworth) on the Soviet Proposal, May 11, 1955.*[24]

Now, for the third time in the subcommittee meetings this year, the Soviet Union has reversed its line and this time seems to be using ideas and language which are similar in many respects to the views put forward for many years—by Canada, France, the United Kingdom, and the United States. My immediate reaction is that ideas which have been advocated by Western powers as long ago as 1947 are at last being seriously considered by the Soviet Union. Clearly, our patience and persistence is paying off on some points. We welcome this development.

The Soviet Union now also seems to recognize that progress on the issue of disarmament is closely related to progress in other areas of international relations—a point the United States has long emphasized. Obviously the subcommittee was not created to deal with many of these issues, and I would therefore think it improper to comment on the wide range of problems brought in. They affect the interests of a good many states not represented in the subcommittee.

However, many questions must be asked and we hope will now be answered. For example, if we do not provide a really effective means of seeing to it that agreements reached are carried out in fact, then we will be deluding not only ourselves but all the peoples of the world who hope and long for real disarmament. In this connection, the sections of the Soviet proposals concerning international control and inspection still appear to fall short of the minimum safety requirements. It is not clear that the control organ's inspectors can go everywhere and see everything necessary to make sure that forbidden munitions are not being manufactured or that nuclear weapons are not being secreted. It will require some time before we will know what is the true Soviet position on this crucial question of controls.

The United States wants to see force and the threat of force, in all its forms, ended as an instrument of international

[24] *Department of State Bulletin,* v. 32 (May 30, 1955), p. 900.

relations. We recognize the urgency of the problem, and we recognize too its difficulty. We will neither be deterred by difficulty, nor accept shadow for substance, in a matter so gravely affecting the freedom and the security of all men.

In this spirit we will give the Soviet position the most responsible consideration.

o. *Subcommittee Agreement to Recess Talks: Statement by the United States Representative (Wadsworth), May 18, 1955.*[25]

In concert with the other members of the subcommittee, it has been agreed that a pause at this point would be valuable. We plan to resume our discussions in New York on June 1. Our subcommittee has been meeting for almost 3 months. We have examined a great many of the complex issues which must be solved in order to achieve the end of a general disarmament program called for by the United Nations, a program which will protect the interests of all states.

I have called attention to the fact that the Soviet Union's proposals of May 10 present, in many respects, the Soviet version of proposals previously made by various of the Western Powers. However, the important fact is not the original authorship of many of these ideas. What is important is the fact that, to a measurable degree, the gaps between us seem to have been lessened. The United States is pleased to have helped bring this about.

Much remains to be done. In doing it, one of our major jobs will be to provide a really effective system of safeguards, to make sure that both nuclear and conventional disarmament is being carried out. This is one important way to contribute to international trust and confidence. This trust, this confidence, cannot be created overnight by words alone; it will require much more than that. President Eisenhower said recently, "There can be no true disarmament without peace, and there can be no real peace without very material disarmament." We hope that progress in settling outstanding international problems and progress toward disarmament will go hand in hand. The United States will continue—patiently, realistically, persistently—to work for this progress.

[25] *Ibid.*, p. 901.

2. *Further Meetings of the Subcommittee of the United Nations Disarmament Commission, New York, August 29—October 7, 1955.*

a. *Statement by the United States Representative to the United Nations (Lodge) on the President's Proposal for Disarmament and Aerial Inspection, August 29, 1955.*[26]

(Excerpts)

* * *

We believe . . . that the heart of the disarmament problem is inspection, that no nation—not the United States, not the Soviet Union, nor any other nation—can afford to cut its strength under an international agreement unless and until an inspection system is created which will support every portion of such an agreement and upon which humanity can rely.

President Eisenhower's proposal[27] was made with all the strength and sincerity and hope of the 160 million Americans for whom he spoke.

* * *

The word "blueprint" in the President's plan includes, first, the identification, strength, command structure, and disposition of personnel, units, and equipment of all major land, sea, and air forces, including organized reserve and paramilitary; second, a complete list of military plants, facilities, and installations with their locations.

No nation, of course, could furnish such information without assurances of complete reciprocity and of simultaneous delivery of similar types of information. There must be effective means for verifying the reports of the participating states by air, ground, and sea observation.

In implementation of the aerial photography in the President's plan, each country would permit unrestricted but monitored aerial reconnaissance by the other country.

In order to provide fully against major surprise assault, the United States believes that the plan should provide particularly for safeguards against attack by long-range striking forces of both countries through observation and inspection

[26] *Ibid.*, v. 33 (September 12, 1955), pp. 438-440.
[27] See above, pp. 213-216.

of these forces and their support, and through measures to detect preparation for such an attack. The Untied States believes further that the exchange of information under the President's plan should proceed in progressive stages from the least sensitive aspects to the more sensitive, covering those items most likely to provide against the possibility of surprise.

Further details will be supplied to you concerning the methods by which mutual aerial reconnaissance would be conducted. Among other things, each inspecting country would utilize its own aircraft and related equipment, including visual, photographic, and electronic means of observation. Personnel of the country being inspected would be aboard each reconnaissance aircraft during all over-flights.

The United States contemplates that the lists of military installations which are exchanged would include the designation of one or more airfields or bases which would be made available for the support of reconnaissance aircraft and crews.

There would be provision for adequate communication facilities, as required for rapid and direct reports by observers to their home governments.

Each government would arrange to designate ports of entry and egress for observers and aircraft; to clear observers, aircraft, and crews to and from home territory; and to check and identify personnel and equipment engaged in these operations.

Each country being inspected would be responsible for air traffic control of inspecting aircraft.

The United States is prepared to submit a paper setting forth in more details the manner in which all these operations should be carried out. The details, of course, are negotiable. We are prepared to join with other governments in studying all aspects of the plan.

The summary which I have just given is to be considered only in the context of and as an integral part of such a paper.

The plan which I have described obviously involves far-reaching undertakings for the participating states. The American people will, I am sure, gladly accept their share of the burdens of an equitable plan which will in all truth add greatly to world security and which will brighten the prospects of a durable and just peace by limiting the dangers of surprise attack, thus opening the way to a general agreement on the regulation and reduction of armaments.

* * *

b. *Outline Plan for the Implementation of the President's Prosposal for Disarmament and Aerial Inspection, Submitted by the United States Delegation, August 30, 1955.*[28]

1. *Purpose.* The purpose of this outline plan is to translate the proposal made by President Eisenhower on 21 July at Geneva into terms of reference, a concept, and an outline of procedures. The details are subject to negotiation within the principles stated by the President.

2. *Terms of Reference.*

a. The term "blueprint of military establishments" is defined as consisting of the identification, strength, command structure and disposition of personnel, units and equipment of all major land, sea and air forces, including organized reserves and para-military; and a complete list of military plants, facilities, and installations with their locations.

b. Each nation has recognized the need for ground observers and these will be stationed at key locations within the other country for the purpose of allowing them to certify the accuracy of the foregoing information and to give warning of evidence of surprise attack or mobilization.

c. Each country shall permit unrestricted, but monitored, aerial reconnaissance by visual, photographic, and electronic means by the other country.

3. *Concept.* The United States and the USSR will exchange all data relative to military forces and installations which, coupled with measures for verification and surveillance, are essential to provide against the possibility of surprise attack. This exchange is to be accomplished in progressive steps as mutually agreed upon by the two Governments. Among the elements of information considered essential to preclude surprise attack and to be sought by an exchange between the Governments and to be verified and maintained under surveillance are:

a. Weapons and delivery systems suitable for surprise attack.

b. Transportation and telecommunications.

c. Armed forces, structure and positioning of armed forces.

d. Additional facilities as mutually agreed upon by the two Governments.

[28] United Nations Document DC/SC.1/31, dated August 30, 1955.

4. *Initial Procedure.*

a. Exchange of "blueprints" of military establishments.

(1) The Governments of the United States and the USSR will each prepare lists of major military forces and establishments, showing the deployment of forces and the locations of installations and facilities by geographical coordinates.

(2) Schedules will be drawn for time phasing of exchanges to assure simultaneous delivery of similar types of information by each Government, and completion of verification by each side before progressing to a subsequent phase. Provision for immediate spot-checking will be included.

b. Verification of "blueprints" of military establishments.

(1) Arrangements will be made for the posting of on-the-spot observers with operating land, sea, and air forces, at their supporting installations, and at key locations as necessary for the verification, continued observation, and reporting of each category of information. The number and location of the observers will be as mutually agreed upon prior to the exchange of information, and provisions will be made for changes in the location should the initial arrangements prove to be inadequate.

(2) Aerial reconnaissance will be conducted by each inspecting country on an unrestricted, but monitored, basis to augment the efforts of the posted observers. Each inspecting country will utilize its own aircraft and related equipment. Liaison personnel of the country being inspected will be aboard each reconnaissance aircraft during all overflights.

c. Facilities and services to be provided.

(1) Each sub-list of military installations will include the designation of one or more airfields or bases at which facilities will be made available for support of the aerial reconnaissance aircraft and crews.

d. Checks and controls.

Procedures will be established for:

(1) Designation of ports of entry and egress for incoming and departing observers and reconnaissance aircraft.

(2) Clearance of incoming and departing observers, aircraft and crews and arrangements for monitored passage to and from home territory.

(3) Check and identification of observers and reconnaissance aircraft, personnel and equipment engaged in this activity.

(4) Orientation of observers and reconnaissance personnel.

(5) Air traffic control of inspecting aircraft by host Government.

c. *United States Memorandum Supplementing the Outline Plan for the Implementation of the President's Proposal, October 7, 1955.*[29]

Importance of Inspection and Control System in a Disarmament Program

All five of the Governments represented in the Subcommittee of the Disarmament Commission have recognized the crucial importance of effective inspection and control in providing the assurance that commitments to reduce and limit and regulate armaments and armed forces will be honored. President Eisenhower in his statement on disarmament made at Geneva on July 21, 1955 reaffirmed the desire of the United States to introduce "a sound and reliable agreement making possible the reduction of armaments." The President said "No sound and reliable agreement can be made unless it is completely covered by an inspection and reporting system adequate to support every portion of the agreement. The lessons of history teach us that disarmament agreements without adequate reciprocal inspection increase the dangers of war and do not brighten the prospects of peace."

The Prime Minister of the Soviet Union, Marshal Bulganin, on August 4, 1955 told the Supreme Soviet that "the President of the United States justly remarked that each disarmament plan boils down to the question of control and inspection."

Foreign Minister Pearson of Canada, Foreign Minister Pinay of France, Prime Minister Eden of the United Kingdom, have all within the last few months emphasized the need for the kind of control and inspection which would give a basis for confidence that disarmament agreements would be observed, and have all stressed the primary importance of inspection and control of agreements to reduce and limit armaments.

Difficulties of Assuring by Effective Inspection and Control That All Nuclear Weapons Are Eliminated

Together with this recognition of the absolute need for a control system adequate to support every portion of a dis-

[29] *Department of State Bulletin*, v. 33 (October 31, 1955), pp. 708-711.

armament agreement, the Governments represented in the Disarmament Subcommittee have recognized the problems caused by the vast technological developments in an expansion of nuclear energy materials. The Soviet Union, in its proposals of May 10, 1955, noted that "there are possibilities beyond the reach of international control for evading this control and for organizing the clandestine manufacture of atomic and hydrogen weapons, even if there is a formal agreement on international control. In such a situation, the security of the States signatories to the international convention cannot be guaranteed, since the possibilities would be open to a potential aggressor to accumulate stocks of atomic and hydrogen weapons for surprise attack on peace-loving States."

In President Eisenhower's statement on disarmament at Geneva on July 21 this year, he said, "We have not as yet been able to discover any scientific or other inspection method which would make certain of the elimination of nuclear weapons. So far as we are aware no other nation has made such a discovery. Our study of this problem is continuing." The representative of Canada, Mr. Martin, the representative of France, M. Moch, and the representative of the United Kingdom, Mr. Nutting, have all many times during the discussions of the Subcommittee noted the danger of inadequate control of fissionable material, that all our previous concepts have been rendered obsolete by new scientific developments, and that it was necessary to consider facts as they are today and not as they were yesterday or the day before.

Mr. Nutting at the Subcommittee meeting of October 5, 1955 summed up the views of all the delegations when he referred to the "barrier of science which prevents us at this moment, on the admission of the Soviet Union, the United States and every other delegation represented at this table, from making nuclear disarmament the safe hope for the world that we would wish it to be."

The present impossibility of establishing an effective inspection and control method that would completely account for nuclear weapons material is of exceptional importance. It means that no nation has as yet been able to find any scientific or other inspection method that would account for all nuclear weapons material. It means that the amount of unaccountability is of such magnitude as to be an unacceptable unknown quantity of vast destructive capacity.

What Should Be Done?

In the light of these circumstances, the United States believes that two steps should be taken to meet the issues posed by these facts. The first is to continue the search for the method by which complete accountability of nuclear materials and reliable inspection and control might be attained. The United States is already engaged in this search. The United States has placed a number of its ablest scientists in continuing work on this problem. The United States Government welcomes efforts by any other nation in this regard and invites the scientists and officials of any nation in the world, if they believe they have a method which can completely account for past and present production of fissionable materials and to insure against improper diversion of nuclear weapons, to come forward and advance for consideration such a method.

Second, in addition to such continuing study and research there must be a joint effort to reach agreements which can reduce the possibility of war, and in particular, and as a first priority provide against the possibility of a great surprise attack.

President Eisenhower's Proposal

It is against this background that President Eisenhower on July 21 proposed at Geneva that steps be taken now, which would have an immediate effect, which would be practical, and which would strike at the very core of the disarmament problem—the suspicion and fear which are the great causes of international tensions. The Eisenhower proposal called for an exchange of blueprints of their military establishments between the Soviet Union and the United States and the provision of facilities for reciprocal aerial reconnaissance from one end to the other of these two countries. The purpose of this exchange is to provide against the possibility of a great surprise attack, particularly with nuclear weapons, the importance of this having been previously recognized by the Soviet Union as well as by the United States.

In expounding these proposals made by the President, in the Outline Plan presented by the United States in the Disarmament Subcommittee on August 30, 1955,[30] in order to take into account the views of the Soviet Union expressed in its May 10, 1955 proposals and at Geneva, as well as certain

[30] See above, pp. 434-436.

views of the other members of the Disarmament Subcommittee, the United States noted, "Each nation has recognized the need for ground observers, and these will be stationed at key locations within the other country for the purpose of allowing them to certify the accuracy of the foregoing information and to give warning of evidence of surprise attack or of mobilization."

In introducing this August 30 Outline Plan, the United States also recognized that the danger of great surprise attack is a matter of concern to each of the Governments represented in the Subcommittee and to all nations of the world. It is further realized that the carrying out of the President's proposal will involve the cooperation of each of the Governments represented in the Disarmament Subcommittee, and the question arises whether this exchange of military blueprints and aerial reconnaissance should be confined to the territorial limits of the United States and the Soviet Union. It is the belief of the United States that it is most essential that a beginning should be made on the President's proposal by agreement between the Soviet Union and the United States, but that this agreement between these two countries putting the President's plan into effect without delay might also provide for the adherence and participation, as agreed, of designated countries on an equitable basis, once the plan is in operation between the Soviet Union and the United States.

Furthermore, it should be clear that the President's proposal is directed toward providing against the possibility of a great surprise attack of any kind with any weapon. So far as the information to be exchanged is concerned, it will consist of the identification, strength, command structure and disposition of personnel, units and equipment of all major land, sea and air forces, including organized reserves and paramilitary; and a complete list of military plants, facilities, and installations with their locations. It is not contemplated that the blueprints of military establishments would include every specific detail. Similar information would be simultaneously exchanged by each Government, as mutually agreed upon by the two Governments, within the framework of the United Nations. This exchange of information would be directed toward safeguarding against the possibility of a great surprise attack, and the details of information to be exchanged are subject to negotiation.

So far as aerial reconnaissance is concerned, however, the United States would not consider that there are prohibited areas. In the words of President Eisenhower, the United States "would allow these planes, properly inspected, peaceful planes, to fly over any particular area of the country that they wanted to, because in this—only in this—way could you convince them there wasn't something over there that maybe was by surprise ready to attack them."

Reduction of the Burden of Armaments

The United States believes that the taking of this practical step to provide against the possibility of surprise attack, as suggested in the President's proposals, will lessen danger and relax international tensions.

By this very fact, a system guarding against surprise attack as proposed by the United States should make more easily attainable a broader disarmament agreement. The lessons learned through the mutual exchange of military blueprints and through reciprocal aerial reconnaissance will help measurably in the joint efforts of the Disarmament Subcommittee to find an effective inspection and control system which will fully support agreements to reduce, limit and regulate armaments and armed forces.

It is the firm policy of the United States Government that the relaxation of international tensions through concrete deeds should proceed concurrently with efforts to find a solution to the problem of armaments. As President Eisenhower said at the Geneva Conference of Heads of Government, "The United States Government is prepared to enter into a sound and reliable agreement making possible the reduction of armament."

The United States earnestly seeks an agreement for the reduction of all armaments and armed forces, concurrent with the relief of international tensions and when a reliable system of inspection and control is devised. The problems of disarmament have become increasingly complicated because of the changed technical circumstances which have been previously described. These technical circumstances must be taken into account, not only in devising a system of inspection and control, but also in relation to the scale, timing and ratio of any reductions which might be agreed upon.

While these considerations are being studied, and while our scientists are trying to find methods by which complete accountability for nuclear material and reliable inspection and control might be attained, it is imperative that we find the means to provide against surprise attack and to attain that degree of international trust indispensable to a broad disarmament program supported by effective inspection and reporting. The United States believes that the Eisenhower plan is the gateway to agreement in these further fields and in itself provides a great assurance against war.

It is the hope of the United States that, upon further consideration of the proposal of the President of the United States at Geneva on July 21, the Outline Plan in implementation of the Presidential proposal submitted to the Disarmament Subcommittee on August 30, and the further explanations made during the course of the Subcommittee discussions and summed up in this memorandum, that the members of the Subcommittee, the Disarmament Commission and the United Nations General Assembly may decide that the early execution of this plan would contribute to the reduction of present international tensions, would provide safeguards against major surprise attack, would lessen the fear of war, would assist in the development of a comprehensive international agreement for the regulation, limitation and balanced reduction of all armed forces and armaments, and would advance the cause of peace. It is the further hope of the United States that agreement could be reached to place the proposal of the United States into effect at the earliest opportunity, and that the members of this Subcommittee would continue their efforts to reach agreement on an effective system of international inspection and control and upon a general program for reduction and limitation of armament.

3. *Exchange of Views on Aerial Inspection between the President and the Chairman of the Council of Ministers of the Soviet Union (Bulganin).*

a. *Letter by the Chairman of the Council of Ministers of the Soviet Union (Bulganin), September 19, 1955.*[31]

SEPTEMBER 19, 1955

DEAR MR. PRESIDENT: I feel I must sincerely and frankly exchange opinions with you on a subject which at the present time has acquired particular importance. I have in mind the question which is being discussed now by our representatives in the subcommittee of the U.N. Disarmament Commission.

In the course of our memorable meetings in Geneva we agreed to work jointly for elaboration of an acceptable system

[31] *Department of State Bulletin,* v. 33 (October 24, 1955), pp. 644-647.

of disarmament. When we approved directives to our Ministers of Foreign Affairs on this score, I thought a great deal had been accomplished. Now the representatives of our countries, guided by these directives and taking into account in their work the opinions and proposals put forth by the heads of the four governments in Geneva, can and must achieve definite progress.

I and my colleagues thought that even at the very beginning of their work our representatives would be able to reach general agreement on those basic questions on which our viewpoints either coincided or had already appreciably approached each other. I have in mind first of all the question of the levels of armed forces of the five great powers, the question of dates for introducing into force the prohibition of atomic weapons, and the question of international control. In this manner there would be created a solid foundation for further work during which it would be possible to make more precise all the details of the necessary agreements concerning the working out of an acceptable system of disarmament.

However, the first weeks of the work of the subcommittee so far have not yet produced those results for which you and I were fully entitled to hope, and I must frankly say that the delay is occasioned to a considerable degree by the fact that the members of the subcommittee so far do not know the position of the representative of the United States with regard to those provisions which we had all the grounds to consider as agreed. As is known, the representative of the United States completely put aside the questions of reduction of the armed forces, of armaments, and prohibition of atomic weapons, having expressed the desire to discuss first of all and mainly your proposal concerning the exchange of military information between the U.S.S.R. and the U.S.A. as well as of the mutual exchange of aerial photography of the territories of both countries. In this manner the impression is left that the entire problem of disarmament is being confined by him to these proposals.

I think to put the question in this manner would not satisfy the aspiration of peoples, even though I fully recognize the importance of the proposals introduced by you in Geneva.

However, since I and my colleagues have received the above-mentioned impression, I consider it my duty once more to share with you, esteemed Mr. President, certain primary considerations.

We feel that the main problem for us is to use further efforts to look for ways which would permit us to move the problem of disarmament away from dead center, which problem has vital importance for the peoples of the U.S.S.R. and the U.S.A. as well as peoples of the entire world.

In connection with this allow me to touch upon the proposals put forward by you at Geneva. We regard these proposals as testimony of your sincere desire to find a way to settle the important problem of the international control and inspection and to contribute personally to general efforts for the normalization of international relations.

Upon our return from Geneva we with all carefulness have studied your proposal of July 21 which was introduced on August 30 by Mr. Stassen into the disarmament subcommittee. In the course of this study several questions have arisen about which I would like to express to you my thoughts.

First of all, about the mutual exchange by the United States of America and the Soviet Union of information concerning their armed forces and armaments.

In principle, we have no objections to this proposal. I think that at a definite stage the exchange of such information between states is necessary. It would be better, however, if such information concerning armaments were submitted by all states, and not only by the U.S. and the U.S.S.R., to the international organ of control and inspection, concerning the creation of which we should reach an agreement. In order to avoid misunderstandings, it is self-evident that information on all kinds of armaments, conventional as well as nuclear, must be submitted in order to avoid misunderstanding [*sic*]. If these considerations are valid, we should carefully discuss exactly when this full information on armaments of states should be presented and first of all information concerning the armaments of great powers.

It is self-evident that the submission of the above-mentioned information to an international control organ would become significant only if agreement is achieved on the reduction of armaments and on taking measures for the prohibition of atomic weapons.

It seems to me that the problem of the creation of an international control organ which would satisfy the requirements of the problems of disarmament should be considered in indissoluble unity with decisions for putting into effect a plan for gradual disarmament. At the same time it is necessary to keep sight of the fact that achievement of a really valuable exchange of military information will become really effective to the degree that mutual trust among states is strengthened.

Now I would also like to express my opinion about the problem of aerial photography.

I do not doubt that when you introduced your proposal for photographing from the air the territories of our two countries, you were guided by a legitimate desire to create confidence that neither of our two countries would be subjected to attack by the other.

However, let us be frank to the end. Under present international conditions both our countries are not acting singly. The United States of America, as is known, heads all military groupings which exist in the West and in the East, and what is more their armed forces are stationed not only on American territory; they are also stationed in England, West Germany, Italy, France, Spain, North Africa, Greece, Turkey, in several countries of the Near and Middle East, in Japan, on Taiwan, in the Philippines, etc.

To this should be added the fact that the armed forces of several states are organically connected with the military forces of the United States through inclusion under a single command.

Under these conditions, the Soviet Union on its side has united militarily with several allied states.[32]

It is impossible not to see that the proposal introduced by you completely omits from consideration armed forces and military installations which are outside the area of the United States and the Soviet Union.

And yet it is perfectly self-evident that aerial photographing should also be extended to all armed forces and military installations located on the territories of those other states.

This presents an entirely new problem: Would the governments of such states permit their sovereign territory to be photographed from the air by foreign aircraft?

All this shows that the problem of aerial photography is not a question which, under present conditions, would lead to effective progress toward insuring security of states and successful accomplishment of disarmament.

This conclusion is suggested by the fact that your proposal,

[32] The reference is to the Warsaw Pact concluded by the Soviet Union with seven other Communist governments on May 14, 1955.

unfortunately, does not mention the necessity for reduction of armaments and prohibition of atomic weapons.

It is therefore natural that people should ask more and more often what the proposal for aerial photography and the collecting of such information would really do to end the arms race. If such a proposal does not promote the ending of the arms race, then it means that it does not remove the threat of a new war. It does not lighten the burden which the peoples are bearing in connection with this arms race. Would such a proposal satisfy the expectations of the people of our states and those of all countries?

Finally, it is impossible not to stop and think about what would happen if we occupy ourselves with the questions of aerial photography and the exchange of military information without taking effective measures for reduction of armaments and prohibition of atomic weapons.

I have apprehensions which I cannot help but share with you. Would not such a situation lead to the weakening of vigilance toward the still existing threat of violation of the peace generated by the arms race?

My remarks do not at all mean that we cannot achieve an agreement on important aspects of the disarmament problem. I would like to call your attention to the fact that on very substantial aspects of this problem our positions have become so close that we would be able to reach a definite agreement.

Let us take such a question as the establishment of levels of armed forces for the great powers.

It is generally recognized that this is a question of great importance. Originally, the idea of establishing levels to which armed forces of the Big Five should be reduced, as is known, was put forth by your Government together with the Governments of Great Britain and France in 1952.[33] In the interest of achieving general agreement on this matter, which is so important for the problem of disarmament, we decided to adopt this joint proposal of the U.S., England, and France as a basis for discussion. Consequently we have a common point of view on this question. It is very important for us to arrive at agreement on this point.

On the question of atomic weapons, we must remember that at the present, when the greatest armies of the world have at their disposal such means of mass destruction as atomic and hydrogen weapons, it is impossible, of course, to talk about

[33] *Documents on American Foreign Relations, 1952,* pp. 369-372.

disarmament without touching on this important subject. Therefore, we have always attached paramount importance to the problem of prohibition of atomic weapons. In the discussion of this problem, one of the substantial subjects of disagreement was the question of dates when the prohibition against the use of atomic weapons would go into force. In our desire to bring the opposition positions closer and to thereby facilitate and expedite the achievement of agreement on this subject, we agreed to accept the dates for putting into force the prohibition on the use of atomic weapons which were proposed by the representatives of England and France in the subcommittee of the U.N. Commission on Disarmament in London in April 1955.[34]

I think you will agree that the proposal concerning the stage at which prohibition against the use of atomic weapons would come into force, as proposed by England and France, and accepted by the Soviet Union, satisfies our common interests.

It would be desirable—and I think completely feasible—to reach an agreement also on this question.

It also seems expedient for us to reach agreement at this time on putting into effect several measures designed to prevent sudden attack by one state or another. We feel that this measure would be in accord with the interests of maintaining peace and security of nations and in this respect it would be possible to reach agreement also concerning the form of control suitable to the above-mentioned problem.

You, Mr. President, as a military man, know from your own experience that modern war requires drawing into military action armies of many millions and an enormous quantity of technical combat equipment. In this connection great importance has now been acquired by the definite locations where concentrations of large military groups can take place and whose armaments would include all this technical combat equipment. The system of control proposed by us, namely the creation of control posts in large ports, at railroad junctions, on automobile highways, and at airfields, is designed to prevent dangerous concentrations of troops and combat equipment on large scale and thereby remove the possibility of sudden attack by one country against another. Establishment of such posts would be an important step toward relaxation of international tension and the establishment of trust among states.

[34] See above, pp. 413-414.

In my opinion our proposal concerning control posts has the advantage that it provides a definite guaranty against a sudden attack by one state against another.

I think you will agree that the proposals introduced by us concerning levels of armed forces, the dates for coming into effect of the prohibition of nuclear weapons and for the establishment of control posts can promote the reduction of tension in international relations and strengthening of peace. I do not see, therefore, any reasons why we could not arrange to reach agreement on these questions. Such joint decisions of the Four Powers would have tremendous importance because they would put into the hearts of millions of people the assurance that disarmament is fully realizable and that real steps are being taken in this direction. An agreement on these questions would open the way toward solution of other questions which concern the problem of disarmament. It would encourage the strengthening of that atmosphere of cooperation and mutual understanding which we initiated at Geneva, and it would create favorable conditions to put into practice a broader program of disarmament and control over this disarmament.

In presenting ideas to you, Mr. President, I am inspired by the sincere desire to achieve through a frank exchange of opinions on the problem of disarmament better mutual understanding which may facilitate reaching agreed decisions on this most important problem.

Inasmuch as the solution of these questions depends mainly on the four great powers who participated in the Geneva Conference, I have taken the liberty of sending copies of this letter to Mr. Eden and Mr. Faure and hope that you will not misunderstand this action.

I hope soon to receive your ideas on the questions touched upon in this letter.

With sincere respect,
N. BULGANIN

b. *Reply by the President, October 11, 1955.*[35]

DENVER, COLORADO
October 11, 1955

DEAR MR. CHAIRMAN: I wish to thank you for your letter of September 19, 1955 about my Geneva proposal of July 21 that we exchange information about military establishments

[35] *Department of State Bulletin,* v. 33 (October 24, 1955), pp. 643-644.

and permit reciprocal aerial inspection over our two countries.

You raise a good many questions, and I shall not be able to reply to them until the doctors let me do more than at present. In any event, a full reply calls for preliminary work by my advisers and this is actively under way.

Let me now say, however, that I am encouraged that you are giving such full consideration to my Geneva proposal. I hope that we can agree on it, not as a cure-all, but, as I said at Geneva, to show a spirit of non-aggressiveness on both sides and so to create a fresh atmosphere which would dispel much of the present fear and suspicion. This, of itself, would be worthwhile. It would, I believe, make it more possible to make progress in terms of comprehensive plans for inspection, controls and reductions of armament, which will satisfy the high hopes of our peoples, and indeed of all the world.

I have not forgotten your proposal having to do with stationing inspection teams at key points in our countries, and if you feel this would help to create the better spirit I refer to, we could accept that too.

With best wishes,

Sincerely,
DWIGHT D. EISENHOWER

4. *General Assembly Action on Disarmament.*

a. *Statement by the United States Representative to the United Nations (Lodge), December 5, 1955.*[36]

(Excerpt)

* * *

The heart of the [President's] plan is unrestricted—but monitored—reciprocal, aerial inspection, by visual, photographic, and electronic means. Personnel of the country being inspected may be aboard the aircraft.

Modern aerial reconnaissance has phenomenal capabilities. Two standard jet photo planes can photograph a band of terrain 490 miles wide and 2,700 long, the distance from New York to Los Angeles, in only two hours.

A country the size of the United States or the Soviet Union can have its picture taken, mile by mile, field and factory, in considerably less than six months. The information can be kept current week by week. Extremely accurate results are possible at night and under adverse weather conditions.

[36] *Department of State Bulletin,* v. 34 (January 9, 1956), pp. 55-61.

The costs of the operation are slight for the boon it would confer. For a whole year, the expenses could be compared to the cost of only 2 or 3 days of World War II. And if we include in the account the unspeakable suffering, the blight on the future, the deaths, and the broken lives in another war, no cost would be too great.

The United States has offered to extend this plan to other countries and to bases abroad if acceptable to the nations involved. We have agreed to add to it Mr. Bulganin's plan for ground observers.

The United States regrets that the Soviet Union has still not approved President Eisenhower's plan. But we continue to hope that further discussions will lead it to recognize the value of the proposal.

Here is the background against which it was made.

Inspection is the crux of the problem of disarmament by international agreement—inspection to see that what is promised is actually performed. When disarmament is undertaken *without* adequate inspection, as it was in Germany and Japan between the two World Wars, the result is a war-breeding fiasco.

President Eisenhower at Geneva declared[37] that—

"No sound and reliable agreement can be made unless it is completely covered by an inspection and reporting system adequate to support every portion of the agreement. The lessons of history teach us that disarmament agreements without adequate reciprocal inspection increase the dangers of war and do not brighten the prospects of peace."

The other Heads of State [sic] at Geneva and leaders in other countries have said very much the same thing.

Marshal Bulganin put it in a nutshell when he told the Supreme Soviet on August 14 [4], 1955, that "each disarmament plan boils down to the question of control and inspection." [38]

But the Soviet Union does not mean the same thing by control and inspection that we do. It will not allow the kind of forehanded, permanent, and thorough inspection which the other countries on the United Nations Subcommittee[39] would accept, which is necessary to ease the arms burden and to permit the full flowering of atomic energy for peace.

This is the issue which has divided the Soviet Union from

[37] See above, p. 214.

[38] *New Times*, No. 33, August 11, 1955, Special Supplement.

[39] The reference is to the Subcommittee of the U.N. Disarmament Commission, whose members are Canada, France, the U.S.S.R., the U.K. and the U.S.

the overwhelming majority in the United Nations ever since 1946. Meanwhile, the problem has become steadily more difficult and more urgent.

The production of nuclear material has been under way for a decade under no international control whatsoever. During all of this time it has been possible to hide atomic weapons. The telltale radioactivity of nuclear materials can be shielded by containers, beyond the range of any presently known detection device.

As the stockpile grows, the danger mounts. Because of the margin of error in accounting, with each year that passes, the amount of material available for hidden weapons has increased. With the passage of time we were bound to reach a crucial point at which this margin of error represented a dangerous potential in nuclear weapons. That point has now been reached.

This is the scientific background of the Eisenhower project.

It means that the older plans for inspection of nuclear material based on total accounting for production are unrealistic.

The situation thus created required two things: an intensive review of the inspection problem, and some new and radical conception which would offer the world time, security, and confidence while it tackled its problem.

The President moved to meet the first by mobilizing a number of our most eminent physicists, military men, industrialists, and scholars to work on all aspects of the problem under the direction of Mr. Harold E. Stassen.[40] The United States considers that such studies should be the subject of appropriate consultation between governments.

To meet the second vital requirement for increased international security, and as a demonstration of American sincerity, the President put forward his proposals.

The plan of aerial inspection for peace is designed primarily to provide against great surprise attack. Since we can no longer keep track of all nuclear munitions, it focuses more sharply on controlling the means for delivering them in war.

If we succeed in shackling surprise attack, we may set a seal against war itself.

The Soviet Union in its May 10 proposals[41] also recognized very clearly the danger of mounting stockpiles in the changed

[40] *Department of State Bulletin,* v. 33 (October 31, 1955), p. 706.
[41] See above, pp. 417-430.

technological picture. It also claims to see the increased necessity of guarding against surprise attack.

The Soviet May 10 proposals contain these words:

"There are possibilities beyond the reach of international control for evading this control and for recognizing the clandestine manufacture of atomic and hydrogen weapons, even if there is a formal agreement on international control. In such a situation, the security of states signatories to the international convention cannot be guaranteed, since the possibility would be open to a potential aggressor to accumulate stocks of atomic and hydrogen weapons for a surprise atomic attack on peace-loving states."

But the Soviet Union prescribes no new remedy to fit this clear diagnosis. Moreover, it continues to call for measures of disarmament which could not be backed up by the only kind of inspection which it would permit.

In spite of repeated inquiries put by the members of the Subcommittee, the Soviet Union would give no assurance that inspectors would be in the field and ready to operate before disarmament began. It will not specify in any detail those things which the inspectors would be allowed to inspect. It would allow inspection from the air only at the very end of a disarmament program.

These Soviet proposals are quite inadequate to guard against surprise attack. Nor are they sufficient to support a comprehensive program of arms limitation.

This is what the Soviet position on inspection boils down to after we examine the confused and contradictory record of the past year—a year marked by alternating hope and disappointment for the rest of us.

The Soviet Government knows as well as anyone how illusory the prospect for total prohibition of nuclear weapons material is under present conditions. Yet it would pledge every country to a program vitally affecting its national security without providing the means to insure that the provisions of an agreement are carried out equally by all.

To continue to call for elimination of nuclear weapons as an immediate objective in the light of inescapable scientific facts is to ignore the cardinal principle that any disarmament progıam must be fully supported by effective control. We cannot lend ourselves to this hyprocrisy and obscurantism. A new solution must be found which will fit the facts.

Mr. Chairman, I am sure that most of you recall a story about Marshal Potemkin, the Viceroy of Catherine the Great of Russia. When the Czarina went out to tour her domain, the Marshal, in order to create the illusion of prosperity under his regime, built false villages along her route. The Czarina's party was hurried through without time for a closer look behind the false façades.

Mr. Chairman, we will not accept illusions. We want no Potemkin village of disarmament.

Mr. Kuznetsov[42] is apparently disturbed because the United States position evolves and is not static. He would have you believe that the United States is less eager for disarmament because it has *some* reserves about *some* of the ideas we have contributed to these discussions in the past.

It is true that we are appraising past theories in the light of changing political and scientific conditions. It is true that we believe that whatever may be eventually agreed with respect to levels of armed forces or the reductions of conventional weapons will have to be calculated in relation to what can be done about nuclear weapons.

In a field so complex, dynamic, and dangerous, we cannot afford to be doctrinaire. Each country has a positive obligation to test and revise its policies constantly. We believe that this is an honest and logical course of action.

But if the test of policy be *lack* of change, let us see how that applies to the Soviet position.

From 1946 to 1954 the Soviet Union in effect called for prohibition and elimination of atomic weapons, by mere declaration, with inspection second. Theirs was a platform of "ban the bomb, trust the Russians." But disarmament cannot be built on a platform of trust alone. It must be supervised by rigorous, unremitting, reciprocal inspection under rigid, agreed standards.

In October 1954 the late Mr. Vyshinsky surprised the General Assembly with an apparent change in the Soviet position. He said his country would accept as a "basis for discussion" the Anglo-French proposals of June 11, 1954[43] which stipulated real inspection from the outset and throughout each stage of a progressive program of arms reduction. But the Soviet Union still could not say whether inspection would be intermittent or continuous, permanent or periodic, or whether it could operate from the beginning.

The London talks [of the Disarmament Subcommittee] in

[42] The reference is to the Soviet representative in Committee I of the General Assembly, Vasily V. Kuznetsov.

[43] *Documents on American Foreign Relations, 1954,* pp. 457-459.

1955 occurred during a mysterious period of change in the Soviet Government. The Soviet disarmament position was obviously in a state of flux. Mr. Gromyko opened in February with a remarkable proposal for immediate "destruction" of all nuclear weapons, *without* inspection and with no provision for stopping nuclear weapons production.[44] This scheme bore no relation to Mr. Vyshinsky's idea. It was not disarmament. It was really a proposal for a built-in nuclear arms race, rigged to let the Soviet Union start even.

For weeks the other members of the Subcommittee wondered what this really involved. Then in mid-March, the Soviet Union just as suddenly switched back to the Vyshinsky position,[45] but it neither abandoned nor affirmed the Gromyko proposition. Instead we were told that it had something called "independent significance." For all we know, it still does; but just what it signifies for our present discussions, or for real disarmament, we do not know.

Then, overnight, on May 10, the Soviet Union took up what we are told is its present position. It ostensibly accepted some Western suggestions—which it was still violently attacking only 2 or 3 days earlier—but on the key issue of inspection it still did not and does not state in any useful detail what it would allow to be inspected, or what the rights, duties, and immunities of the inspectors would be, or when they could begin their task. It has not specified whether the control teams would be mobile or stationary. It has not explained how inspectors could mount an effective guard against surprise attack if they were tied down to fixed control posts.

Thus, Mr. Chairman, in spite of a confused shifting back and forth in Soviet ideas, there has been very little evolution where it is most needed—in the vital matter of inspection and control.

The United States stands firm on the need for genuine inspection. But it is always ready to study new methods to fit the facts. My Swedish colleague, Mr. Sandler, the other day expressed the hope that what he called our "reserved attitude" was "a question of preliminary measures proposed so as to facilitate genuine disarmament in due course." I am glad to assure him that that is exactly the case.

Even where effective controls can be devised, international distrust may block their application. The other states repre-

[44] See above, pp. 401-402.
[45] See above, pp. 408-410.

sented in the Subcommittee also recognize this condition. In its proposals of May 10 the Soviet Union says:

"The necessary conditions for the institution of a control system which would enjoy the trust of all states and would fully meet the requirements of international security do not at present exist."

The solution to the problem is not to jettison all attempts to establish effective control. The answer is to attack the problem at its heart, to try to reach agreement on measures to dispel distrust, and to create conditions for more fruitful discussion of disarmament.

President Eisenhower declared at Geneva that—

"The United States is ready to proceed in the study and testing of a reliable system of inspection and reporting and, when that system is proved, then to reduce armaments with all others to the extent that the system will provide assured results."

The President's plan was not intended to be a substitute for an overall program for the limitation and reduction of armaments and armed forces. Rather, it was intended to make one possible.

The resolution which we have sponsored with our colleagues of the United Kingdom, France and Canada[46] demonstrates clearly the importance and priority we assign to this objective.

The President's plan would provide practical experience in many of the control measures required to supervise a disarmament agreement. More important, it would promote that international confidence which is indispensable to such an agreement.

The United States is pledged to work for, earnestly desires, and energetically seeks a comprehensive, progressive, enforceable agreement for the reduction of military expenditures, arms, armaments, and armed forces under effective international inspection and control.

It believes that these reductions should be of such character and the machinery for inspection and enforcement so effective that no one nation anywhere in the world would be in a position to launch sudden, successful aggression against any other nation anywhere in the world. At the same time, every nation must have the strength to assure its internal security,

[46] United Nations Document A/C.1/L 150, introduced by the delegate of the U.K. (Nutting) on December 2, 1955.

to meet its international obligations, and to discourage predatory designs.

The Eisenhower plan would lead promptly and directly to the achievement of all these objectives.

The United States further believes that, if agreement can be reached to eliminate or limit nuclear weapons within the framework of an effective system of disarmament and under proper safeguards, there should be corresponding restrictions on the testing of such weapons.

The United States intends that a general disarmament agreement should affect broad elements of armed strength, including military bases. This applies to those bases which, by the desire and at the request of other countries, have been placed at the disposition of the United States abroad. It should apply as well to the bases of the Soviet Union at home and abroad, even though the Soviet Union, proclaiming that it no longer has any foreign bases, apparently persists in regarding its military installations in other countries as domestic establishments.

You will find in the record concrete evidence of the readiness of the United States to reduce its armaments while not merely maintaining but actually increasing the prosperity not only of its own citizens but of its friends elsewhere in the world. The record contains the figures for United States strength year by year since the end of the war. From a military force of twelve and a half million in the last year of World War II we came down to a million and a half men before the Korean War.

You will not find in the record any comparable figures for the Soviet armed forces. You will not be able to fix any base line for Soviet strength against which to measure the arms cuts recently reported by the Soviet Union.

Whether the United States reduces its forces further or alters their composition in any way, whether agreement on disarmament comes late or soon, the world may be sure of this: The United States will not use atomic weapons or any other weapons—be they guns, tanks, airplanes, rifles, or anything else—in any way except in accordance with the charter of the United Nations and in defense against aggression.

The Eisenhower conception is as simple as it is bold. The United States readily understands that any government would want to weigh its effect most carefully. But we must all be aware that the longer a start on this problem is delayed, the more difficult it will become.

The Soviet Union has expressed what must be its considered objections to the plan through Mr. Molotov at Geneva, through Mr. Sobolev in the Disarmament Commission, and through Mr. Kuznetsov.

What are these objections?

First, the Soviet Union says that the President's plan has nothing to do with disarmament. The fact is that the proposal was made as a prelude to reduction in armament, after 9 years of discussion of other methods had failed to produce a solution. The resolution introduced on December 2 by the United Kingdom, France, Canada, and the United States declares our resolve to seek early agreement on both the President's proposals and on such adequately safeguarded measures of a disarmament plan as are now feasible. We shall continue to strive for a comprehensive agreement.

Second, the Soviet delegation at Geneva objected that the plan was limited to the territory of the United States and the Soviet Union. That is, in fact, the logical place to begin. These two countries hold the preponderance of nuclear weapons which the world fears may be loosed in war. They also maintain the greatest portion of their armed strength within their own borders.

The President spoke only for his own country when he made his proposal to the Soviet Union. But we are ready to negotiate both with other sovereign states involved and with the Soviet Union for the extension of the Eisenhower plan and the Bulganin plan for ground control posts to overseas bases and the forces of other countries. They are sovereign states; it is up to them. My guess is that they will authorize it.

Third, the Soviet Union says that the plan might involve "enormous expenditures." I have already dealt with that point, and it is perfectly true that some expense would be involved. We can afford it and we believe that the Soviet Union could afford it. It is a trifling premium to pay for an insurance policy against war.

Fourth, the Soviet Union to our surprise still claimed at Geneva that the plan did not provide for ground observers at key points. The fact is that President Eisenhower told Mr. Bulganin in his letter of October 11 that,[47]

"I have not forgotten your proposal having to do with

[47] See above, p. 448.

stationing inspection teams at key points in our countries, and if you feel this would help to create the better spirit I refer to, we could accept that too."

Finally, Mr. Molotov at Geneva[48] and Mr. Khrushchev in India[49] have argued that the Eisenhower plan would increase the risk of war because it would give each country access to military information about the other which it might put to use in launching a surprise attack. The fact is, as Secretary Dulles pointed out at Geneva, that lack of information is not what inhibits hostilities. What is lacking is the deterrent to attack which would result if this plan is put into effect, depriving the aggressor of the benefit of surprise.

These are the sum of the Soviet arguments against the Eisenhower proposals. In all candor, they do not appear impressive—or insuperable. This is lucky, because the outlook would be bleak indeed if we were constrained to accept them as the Soviet last word.

The outlook would be far brighter if the Soviet Union would answer these four questions:

1. When will the Soviet Union join us in a policy of openness which would reassure the world and advance the cause of disarmament?

2. Why does the Soviet Union continue to advocate elimination of atomic weapons as an immediate objective, when it has told the world so clearly that this is impossible?

3. Why would the Soviet Union commit states to a whole series of actions vitally affecting their national security without providing the means of inspection and control to see that they are carried out equally by all?

4. Why, if the Soviet Union is sincere in its concern about the possibility of attack from the West, is it not willing to join in an immediate practical program to proscribe surprise attack by either side?

If it is the Soviet aim to lull the defenses of the free world with a smile and to promote the dissolution of free-world alliances which have been created in response to the Soviet Union's postwar policy and action, then a specious disarmament program unsupported by inspection would serve that

[48] The reference is to the Geneva Meeting of Foreign Ministers, October 27—November 16, 1955.

[49] The reference is to a visit of the Chairman of the Council of Ministers of the U.S.S.R. (Bulganin) and of the First Secretary of the Communist Party of the Soviet Union (Khrushchev) to India and other Asian countries in November and December 1955.

end. But we are loath to think that this is the answer to our questions. Gentlemen, let us have clear answers; the world deserves them.

In spite of recent discouraging developments, the United States is not ready to accept melancholy conclusions about Soviet policy.

We still hope that with further reflection and discussion the Soviet Union will see that the Eisenhower plan is in the world's interest and in its own.

We are glad to note that understanding has been reached on at least some points. All of us agree that nuclear material can now be concealed in significant quantities. All agree that there must be new emphasis on preventing surprise attack.

We note that the Soviet Union, after rejecting aerial inspection for 10 years, now seems to say it would accept it, at least "at the concluding stage" of a disarmament program. We hope that it will agree that such inspection as proposed by President Eisenhower should occur as a *beginning* step, when it would do most to lessen tension and open the path to further measures of inspection and control of armaments.

This would not be the first time that the Soviet Union has reacted negatively to new proposals, only to adjust its thinking as time went on. We remember the welcome evolution of its views concerning the atoms-for-peace plan.

The United States hopes the Soviet delegate will choose the platform of this General Assembly to announce an advance in Soviet thinking on this problem. We believe the General Assembly will want to go on record for the principles of the Eisenhower proposals as well as for the constructive suggestions made by the British, French, and Soviet Governments.

Mr. Chairman, I conclude:

On November 26 last, Mr. Khrushchev spoke to an Indian audience. "Just imagine," he is reported to have said, "Soviet planes flying over the United States and United States planes flying over the Soviet Union."

Mr. Khrushchev seemed to find this picture fantastic.

We Americans do not. We believe that many, many others do not.

We believe that this vision of "sentinels of peace" crossing each other in the "open skies" is something which millions of everyday people in every country can see plainly.

It will be as reassuring as the sight of the policeman on his beat. We hope that there will be the vision and the statesmanship to enable the Soviet leaders also to see it.

We hope, finally, that this Assembly of the United Nations will endorse this plan for aerial inspection and that this endorsement will lead to its being put into effect soon. The day that these "sentinels of peace" start their flights will indeed be the most brilliant day in the history of the United Nations.

b. *General Assembly Resolution 914 (X), Adopted December 16, 1955.*[50]

The General Assembly,

Recalling its resolution 808 (IX) of 4 November 1954,[51] which established the conclusion that a further effort should be made to reach agreement on comprehensive and co-ordinated proposals to be embodied in a draft international disarmament convention providing for:

(a) The regulation, limitation and major reduction of all armed forces and all conventional armaments,

(b) The total prohibition of the use and manufacture of nuclear weapons and weapons of mass destruction of every type, together with the conversion of existing stocks of nuclear weapons for peaceful purposes,

(c) The establishment of effective international control, through a control organ with rights, powers and functions adequate to guarantee the effective observance of the agreed reductions of all armaments and armed forces and the prohibition of nuclear and other weapons of mass destruction, and to ensure the use of atomic energy for peaceful purposes only, the whole programme to be such that no State would have cause to fear that its security was endangered,

Expressing the hope that efforts to relax international tensions, to promote mutual confidence and to develop co-operation among States, such as the Geneva Conference of the Heads of Government of the four Powers, the Bandung Conference of African and Asian countries and the United Nations tenth anniversary commemorative meeting at San Francisco, will prove effective in promoting world peace,

Desirous of contributing to the lowering of international tensions, the strengthening of confidence between States, the removal of the threat of war and the reduction of the burden of armaments,

[50] United Nations General Assembly *Official Records, Tenth Session,* Supplement No. 19, pp. 5-6. The resolution was adopted by a vote of 56-7, with the Soviet bloc countries, including Hungary and Rumania, voting against.
[51] *Documents on American Foreign Relations, 1954,* pp. 461-462.

Convinced therefore of the need to continue to seek agreement on a comprehensive programme for disarmament which will promote international peace and security with the least diversion for armaments of the world's human and economic resources,

Welcoming the progress which has been made towards agreement on objectives during the meetings in 1955 of the Sub-Committee of the Disarmament Commission,

Noting that agreement has not yet been reached on the rights, powers and functions of a control system, which is the keystone of any disarmament agreement, nor on other essential matters set out in General Assembly resolution 808 (IX),

Noting also that special technical difficulties have arisen in regard to the detection and control of nuclear weapons material,

Recognizing further that inspection and control of disarmament can best be achieved in an atmosphere which is free of fear and suspicion,

1. *Urges* that the States concerned and particularly those on the Sub-Committee of the Disarmament Commission:

(a) Should continue their endeavours to reach agreement on a comprehensive disarmament plan in accordance with the goals set out in General Assembly resolution 808 (IX);

(b) Should, as initial steps, give priority to early agreement on and implementation of:

(i) Such confidence-building measures as the plan of Mr. Eisenhower, President of the United States of America, for exchanging military blueprints and mutual aerial inspection, and the plan of Mr. Bulganin, Prime Minister of the Union of Soviet Socialist Republics, for establishing control posts at strategic centres,

(ii) All such measures of adequately safeguarded disarmament as are now feasible;

2. *Suggests* that account should also be taken of the proposals of the Prime Minister of France for exchanging and publishing information regarding military expenditures and budgets,[52] of the Prime Minister of the United Kingdom of Great Britain and Northern Ireland for seeking practical experience in the problems of inspection and control,[53] and of the Government of India regarding the suspension of

[52] See above, pp. 217-220.
[53] See above, pp. 216-217.

experimental explosions of nuclear weapons and an "armaments truce";[54]

3. *Calls* upon the States concerned, and especially those on the Sub-Committee of the Disarmament Commission, to study the proposal of the Prime Minister of France for the allocation of funds resulting from disarmament for improving the standards of living throughout the world and, in particular, in the less-developed countries;

4. *Recommends further* that scientific research should be continued by each State, with appropriate consultation between Governments, for methods that would make possible thoroughly effective inspection and control of nuclear weapons material, having as its aim to facilitate the solution of the problem of comprehensive disarmament;

5. *Suggests* that the Disarmament Commission reconvene its Sub-Committee and that both pursue their efforts to attain the above objectives;

6. *Decides* to transmit to the Disarmament Commission, for its information, the records of the meetings of the First Committee at which the disarmament problem was discussed during the tenth session of the General Assembly, and requests the Disarmament Commission and the Sub-Committee to give careful and early consideration to the views expressed in those documents.

B. Peaceful Uses of Atomic Energy.

1. *Meeting the Human Problems of the Nuclear Age: Address by the President at the Centennial Commencement Ceremonies of Pennsylvania State University, University Park, Pennsylvania, June 11, 1955.*[1]

(Excerpts)

* * *

Nuclear energy is too new for any man to chart its limits or predict its course with accuracy. But in 10 short years the curtain has been pushed aside sufficiently to afford glimpses that have aroused atomic hopes commensurate with the awful dimension of atomic fears.

The extent of the economic and industrial changes that we can anticipate is indicated by estimates that world sources of uranium potentially available contain as high as 20 times the

[54] Not printed.

[1] *Department of State Bulletin,* v. 32 (June 27, 1955), pp. 1027-1030.

energy of the known world reserves of coal, petroleum and natural gas combined. But power is only one of the results of nuclear fission. Many engineers and scientists believe that radiation and radioactive isotopes may provide even greater peacetime benefit. They are already opening new horizons in medicine, agriculture, and industrial processes.

Our nation has no desire for a monopoly on the knowledge and practice of these possibilities. We want the world to share —as we always have. Moreover, we know that the human talents essential to the advancement of science are not restricted to this country. Throughout the free countries there are men and women of great ability who, given the opportunity, can help further to advance the frontiers of knowledge and contribute to the peace and progress of the peoples of all nations.

Progress to date in nuclear science is not, of course, exclusively an American achievement. An international cooperative effort broke the barriers and made possible man's use of atomic energy. For maximum progress in the future, we must work for a continued partnership between the world's best minds—in science, engineering, education, business, and the professions.

In recognition of these facts, I proposed before the General Assembly of the United Nations on December 8, 1953, that governments begin then and continue to make joint contributions from their stockpiles of fissionable materials to an International Atomic Agency.[2] Although a year later the United Nations adopted the resolution recommending the formation of such an international agency,[3] the Soviet Union has indicated no willingness to share any part of its nuclear stockpile with such an agency. Our offer still stands.

But we cannot wait on Soviet decisions. Already we have made substantial progress under congressional authority toward agreements with friendly foreign governments for participation with us in the task of forwarding peaceful atomic progress. Agreements with Turkey,[4] Lebanon, Israel, Italy, Spain, Switzerland, Denmark, Colombia, Brazil, and the Argentine Republic have been initialed. Others are being negotiated.

Now we move in further action. We have developed two new programs that I shall submit to the Congress in the

[2] *Documents on American Foreign Relations, 1953,* pp. 45-52.
[3] *Ibid., 1954,* pp. 494-496.
[4] *Department of State Bulletin,* v. 32 (May 23, 1955), p. 865.

conviction that they reflect the spirit and intent of law and of the American people.

First: We propose to offer research reactors to the people of free nations who can use them effectively for the aquisition of the skills and understanding essential to peaceful atomic progress. The United States, in the spirit of partnership that moves us, will contribute half the cost. We will also furnish the acquiring nation the nuclear material needed to fuel the reactor.

Second: Within prudent security considerations, we propose to make available to the peoples of such friendly nations as are prepared to invest their own funds in power reactors, access to and training in the technological processes of construction and operation for peaceful purposes.

If the technical and material resources of a single nation should not appear adequate to make effective use of a research reactor, we would support a voluntary grouping of the resources of several nations within a single region to acquire and operate it together.

Our purpose is to spark the creative and inventive skills latent in the free world, to pool them, and to put them to work for the betterment of the conditions under which men must live. The research reactors acquired under this program will be fertile seeds for progress sown in the receptive soil of the free nations. The cost to the people of the United States will be small indeed when measured against the certain returns, tangible and intangible.

The second proposal will be of immediate interest mainly to the power-short areas of the world where atomic power may be economically feasible even today. Some of the countries, however, lack the knowledge and experience needed to construct and operate a commercial power reactor. This we can share for constructive purposes with friendly countries without real risk to our national security. Such sharing is expressly contemplated by the new Atomic Energy Act.

Together, these two provisions are designed, within the limits of prudence, to clear away some of the obstacles that have impeded progress in nuclear science and to permit its peaceful application by all who propose to make it serve mankind. Here is an invitation—to scientists and engineers, to industries and governments—to pool their energies and creative talents that this great achievement of the human mind may bear the fruit of its infinite promise.

The people of the United States instinctively reject any

thought that their greatest scientific achievement can be used only as a weapon. Our increasing progress in its peaceful applications is evidence of that fact.

While we build atomic-powered ships for war—because we must—we have the desire, the determination to build atomic-powered ships for peace. And build them we shall! The first atomic-powered merchant ship, at its ports of call, will be a laboratory demonstration that man can harness this unlimited energy for normal, peaceful, prosperous life.

While we design bombs that can obliterate great military objectives—because we must—we are also designing generators, channels, and reservoirs of atomic energy so that man may profit from this gift which the Creator of all things has put into his hands. And build them we shall!

The two proposals I have outlined here are the gateway to a broad avenue of world progress in the peaceful uses of atomic energy.

Surely those of the Russian people who, despite their Communist overlords, still think for themselves and who still retain respect for human dignity are moved by the same feelings as we. I still hope earnestly that the Soviet Union may join in an international effort to harness the atom for man's good. But I have such unlimited confidence in the creativeness of free minds and in the capacity of free men that I know we will, with or without the Soviets, achieve a more abundant life for those who join together in this historic venture.

* * *

The peoples of this earth share today a great aspiration. They all have a common dream of lasting peace with freedom and justice. But the realization of the dream calls for many types of cooperation based upon sympathetic and thoroughly mutual understanding. In turn, such understanding is dependent on education that produces disciplined thinking.

Throughout the world mutual suspicions flourish in ignorance and misunderstanding. They can be dispelled only with knowledge and wisdom.

If we are to have partners for peace, then we must first be partners in sympathetic recognition that all mankind possesses in common like aspirations and hungers, like ideals and appetites, like purposes and frailties, a like demand for economic advancement. The divisions between us are artificial and transient. Our common humanity is God-made and enduring.

* * *

2. *Conference on the Peaceful Uses of Atomic Energy, Geneva, August 8-20, 1955.*[5]

a. *Message from the President to the Conference, Delivered by the Chairman, United States Atomic Energy Commission (Strauss), August 8, 1955.*[6]

MEMBERS OF THE CONFERENCE:

Please accept my warmest greetings and sincere good wishes, on behalf of the people of the United States, for the success of this first international conference on the peaceful uses of atomic energy, held under the auspices of the United Nations.

You—the world's foremost nuclear scientists and engineers, who are penetrating the mysteries of atomic energy—most surely know how the atom stands ready to become man's obedient, tireless servant, if man will only allow it.

The knowledge and vision which you possess carries with it a great opportunity—and a great challenge. Your lives are dedicated to the search for knowledge and truth. You hold the respect of your peoples because they look to you for words of calm, unadorned scientific fact.

You can best unfold to the peoples of the world the bright promise of the benign atom.

You meet in Geneva under conditions favorable to this great purpose.

No other scientific gathering of such scope and importance, or of such widespread interest, has ever taken place. The peoples of the world are represented. At hand is a rich opportunity to restore old lines of free scientific communication which have been disrupted for so many years. The knowledge and skills which each of you has acquired in his own country to put the atom to work for peaceful purposes will be circulated and shared in the friendly atmosphere of hospitable Switzerland with its age-old tradition of freedom.

This atmosphere is encouraged also by the fact that the United Nations Resolution of last December 4, which created your Conference, limited its concern to scientific and technical matters. It is expressly non-political.

You meet, therefore, as free men of science, interested only in enriching man's store of knowledge about this wonderful discovery.

[5] The conference was held in accordance with a decision embodied in General Assembly Resolution 810 (IX), adopted December 4, 1954. See *Documents on American Foreign Relations, 1954,* pp. 494-496.

[6] *Department of State Bulletin,* v. 33 (August 22, 1955), pp. 300-301.

Science speaks in many tongues. The advancement of the nuclear arts has been the work of men of many nations. That is so because the atom itself is non-political. It wears no nationality and recognizes no frontiers. It is neither moral nor immoral. Only man's choice can make it good or evil. The phenomenon of nuclear fission having been revealed to man, it is still left to him to determine the use to which it shall be put.

On December 8, 1953, I had the privilege of addressing the General Assembly of the United Nations on the subject which occupies this conference—world cooperation for the peaceful uses of atomic energy.

I stated then, and I reaffirm now, that the United States pledges its determination to help find ways by which the miraculous inventiveness of man shall not be dedicated to his death, but consecrated to his life.

This pledge which we gave twenty months ago has become the law of our land, written into our statutes by the American Congress in the new Atomic Energy Act of 1954. The new Act states in forthright language that we recognize our responsibilities to share with others, in a spirit of cooperation, what we know of the peaceful atomic art. To further encourage such cooperation with other nations, the new Act relaxed the previously existing restrictions on independent atomic research and development by private industry, thereby further clearing the way for cooperation with others.

Since our new Atomic Energy Act became law a year ago, we have striven in many ways and ever in a spirit of good will to translate its words and its purpose into concrete action.

That is the way we interpret our responsibility and the responsibility of all nations of good will.

We appeal not alone to governments to join with us in this cooperative endeavor. We are hopeful also that business and professional groups throughout the world will become interested and will provide incentives in finding new ways that this science can be used.

All of the enlightened nations of the world are spending large sums every year on programs of health, education and economic development. They do so because they know that disease, ignorance and the lack of economic opportunity are the dark breeding places of disorders and wars.

Every scientific tool available has been brought to bear in this effort.

Atomic science is the newest and the most promising tool of all.

In your capable hands, I am confident it can be made to perform greatly for the betterment of human living.

DWIGHT D. EISENHOWER

b. *Address by United States Representative to the Conference (Libby), August 20, 1955.*[7]

(Excerpts)

We have had a momentous and fruitful 2 weeks together here at this first International Conference on the Peaceful Uses of Atomic Energy.

The benefits of this meeting have been great. Scientists knowing the same things separately increase their total knowledge in conferring with one another. Though possibly unable to tell one another anything new, the fact that another scientist has discovered the same knowledge working independently constitutes the final necessary scientific proof of essential truth. In this way has our total knowledge been greatly increased by this Conference. Let us hope that we shall meet again, perhaps in 3 years, to describe the progress made in the interim.

President Eisenhower, in his memorable address to the United Nations General Assembly on December 8, 1953, proposed that an International Atomic Energy Agency be established under the aegis of the United Nations. He proposed such an agency as an instrumentality to spread throughout the world knowledge which had been acquired by those nations with advanced atomic energy programs. Last September the United States and a number of other nations, believing the worldwide sharing of atomic knowledge to be imperative, agreed to press forward with the creation of an international agency. Since that time, a draft statute has been prepared and discussed by those nations, and it is my understanding that this draft statute will be ready for consideration in the immediate future.[8] These preliminary discussions were held by Australia, Belgium, Canada, France, Portugal, the United Kingdom, the Union of South Africa, and the United States of America.

However, the United States has taken steps to spread

[7] *Ibid.* (September 5, 1955), pp. 381-384.
[8] See below, p. 479.

atomic knowledge in advance of the formation of the international agency. During the last 6 months it has been disclosing to the world a good deal of its fund of information gained through the American people's immense outlay of time and treasure and energies. We hope that the accomplishments of this Conference will increase the tempo of international cooperation in atomic energy. We are sure that this Conference has contributed in large measure to an improved understanding on the part of all nations of the present and future prospects for the peaceful uses of atomic energy. Such understanding is certain to be followed by constructive, cooperative action to develop these uses throughout the world.

Most of you here are aware of the effort which the United States is making to assist other peoples to develop their own atomic energy programs. However, the extent and variety of the measures which we are taking may not be fully known to all of you. I would like to review the present status and future possibilities for United States cooperation in training of technical personnel and exchange of technical data, materials, and equipment. By bringing this to your attention now, we hope that in the months to come there will be a marked increase in the opportunities for cooperative endeavors presented to the United States.

Forty-seven countries now receive shipments of radioisotopes from Oak Ridge. It is intended to facilitate this foreign distribution by an early substantial liberalization of the regulations applying. For some time, the Oak Ridge Institute of Nuclear Studies has been offering a course in the handling of radioisotopes. In May of this year a special 4-week course began at Oak Ridge, with 30 scientists and technicians from 21 nations in attendance. The training they received was identical with that given to American scientists at the same school. In the future, a substantial percentage of the total enrollment in the course on radioisotope techniques will be reserved for students from countries other than the United States. The next course for foreign scientists will be offered in October.

* * *

Since an increasing level of power generation is one of the prime factors in improving living standards, it is hardly surprising that the interest of people throughout the world is focused on the utilization of nuclear energy in the production of electric power.

Remembering that this use of the atom is new, we must caution that the development of conventional power sources should not be neglected. For the next few years the atom will not be a major source of power. It is in the future—perhaps 10 years from now—that we see it taking its rightful place as a primary source of power.

It is the aim of the United States to help other countries proceed, as rapidly as possible, toward the economic production of electric power from the atom. Harnessing a nuclear chain reaction, however, is a highly complex undertaking. The design and operation of a reactor requires scientific and technical personnel who are familiar with this new and complicated technology.

In recognition of this need, the United States has established a School of Nuclear Science and Engineering at Argonne National Laboratory near Chicago.[9] The purpose of the school is to provide advanced instruction in reactor technology. The school opened in March of this year with 30 students from 19 countries in addition to the American students in attendance. During the 7-month course the students receive instruction in reactor physics, reactor engineering, metallurgy of reactor materials, chemistry of the lanthanide and actinide elements, principles of separation processes, instruments, remote control, experimental reactor physics, and analytical procedures. A second course will begin in November and a third next March. When these men return to their homes, they will form nuclei around which may develop indigenous groups of atomic specialists.

The Government of the United States has concluded agreements for cooperation in the civil uses of atomic energy with more than 25 nations and is prepared to conclude similar agreements with many more.[10] The agreements call for exchanges of information in the application of atomic energy to biology, medicine, and agriculture. In addition, under these agreements the United States aids in the construction of research reactors, will contribute half the cost of the first reactor in each country, and furnishes the necessary fuel for these reactors.

[9] *Department of State Bulletin,* v. 32 (April 4, 1955), p. 553.

[10] Bilateral Agreements for Cooperation were signed with nineteen countries (Turkey, Brazil, Colombia, Lebanon, Israel, Argentina, Spain, Italy, Denmark, Switzerland, Portugal, China, Netherlands, Philippines, Venezuela, Pakistan, Chile, Japan, Greece). Agreements were initialed with five additional countries (Uruguay, Peru, Korea, Sweden, Thailand), but these did not become effective prior to the adjournment of Congress.

Nearly a year ago the President authorized the Atomic Energy Commission to allocate 100 kilograms of enriched uranium for use in research reactors abroad and last June this amount was increased to 200 kilograms. Agreements for the sale of heavy water have been made with a number of countries at a price of $28 per pound. The enriched uranium containing as much as 20 percent U-235 is to be leased at 4 percent per annum on the basis of $25 per gram of contained U-235. A charge at this rate will be made for the U-235 consumed. Ordinary uranium metal will be sold at $40 per kilogram. All of these prices and values are estimated so that the United States Government neither gains nor loses financially.

Research reactors, as you know, have many uses in themselves. These include production of radioisotopes; medical therapy; solid-state physics research; studies on nuclear properties of matter, such as cross sections for capture or scattering of neutrons, gamma ray spectrum induced by neutron capture, and radiation attenuation; reactor physics measurements; and reactor engineering experiments. The "swimming pool" reactor at the United States exhibit, which has been sold and transferred today to the Swiss Government, is one of the types of research reactors which the United States will help to build.

I should like to emphasize that each of these bilateral agreements states that it is the hope and expectation of both parties that the initial agreement for cooperation will lead to consideration of further cooperation extending to the design, construction, and operation of power reactors.

The United States has no wish that any nation be dependent on American technicians for the operation of a nuclear power program. Experience in the operation of research reactors will provide a reservoir of trained engineers and scientists in the countries where such specialists are now lacking.

President Eisenhower, in his notable speech of last June 11, said:

"If the technical and material resources of a single nation should not appear adequate to make effective use of a research reactor, we would support a voluntary grouping of the resources of several nations within a single region to acquire and operate it together."

These are regions throughout the world where governments well might consider the establishment of such cooperative ventures in the operation of research reactors.

The following countries have negotiated agreements for cooperation with the United States, received technical libraries, or have had students participating in one or more of our training programs: Argentina, Australia, Austria, Belgium, Brazil, Burma, Canada, Chile, Republic of China, Colombia, Cuba, Denmark, Egypt, Finland, France, Germany, Greece, Guatemala, India, Indonesia, Israel, Italy, Japan, Republic of Korea, Lebanon, Mexico, the Netherlands, Pakistan, Peru, the Philippines, Portugal, Spain, Sweden, Switzerland, Thailand, Turkey, Union of South Africa, United Kingdom, Uruguay, and Venezuela.

Making the atom serve man is a long and laborious task. Atomic scientists and technicians must first be trained and given experience. Experimentation and development work must be carried on continuously. The job is not a short one, but with large measures of patience, faith, and imagination we can confidently anticipate the time when all men will realize the full potential of the atom.

c. *Report on the Conference: Address by the Chairman, United States Atomic Energy Commission (Strauss) before the Atomic Industrial Forum and the American Nuclear Society, Washington, D.C., September 28, 1955.*[11]

The posture of a nation is a composite of the words of its leaders and the deeds of its people. The Atomic Energy Conference had its origin in President Eisenhower's unforgettable words to the United Nations in December of 1953 when he told of the great promise in store for peoples everywhere if the world's scientists and engineers could be free to devote themselves fully to the benign uses of the atom.

Four months later we moved to translate the President's vision into deeds. We proposed a world conference to compare notes on the peaceful atom, for we were convinced that such a conference would give to the peoples of the world a clearer understanding of the paramount problem of this age —a realization of the blessings denied to all of us by reason of the fact that atomic armament must have first call upon the resources, intellectual and material, of a world precariously at peace.

The problem is not a new one. As children, we all grew up with the Arabian Nights story of the fisherman who found

[11] *Department of State Bulletin,* v. 33 (October 10, 1955), pp. 555-559.

a bottle in his nets, uncorked it, and released a great cloud which rapidly transformed itself into the monstrous and threatening Djinn. The story ended happily, as you recall, by the fisherman's artifice in inducing that unwelcome apparition to return to the bottle and become captive once more.

This fable, even to the illustrations of the great mushroom cloud from which the Djinn materialized, is like the situation we face today—how to render atomic energy harmless, how to get it back into its bottle, under control, so we may make it fulfill our wishes for good purposes only.

The Geneva conference was a step toward that goal, but only a step. The press of the world, which sent some 800 reporters to Geneva, was enthusiastic and generous in its appraisal of the proceedings. They were described as a resounding triumph of "atoms for peace." But this should not conceal for us the fact that the conference was only a preliminary move in a right direction and that succeeding steps will have to be taken if any permanent good is to result.

But it was a truly gratifying beginning. The enthusiasm and cooperation which it inspired among the nations, great and small, surpassed the expectations of those whose task it was to set up the conference machinery. They had anticipated that the conference might attract some 400 scientists and that perhaps 300 papers would be submitted. Actually we found that 72 nations were eager to participate and that, not 400 scientists and engineers, but 1,400 would attend. The number of reports and papers submitted was not 300, but nearly four times as many—so many in fact that only a fraction could be presented orally. But most of them, brilliant works, will be published.

The day is not yet here for a precise evaluation of these more than 1,100 papers and discussion sessions. However, enough time has perhaps elapsed for a reminiscent look at the conference, to appraise its more obvious and immediate effects and some of the initial benefits gained from it. Within those limits I would like to give you my impressions, admittedly from the viewpoint of a prejudiced observer.

First, I might say something about our own participation. Our United States delegation was selected with great care and numbered 384 persons, of whom 239 were scientists and engineers, the remainder being the necessary staff to operate the exhibits, the reactor, and other services.

Of the 1,110 papers presented to the conference by all the

participating countries, either orally or for inclusion in the published proceedings, approximately one-half—to be precise, 48.2 percent—were submitted by the United States. All our papers had been prepared months in advance and carefully reviewed to make certain that no maters of military significance were compromised.

The nations having atomic energy programs of any magnitude had impressive technical exhibits at the conference, but incontestably the star attraction was our operating research reactor, built at our Oak Ridge Laboratory, flown to Geneva, and erected on the grounds of the Palace of Nations. The attractive redwood structure we put up to house the reactor quickly acquired the nickname of "The Tennessee Chalet," and it was visited by more than 63,000 persons during the 2 weeks of the conference. Incidentally, for most of the delegates from other countries, including scientists and engineers come to deliver learned papers on atomic energy, it was their first opportunity to see an actual atomic reactor of any kind, much less to operate its controls as very many of them did. We also had in our main exhibit an outstanding demonstration of what Americans are doing in pure science, industry, medicine, and biology, and more about power development. Many of you here tonight contributed to this exhibit and are familiar with it. Some of those exhibits, brought from Geneva, are included in the Trade Fair on exhibition here.

At a trade exposition in another section of Geneva, industrial firms of several countries—the Soviets excepted—showed their products to good effect, but we made it clear that we had not come to Geneva to boast of our scientific prowess or, in other words, that we had not entered with the spirit of carrying off all the laurels in a sort of atomic Olympic Games.

The Soviet had a large technical exhibit which was chiefly remarkable, from my point of view, for the fact that it was there at all. We have had "atoms for peace" exhibits circulating around the world for more than a year. But, until this conference, we had seen nothing of Russian progress in this field. Therefore, great interest and conjecture attached itself to anything they proposed to show. Because the rest of the world knew so little of what the Russians were doing with the peaceful atom, it was clear that whatever they exhibited, or even reported, would be in the nature of a revelation.

Let me at this point say that they did come up with a great deal. There was no evidence, however—photographic or otherwise—to support the statement made by Soviet official spokesmen a few years back to the effect that, whereas the United States was engrossed with atomic energy to make bombs, they, the Soviets, were using atomic energy to change the courses of rivers and to remove mountains. On the other hand, their exhibits in areas of biology, in certain industrial applications, and in general instrumentation were not unimpressive and occasionally not greatly dissimilar from our own.

However, it was electrical power generation from atomic energy that attracted particular interest in the Soviet exhibit. They demonstrated a scale model of their 5,000-kilowatt reactor and a motion picture of the reactor itself, well photographed and accompanied by a narration in English. They also indicated that larger power reactors of a different design were planned. We, of course, have had units substantially larger than the Soviet plant operating for a considerable time, and far larger ones are building.

Soviet written reports to the conference showed careful preparation and a considerable amount of detail. But it became apparent early in the proceedings that, in answering the questions of delegates, they were not prepared to engage in the same degree of frankness as other delegations.

The Russian delegation, of whom some 79 were technicians, impressed our people as generally competent and, in some instances, as exceptional men. We have no way of knowing whether it was their first team, but as one of our people said, "They were good enough to be a first team."

It is the general impression among the members of our delegation that, on the basis of Geneva, we are well ahead of other nations—all other nations—in both the scope and the state of our technology in using atomic energy for peaceful purposes. This, however, was to be expected since we appear to have a considerably larger program than any other country and we have been engaged upon it for a longer time.

In this connection it is interesting to note, however, that at least one of the Russian papers presented at the conference bore the date of 1943, indicating that they had been seriously concerned with the subject for a longer time than many of us realize.

While what the Russians revealed at Geneva did not contain anything new or startling, it did give some insight into their working methods and into the caliber of their research. On the basis of their role at Geneva, they appeared stronger in basic research than in its practical applications.

The fact that we appear to be ahead in the peaceful applications of atomic energy—perhaps by a scant few years—certainly offers no justification for complacency. To the contrary, the situation must be regarded as a serious challenge. The Soviets have not outstripped nor equaled us in any peaceful application, but at the same time—and this is important—we did not show anything at Geneva which they cannot have in a few years, given the talent and zeal which we believe them to possess.

Too many of us have been thinking of the Russians, either by education or temperament, as not quite equal to us in the technological sense. Despite the many things wrong with their political system from our point of view, let us not fall into the easy attitude of assuming that they cannot compete with us in mastering atomic energy. The early date at which they produced nuclear weapons should be a constant reminder of the fallacy and danger of such an attitude on our part. We can never let down our research without letting down our guard at the same moment.

Also, the belief that science cannot thrive under conditions designed solely to protect the security of data already in hand and deemed important to national defense would seem to be brought into question by the degree of Soviet progress. This progress was achieved under security provisions which are part of a complete tyranny where communication is rigidly controlled and the individual has no rights. Since *we* proceed under the policy of removing information from classification as rapidly as possible, the Soviet results present something of a paradox.

With respect to power from atomic energy, the Geneva conference made it evident that, while others are engaged in extensive undertakings, our program is presently substantially ahead in extent and in the versatility of its approach. As you know, we are relatively close in the United States to the production of economic, electrical energy. Even today, the kilowatts we are producing in our reactors would be economic in some parts of the world.

But different countries are taking different paths to power development, depending upon varying economic factors. England, for example, foresees the end of her increasingly expensive coal. For England, therefore, time is of the essence; she cannot afford to wait for development of the ultimate reactor of maximum efficiency.

Soviet Russia has no private industry interested in developing the peacetime uses of atomic energy and no spirit of competitive free enterprise. In Russia the whole show is a government monopoly. It will be interesting to see how this will affect the search for a more economic and efficient power system than the one they exhibited.

We, in the United States, are fortunate in that we face no urgent shortage of conventional fuels. We have time and the opportunity to attack the problem from every side and to experiment simultaneously with a whole variety of atomic power systems. That is exactly what we are doing. Last week the Commission took another step forward and invited proposals from industry and other groups for the design and construction of small atomic power plants. This marks the second round of a partnership program designed to speed the development of efficient, economic nuclear power. Our first power demonstration reactor program began, as you know, earlier this year and produced proposals for large plants. American industry is dedicating risk capital in a conservative race to produce the best and most efficient means of atomic power—knowing full well that the first plants will not be economic.

To sum up, we did not go to this conference in an effort to carry away all the honors. If there was some semblance of a contest, in the technical exhibits and in the papers presented, no one lost in this competition. All the nations gained, and the winner was mankind.

From the viewpoint of our national self-interest, however, the conference was certainly a victory for fundamental American policy. We achieved new understanding abroad of our earnest effort to promote a decent and enduring peace.

As a people, knowing full well the sincerity of our own desire for peace, we have not always appreciated how the rest of the world regarded us. Sometimes even nations whose safety from aggression has depended upon our possession of nuclear weapons have shown a tendency to view us with suspicion. Too often, in the past, Communist propaganda has had some success in depicting us as warmongers interested in the atom only to make bombs and ready to use them to gain our supposed imperialist aims. This myth was effectively demolished at Geneva and without our having to brand it as a myth. Our scientists and engineers who went to Geneva and who unfolded there a factual account of our purpose and efforts to use the atom for man's benefit were ambassadors of peace, plenipotentiary and extraordinary.

The conference was convened without any political objective. Nor did it, in its 162 hours of sessions, encounter any political complications. Under its "ground rules" any discussion of political topics or of atomic weapons was out of bounds by common consent, in advance. The fact that no violations of either the letter or the spirit of the conference occurred is one of the principal explanations for its success. But notwithstanding the absence of politics from the conference, it is bound to have a profound international political impact.

What were its chief results? It would appear that there were several, both immediate and for the not-distant future:

First, the free world—perhaps even the Soviet—has a new understanding of the absolute sincerity of our desire to strip the atom of its "military casing" and "adapt it to the arts of peace." The conference substantially advanced the President's program of "atoms for peace." Any suspicion of our motives, imported to the conference, could not have survived the 2 weeks of Geneva, and many delegates volunteered that statement to me in similar words.

Second, communication was reestablished between men of science who for many years had experienced the isolation of finding those lines down. As a result, much cross-fertilization of ideas will occur and that, inevitably, will stimulate new inventions in many phases of the atomic art during the next year or two.

Third, there can no longer be any talk of nations which, from the point of view of possessing information for the peaceful applications of atomic energy, are "have not" nations. The smaller nations were impressed by the fact that the development of atomic power is a very complex and expensive undertaking—an undertaking which requires, first of all, a grounding in the basic technology and then a substantial body of trained scientists and engineers. The notion that all they have to do is place an order for a reactor out of a catalog and be immediately in business to provide electrical energy from atomic power—if such a notion existed—was, or should have been, dispelled at Geneva.

Fourth, we gained much information of value to ourselves from the conference. One byproduct, I believe, was a rebirth of humility. We learned not to underrate the competence of others and to cease to think of ourselves—those of us, that is, who were so inclined—as especially and exclusively gifted with imagination and ability in exploring the possibilities of the new worlds that lie ahead. This realization could save us in the future from some grievous error of judgment.

Fifth, all of us were impressed by the disturbing fact that Russia appears to be training scientists and engineers at a faster rate than we are. Mr. Allen Dulles, the distinguished Director of our Central Intelligence Agency, has publicly stated that, between 1950 and 1960, Soviet Russia will have graduated 1,200,000 scientists and engineers, compared with about 900,000 in the United States in our present program. Those figures would not be so important did we not know that our own colleges and universities are turning out only about half the number of engineers we require today. Unless corrected, this situation, a generation hence, will become a national calamity, imperiling our security and freedom in an age of expending dependence upon science and technology. This is a most serious subject and demands prompt consideration and more emphasis than I can give it in this general report.

Sixth and finally, in this listing of the results of the world's first Conference on the Peaceful Uses of Atomic Energy, I come to the brightest, most appealing of all its accomplishments. As our story of the peaceful atom was printed widely overseas, the result was that for millions of people all over the world Geneva cast off the mesmerism of the bomb. No other event that has occurred has done so much toward taking the horror—the terror—out of the atom.

The first decade of man's mastery of the atom, in its actual application, began on an early morning in July of 1945 in a blinding flash over the sands of Alamogordo. The monstrous Djinn had been released from the bottle. The second decade of the atom may be said to have begun in Geneva, 10 years later, but this time it emerged, not as a terrifying monster, but as the powerful, obedient servant of man. Wider horizons of grander view were opened. To many, it must have seemed that, overnight, the atom had been transformed from a thing of fear and terror to a promise of great blessing.

History may record that in Geneva, at the opening of this second decade of the atom, mankind's stake in peace was lifted out of the paralysis of fear to a vision so compelling as to render unthinkable the very notion of another major war. If the conference produced such a vision, it made a good and auspicious beginning. We must not allow that vision to fade —either for us or for other men.

3. *The International Atomic Energy Agency.*

a. *Draft Statute, Circulated by the United States, August 22, 1955.*[12]

[The Draft Statute circulated by the United States, served as a basis for discussion among serveral nations. The text of the Draft Statute is not reproduced here because it was modified in subsequent negotiations.]

b. *Announcement Concerning United States Invitation of Eleven Nations to Participate in Consideration of the Draft Statute for the International Atomic Energy Agency, October 21, 1955.*[13]

The United States Government has today invited the Governments of Australia, Belgium, Brazil, Canada, Czechoslovakia, France, India, Portugal, Union of South Africa, the Union of Soviet Socialist Republics, and the United Kingdom to participate in a working level meeting in Washington in December for the purpose of considering the text of the draft Statute for the International Atomic Energy Agency. The establishment of such an agency was originally proposed by President Eisenhower on December 8, 1953.

Brazil, Czechoslovakia, India and the Union of Soviet Socialist Republics are being invited to participate in this meeting with the eight States which negotiated the draft Statute. This Statute was circulated on August 22, 1955 for comment to all States Members of the United Nations or of the Specialized Agencies. It is expected that a preparatory meeting will be held shortly in Washington to agree upon an agenda and other procedural matters.

4. *Peaceful Uses of Atomic Energy: General Assembly Resolution 912(X), Adopted December 3, 1955.*[14]

The General Assembly,

Desiring that mankind should be enabled to make the fullest use of atomic energy for peaceful purposes,

[12] *Department of State Bulletin,* v. 33 (October 24, 1955), pp. 666-672.
[13] Department of State Press Release 617, dated October 21, 1955.
[14] United Nations General Assembly *Official Records, Tenth Session,* Supplement No. 19, pp. 4-5. The resolution was adopted by a vote of 58-0.

Desiring to promote energetically the use of atomic energy to the end that it will serve only the peaceful pursuits of mankind and ameliorate their living conditions,

Recognizing the deep interest of all Members of the United Nations in achieving these ends,

Recalling its resolution 810 (IX) of 4 December 1954[15] concerning international co-operation in developing the peaceful uses of atomic energy, and recognizing that, in accordance with that resolution, significant progress is being made in promoting international co-operation for this purpose,

Having considered the report[16] of the Secretary-General, submitted pursuant to paragraph 8 of section B of the abovementioned resolution, on the International Conference on the Peaceful Uses of Atomic Energy held in Geneva from 8 to 20 August 1955,[17]

Recognizing the necessity of ensuring that the facilities of the International Atomic Energy Agency and such fissionable material as may be placed at its disposal are not used for, or diverted to, other than peaceful purposes,

Believing that continuing international co-operation is essential for further developing and expanding the peaceful uses of atomic energy,

I

CONCERNING INTERNATIONAL CONFERENCES ON THE PEACEFUL USES OF ATOMIC ENERGY

1. *Expresses its satisfaction* with the proceedings of the International Conference on the Peaceful Uses of Atomic Energy convened in accordance with General Assembly resolution 810 (IX), and commends the participants therein for the high scientific quality of the papers and discussions, and for the spirit of co-operation which prevailed at the Conference;

2. *Notes* the impressive results achieved by the Conference in facilitating the free flow of scientific knowledge relating to the production and peaceful uses of atomic energy and in laying a foundation for the fuller exchange of information on the development of atomic energy for the aims of human welfare;

[15] *Documents on American Foreign Relations, 1954,* pp. 494-496.
[16] United Nations General Assembly *Official Records, Tenth Session,* Annexes, agenda item 18.
[17] See above, pp. 465-478.

3. *Expresses its appreciation* of the work of the Secretary-General and of the Advisory Committee established under paragraph 5 of section B of resolution 810 (IX) in preparing and organizing the Conference;

4. *Recommends* that a second international conference for the exchange of technical information regarding the peaceful uses of atomic energy should be held under the auspices of the United Nations in two to three years time;

5. *Requests* the Secretary-General, acting upon the advice of the Advisory Committee referred to in paragraph 7 of section I of the present resolution and in consultation with the appropriate specialized agencies, to determine an appropriate place and date, to issue invitations to the conference in accordance with paragraphs 3 and 7 of section B of resolution 810 (IX), to prepare and circulate an agenda, and to provide the necessary staff and services.

6. *Invites* the specialized agencies to consult with the Secretary-General and the Advisory Committee with a view to ensuring proper co-ordination between the conference referred to in paragraph 4 above and such technical conferences as they or their affiliated non-governmental scientific organizations may convene on the more specialized aspects of the peaceful uses of atomic energy;

7. *Decides* to continue the Advisory Committee established under paragraph 5 of section B of resolution 810 (IX) in order that it may assist the Secretary-General in carrying out the provisions of the present resolution;

II

CONCERNING AN INTERNATIONAL ATOMIC ENERGY AGENCY

1. *Notes with satisfaction* that substantial progress has been made toward negotiation of a draft statute establishing an International Atomic Energy Agency and that this draft has been circulated to Governments for their consideration and comment;

2. *Welcomes* the announced intention of Governments sponsoring the Agency to invite all States Members of the United Nations or members of the specialized agencies to participate in a conference on the final text of the statute of the International Atomic Energy Agency;

3. *Further welcomes* the extension of invitations to the Governments of Brazil, Czechoslovakia, India, and the Union of Soviet Socialist Republics to participate, as Governments

concerned, with the present sponsoring Governments in negotiations on the draft statute of the International Atomic Energy Agency;[18]

4. *Recommends* that the Governments concerned take into account the views expressed on the Agency during the present session of the General Assembly, as well as the comments transmitted directly by Governments, and that they take all possible measures to establish the Agency without delay, bearing in mind the provisions of the present resolution;

5. *Requests* the Secretary-General, in consultation with the Advisory Committee referred to in paragraph 7 of section I of the present resolution, to study the question of the relationship of the International Atomic Energy Agency to the United Nations, and to transmit the results of their study to the Governments concerned before the conference referred to in paragraph 2 of section II above is convened;

6. *Requests* the Governments concerned to report to the General Assembly as appropriate;

7. *Suggests* that the International Atomic Energy Agency, when established, consider the desirability of arranging for an international periodical devoted to the peaceful uses of atomic energy.

5. *Effects of Atomic Radiation: General Assembly Resolution 913 (X), Adopted December 3, 1955.*[19]

The General Assembly,

Recognizing the importance of, and the widespread attention being given to, problems relating to the effects of ionizing radiation upon man and his environment,

Believing that the widest distribution should be given to all available scientific data on the short-term and long-term effects upon man and his environment of ionizing radiation, including radiation levels and radio-active "fall-out,"

Noting that studies of this problem are being conducted in various countries,

Believing that the peoples of the world should be more fully informed on this subject,

1. *Establishes* a scientific Committee consisting of Argentina, Australia, Belgium, Brazil, Canada, Czechoslovakia, Egypt, France, India, Japan, Mexico, Sweden, the United

[18] See above, p. 479.

[19] United Nations General Assembly *Official Records, Tenth Session,* Supplement No. 19, p. 5. The resolution was adopted unanimously.

Kingdom of Great Britain and Northern Ireland, the United States of America and the Union of Soviet Socialist Republics, and requests the Governments of these countries each to designate one scientist, with alternates and consultants as appropriate, to be its representative on this Committee;

2. *Requests* the Committee:

(a) To receive and assemble in an appropriate and useful form the following radiological information furnished by States Members of the United Nations or members of the specialized agencies:

(i) Reports on observed levels of ionizing radiation and radio-activity in the environment;

(ii) Reports on scientific observations and experiments relevant to the effects of ionizing radiation upon man and his environment already under way or later undertaken by national scientific bodies or by authorities of national Governments;

(b) To recommend uniform standards with respect to procedures for sample collection and instrumentation, and radiation counting procedures to be used in analysis of samples;

(c) To compile and assemble in an integrated manner the various reports, referred to in sub-paragraph (a) (i) above, on observed radiological levels;

(d) To review and collate national reports, referred to in sub-paragraph (a) (ii) above, evaluating each report to determine its usefulness for the purposes of the Committee;

(e) To make yearly progress reports and to develop by 1 July 1958, or earlier if the assembled facts warrant, a summary of the reports received on radiation levels and radiation effects on man and his environment together with the evaluations provided for in sub-paragraph (d) above and indications of research projects which might require further study;

(f) To transmit from time to time, as it deems appropriate, the documents and evaluations referred to above to the Secretary-General for publication and dissemination to States Members of the United Nations or members of the specialized agencies;

3. *Requests* the Secretary-General to provide the Committee with appropriate assistance in organizing and carrying on its work, and to provide a secretary of the Committee;

4. *Calls upon* all concerned to co-operate in making available reports and studies relating to the short-term and long-

term effects of ionizing radiation upon man and his environment and radiological data collected by them;

5. *Requests* the specialized agencies to concert with the Committee concerning any work they may be doing or contemplating within the sphere of the Committee's terms of reference to assure proper co-ordination;

6. *Requests* the Secretary-General to invite the Government of Japan to nominate a scientist, with alternates and consultants as appropriate, to be its representative on the Committee;

7. *Decides* to transmit to the Committee the records of the proceedings of the General Assembly on the present item.

INDEX

This is a selective index intended to supplement the detailed table of contents which appears at the head of this volume. Listings are restricted to the names of personalities who are connected with major documents in the text and to a small number of topical entries covering subjects which are either not independently listed elsewhere or may be difficult to locate through the table of contents.

Date Du